All the Money
in the World

Contributors

Paul Berger

Anna Isgro

Gwen Kinkead

Alex Ulam

All the Money in the World

*How the Forbes 400
Make—and Spend—
Their Fortunes*

EDITED BY

Peter W. Bernstein

AND

Annalyn Swan

Alfred A. Knopf New York 2007

THIS IS A BORZOI BOOK
PUBLISHED BY ALFRED A. KNOPF

Library of Congress Cataloging-in-Publication Data
All the money in the world : how the Forbes 400 make—and spend—
their fortunes / edited by Peter W. Bernstein and Annalyn Swan.
p.   cm.—(A Borzoi book)
Includes bibliographical references and index.
ISBN 978-0-307-26612-5 (alk. paper)
1. Rich people—United States.   2. Millionaires—United States.
3. Wealth—United States.   I. Bernstein, Peter W.
II. Swan, Annalyn.   III. Forbes Inc.
HC110.W4A436 2007
305.5'2340973—dc22   2007015676

Contents

Acknowledgments

For the past twenty-five years, *Forbes* magazine has compiled its now legendary list of the four hundred wealthiest Americans and considered the state of the nation's vast fortunes. Its issues on the subject have been rich in facts and figures, on who's up and who's down, on whether Bill Gates (or Donald Trump) has a billion more or less. But the list is perforce numbers-driven; the issues focus less on the character of the people and the peculiar world they inhabit. What makes the Forbes 400 members tick? Who gets to the top—and why? How different are they from more average Americans? Are they happy? What lessons about money and life can we glean from them?

In *All the Money in the World: How the Forbes 400 Make—and Spend—Their Fortunes,* we set out to answer these questions and to create a collective profile of America's superrich over twenty-five years. While this book was created in collaboration with *Forbes,* much of the information comes from our own interviews, original research, and never-before-compiled data.

When we first approached Tim Forbes, the company's chief operating officer, with the idea for the book, he enthusiastically endorsed it. Throughout the research and writing, many at the magazine eased our way, sharing insights, opening archives and files, providing phone numbers and e-mail addresses, and helping in every way possible. Pete Newcomb, the longtime editor of the Forbes 400 list, was an inexhaustible source of information about members of the 400, as was his successor, Matthew Miller. James Michaels, the first editor of the Forbes 400, shared with us information, anecdotes, and insights from the early years. Additionally, Mitchell Rand, director of information technology, provided original and insightful analysis of Forbes 400 data over the last twenty-five years, while Barbara Strauch, director of *Forbes*'s book division, reviewed the data and manuscript and compiled the definitive list of all Forbes 400 members. Their efforts are immediately evident in the many charts, graphs, and tables throughout the book, to which designer Nigel Holmes has brought his distinctive flair.

At the heart of *All the Money in the World* are the voices of the Forbes 400 members themselves, as well as those of their families. Many gave us extensive interviews. (A few requested anonymity; we honored their wishes.) Others responded—sometimes at length—to a questionnaire we sent. Still others maintained an e-mail correspondence with us. We are most grateful to them for their time and insights into every aspect of Forbes 400 careers, philanthropic causes, and much more: Sheldon Adelson, John E. Anderson, Leon Black, Timothy Blixseth, Michael Bloomberg, Eli Broad, Peter Buffett, Susie Buffett, S. Truett Cathy, Jim Clark, Mark Cuban, David Duffield, Red Emmerson, Ken Fisher, Ted Forstmann, Daniel Gilbert, David Gold, Stanley S. Hubbard, J. B. Hunt, Jon Huntsman Jr., Michael Huffington, Wayne Huizenga, David Kaplan, Vinod Khosla, Charles Koch, David Koch, Jerome Kohlberg, Herbert Kohler Jr., Bruce Kovner, Ronald Lauder, John Malone, Ross Perot, Ross Perot Jr., T. Boone Pickens, Marc Rich, Julian Robertson, Arthur Rock, Wilbur L. Ross, Richard Mellon Scaife, Charles Schwab, Steve Schwarzman, Charles Simonyi, Ram Shriram, Robert F. X. Sillerman, John Sobrato, James Tisch, Donald Trump, Ivanka Trump, Mortimer Zuckerman.

This book has also benefited greatly from the wisdom of many writers, professors, and analysts who have thought and written about wealth. Each is credited in the Notes section, at the top of the chapters in which they are quoted. We owe a number of them special thanks: the writers Nelson W. Aldrich Jr., Ken Auletta of *The New Yorker,* Dr. Paul Babiak (industrial psychologist and author), Ron Chernow, Richard Conniff, Edward Jay Epstein, David A. Kaplan of *Newsweek,* Dr. Michael Maccoby (psychoanalyst and author), *Washington Post* business columnist Steven Pearlstein, Matthew Symonds of *The Economist,* and Thayer Cheatham Willis. A number of professors gave generously of their time and insights: Raphael Amit (Wharton School, University of Pennsylvania), Joseph Astrachan (Kennesaw State University), John C. Coffee (Columbia University Law School), Pablo Eisenberg (Public Policy Institute, Georgetown University), K. Anders Ericsson (Florida State University), Charles Geisst (Manhattan College), Alexander Horniman (Darden School of Business, University of Virginia), Christopher Jencks (Harvard University), Steven Kaplan (University of Chicago Business School), Andrew Keyt (Chicago Family Business Center, Loyola University), Josh Lerner (Harvard Business School), Anthony Mayo (director, Leadership Institute, Harvard Business School), Eli Noam (Columbia University Business School), Peter Singer (Princeton University), David A. Skeel Jr. (University of Pennsylvania), George Smith (Stern School of Business, New York University), James Allen Smith (Georgetown University), Roy C. Smith (New York University), Robert J. Sternberg (dean of the School of Arts and Sciences,

Tufts University), Jonathan Taplin (Annenberg School for Communication, University of Southern California), David Waterman (Indiana University), and Jerry White (Caruth Institute of Entrepreneurship, Cox School of Business, Southern Methodist University). In many cases, they are also the authors of well-known books, which are listed in the Notes section.

A major theme of *All the Money in the World* is how the Forbes 400 spend their money. Many are philanthropists and have created foundations of their own. Others try to influence politics. Several people were particularly helpful in describing the universe of charitable giving and the ways in which money can buy power. William Luers, former president of the Metropolitan Museum of Art in New York and now head of the United Nations Association of the USA, was a valuable guide, as was Vartan Gregorian, president of the Carnegie Corporation. Others whose insights enrich the book included Rich Avanzino, president, Maddie's Fund; Joe Breiteneicher, president, The Philanthropy Initiative; Kathy Bushkin, chief operating officer, United Nations Foundation; Chuck Collins, cofounder of Responsible Wealth; William Dietel, president, F. B. Heron and Pierson/Lovelace Foundation; Joan DiFuria and Stephen Goldbart, codirectors, Money, Meaning & Choices Institute; Sara Hamilton, of Family Office Exchange; Dr. Lee Hausner, of the family-wealth consulting firm IFF Advisors; John Healy, former president, Atlantic Philanthropies; Todd Millay, executive director, Wharton Global Family Alliance; Aryeh Neier, president of the Open Society Institute; Judith Stern Peck, director of the Money, Values and Family Life Project, Ackerman Institute for the Family; Tim Stone, president, and Ryan Nguyen, research manager, NewTithing Group; Celia Wexler, vice president for advocacy, Common Cause; and Rod Wood, Wilmington Trust.

The "Beyond Wall Street" chapter benefited, in particular, from the advice of experts who helped us navigate the often arcane world of high finance. We are grateful to John K. Castle, former president of famed Wall Street investment-banking firm Donaldson Lufkin & Jenrette and now chairman of Castle Harlan, for giving us the benefit of his encyclopedic knowledge of the history of Wall Street and of the various financial developments of the past twenty-five years. Also providing insight were Zachary Bagdon, executive director, International Center for Finance, Yale School of Management; Steve Drobny, cofounder and partner of Drobny Global Advisors and author of *Inside the House of Money;* Steve Greenberg of Allen & Company; Erik Hirsch, chief investment officer, Hamilton Lane; Michael Karagosian, MKPE Consulting; Alan Kosan, managing director, RogersCasey; Dick Kramlich, cofounder and general partner of New Enterprise Associates; Bruce McGuire, president of Connecticut Hedge Funds Association; Michael Peltz, executive editor, *Institutional Investor* and *Alpha;* Charles Taylor, National Venture Capital Association; and David B. Williams, managing partner, Williams Trading LLC.

We are also grateful to the following for their help on an array of subjects, ranging from how money works in Hollywood to how members of the Forbes 400 enjoy themselves and invest their money: Banker Mark Buchman; Diane Byrne, editor, *Power & Motoryacht;* George Cooke, entertainment lawyer, Manatt, Phelps & Phillips, LLP; Janet Healy, former Walt Disney Company studio executive and producer; Gregg Kilday, film editor at *The Hollywood Reporter;* Tobias Meyer, worldwide head of contemporary sales, Sotheby's; Craig Moffett, Stanford C. Bernstein entertainment analyst; Tom Pollock, ex-chairman of MCA/Universal Pictures and co-owner of Montecito Picture Company; Farhad Vladi of Vladi Private Islands; William D. Zabel, founding partner, Schulte Roth & Zabel, LLP. Additionally, Louise Grunwald and Mary Sharp Cronson provided insights into the manners and mores of the wealthy world. Family and friends not only shared stories and offered support but in many cases helped with contacts and arranging interviews.

Throughout our work on the book we were aided by a number of talented young researchers. Karl Moats, a student at Columbia University, proved indefatigable in compiling vast lists of data about everything from which sectors create the most wealth to the number of immigrants and women on the list. He was ably assisted by Erin Gaetz, Courtney Myers, and Mary-Catherine Lader, all members of the *Forbes* summer intern program for college students. Whenever we encountered problems in running facts or people to ground, we consulted Anne Mintz, director of knowledge management at *Forbes.* In the final stages of editing we benefited from the fact-checking of Cesar Suero and Jason Storbakken at *Forbes.* We are also grateful to Monie Begley Feurey and Laurie Baker at *Forbes* for their interest in, and promotion of, the book.

At Knopf we were fortunate to work with Erroll McDonald, a superb editor in every sense of the word. His suggestions about how to use the fascinating data compiled from twenty-five years of Forbes 400 issues proved especially important to the collective portrait that emerges from these pages. Against all odds Robin Reardon mastered the many moving pieces—manuscript, charts, graphs, boxes—and kept us on course, as did Kathy Hourigan, Ellen Feldman, Andy Hughes, and Tracy Cabanis. Virginia Tan's design elegantly weds the two parts of the book—the running text and the graphic elements—and Peter Mendelsund's cover design is both classy and powerful. Knopf publicists Paul Bogaards and Erinn Hartman gave enthusiastic support to the project. And from the beginning, our lawyer, Robert Barnett, was there behind us, supporting the idea in every way.

Above all we are deeply grateful to the wonderful team of writers and reporters who spent months fleshing out the themes of the book in the various chapters, and then helped us through the endless checking of every detail. Their knowledge and command of their subjects illuminate every page: Paul Berger, Anna Isgro, Gwen Kinkead, and Alex Ulam. A brief biographical sketch of each writer is included below. To them all, our deepest thanks.

Paul Berger is a British freelance writer based in New York. His work has appeared in the *New York Times,* the *Washington Post, U.S. News & World Report, Online Journalism Review,* and Denmark's *Weekendavisen.* He is a contributing editor to three books, including the *New York Times* best seller *Secrets of the Code.* (Chapters 2, 3, 9, 10, 11, 13)

Anna Isgro, a freelance writer and editor based in the Washington, D.C., area, was an associate editor at *Fortune* magazine and editor of *US News Business Report.* She has contributed to a variety of book projects, including *The New York Times Practical Guide to Practically Everything* and the *TurboTax Income Tax Handbook.* (Chapters 1, 5, 11, 12)

Gwen Kinkead, a prizewinning journalist and author, was a senior editor at *Worth* and *Fortune* magazines, and has contributed to *The New Yorker* and the *New York Times.* (Chapters 4, 7, 8)

Alex Ulam is a New York City–based freelance writer who specializes in architecture and urban planning. His work has appeared in *Architectural Record, Landscape Architecture, Wired, Archaeology,* and the *National Post* of Canada. (Chapter 6)

All the Money in the World

Introduction

The Forbes 400 is the dominant symbol of wealth in America. It recalls the earlier 400 list of Mrs. Astor but differs from hers in one telling respect. Whereas the original 400 referred to the collection of socially prominent New York families who filled the ballroom of Mrs. Astor in the late nineteenth century, the Forbes index spotlights individual wealth. It measures the size of this or that personal fortune. It asks not where you came from or who you work for, but who's richer? It's the big-banana index—simple, primal, direct—and for those reasons irresistible.

Malcolm Forbes, a passionate believer in fortune-making, established the list in 1982. There was nothing elitist in his ebullient approach to wealth. Forbes was unashamed by his fortune; he relished the idiosyncratic (and he knew the value of publicity in promoting his brand). His favorite form of transportation was neither the everyman's Chevy nor the aristocrat's polo pony, but a motorcycle and a hot-air balloon—both of which kept him and his eponymous magazine, *Forbes,* in the news. Several years before the creation of the 400 list, *Forbes* developed a Cost of Living Extremely Well Index (CLEWI), a cheeky riff on a traditional Cost of Living Index, which measures the price of staples. The CLEWI (see page 207) charted the changing prices of yachts, caviar, cigars, and private planes. Similarly, *Forbes* presented its 400 as celebrities, treating them the way *People* treated actors or *Sports Illustrated* home-run hitters. The reported numbers had a kind of celebrity flash: A fortune was a batting average.

It seems remarkable that the Forbes 400 list, today endlessly quoted around the world, is only twenty-five years old. (B. C. Forbes, Malcolm's father and the magazine's founder, published a brief precursor of the list in 1918, naming the thirty richest Americans of the time, but it did not take hold.) The Forbes 400 is a particular product of its era, a living reflection of recent history. It captures a period of extraordinary individual and entrepreneurial energy, a time unlike the extended postwar years, from 1945 to 1982, when American society emphasized the power of corporations. The gross domestic product (GDP) in the United States has more than doubled since 1982, and may soon triple. The size of American personal fortunes has more than kept pace. In 1982 only thirteen billionaires were on the Forbes list, and you needed $75 million to make the cut. Today you must be a billionaire. In 1982 the combined net worth of the 400 represented 2.8 percent of the GDP. By 2006 that figure had risen to 9.5 percent. (The percentage actually reached 12.2 percent of the GDP in 2000, during the Internet boom.) More generally, in 2005 the wealthiest 1 percent of Americans claimed a percentage of the national income not equaled since 1928. Only the Gilded Age, the period from the Civil War to the 1890s, and the 1920s can withstand comparison to the last twenty-five years in terms of wealth accumulation.

For many people (not least, before his death, Malcolm Forbes himself) the Forbes 400 represents a powerful argument—and sometimes a dream—about the social value of wealth in contemporary America. In this view, great wealth does not (at least in the United States) suggest an aristocratic or privileged group of people who inherited their positions. It means enterprising individuals, a marvelous meritocracy of money. Those who make fortunes are an ever-changing, ever-churning group of remarkable people who flourish in the land of opportunity. They bring jobs, energy, ideas, and even joy to their society. They have been responsible, in the late twentieth century, for extraordinary advances in technology, the invention of new financial instruments, and the efficient restructuring of American industry. Money is fluid. Money is restless. In 1982 twenty-four Du Pont heirs were among the four hundred wealthiest Americans. By 1999 no Du Ponts remained on the list. New money was supplanting old. It was wealth's way.

To be sure, many take the other side of the argument. Why commemorate greed, competition, and dollar one-upmanship? What does it say about America that the wealth of four hundred individuals should, in 2006, equal almost one-tenth of the annual output of a nation of 300 million people? To skeptics, the Forbes 400 symbolizes a period of avarice, excess, and selfishness.

All the Money in the World does not join in these arguments. Instead it recounts a more nuanced and personal story. At times anecdotal, at times

The rich are getting much richer

Since 1982 the total net worth of the Forbes 400 has increased from $91.8 billion to $1.25 trillion in 2006. Over the 25-year period, there have been only two down years for the 400 as a whole (2001 and 2002). The average net worth of a 400 member (not adjusted for inflation) has jumped from $230.8 million to $3.14 billion. To make it onto the list in 1982, you had to have at least $75 million; in 2006 you had to be a billionaire. To put these mind-boggling numbers into some perspective, the average annual increase in the 400's total net worth from 1982 to 2006 is 11.5%, while the average annual increase in the S&P 500 was 13.2% (with dividends reinvested).

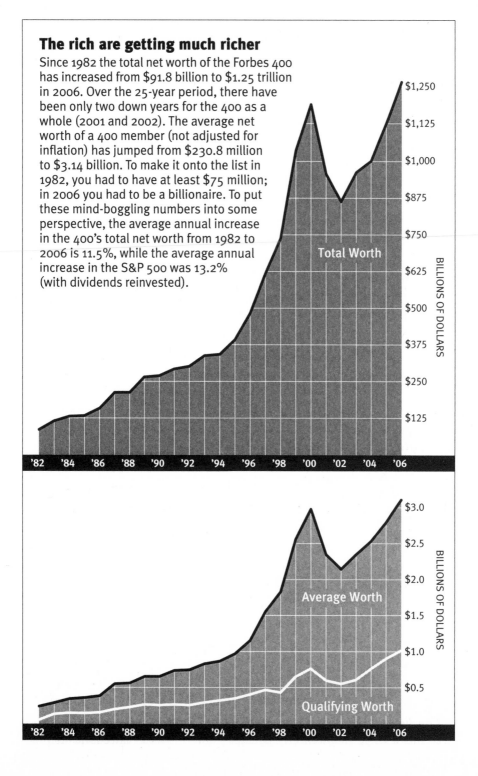

analytical, *All the Money in the World* tells the story of the individuals who actually made the money, many of whom were interviewed for the book. Taken together, their stories illuminate how fortunes are made, lost, and spent today. The book is organized into three sections. The first, What It Takes, examines the character of fortune-makers, looking at such factors as risk taking, luck, and education in helping them get ahead. The second, Making It, explores how their money was made, with particular emphasis given to the booming fields of technology, finance, and entertainment and media (while also reporting on the more traditional, so-called blue-collar fortunes). The third, Spending It, looks at what the wealthy do with their money, focusing on conspicuous consumption, heirs, family feuds, and philanthropic and political activities.

All the Money in the World also contains a rich collection of charts and graphs that detail intriguing facts about wealth (many analyzed here for the first time) gleaned from the twenty-five years of the list. A few of the highlights:

- In the first Forbes 400, oil was the source of 22.8 percent of the fortunes, manufacturing 15.3 percent, finance 9 percent, and technology 3 percent. By 2006 oil had fallen to 8.5 percent and manufacturing to 8.5 percent. Technology, however, had risen to 11.75 percent and finance to an extraordinary 24.5 percent.
- With the emergence of new technology-based and financial fortunes, the geography of American wealth has changed. In 1982 New York had 77 members on the list, California 48. Today California has 89 members. (At its peak, before the Internet bubble burst in 2000, California had 107 people on the list.) New York now has 56 members, a decline of 27 percent over the life of the index. But New York City has more 400 members (45) than any other American city. Texas had 65 members on the list in 1982 and 36 in 2006. The flow of fresh money to California is mostly concentrated in Silicon Valley, near San Francisco. In the last twenty-five years, Silicon Valley has joined Wall Street, Hollywood, and the Texas oil patch as a storied and almost mythical source of American riches.
- In the last twenty-five years, 97 immigrants have made the list. Only 13 working women have made the cut, and this small number includes several who began life with substantial advantages, such as Katharine Graham and Abigail Johnson, each of whom inherited a large fortune. (The fortunes of Oprah Winfrey; Martha Stewart; Pleasant Rowland, founder

Where are the women?

Surprisingly, as the number of women in the workplace has increased over the last 25 years, the number of women on the 400 list has slipped dramatically, as has the percentage of overall 400 wealth controlled by women.

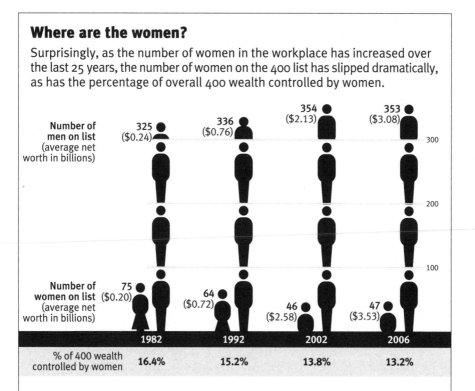

Number of men on list (average net worth in billions)

325 ($0.24) — 336 ($0.76) — 354 ($2.13) — 353 ($3.08)

Number of women on list (average net worth in billions)

75 ($0.20) — 64 ($0.72) — 46 ($2.58) — 47 ($3.53)

1982   1992   2002   2006

| % of 400 wealth controlled by women | 16.4% | 15.2% | 13.8% | 13.2% |

The very richest . . .

Of the richest women on the 400 over the last 25 years, only one (Doris Fisher, cofounder of the Gap with her husband) didn't inherit her money from a family or spouse.

	Peak value in billions	Year	Years on list
Alice Walton	$20.5	2003	18
Helen Walton	$20.5	2003	15
Christy Walton	$15.7	2005	2
Abigail Johnson	$13.0	2006	12
Barbara Cox Anthony	$12.6	2006	25
Anne Cox Chambers	$12.6	2006	25
Jacqueline Mars	$10.5	2006	21
Martha Ingram	$4.7	1998	12
Doris Fisher	$4.1	1999	15
Barbara Davis	$4.0	2005	1
Joan Tisch	$3.4	2006	1
Joan Kroc	$3.2	1999	20
Mary Malone	$3.0	1998	18

. . . and the working rich

Most of the working women on the 400 are heiresses. But some, like eBay's Margaret Whitman, Pleasant Rowland (creator of the American Girl doll empire), Oprah Winfrey, and Martha Stewart are self-made.

	Peak value in billions	Year	Years on list
Abigail Johnson	$13.0	2006	12
Martha Ingram	$4.7	1998	12
Leona Helmsley	$2.5	2006	10
Barbara Gage	$2.0	2006	8
Maggie Magerko	$2.0	2006	9
Marilyn Nelson	$2.0	2006	8
Phyllis Taylor	$1.6	2006	2
Margaret Whitman	$1.6	2004	8
Oprah Winfrey	$1.5	2006	12
Estee Lauder	$1.0	1995	14
Martha Stewart	$1.0	2000	3
Katherine Graham	$0.9	1987	9
Pleasant Rowland	$0.7	1998	1

of the American Girl doll empire; and Meg Whitman, the chief executive officer of eBay, are entirely self-made.)

- The average net worth in 2006 of Forbes 400 members without a college degree was $5.96 billion; those with a degree averaged $3.14 billion. Four of the five richest Americans—Bill Gates, casino owner Sheldon Adelson, Oracle's Larry Ellison, and Microsoft cofounder Paul Allen (whose combined net worth was $110 billion in 2006)—are college dropouts. The fifth, Warren Buffett, has an undergraduate degree from the University of Nebraska—and subsequently got a master's degree in economics from Columbia University. A broader study of the Forbes 400 over the last twenty-five years indicates that in any given year about 10 percent of the members dropped out of high school, possess only a high school diploma, or never completed college.

While Ronald Reagan wasn't solely responsible for the historic economic boom reflected in the Forbes 400, there can be little doubt that he created the environment in which the list took root and flourished. Elected to the presidency in 1980, two years before the list was invented, Reagan was in certain respects a characteristic voice of the corporate fifties: After his movie career faded, he became well-known as a spokesman for General Electric (GE) and as the genial program host for its hit television show, *General Electric Theater.* The United States was developing at this time into a mass society with a vigorous consumer culture. The country had united as never before during World War II, marshaling its industry to defeat a common enemy. In the postwar period its energetic corporations defined what was meant by economic success. The company man (and shareholder) came into his own; it would have seemed selfish, with the Cold War intensifying and memories of the Depression and World War II still fresh, to overemphasize individual riches. The chief executive officers (CEOs) of IBM, General Motors (GM), and AT&T were kings of the American hill.

Nobody better symbolized corporate America than Robert McNamara, a man driven less by his belief in individual glory than by his faith in rational planning and the social utility of institutions. Ford Motor Company had, of course, been founded by the industrialist Henry Ford. That McNamara rather than a Ford heir rose to the top of this legendary family company symbolized the ascendancy of a corporate ideal that appeared to many people of the time at once sensible and visionary. It seemed natural that the young, newly elected president John F. Kennedy would, in 1960, ask a man of the new forward thinking to modernize the military as he might a corporation. What happened to McNamara as secretary of defense during the 1960s—as American culture was shocked in turn by the assassination of a president, a failed war, and the rise of the counterculture—helped bring this idealization of the corporation to an end. The company man became, in the eyes of many, a soulless automaton. In the aftermath of the Vietnam War, moreover, a frightening inflation ripped through the economy, destroying public faith in the weight and stability of the dollar.

As president, Ronald Reagan inherited a nation that had lost its confidence in business. He instinctively knew that the country was not in a mood to restore the corporation to iconic status. Instead, he invoked a simpler era, exalting individual pluck over institutional power. It was the entrepreneur, not the bearer of a famous name or the holder of a corporate title, who represented the true spirit of wealth in America. The individual American entrepreneur must be newly unshackled, liberated from both government regulation and the lingering cultural distaste for riches found in certain elite circles. Someone who made his own way deserved to enjoy the fruit of his labors: Wasn't that fair and reasonable? America was once again prepared to lionize the self-made man.

Reagan did not just change minds; he changed means. He came into office as Federal Reserve chairman Paul Volcker was fiercely attacking double-digit inflation. Reagan then cut taxes sharply. The economic landscape began to shift tectonically, a shift chronicled here in the section entitled Making It. Two vast fields opened up for fortune makers of the time, one based upon financial acumen—in particular, the borrowing of money to buy undervalued assets—the other upon investment in rapidly evolving digital and computer technologies. These two sectors, more than any others, represented "Oklahoma" in the money rush of the last twenty-five years. More traditional fields for making big money, such as oil and manufacturing, grew at a much slower rate.

In the 1980s, as the chapter on finance, Beyond Wall Street, chronicles, corporate raiders dominated the news, with Michael Milken (the so-called junk bond king) becoming the financial poster boy of his generation. Milken and other leveraged buyout (LBO) players would, in the popular phrase, "unlock" the value of the American corporation; typically, they would buy a company with borrowed money and then sell off some of its pieces and ruthlessly streamline others until they repaid their debt and made back their investment many times over. It was not just the LBO kings, however, who accounted for the ongoing financial boom. In the 1990s, the dollar remained strong even as the Federal Reserve maintained a generally easy stance, pumping dollars into the economy. Interest rates stayed low. Fresh financial ideas and wrinkles (derivatives, various ways of packaging debt, carry trades, computer-driven arbitrage) led to the pooling of vast sums of money. The biggest paychecks went not to officials at the big Wall Street firms, who were paid very well, but to individuals who established hedge funds to invest the new cash. Seventeen of the eighty-three financiers on the 2006 list started hedge funds. (Only five hedge-funders were on the list in 2001.) The founders of these largely unregulated pools of capital funds pay themselves a managing fee and whatever percentage of fund profits the market will tolerate; and the market, not surprisingly, tolerates just about anything if the fund still offers a good return. The founders of hedge funds were not known, as a group, for a modest assessment of their own talents. In 2006 the highest-paid founder of a hedge fund was James H. Simons. His paycheck was $1.7 billion.

If Michael Milken symbolized the emergence of new financial fortunes, Bill Gates, the founder of Microsoft, played that part for the tech revolutionaries—and, unlike Milken, he has remained a powerhouse over the last twenty-five years. He joined the list in 1986 and has been number one since 1994. His fortune now equals the combined GDP of eleven African countries (Burundi, Niger, Ethiopia, Tanzania, Central African Republic, Lesotho, Liberia, Namibia, Sierra Leone, Malawi, and the Congo), with a population totaling 226 million. Tech entrepreneurs like Gates made fortunes mainly by forming new companies instead of working within the sclerotic bureaucracies of established corporations. As the West Coast Money and Entertainment and Media chapters demonstrate, however, the tech revolution (like its financial cousin) has many aspects. The rapid evolution of digital technologies led not only to a computer in every home but also to a transformation of the media, entertainment, and communications industries—notably through the Internet—that opened fresh opportunities for entrepreneurs.

Old Hollywood remains important, to be sure: The venerable movie studios still make profitable films, and an entertainer such as Oprah Winfrey can still become enormously wealthy by capturing the popular American imagination. But the largest fortunes of this era rarely have gone to what Hollywood likes to call "the talent." They go to the people who buy, market, and distribute the talent—that is, to salesmen, consolidators, and distributors. Successful athletes, actors, inventors, artists, and rock stars earn large salaries, but they make far less, as a rule, than the empire builders. In 1982 Bob Hope

Counting Bill Gates's billions: It takes a continent

The Microsoft billionaire has been on the 400 list for 21 years—debuting in 1986. At the height of the tech boom in 1999 and before he started giving some of his fortune to the Gates Foundation, he was worth $85 billion. Here's how his wealth compares to the gross domestic product (GDP) of several African countries.

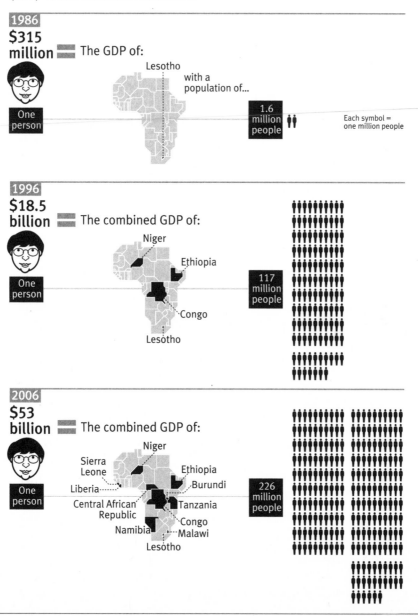

1986

$315 million ≈ The GDP of:

One person

Lesotho
with a population of...

1.6 million people

Each symbol = one million people

1996

$18.5 billion ≈ The combined GDP of:

One person

Niger
Ethiopia
Congo
Lesotho

117 million people

2006

$53 billion ≈ The combined GDP of:

One person

Niger
Sierra Leone
Liberia
Central African Republic
Namibia
Ethiopia
Burundi
Tanzania
Congo
Malawi
Lesotho

226 million people

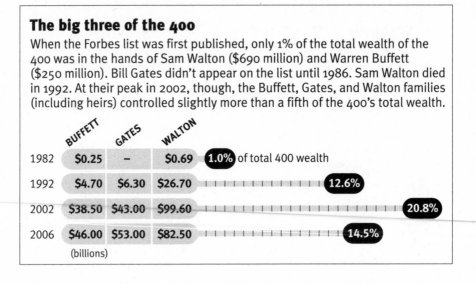

The big three of the 400

When the Forbes list was first published, only 1% of the total wealth of the 400 was in the hands of Sam Walton ($690 million) and Warren Buffett ($250 million). Bill Gates didn't appear on the list until 1986. Sam Walton died in 1992. At their peak in 2002, though, the Buffett, Gates, and Walton families (including heirs) controlled slightly more than a fifth of the 400's total wealth.

	BUFFETT	GATES	WALTON	
1982	$0.25	–	$0.69	**1.0%** of total 400 wealth
1992	$4.70	$6.30	$26.70	**12.6%**
2002	$38.50	$43.00	$99.60	**20.8%**
2006	$46.00	$53.00	$82.50	**14.5%**

(billions)

was a member of the Forbes 400, but his fortune stemmed less from one-liners than from investments in Palm Springs real estate. Of today's showbiz members on the list, Steven Spielberg may owe as much to his role as a founder of DreamWorks, whose animated movies depend upon digital technologies, as to his day job directing movies. David Geffen credits the scale of his financial success, in part, to the return he received on a $200 million investment in a hedge fund. Meanwhile, much of the energy in media has come from master builders such at Rupert Murdoch. As *Forbes* noted in October 2006, after Murdoch's acquisition of MySpace.com, "Time and again he's confounded skeptics by making acquisitions and investments that at the time look extravagant and overly ambitious but go on to yield very impressive gains."

Despite these dramatic changes, the Forbes 400 has retained certain old-fashioned qualities. Over its twenty-five years, at least 175 "blue-collar billionaires," whose stories are told in the chapter of that name and who depend upon unglamorous businesses such as hogs, shoes, dollar stores, hauling, and tree trimming, have made the list. Typically, the blue-collar fortunes have taken many years to create. They are often well-tended family enterprises. Wal-Mart is the standard. (In 2006, the year before her death, Sam Walton's widow, Helen, his children, and his daughter-in-law occupied positions number 6, 7 [a tie], 9, and 11 on the list, with a combined net worth of $77.7 billion.) By contrast, tech fortunes often seem made in a nanosecond. Sergey Brin and Larry Page of Google were thirty-one and thirty-two, respectively, when manna fell from heaven; Steve Jobs of Apple was twenty-seven.

And what of the character traits that helped the 400 get to the top? Historically, the fundamental characteristics—the subject of the What It Takes section—do not seem to change much over time. Very often, the self-made were willing to take enormous risks (sometimes again and again and again, seemingly against all reason) until they hit their jackpot; not surprisingly, many financiers, Warren Buffett among them, relish poker. Vices are also virtues. A person who builds a company from the ground up often loves his creation as himself and can develop a kind of maniacal energy and obsessive focus. He may become competitive to the point of ruthlessness. Companies routinely buy out, and sometimes close, other companies to control markets. Microsoft didn't become Microsoft by welcoming competition and encouraging other up-and-coming Bill Gateses; it was an elephant happy to step on the mice.

Often members of the 400 are as competitive personally as they are when dealing with their business. As Paul Johnson pointed out in the 2004 Forbes 400 issue of the magazine, in an article entitled "When Are You Seriously Rich?": "My experience is that the rich are extremely interested (and competitive) about wealth totals." It should be noted that many members of the list have disagreed over the years with *Forbes*'s estimate of their worth: How can an outsider calculate, for example, the value of a privately held trust or corporation? But for the purposes of the social portrait contained in *All the Money in the World*, it does not matter if number 183 should be number 242. In general, Forbes 400 members seem to make their own good luck through a combination of hard work, homework, and the sheer drive to succeed. "What I do is work," the late Kenneth W. Ford, a timber baron, once said. "I don't do anything else. I work."

Over the years, *Forbes* has celebrated the fluidity of big money. The 400 issue of 2001 noted that "energy, mobility, change are the constants. Today's success is no guarantee of success tomorrow." It is true that big money in America is ever changing—but only up to a point. (The total number of peo-

---

A group snapshot of 400 money

Since 1982, 1,302 individuals have appeared on the Forbes 400 list. The overwhelming number of them have been white males. Only 202 women (15.5%) have made the list over its 25-year history. Forbes does not collect information about the ethnic background of 400 members. But a rough calculation indicates that the number of minorities gaining a berth on the list is small—fewer than 10 African Americans and Hispanics and 30 or so Asians.

ple to make the list, for example, is 1,302 out of a possible 10,000; in 2006 only 29 members were first-timers.) Still, self-made money regularly flows toward the top; inherited money slowly subsides. Twelve families who possess "old money"—bearing names such as Du Pont, Ford, Frick, Rockefeller, Harriman, Hunt, Hearst, and Whitney—represented 21.4 percent of the list in 1982. They had declined to 1.7 percent in 2006. In addition to the departing Du Ponts, there is only 1 Mellon (down from 6 in 1982), and only David Rockefeller remains to represent his clan (down from 14 in 1982). Inherited money is, as a rule, not invested particularly well and dwindles over generations, as more heirs make demands on less capital. Among the 400 founders (i.e., those who have been on the list from the beginning), 40 percent have done better and 60 percent worse than the S&P 500 over the last twenty-five years. The decline of inherited money also has led to a major reduction in the total number of women on the Forbes 400 list. In 1982 there were 75 women on the list whose combined wealth amounted to 16.4 percent of the total holdings of the 400. In 2006 only 47 women remained on the list, and they possessed 13.2 percent of the total wealth.

Inherited money remains, nonetheless, a very powerful factor in American society. While the Du Ponts have left the list, they are hardly poor; in 2000 *Forbes* estimated the Du Pont family's total net worth at an unmeasly $14 billion, the Mellons' at $10 billion, and the Rockefellers' at $8.5 billion. The old inherited money is today being replaced by newly inherited money, which will be old soon enough, in families such as the Waltons. If you include among the self-made those second- and third-generation heirs who aggressively increase the value of the money they inherited, then the percentage of inherited money on the list falls over time. By this reckoning, a businessman such as Donald Trump, who inherited a real-estate fortune, is placed on the "self-made" side of the ledger. (To be fair, the easiest way to make money is to begin with money. Like loves like; fortune begets fortune.) But even when heirs who increased the family fortune are counted on the "inherited" side of the ledger, that number continues to fall against the self-made. In 1982, 212 members of the 400 created their own fortunes—just over half the entire number. By 2006 the number of "self-made" fortunes had risen to 280, with the heirs dwindling to less than a third of the list. As the 2001 Forbes 400 issue noted, "Some critics carp that a third of our listees inherited wealth. So what? But what they do with it—enhance it, diminish it, give it away—is intriguing."

Since 1982, American society has increasingly celebrated the innovator over the steward and the self-made over the inherited. This represents a remarkable shift of historical emphasis. Earlier periods were no less competitive, but before the present day, money was rarely thought of in the direct, bottom-line terms presented in the Forbes 400. For the nineteenth and much of the twentieth century, a person's social station did not depend entirely upon wealth; money inherited continued to matter more than money made. Many fortune makers during the Gilded Age assumed the aristocratic European manners and accoutrements typical of Mrs. Astor's 400. (The American heiress who marries the impoverished European aristocrat—exchanging means for manners and manners for means—remained a stock figure well into the twentieth century.) The rich who did not cultivate European airs, or heirs, often covered their money in Calvinist qualms. For Protestants such as John D. Rockefeller and his son, the family fortune was also God's business: Philanthropy could transfigure the naked fact.

Many of the big money heroes of today, however, particularly the ones based on the West Coast, do not seem to aspire to the old-money standards: They dress down (the T-shirt can be more powerful than the suit) and remind no one of parents or traditional authority figures. The financial whizzes have developed a kind of gun-slinging swagger; such techies as Gates and Steve Jobs have displayed, in turn, a boyish brio and a nerdy brilliance. In the 1980s, under the influence of this new kind of hero, college students stopped recoiling from business and became enamored of these fresh role models. The most ambitious began to move into investment banking and the new Internet and tech companies. Some became billionaires in their own right and joined the list.

While the techies have influenced an entire generation, heirs—the subject of their own chapter—continue to hold a particular fascination for many people. It is heirs who often become absorbed in politics and philanthropic giving, although the self-made (such as Bill Gates or George Soros) frequently initiate the process and create the traditions that subsequently guide family giving. It is heirs, too, who tend to fight, which is the focus of the Family Feuds chapter. Divorces, second wives, and sibling rivalries create flash points; the financial stakes are large, so the feuds are often intense. The very public battles of the Koch family of Kansas, played out in numerous lawsuits over the years, are a dramatic case in point. The Koches' squabbling has been called "perhaps the nastiest family feud in American business history." The Rockefellers have proven particularly adept at avoiding such a fate. They have divided the family inheritance into a series of interlocking trusts designed to prevent disagreements. But even they have had their spats.

How the rich disperse their money also continues to fascinate, especially the over-the-top excess chronicled in Conspicuous Consumption. Many of the best examples of excess and pretension during the last twenty-five years have in fact been the work of the lesser rich. Surprisingly few of the Forbes 400 regularly make headlines because of their ostentatious lifestyles. Houses and yachts remain important showpieces, of course, and the competition in both areas is intense: Larry Ellison built a boat that is ninety feet longer than a football field. Few have put on a more ostentatious show than list member Ira Rennert, who constructed a five-building compound in the Hamptons, the centerpiece of which is a sixty-six-thousand-square-foot, twenty-nine-bedroom, Italianate villa by the sea.

At the same time, the very rich can also spend very well, as the chapter Giving It Away details. They support many charities, notable among them environmental, educational, medical, and arts organizations. Their giving is essential. Precisely because they can do as they want and are not bound by convention or legislative constraints, the wealthy can experiment and generate remarkable change. The open-ended tradition of philanthropy in the United States ensures that the government alone is not responsible for developing and supporting new projects that might benefit society. American research universities are today the wonder of the world; they became so mainly through private giving. As for the influence that money can buy, addressed in the Power and Politics chapter, members of the Forbes 400 tend to be less successful at shaping society by running for political office (certain Rockefellers and Michael Bloomberg excepted) than they are at shaping policy from behind the scenes. The rich support think tanks, which can generate ideas and enliven the culture. George Soros, through his Open Society Institute, has set himself the ambitious goal of fostering "civil society" throughout much of the world. A surprising number of 400 members argue for higher inheritance taxes.

Since the Forbes 400 coincides with a period of huge wealth accumulation in the United States, it begs comparison to other periods of accumulation, above all with the late nineteenth century. How do the richest today compare to the richest of years gone by? Is the style in which they live more lavish or more modest? Is the music of life as sweet? Are they as happy?

Such questions have no satisfactory answer. The robber barons are not available to be interviewed, and their society and today's are too different to be evaluated by a common standard. But there are several meaningful ways to compare present fortunes against past ones. The best is probably to contrast relative scale, treating earlier fortunes as a percentage of inflation-adjusted GDP and then translating that percentage into contemporary dollars. By this standard John D. Rockefeller would today be worth $305.3 billion, Andrew Carnegie $281.2 billion, and Cornelius Vanderbilt $168.4 billion. Today's big rich are rather modest by comparison: Bill Gates, at $53 billion, would be the thirteenth richest American of all time.

The grandees of the Gilded Age stood out from their surrounding societies more than today's rich do. In the nineteenth century, the difference that wealth could make in a person's life was enormous, and the division between the haves and the have-nots seemed fundamental; the well-to-do middle class remained small, and the desperate poor, their ranks swollen by waves of immigration, large. For the great mass of people, there was no security and little comfort to be found in the world. Many in the nineteenth century would have regarded the prospect of a hot bath every day as an unimaginable luxury. In modern American society, social gaps of this sort have narrowed. The comfortable middle class has vastly expanded; even the poor can bathe daily. As Dinesh D'Souza argued in a

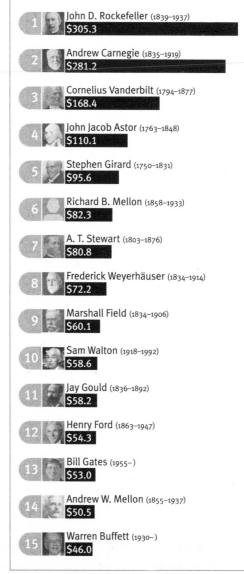

All-time richest Americans

To compile this list, each individual's wealth was calculated (in billions) at its peak. The figure was compared to the U.S. gross domestic product at the time and converted to 2006 dollars. So if John D. Rockefeller were alive today, his wealth would be many times greater than Bill Gates's.

1. John D. Rockefeller (1839–1937) — $305.3
2. Andrew Carnegie (1835–1919) — $281.2
3. Cornelius Vanderbilt (1794–1877) — $168.4
4. John Jacob Astor (1763–1848) — $110.1
5. Stephen Girard (1750–1831) — $95.6
6. Richard B. Mellon (1858–1933) — $82.3
7. A. T. Stewart (1803–1876) — $80.8
8. Frederick Weyerhäuser (1834–1914) — $72.2
9. Marshall Field (1834–1906) — $60.1
10. Sam Walton (1918–1992) — $58.6
11. Jay Gould (1836–1892) — $58.2
12. Henry Ford (1863–1947) — $54.3
13. Bill Gates (1955–) — $53.0
14. Andrew W. Mellon (1855–1937) — $50.5
15. Warren Buffett (1930–) — $46.0

2000 *Forbes* article entitled "The Moral Limits of Wealth," "The traditional mantra about inequality is that the rich are getting richer and the rest are getting poorer. In the past two decades, however, the rich have gotten richer and the rest have also gotten richer, although not at the same pace."

The difference in the way of life of a billionaire and a middle-class professional, while significant, no longer seems so striking. A member of the Forbes 400 will fly to his large villa in the Caribbean on a private jet; a lawyer will fly first class to the Caribbean, stay in a fine hotel, and play on the same golf course as the billionaire. The rich of today have extraordinary apartments in New York City, but not a parade of mansions down Fifth Avenue. (The Vanderbilts alone possessed several mansions on Fifth, the most spectacular of which was modeled on a sixteenth-century château and took one thousand workers three years to build: The main hall evoked the interior of a Gothic cathedral.) Today's rich can be just as grand as yesterday's, but they cannot summon the same grandeur. Louis Auchincloss, writing in *Forbes,* recalled: "I remember an old gentleman in Newport at a dance at the Breakers in 1936 viewing with nostalgic eyes the vast marble stairway and telling me of a party 30 years before, where a flunky in maroon livery was perched on every step."

In 1991 Kevin Phillips wrote an essay in which he predicted that the current period of rapid wealth accumulation was ending. Such periods in American history have always been cyclical, he argued, and the pendulum was set to swing again. His timing was wrong—the boom would continue, despite some interruptions, for at least another fifteen years. While it rarely pays to underestimate the American economy, he was surely right that this period will not go on forever. He cited three factors that indicated a change was coming, all of which seem to be increasingly important elements in contemporary American culture. First, he wrote, "it becomes obvious to ordinary Americans that wealth is surging at the top, but not in the middle. Second, more and more citizens perceive wealth as a reward for abuse, not achievement. . . . Finally, there comes the disenchantment of a significant economic downturn relating to the implosion of the debt-and-speculative bubble pumped up during the go-go period."

When future historians look back at the era that produced the Forbes 400, they will certainly recount its great financial and technological achievements. They will talk about the end of the twentieth century and the beginning of the twenty-first century as a time of entrepreneurial vision. But they will also look for a more elusive kind of contribution: something the otherworldly rich have done that can seriously elevate or excite the public imagination—an act, gesture, or creation that's visionary. Naturally, this is rarely found in any period. But there are exceptions. Andrew Carnegie said 120 years ago that "to die rich was to die disgraced." His funding of three thousand public libraries was more than just philanthropy; it was a kind of existential gesture. Louis Comfort Tiffany's Laurelton Hall and George Washington Vanderbilt II's Biltmore estate in North Carolina—the largest private home ever built in America—bewitched the American mind. A speculative boom on Wall Street helped put the liberating roar into the Roaring Twenties, and Howard Hughes raised eyes with the H-4 Hercules aircraft, better known as the Spruce Goose. In the era of the Forbes 400, nothing comparable to those feats of the imagination has yet emerged. But many of the fortune makers are relatively young. They're part of a new century. They're looking ahead.

PART·ONE

What It Takes

1

Education, Intelligence, Drive

The notion of a good education as a ticket to the good life is deeply ingrained in the American psyche. Studies show over and over that there's a strong correlation between schooling and future earnings. It's a central tenet of billionaire Michael Bloomberg, New York City's 108th mayor, who has taken on the city's failing education system with gusto. "Nothing is more important than education," says Bloomberg, "so you're seeing the better educated getting the greater percentage of the wealth. And education is only going to become more important as we get into a more and more complex world."

If this is so, how did David Murdock, son of a traveling salesman and a high-school dropout, amass a net worth of more than $4 billion in real-estate development and the food business? What transformed onetime welfare recipient Tim Blixseth, a high-school grad, into a billionaire timber lord? And what turned eighteen-year-old Thomas Flatley, who left Ireland with $32 in his pocket and no advanced education, into a $1.3 billion real-estate mogul? One thing is certain: It was not the hallowed halls of an ivy-covered university.

For members of the Forbes 400, who have reached the financial apex, you would expect a basic requisite to be a college diploma, if not an MBA—assuming, of course, they didn't inherit their riches. Yet Murdock, Blixseth, and Flatley all made fortunes with little formal schooling. And they aren't alone. Four of the five richest Americans on the 2006 Forbes 400 list—software king Bill Gates, casino impresario Sheldon Adelson, Oracle's Larry Ellison, and Microsoft cofounder Paul Allen, whose combined net worth in

2006 came to a staggering $110 billion—are all college dropouts. The only university grad among the top five is America's second-richest man, genius investor Warren Buffett, who graduated from the University of Nebraska in 1949. In fact, in any given year over the past twenty-five years, about 10 percent of the Forbes 400 either dropped out of high school, only graduated from high school, or never finished college.

If you ask the nation's richest man, Bill Gates, what's behind his success, he'll attribute his accomplishments to a sort of chaos theory: "My success just proves that life is chaotic . . . some butterfly did the right thing for me." Buffett uses a different metaphor but holds out a similar explanation for his success (and it doesn't refer to his 1951 master's degree in economics from Columbia University). As Buffett puts it: "I was wired at birth to allocate capital." But of course, success is not as simple, or as elusive, as those responses suggest.

To begin with, there's the matter of raw intelligence. For most of the decades prior to the early 1990s, the notion of intelligence quotient, or IQ, was paramount in explaining why some people excelled at certain tasks. But the use of IQ scores as a measure of future success, except for gauging results on academic tests, has since fallen out of favor. It seems hard to argue that IQs don't matter when you consider that Bill Gates's score is reportedly a mind-boggling 170, far above the 130 or so required to become a member of Mensa, the high-intelligence society, and even higher than Albert Einstein's reputed 160. What's more, Gates's successor-to-be at Microsoft, Steven Ballmer (2006 net worth: $13.6 billion), is said to have an equally impressive score. But one of the failings of such tests becomes obvious when you consider that not all high-IQ individuals achieve the financial status of Gates and Ballmer, while many people who score poorly turn out to be megabillionaires. "It's not a magical measure of people's capacities, but just one more test that you can be good or not good at," says K. Anders Ericsson, psychology professor at Florida State University.

Many researchers, such as Robert Sternberg, author of *Successful Intelligence: How Practical and Creative Intelligence Determine Success in Life* and dean of the School of Arts and Sciences at Tufts University, agree that the notion of general intelligence alone has little value. "Just as low scores on intelligence tests don't preclude success," says Sternberg, "neither do high scores guarantee it." The whole concept of relating IQ to life achievement is misguided, Sternberg believes, because "IQ is a pretty miserable predictor of life achievement." Research shows, in fact, that IQ counts for only 10 to 20 per-

Where *A* Is for Apple, *B* Is for Billionaire . . .

How many grammar and high schools can lay claim to four slots on the Forbes 400 and a raft of other notable grads? For the moment, Lakeside School, on an ersatz New England campus in Seattle—and with fewer than eight hundred students in grades 5 to 12—is the clear winner.

Bill Gates and Microsoft cofounder Paul Allen (2006 combined net worth: $69 billion), its two most famous grads, got their start at the school on a computer provided partly by Lakeside's Mothers' Association. A 1968 grad, Craig McCaw (2006 net worth: $2.1 billion), subsequently turned a family business into a cell-phone empire before selling it to AT&T. And the Pigott family (1995 net worth: $777 million), which controls the Paccar heavy-machinery company, counts a dozen family members as Lakeside grads, including Charles Pigott, Paccar's chief executive for nearly thirty years.

Aside from Forbes 400 superstars, Lakeside has spawned other successes in a variety of fields. Among them: Adam West, TV's Batman; magazine writer and author Po Bronson (latest book: *Why Do I Love These People?: Honest and Amazing Stories of Real Families*); former Washington governor Booth Gardner; and art critic and Princeton art professor Hal Foster. Needless to say, with such illustrious alums the school is flush with endowments, including a fairly recent $40 million gift from Gates alone. Said Gates as he made the donation: "I can say that without Lakeside, there would be no Microsoft, and I'm here to say thank you."

cent of career success. More than a decade ago, therefore, researchers shifted their focus to other types of intelligence. Daniel Goleman, author of *Emotional Intelligence: Why It Can Matter More Than IQ,* says you need to factor in aptitudes such as empathy, interpersonal skills, and self-control. "The road to success will, of course, always include enough general intelligence to do the job," but being a star also requires a hefty dose of social skills, argues Goleman. As one executive headhunter puts it, "CEOs are hired for their intellect and business expertise—and fired for a lack of emotional intelligence."

But even a lack of emotional intelligence is sometimes no deterrent to success. One look at the Forbes 400 list and it's easy to spot bosses with reputations for being physically and emotionally removed from their employees. You have to consider other factors, too, says Sternberg—such as knowledge, thinking style, personality, and the business environment. What he terms *successful intelligence* is actually a "confluence of strong analytical, creative, and practical abilities." That doesn't mean superachievers have to shine in all three, but they do have "to find a way effectively to exploit whatever pattern of abilities they may have," he says. What sets apart the megastars from the mediocre, then, is not one trait or even a bundle of specific traits, but an alchemic convergence of a variety of strengths—as well as the know-how to use them.

Yet even when all these forms of intelligence are present, researchers say, success won't happen without a few other key ingredients, including determination and hard work. "It all has to come together for people to reach the Forbes list," says Anthony Mayo, director of the Leadership Initiative at Harvard Business School. "But, assuming they made it on their own, they had to have had ambition and drive." While drive alone won't propel a dullard to success, of course, without it even the most educated, analytic, creative minds won't get an idea off the ground. All of which goes a long way toward explaining how Murdock, Blixseth, Flatley, and others without advanced degrees managed to strike it rich.

Academic underachievers who go on to great business success often have a couple of things in common. They started working at a very young age; and while school may not have been good for their egos, working was. David Murdock is a classic example. As a high-school dropout, Murdock had entrepreneurial drive that more than compensated for his stunted schooling. The son of an often unemployed traveling salesman who peddled everything from insurance to small electric generators, young Murdock, born in 1924, experienced the misery of the Depression years firsthand in rural Wayne, Ohio. At sixteen he dropped out of school. But by the time he would have celebrated his twentieth high-school reunion, Murdock was worth $100 million. As a fit, sharp, and energetic octogenarian who only half jokes about living to 125, Murdock is the sole owner of two huge enterprises: Dole Food, the nation's largest fruit and vegetable company, and real-estate development company Castle & Cooke. His net worth in 2006: $4.2 billion.

A hard-charging businessman, Murdock has a complicated relationship with his past: He once suggested to a potential biographer that a book about his life start at age forty-three. As a child Murdock was short and uninterested in sports, making him a target for bullies. This constant taunting may be what motivated him to do great things. His response to the bullies was, according to his sister, "I'll make money. I'll be as big as you are."

Just why Murdock dropped out of high school remains unclear. He has offered several accounts over the years. "I wasn't motivated," he once said. A later explanation was that he suffered from dyslexia. It's also possible that he quit to help out his family financially after a kerosene fire burned down their modest home and seriously burned his mother. Whatever the case, Murdock *was* motivated to work hard at moneymaking pursuits: at the local duck hatchery, pumping gas, and as a riveter just before he was drafted into the army. It was during military service that Murdock realized several key things about himself. One was that he didn't want to take orders from anyone. He also learned that although he was a high-school dropout, he was not dim-witted. He once mentioned that he got a "very high rating" on an intelligence test the army gave him. For much of World War II, Murdock was a gunnery instructor traveling from post to post. Along the way an army buddy got him interested in books, especially biographies of business titans like Andrew Carnegie and Henry Ford. "They excited my mind incredibly," Murdock recalled—so much so that he allegedly began to keep files on the nation's richest people in an attempt to fathom the secrets to their success.

Once out of the military, Murdock bounced around the country and landed in Detroit, where he borrowed a few thousand dollars to buy a small diner. It was his first entrepreneurial success: He sold it two years later, nearly doubling his money. Then, barely twenty-three, Murdock and his young wife drove their trailer home to Phoenix. The city was booming, fueled by the postwar Western migration. He teamed up with a carpenter and started building houses literally from the ground up: He dug ditches, poured concrete, scrapped together construction materials. "Dave was a bulldog with ambition, who struck some people as obnoxious," a colleague from the early days noted, "but he knew how to take an idea and make it go." As Phoenix grew, so did Murdock. And as Murdock grew, so did his drive to succeed and to overcome his hardscrabble roots.

By the early 1960s, Murdock had arrived. He built up a publicly traded holding company for his thriving commercial real-estate and banking ventures. *Time* magazine called him one of the West's brightest entrepreneurs. He formed his own private club, which attracted Phoenix's financial elite, and he hobnobbed in Rome with an international set. "It was very important to him to be around a certain class of people," a friend later recalled. But Murdock's empire collapsed a few years later, when the overbuilt Phoenix real-estate market tanked. That, combined with alleged fraud by a company official (the indictment was later dismissed), forced Murdock to liquidate most of his holdings to pay off debts.

"I had all my eggs in one basket and I didn't even know it," Murdock admitted about those years. But Murdock, like many entrepreneurs, is nothing if not resilient. He took $3 million in cash that he had stowed away from his private construction company and moved to Los Angeles. This time he invested shrewdly in what to him were sure things—asset-rich, undervalued, and overlooked companies. The strategy worked: By 1982 Murdock's new empire brought him a $400 million fortune, enough to secure him a place on the first Forbes 400 list.

Like Murdock, California billionaire and college dropout Timothy Blixseth is a youthful underachiever who made good. He is the first to tell you that his success in the timber and real-estate industries has nothing to do with talent or formal education. "Some people say you're just born with certain talents. I'm not sure I have any," he says matter-of-factly. That's why he got into timber, he says, the only work he was familiar with while growing up in the lumber town of Roseburg, Oregon. "No one taught me. I had to teach myself by working and learning, working and learning. And I made a lot of mistakes. I say I graduated from UHK, the University of Hard Knocks."

Like Murdock, Blixseth grew up poor, in a family of five children. His father had a heart condition, the result of a serious childhood illness, and couldn't provide for the family. But unlike Murdock, Blixseth talks freely and humorously about his early hardships. "I was born on welfare," he says. "I can't tell you how many ways you can eat Spam." Ask Blixseth what his nickname was in school and he quips: "I was so poor they wouldn't give me one." Boyish and casual,

1982

from the pages of *Forbes*

Forrest Mars Sr. led top brass in prayer at his first meeting after taking over the U.S. operation: "I pray for Milky Way, I pray for Snickers . . ." (1982 net worth: $1 billion)

Malcolm Forbes, publisher of *Forbes* magazine, hot-air balloonist, and motorcyclist, collects Fabergé eggs and toy soldiers. (1982 published net worth on first Forbes 400 list: $1)

Sandra Ferry, daughter of John D. Rockefeller III and sister of (now senator) Jay Rockefeller, dropped the family name and lives as a recluse. (1982 net worth: $100 million)

Yoko Ono, widow of Beatle John Lennon, reportedly bases business decisions on astrology. (1982 net worth: $150 million) the fiftysomething Blixseth can, of course, laugh these days about his family poverty—now that he dines regularly at the swanky Beverly Hills restaurant Spago, takes his Gulfstream G550 from Los Angeles to Paris, and skis at his own Yellowstone Club in Montana, an exclusive members-only retreat.

Not bad for a kid who, also like Murdock, was humiliated daily in school. At lunchtime, as Blixseth tells it, teachers separated the students on welfare who got a free lunch from those who could afford to pay. "The kids in the welfare line got heckled every single darned day," Blixseth says. Finally, "A spark plug went off and I said, 'This is not what I want to do. I'm going to show you guys that I'm as good as you are.'" After school let out, Blixseth took whatever odd jobs he could find, from boxing groceries to working at a nearby lumber mill on the four-p.m.-to-midnight shift. He started honing his marketing skills as a teenager. Every day he perused the classifieds looking for ways to make money, sometimes by adding value to goods he could buy on the cheap and sell at a profit. For example, Blixseth turned an easy profit by buying donkeys and creatively reselling them as pack mules (which resemble donkeys but are more reliable and durable on the trail).

Such creativity and freethinking weren't encouraged in the Blixseth household. His father was a minister in a restrictive "offbeat religion, a kind of minicult," as Blixseth describes it, which prohibited watching television, listening to music, dancing, even taking out insurance. But Blixseth says he didn't buy into his parents' beliefs, and at night he listened to music in the dark on a small transistor radio: "Music was my escape; it was freedom to me." Although college wasn't encouraged, Blixseth decided to give it a try. He lasted one day at Roseburg's Umpqua Community College: "The guy started talking about philosophy and I thought, 'That's great, but it won't help me make a living.'" He never returned.

By this time, however, he was getting a taste of the potential that lay in the tall timbers around Roseburg. At eighteen, he made a quick $50,000 by putting down $1,000 on timberland that he knew a nearby company had been eyeing, and then selling the contract to the company. For a while he used the proceeds to underwrite car trips between Roseburg and Hollywood, where he hoped to make it in his dream career, songwriting. But he never lost sight of the timber business. Whenever he returned home, he spent entire days researching potential deals, trying to match timberland sellers with possible buyers, taking loans, and gambling that he could sell the land at huge profits. His gambles paid off: By the time he was twenty-five Blixseth had made millions.

But again like Murdock, he took his eyes off the larger economic picture.

When he was thirty-two timber values plunged, interest rates soared, and Blixseth lost everything. "There's nothing worse than to be born into welfare, want to get out, hit the home run, and then end up broke again," says Blixseth. "It's very humbling." After a bit of "soul-searching," he decided to rebuild and take more calculated risks. He also realized the appeal of appreciating land values and decided to buy rather than broker property. Eventually, he built up another timber fortune and in the 1990s started branching out into real estate, buying more than 130,000 acres in Montana. He later turned some 13,000 acres near Big Sky into his exclusive Yellowstone Club golf and ski resort. He now scours the globe in search of outstanding properties that he can develop to expand his Yellowstone Club franchise worldwide. It's perhaps the most expensive vacation resort club ever created, with memberships starting at $1.5 million. This, he believes, is a far more creative enterprise than simply owning timberland. And it's one that adds value to his investment—not unlike the business of turning donkeys into pack mules, he claims.

Like Blixseth, who walked away from education, many successful dropouts believe that further education would not have helped—and could possibly have hindered—their rise to the top. Timber baron Archie Aldis "Red" Emmerson (2006 net worth: $1.6 billion) is one such case. "I can at least say I finished high school, but I don't know what good it did me," says septuagenarian Emmerson, who relishes telling the story of how he almost didn't make it to graduation day. Sent to a religious high school by his parents (he worked forty hours a week at the school to help pay his way), Emmerson was kicked out after taking part in a prank that involved pinning a condom to the school bulletin board. He left town and went to work on a cattle ranch until a friend convinced him to return to school in California. Emmerson did so but claims he has no regrets about not having pursued a college diploma. "I'm sure with four years at college I could have learned some things I've never learned. But on the other hand," he says, echoing Blixseth, "I've just learned from doing it."

Arkansan truck driver J. B. Hunt, who died in 2006, was convinced that his success actually sprang from his limited schooling. A sharecropper's son, he started working in sawmills at age ten and quit school in the seventh grade. "Education was not on the top of people's lists in those days—just surviving and not starving to death," he said years later; yet two of his siblings graduated from college and became schoolteachers. "But it seems like they have got boundaries that they stay in and those are boundaries I don't have,"

The value of a college degree

An accepted fact in modern society is that the better educated you are, the better your chance of success, and the Forbes list mirrors that—but with an interesting caveat. Most Forbes 400 members have undergraduate college degrees—at least 244 in 2006. (Forbes doesn't have educational information on every 400 member.) And of those, 132 had graduate degrees, as well. But in 2006, 45 members of the Forbes 400— 11.25%—had never graduated from college. Bill Gates, number 1 on the Forbes list for many years, is, of course, the most famous college dropout. He quit Harvard during his junior year. But he has plenty of company. The number of 400 members without a college degree has hovered between 40 and 50 each year since at least 1990, according to Forbes statistics. The peak year was 2002, when 56 members of the 400 didn't have a college diploma. And a sprinkling never graduated from high school.

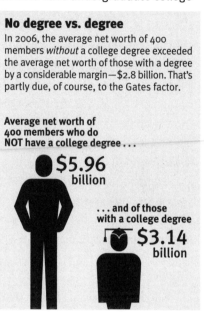

No degree vs. degree
In 2006, the average net worth of 400 members *without* a college degree exceeded the average net worth of those with a degree by a considerable margin—$2.8 billion. That's partly due, of course, to the Gates factor.

Average net worth of 400 members who do NOT have a college degree . . .

$5.96 billion

. . . and of those with a college degree
$3.14 billion

explained Hunt shortly before his death. "If they don't read something in a book they don't believe it can be done. The whole world belongs to me because I don't have any boundaries." Had he gone to college, Hunt believed he "probably would have ended up keeping the books for Tyson Foods or Wal-Mart," two other Arkansas companies. Instead, he built up a net worth of $335 million by 1994, the last time he made the Forbes 400 list.

Fred DeLuca, billionaire founder of Subway, never made it through college and has the same innate suspicion of advanced education as Hunt. As a high-school grad looking for a way to pay for college, DeLuca borrowed $1,000 from family friend Peter Buck to start a submarine-sandwich shop. At seventeen he opened up a sliver of a store in Bridgeport, Connecticut, without even getting a license. Thirty years later, Subway is one of the world's largest privately held companies; DeLuca's worth in 2006 was $1.5 billion. (Buck's original investment also garnered him a spot on the Forbes 400, with a net worth of $1.5 billion in 2006.) Not going to college may have been the best thing DeLuca ever did: "I was willing to try solutions that other people may not even have thought of—I'm not saying they were all smart solutions, but I tried them. I didn't know enough about business to realize how bad we were doing."

Dell Computer Corporation* founder Michael Dell also found he was more adept at making money than at schoolwork. At the insistence of his parents, Dell was studying medicine at University of Texas–Austin in 1983, but it was business that was on his mind. Even as a young boy growing up in Houston, Dell talked about making "more money than any other kid in school." As a freshman, Dell put together hard-drive kits that he sold to computer nerds who wanted to upgrade their IBM personal computers (PCs). By the end of the first semester Dell still hadn't bothered to buy textbooks, but by the end of the year he had grossed nearly $400,000. He dropped out at nineteen to start a computer mail-order business. By the time he would have received his college diploma, revenues for Dell Computer came to $34 million; his net worth in 2006 was estimated at $15.5 billion. Though Dell never graduated from UT Austin, he has given some $50 million to the college, which will name three new research centers on campus after him.

Well-known successes aside, the reality is that the diploma-deprived have succeeded against the odds. For every high-school dropout who has reached the zenith, there are millions who did not and never will, as an increasingly high-tech and sophisticated world demands more educational training. Harvard Business School's Anthony Mayo and Nitin Nohria, a business administration professor at the school, studied one thousand influential business leaders of the twentieth century—from Henry Ford to Bill Gates—and found that education was not an important factor in the early part of the century, when America was largely a manufacturing nation. But after the 1950s, says Mayo, about half the business leaders had a college degree. The same trend seems to be apparent among the Forbes 400, although educational data was not comprehensively collected in the early years of the list. In 1982 at least 50 of the nation's richest had a college degree. By 2006 the number had jumped to 244. The least educated are aging members of what TV journalist Tom Brokaw calls "the Greatest Generation," who may have experienced the Depression, fought in World War II, and then come home to help build postwar America. For many of them, schooling was not an option.

So what good is higher education if you can make it big without advanced

*The company name was changed to Dell Inc. in 2003.

degrees? For one thing, states Mayo, "There is a difference between intelligence and educational credentials." If you have the intelligence but not the credentials, you can succeed—although it will require more effort. Going to the right school and getting the right degree, says Mayo, simply "mitigates risks and opens doors." Google CEO Eric Schmidt (2006 net worth: $5.2 billion) adds another benefit to that mix. He believes that the United States' high-tech economy demands the type of technical skills acquired through advanced education. "Intelligence and drive have always been basic requirements for success in this country," he has said. "What's different today is that it's getting harder to succeed if you are not extremely well educated." Schmidt himself is laden with diplomas, including an electrical engineering degree from Princeton University and a PhD from Berkeley.

The role of college campuses as breeding grounds for potential businesses is another advantage. A number of companies that later propelled their founders to great riches were, in fact, born in a dorm room. Even though Microsoft founders Bill Gates and Paul Allen both dropped out of college, the seed for what became Microsoft was planted while Gates was still at Harvard. Allen had already dropped out of Washington State University to take a programming job in Boston. The story goes that while visiting Gates, Allen saw a *Popular Electronics* story describing the MITS Altair 8800, the "World's First Minicomputer Kit to Rival Commercial Models," which prompted the duo to talk themselves into dropping every-

1983

from the pages of *Forbes*

Lamar Hunt, son of Texas wildcatter H. L. Hunt, reportedly owns only one suit. (1983 net worth: $500 million)

J. R. Simplot, the Idaho potato king, flies a thirty-by-fifty-foot American flag in front of his house in Boise. (1983 net worth: $500 million)

T. Cullen Davis, heir to an oil field drilling fortune, is the richest man ever tried for murder and acquitted. (1983 net worth: $250 million)

Dapper **Harry B. Helmsley,** whose wealth comes from commercial real estate and hotels, was voted best-dressed businessman. (1983 net worth: $800 million)

thing and starting a company. "Paul saw that the technology was there," Gates later recalled. "He kept saying, 'It's gonna be too late. We'll miss it.'" They teamed up to write a version of BASIC (short for Beginner's All-purpose Symbolic Instruction Code), a compact computer language for the MITS machine, and Microsoft was born.

When Microsoft had about thirty-five employees, Gates and Allen de-

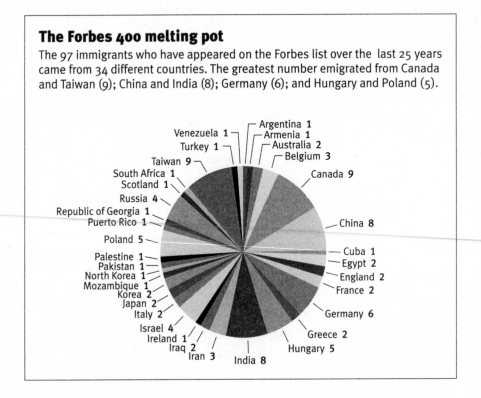

The Forbes 400 melting pot

The 97 immigrants who have appeared on the Forbes list over the last 25 years came from 34 different countries. The greatest number emigrated from Canada and Taiwan (9); China and India (8); Germany (6); and Hungary and Poland (5).

Argentina 1
Armenia 1
Australia 2
Belgium 3
Venezuela 1
Turkey 1
Taiwan 9
South Africa 1
Scotland 1
Russia 4
Republic of Georgia 1
Puerto Rico 1
Poland 5
Palestine 1
Pakistan 1
North Korea 1
Mozambique 1
Korea 2
Japan 2
Italy 2
Israel 4
Ireland 1
Iraq 2
Iran 3
India 8
Canada 9
China 8
Cuba 1
Egypt 2
England 2
France 2
Germany 6
Greece 2
Hungary 5

cided they needed a professional manager. They turned to Steve Ballmer, who had lived down the hall from Gates at Harvard. Unlike Gates, Ballmer, the son of Swiss immigrants, hung around Cambridge long enough to get his Harvard degree in math and economics. Brainy Ballmer then headed to Stanford for a master's, but quit to take the Microsoft job as head of marketing, user education, and systems testing.

Had Patrick McGovern skipped college, he never could have taken the same path to his billions. The son of a construction manager, McGovern had a fondness as a teen for problem solving and a fascination with computers. For a science fair project, he designed a computer program that played tic-tac-toe—not an easy feat in the 1950s. The project attracted the attention of MIT, which offered him a scholarship. It was through a series of random events at MIT that his future solidified. First, his roommate was on the school paper and asked him to help out. "I was amazed that I could pick up the phone and call anyone to ask them their opinion on a topic," he later said. The experience hooked him on reporting. Then, as a junior, he answered a school bulletin-board ad for a job as a technical editor for the

The top 20 richest Forbes 400 immigrants

Over the last 25 years, 97 immigrants to the United States have appeared on the 400 list. Below, the 20 richest.

Name	Country of Birth (nationality)	Years on List	Peak Value (in billions)	Peak Year
1 Sergey Brin	Russia	3	$14.1	2006
2 John W. Kluge	Germany	25	$13.0	2000
3 Rupert Murdoch	Australia	22	$11.0	2000
4 Pierre M. Omidyar	France (Iranian)	8	$10.4	2004
5 Sanjiv Sidhu	India	5	$9.8	2000
6 George Soros	Hungary	21	$8.5	2006
7 E. Deshpande Gururaj	India	1	$7.6	2000
8 Leonard Blavatnik	Russia	3	$7.0	2006
9 Edgar Bronfman Sr.	Canada	24	$6.8	2001
10 Jerry Yang	Taiwan	9	$6.4	2000
11 Ted Arison	Israel	12	$3.7	1993
12 Patrick Soon-Shiong	South Africa (Chinese)	4	$3.4	2006
13 Steven F. Udvar-Hazy	Hungary	14	$3.1	2006
14 Roland Arnall	France	3	$3.0	2006
15 Barbara Piasecka Johnson	Poland	21	$2.8	2006
15 Haim Saban	Egypt	6	$2.8	2006
17 James Kim	Korea	7	$2.7	2000
18 Pradeep Sindhu	India	1	$2.5	2000
18 Mort Zuckerman	Canada	18	$2.5	2006
20 Michael Fribourg	Belgium	17	$2.4	1997

pioneering computer magazine *Computers and Automation*. He got the job, and he honed his reporting and publishing skills. Three years after graduating from MIT, McGovern started his own weekly, *Computerworld*. Today his privately held, Boston-based International Data Group (IDG) puts out more than 300 information technology magazines and newspapers in 85 countries, has 400 technology-related Web sites, and organizes nearly 200 technology conferences a year. All told, McGovern reaches more than 120 million

Immigrants Who Hit the Jackpot

Some of the almost one hundred immigrants who made the 400 list are rags-to-riches tales, but by no means all of them are. Here's how some accumulated their fortunes:

Thomas Flatley (2006 net worth: $1.3 billion): Born and raised in County Mayo, Ireland, Flatley was eighteen when he left for Boston with little more than the proverbial pocket change. Flatley, whose father was American, did a military stint, then used the GI Bill to get a technical education. He never graduated, working instead as an electrician and plumber before easing into real estate. He built his first apartment building when he was twenty-seven, followed by investments in retail development. Now in his seventies, Flatley is one of the country's most prominent landlords.

Teresa Heinz (2004 net worth: $750 million): The daughter of a doctor, Heinz was born in Mozambique (formerly Portuguese East Africa) but moved to the United States to work as a UN translator. (She is fluent in five languages.) She married Pennsylvania senator H. John Heinz III, an heir to the Heinz food fortune, in 1966. Twenty-five years later he died in a plane crash, and in 1995 she married Massachusetts senator and former presidential candidate John Kerry. Heinz is a philanthropist, supporter of the environment, and trustee of the family wealth.

Bob Hope (1982 net worth: $280 million): British-born Leslie Townes Hope, the son of a stonemason and a musically inclined mother, was five years old when his family crossed the Atlantic Ocean in 1908. At age sixteen, he dropped out of school, went into vaudeville and then into comedy and films, and later made some shrewd real-estate deals. Hope died at age one hundred in 2003, still the funny man. A few months before his death, his wife asked Hope where he wanted to be buried. He answered: "Surprise me."

Haim Saban (2006 net worth: $2.8 billion): Saban was born to a Jewish family that moved from Egypt to Israel in 1956, and eventually to the United States. Saban, who likes to describe himself as a former "cartoon schlepper," never made it to college but did land jobs as a television producer, mostly for kids' shows like *Mighty Morphin' Power Rangers* and *Big Bad Beetleborgs*. In

2001 he hit it big with the sale of Fox Family Network, his joint venture with Rupert Murdoch's Fox Television, to Disney, which netted him $1.6 billion. His latest acquisition: Univision, the largest Spanish-language media firm in the United States, for which he paid nearly $13 billion in 2006.

Fayez Sarofim (2006 net worth: $1.5 billion): Also Egyptian-born, Sarofim has a bachelor's degree from University of California–Berkeley and an MBA from Harvard. He borrowed $100,000 in 1958 from his wealthy father to launch his own investment firm and later made a killing by buying stock in such start-up companies as Intel and Teledyne. Nicknamed the Sphinx, Sarofim and his Houston-based firm now manage some $40 billion in assets, mostly from Texas oil money.

Jerry Yang (2006 net worth: $2.2 billion): Yang, who left Taiwan at age ten with his widowed mother and younger brother, originally knew only one word of English: *shoe.* He picked up the language easily enough and went on to get BS and MS degrees in electrical engineering from Stanford. He cofounded Internet company Yahoo in the mid-1990s and became a multibillionaire while still in his thirties.

high-tech fans worldwide. (He sold his immensely popular, often-copied For Dummies series to John Wiley & Sons in 2001.) McGovern's net worth in 2006: $3 billion.

As every business school student knows, FedEx founder Fred Smith was an economics student at Yale when he wrote his senior thesis on improving overnight delivery services through a hub-and-spoke system. The paper only earned a C, but that didn't stop Smith from plowing a $3.2 million inheritance, $8 million of his family's money, and $70 million in venture capital into proving that his idea was viable. It worked so well that he took the company public in 1978 and grew it into the world's largest overnight delivery service. He more than recouped his investment: FedEx brought him a personal net worth of $2.2 billion in 2006.

Yahoo, the popular Web portal, and Google were both born at Stanford, under strikingly similar circumstances. Yahoo founders David Filo and Jerry Yang were Stanford graduate students when they designed a system for operating an Internet directory. The duo found the idea so compelling that they put their PhDs on hold in the mid-1990s to devote full attention to the Yahoo project. Now Filo and Yang are each billionaires twice over. Meanwhile, in 1998 Google cofounders Larry Page and Sergey Brin were working toward their PhDs in computer science at Stanford when they started running the now wildly popular search engine. The pair currently shares the company's presidency; their 2006 net worth came to about $14 billion each.

Even investing legend Warren Buffett directly owes part of his success to college. While a graduate student at Columbia University, Buffett took a course with value-investing icon Benjamin Graham that changed his life. Graham proposed that investors carefully research stocks to identify those selling below their intrinsic value—advice that Buffett has adhered to devoutly. (See "The Greatest Investor of All Time," page 187.) That he landed in Graham's class in the first place was a stroke of serendipity. After receiving an undergraduate degree from the University of Nebraska, Buffett applied to grad programs at both Harvard and Columbia; when Harvard rejected him, he attended his second choice. For his part, Graham was so impressed with the young Buffett that he was the only student to receive an A+ in his class.

Friendships forged at universities were also responsible for hooking up like-minded entrepreneurs who went on to do great things. University of Oregon track star Philip Knight and his track coach, Bill Bowerman, who died in 1999, shook hands on a deal to start an athletic shoe company shortly after Knight got an MBA from Stanford. The duo built up Nike into one of the nation's largest footwear manufacturers and retailers. Knight's 2006 net worth: $7.9 billion.

In yet another case, Harvard grad Scott McNealy and Indian-born Vinod Khosla were buddies at Stanford Graduate School of Business in the late 1970s. In 1982 Khosla asked McNealy's help in starting Sun Microsystems. Khosla became CEO; McNealy, head of manufacturing. "That meant I built the first 25 Suns by hand," he later told an interviewer, "and I had the skinned knuckles to show for it." A few years later Khosla went into semi-retirement at age thirty, and McNealy became Sun's CEO. In a series of public attacks against archrival Bill Gates, McNealy once said, "At least I graduated from Harvard." In 2001, the last time McNealy appeared on the Forbes list, his net worth was nearly $1 billion. Khosla's personal assets in 2003: $700 million.

As Google's Eric Schmidt puts it, "Colleges like Harvard and MIT and Stanford are part of a social network. You can be a brilliant entrepreneur, but

Which college has the richest grads?

Number of Forbes 400 members who graduated from selected schools (†) and their average net worth in billions in 2006.

School	Members	Average net worth
MIT	†††††† 6	$5.7
Harvard	†††††††††† 10	$4.8
U of Michigan	†††††† 6	$4.8
Yale	†††††††††††††† 14	$4.0
Columbia	†††† 4	$3.4
Princeton	††††††††† 9	$3.1
U of Pennsylvania	††††††††††† 11	$2.5
Stanford	†††††† 6	$2.3
UCLA	††††††† 7	$2.3
USC	††††††† 7	$2.1
U of Texas–Austin	†††††† 6	$2.1
Brown	†† 2	$1.8
UC–Berkeley	†††††††† 8	$1.8
Dartmouth	†† 2	$1.7
Cornell	††††††† 7	$1.5

Seven of the top ten richest college grads over the years attended state universities, at least for their first degree.

Warren Buffett	U of Nebraska
Gordon Moore	UC–Berkeley
S. Robson Walton	U of Arkansas
Helen Walton	U of Oklahoma
Philip Anschutz	U of Kansas
Sergey Brin	U of Maryland
Larry Page	U of Michigan

if you go to a no-name school you don't have access to these networks. Take my word for it, the networks count for a lot in this industry." Even aside from the chance to schmooze with the best and brightest, there's another upside to a degree from a fancy school—the public perception that the bearer of the degree inspires confidence. A 2005 study coauthored by associate professor Violina P. Rindova at the University of Maryland came to the conclusion that recruiters consider school reputation to be more important than student achievement. "The school's prominence provides legitimacy in the eyes of the third party," she says.

The richest graduates of selected colleges

Colleges looking for dollars would be wise to check this list of 400 members from the 2006 Forbes list who attended these schools. The largest single gift by a 400 member to an educational institution, according to *The Chronicle of Higher Education,* was $600 million, given to the California Institute of Technology by Intel cofounder Gordon Moore and his wife, Betty.

BROWN U

	2006 worth (in billions)
Ted Turner*	$1.9
W. Duncan MacMillan†	$1.6

COLUMBIA U

	2006 worth (in billions)
Warren Buffett	$46.0
John Kluge	$9.1
Dirk Ziff	$1.5
Daniel Ziff	$1.5
Randolph Lerner	$1.5

CORNELL U

	2006 worth (in billions)
Irwin Jacobs	$1.7
Winnie Johnson-Marquart	$1.6
Helen Johnson-Leipold	$1.6
S. Curtis Johnson	$1.6
H. Fisk Johnson	$1.6
Sanford Weill	$1.5
David Duffield	$1.2

DARTMOUTH C

	2006 worth (in billions)
Anthony Pritzker	$2.0
Steven Roth	$1.4

HARVARD U

	2006 worth (in billions)
Steven Ballmer	$13.6
George Kaiser	$8.5
Sumner Redstone	$7.5
Edward Johnson III	$7.5
Bruce Kovner	$3.0
Penny Pritzker	$2.1
Kenneth Griffin	$1.7
Robert Ziff	$1.5
J. Christopher Flowers	$1.2
George Joseph	$1.0

MIT

	2006 worth (in billions)
Charles Koch	$12.0
David Koch	$12.0
James Simons	$4.0
Patrick McGovern	$3.0
Victor Fung	$1.6
Amar Bose	$1.5

PRINCETON U

	2006 worth (in billions)
Carl Icahn	$9.7
Eric Schmidt	$5.2
Jeffrey Bezos	$3.6
Henry Hillman	$3.0
Peter Lewis	$1.4
John Fisher	$1.3
Margaret Whitman	$1.2
William Fisher	$1.2
Robert Fisher	$1.2

STANFORD U

	2006 worth (in billions)
Charles Schwab	$4.6
Jerry Yang	$2.2
Craig McCaw	$2.1
Leonore Annenberg	$2.0
Ray Dolby	$1.7
William Connor II	$1.2

*Never graduated, but later received an honorary degree.
†Died in 2006.

UC–BERKELEY

	2006 worth (in billions)
Gordon Moore	$3.4
Jess Jackson	$2.2
Michael Milken	$2.1
J. Russell DeLeon	$1.8
Fayez Sarofim	$1.5
Charles Simonyi	$1.0
Sehat Sutardja	$1.0
Weili Dai	$1.0

UCLA

	2006 worth (in billions)
Steven Udvar-Hazy	$3.1
A. Jerrold Perenchio	$3.0
Alfred Mann	$2.2
Henry Nicholas III	$2.0
Henry Samueli	$2.0
John Anderson	$1.9
Louis Gonda	$1.6

U OF MICHIGAN

	2006 worth (in billions)
Larry Page	$14.0
Samuel Zell	$4.5
Joan Tisch	$3.4
Stephen Ross	$2.5
Jorge Perez	$1.8
Charles Munger	$1.6

U OF PENNSYLVANIA

	2006 worth (in billions)
Ronald Perelman	$7.0
Steven Cohen	$3.0
Donald Trump	$2.9
Leonard Lauder	$2.9
Ronald Lauder	$2.7
Charles Butt	$2.2
James Kim	$1.5
George Lindemann	$1.5
Jon Huntsman	$1.5
Phillip Frost	$1.4
Edmund Ansin	$1.2

USC

	2006 worth (in billions)
Bradley Hughes	$4.1
George Lucas	$3.6
Edward Roski Jr.	$1.8
Igor Olenicoff	$1.6
Alan Casden	$1.5
Scott Cook	$1.3
Thomas Barrack	$1.0

U OF TEXAS AUSTIN

	2006 worth (in billions)
Robert Rowling	$5.2
Richard Rainwater	$2.5
Joseph Jamail Jr.	$1.4
Billy McCombs	$1.3
William Moncrief Jr.	$1.0
Jeffrey Hildebrand	$1.0

YALE U

	2006 worth (in billions)
John Mars	$10.5
Forrest Mars, Jr.	$10.5
Robert Bass	$5.5
Herbert Kohler	$4.5
Charles Johnson	$4.5
Edward Lampert	$3.8
Stephen Schwarzman	$3.5
Lee Bass	$3.0
Edward Bass	$2.5
Frederick Smith	$2.2
John Malone	$1.7
Whitney MacMillan	$1.6
Cargill MacMillan Jr.	$1.6
Wilbur Ross Jr.	$1.2

The Forbes 400 lists over the years seem to bear out a slowly rising trend toward graduates of big-name schools, but the number remains well below 10 percent. In the first Forbes 400 list in 1982, at least thirteen members were graduates of Ivy League schools. Their average net worth came to $183 million, and their aggregate fortunes totaled $2.4 billion. By 2006 the number of Ivy Leaguers had risen to thirty; their average worth jumped to $3 billion, and their total worth had escalated to $97 billion.

Still, non-Ivies are the bread-and-butter schools of the vast majority of Forbes 400 college graduates. Some of the list's biggest names went to schools without prestigious names. Famed filmmaker Steven Spielberg, for example, was rejected by film schools at the University of Southern California and UCLA. He went to California State–Long Beach instead, and still managed to eke out a $2.9 billion fortune. Another, lesser-known, success is California investor Charles Brandes (2006 net worth: $2 billion), who got his economics degree from Bucknell University and then did some graduate work at San Diego State. Less than a decade later, as a thirty-one-year-old stockbroker in La Jolla, California, he started his own money management firm. Like Buffett, Brandes is a disciple of Benjamin Graham, following the strategy of investing in high-intrinsic-value companies with low stock prices. Or, as he partly explains his approach in his best-selling *Value Investing Today:* "Buy straw hats in winter."

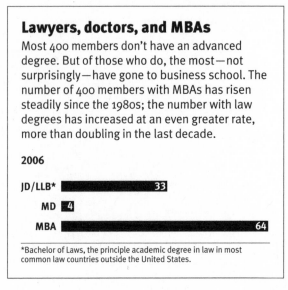

Lawyers, doctors, and MBAs

Most 400 members don't have an advanced degree. But of those who do, the most—not surprisingly—have gone to business school. The number of 400 members with MBAs has risen steadily since the 1980s; the number with law degrees has increased at an even greater rate, more than doubling in the last decade.

2006

JD/LLB* 33
MD 4
MBA 64

*Bachelor of Laws, the principle academic degree in law in most common law countries outside the United States.

As for the MBAs so popular among would-be Wall Street titans, although the number of business degrees granted in the United States has exploded from 26,500 in 1970 to 139,000 in 2004, only 16 percent of those on the 2006 Forbes 400 list had an MBA—meaning that the vast majority did not. When *Forbes* once asked some of America's superrich whether there was any value to having an MBA, opinions varied. Home Depot cofounder Arthur Blank, who has a bachelor's degree from Babson College, reflected the popular viewpoint

The Boys from Budapest

For a country that's the size of Indiana, Hungary has produced more than its share of Forbes 400 members: five. All were originally from Budapest: Investor George Soros, leasing billionaire Steven F. Udvar-Hazy and his business partner Leslie Gonda (Gonda's Venezuelan-born son, Louis Gonda, is also a billionaire), the late real-estate mogul and Holocaust survivor Laszlo Nandor Tauber, and former Microsoft programmer Charles Simonyi.

Simonyi, for one, knew at a young age that Communist Hungary, where he was taught that workers could never own the "means of production," was not where he wanted to be. He showed an early interest in computers, and his father, an electrical-engineering professor, let him tinker with the antiquated vacuum-tube computers used in late-1950s Budapest. Meanwhile, the elder Simonyi was quietly charting an escape route for his son. At age seventeen, Charles left Hungary on his own to work at a Danish computer institute. After one year, he headed for the University of California–Berkeley.

As a student, Simonyi faced a few obstacles, not least of which were his temporary visas, which kept expiring, He couldn't claim residency on the grounds that he had been persecuted by the Communists—"I left Hungary too early to be hurt," he now says. "No one was shooting at me at the Hungarian border." Yet he couldn't get a scholarship as a foreign student. So he began working at Berkeley's computer center to help with tuition. Even before getting his bachelor's degree, Simonyi was hired at Xerox PARC (Palo Alto Research Center), where he developed the Bravo text editor, an early document preparation program. In time, Simonyi also picked up a PhD from Stanford and legal residency in the United States.

Simonyi met Bill Gates in 1980 and, restless at Xerox, decided to join him at Microsoft. The two clicked in a "very intense way," Simonyi says, recalling that colleagues at Xerox were "aghast that I was leaving a preeminent research lab for an unknown start-up led by a twenty-three-year-old who looked more like sixteen. He didn't even wear glasses at that time. But I could see immediately that he was a person with an unbelievable focus and drive—on top of being clever." At Microsoft, Simonyi helped develop the popular Excel and Word programs, gaining a reputation as a programming genius—and a net worth of $1 billion. He left Microsoft in 2002 and now runs his own firm, Intentional Software, focused on improving how organizations write software.

Boyish and fit, Simonyi is also working hard at enjoying his riches. He's often mentioned as Martha Stewart's love interest ("I've known Martha for more than ten years," he says, "and we are best of friends"), and he spends six months a year on his 233-foot yacht. ("Yachts are the closest a commoner can get to sovereignty," he once said.) A pilot with more than two thousand hours of flying time, Simonyi paid $25 million to Russia's space agency for a thirteen-day orbital space flight in spring 2007. To keep himself grounded at home, Simonyi has a machine shop in the basement of his house; there he keeps a lathe and drill press to remind himself of the means of production he was once told he could never own.

that an MBA is only a blip along the learning continuum: "Education is a lifetime process. This is just one step along the way." Las Vegas mogul Phillip Ruffin (2006 net worth: $1.4 billion) says, "It can't hurt, but it's not essential." Ruffin himself is living proof: He dropped out of college to sell hamburgers, got into the real-estate business, and now owns forty-one prime acres on the Las Vegas casino strip. Some, like oil and gas multibillionaire George Kaiser, who has a Harvard MBA, flatly state that the degree is not necessary—at least "not for entrepreneurial business," says Kaiser.

The real value of an MBA, believes Franklin Otis Booth Jr., who graduated from California Institute of Technology and then got an MBA from Stanford, is that it "teaches the conventions by which businesses are conducted." But would Booth have amassed his $1.9 billion fortune without the degree? Quite likely. First, he got a head start with an inheritance from great-grandfather Harrison Gray Otis, founder of the Times-Mirror newspaper publishing company. Then he hit the jackpot with an early $1 million investment in Warren Buffett's Berkshire Hathaway, making him a rare case of a Forbes 400 member who made the list by being a passive investor—a feat with odds about as slim as winning the lottery.

Wharton School management professor Raphael Amit argues that as hard as it is to believe, money really isn't what drives most entrepreneurs. "What we found in a very deep study of entrepreneurs is that wealth is not the primary driver," he says. "No one is saying that they don't like wealth; but what matters more is the innovation, the intense commitment they have to an idea, and the difference it can make. Money is the by-product." Stephen Goldbart, who codirects the Money, Meaning & Choices Institute in Kentfield, California, agrees. "Certainly people who get rich want to be financially rewarded and expect to be." But there's more to it, he says: "Money isn't the only value they see in what they are doing. These are people who love to build."

Often the process of building a company involves embracing a work ethic that most people would find excruciating. "What I do is I work," the late Kenneth W. Ford, another timber lord from Roseburg and an erstwhile Forbes 400 member, once said. "I don't do anything else. I don't have a social life to speak of. I don't read, can't drive a nail in straight. I work. That's what I do." New York's billionaire mayor Michael Bloomberg cannot—simply cannot—imagine ever retiring. "The people I respect are all doing things," says Bloomberg. "They're all workaholics. Not just in their businesses: They're all working on boards or advising. Sure, there are some who retire. But I don't know what the heck they do." Or as media giant John W. Kluge, once the richest man in America (and now worth $9.1 billion), told *Forbes,* "I don't think I've ever 'worked' in my life, because 'work' to me means that you're really doing something that you don't like. I hate to tell you this, but I've never liked the weekend in my life. I was enthusiastic about Monday morning from the day I left college."

2

Risk

Ⅰf there is one cardinal rule of the Forbes 400, it is this: If you don't inherit money, the likeliest route to making a real bundle is by taking a lot of risks. It's not for nothing that the 400 is bursting with card sharks and poker players. Hedge fund honcho Steve Cohen played all-night poker games during high school (his brother Donald said his desk would be stacked with $100 bills in the morning). Media magnate John Kluge spent his college days playing poker and graduated from Columbia University in 1937 with $7,000 in winnings, the equivalent of $97,987 today. Takeover artist Henry Kravis whiled away the hours waiting on a 1986 deal to acquire conglomerate Beatrice Companies by playing poker. "I'd just won a hand and was raking in the pot when the good news came," Kravis said at the time. "This time around, we had a $20 pool to see who could call the time of the announcement closest." And odd couple Bill Gates and Warren Buffett, two of the wealthiest men in U.S. history, are fond of playing poker and bridge together.

Many of the Forbes 400 have been willing to take gargantuan risks, sometimes a number of times, in order to realize their dreams. Toy salesman Ty Warner mortgaged his home and invested his life savings to launch Beanie Babies. Paul Fireman put his home in hock for the U.S. distribution rights to a small British shoe company called Reebok. And billionaire industrialist Dennis Washington spent the first ten years of his career using his house as security on loans so that he could bid on highway contracts. Even when they make it to the top, many of the 400 do not stop gambling. Shipping magnate Daniel Ludwig poured as much as $850 million into building a wood pulp factory in the middle of the Amazon. Donald Trump borrowed hundreds of millions of dollars to build on his father's substantial real-estate empire. And oilman and corporate raider T. Boone Pickens bet his entire company, Mesa Petroleum, which he had spent most of his life building, on his instinct that the falling price of natural gas would eventually go up. (Although the price later went up, it didn't at the time, and Pickens was bought out.)

Big-time entrepreneurs don't just capture the imagination: They embody something of the American Dream. Where else in the world could so many people born of humble origins or who emigrated from foreign shores rise in a short period of time to become among the richest in the country? Among the men who have topped the Forbes 400 are eighth-grade dropout Ludwig and German immigrant Kluge, who grew up with his mother in a Detroit tenement. With the benefit of hindsight it's easy to see how these men succeeded. But at the time their gambles appeared to be edge-of-the-seat risks— if not to the headstrong individuals themselves, then at least to outsiders.

In many cases, Forbes 400 types seem to have a different perception of risk than the average person. Risk takers have to be able to think big, and they have to be able to leverage those big ideas with whatever assets they have at hand: homes, real estate, the shirt off their back. To succeed, they also have to be 100 percent focused on winning and have the confidence to go against the conventional wisdom. Conversely, and this may be the key point for many who have made it onto the Forbes list, they have to know how to avoid disaster, evaluating the risks well enough to ensure that failure doesn't wipe them out. When large corporations are desperate to sell, for example, enterprising members of the Forbes 400 will step in with a lowball offer that guarantees a safety net. Witness Dennis Washington, who bought the Anaconda Copper Mining Company in Butte, Montana, for $13.5 million in 1986. Washington persuaded the desperate seller, Atlantic Richfield Company (ARCO)—which had lost $100 million on the mine in the past sixteen years—to throw in fifty thousand acres of wilderness, recreation, and mining land along with it. "I figured my worst risk at Anaconda was $20 million, and I could have recouped most of that from scrapping the mines," Washington later said.*

---

*The next year, Washington bought the Burlington Northern Railroad's southern Montana rail system for $160 million—quite a risk if he hadn't locked in a guarantee from Burlington that they would run a large amount of traffic over his newly named Montana Rail Link lines. As Texas legend H. L. Hunt once aptly said, "I've never taken a risk so big that if it went against me I couldn't keep right on going."

The biggest winners and losers, year by year

Up a billion, down a billion—so it goes for the Forbes 400, especially the biggest gainers and losers. More interesting, perhaps, than the dollars won or lost are the percentage figures, which show the sometimes huge annual swings in wealth among the 400.

Year	Name	Gain/Loss ($ billion)	Gain/Loss Percentage
1982–1983	Sam Walton	+1.46	+211.6
	Lamar Hunt	−0.50	−50.0
	Perry Bass	−0.50	−50.0
	Sid Bass	−0.50	−50.0
1983–1984	Gordon Getty	+1.90	+86.4
	Daniel Ludwig	−1.50	−75.0
1984–1985	John Kluge	+0.70	+233.3
	Gordon Getty	−3.15	−76.8
1985–1986	Sam Walton	+1.70	+60.7
	William Herbert Hunt	−0.45	−56.3
1986–1987	Sam Walton	+4.00	+88.9
	Gordon Getty	−0.85	−70.8
1987–1988	Henry Hillman	+1.00	+66.7
	Sam Walton	−1.80	−21.2
1988–1989	Warren Buffett	+2.00	+90.9
	John Kluge	+2.00	+62.5
	Sam Walton	−4.90	−73.1
1989–1990	Bill Gates	+1.25	+100.0
	Sumner Redstone	−0.88	−30.6
1990–1991	Bill Gates	+2.30	+92.0
	A. Alfred Taubman	−1.50	−71.4
1991–1992	Rupert Murdoch	+1.50	+136.4
	Bill Gates	+1.50	+31.3
	Henry Hillman	−0.90	−27.3
1992–1993	Warren Buffett	+3.93	+89.2
	Richard DeVos	−0.75	−30.0
	Jan Van Andel	−0.75	−30.0
1993–1994	Edward Crosby Johnson III	+3.40	+200.0
	Sumner Redstone	−1.60	−28.6

Year	Name	Gain/Loss ($ billion)	Gain/Loss Percentage
1994–1995	Bill Gates	+5.45	+58.3
	Edward Crosby Johnson III	−4.10	−80.4
1995–1996	Bill Gates	+3.70	+25.0
	Sumner Redstone	−1.40	−29.2
1996–1997	Bill Gates	+21.30	+115.1
	Stanley Hubbard	−0.91	−50.6
1997–1998	Bill Gates	+18.60	+46.7
	Larry Ellison	−4.30	−46.7
1998–1999	Bill Gates	+26.60	+45.5
	Ronald Perelman	−2.20	−36.7
1999–2000	Larry Ellison	+45.00	+346.2
	Bill Gates	−22.00	−25.9
2000–2001	Warren Buffett	+5.20	+18.6
	Larry Ellison	−36.10	−62.2
2001–2002	Warren Buffett	+2.80	+8.4
	Bill Gates	−11.00	−20.4
2002–2003	Charles Ergen	+4.50	+102.3
	Eli Broad	−1.00	−20.8
2003–2004	Warren Buffett	+5.00	+13.9
	Larry Ellison	−4.30	−23.9
2004–2005	Sheldon Adelson	+8.50	+283.3
	Helen Walton	−2.60	−14.4
2005–2006	Sheldon Adelson	+9.00	+78.3
	Paul Allen	−6.50	−28.9

The saga of Haroldson Lafayette Hunt and the Texas Hunts illustrates both the upside and the downside of the gambling instinct that permeates the Forbes 400. When H. L. Hunt's father died in 1911, the then twenty-two-year-old man from Fayette County, Illinois, set out to earn his fortune. Armed with a $5,000 inheritance, he headed for Lake Village, Arkansas, where he invested in 960 acres of farmland. Hunt wanted to be a cotton farmer, but fate dealt him a different hand: His cotton crop was wiped out in the first flooding to hit the area in thirty-five years. And so the young man was forced to turn to a vocation he already knew well. He had proved to be an ace card player in his previous travels as a teenager, earning himself the nickname Arizona Slim. Hunt stayed afloat through those difficult years in Arkansas playing cards day and night.

Hunt eventually opened a gambling hall in El Dorado, Arkansas, invested in his first oil leases, and struck oil with his first well. But it wasn't until he signed a deal in November 1930 to take over the lease of the Daisy Bradford No. 3, a well in the East Texas oil field, that he hit the jackpot. The well was situated in an extremely productive section of the biggest oil find of the early twentieth century. And it was the basis for Hunt's future oil empire, which would later be estimated at $2 billion.

In his biography of the Hunt family, *Texas Rich: The Hunt Dynasty, from the Early Oil Days Through the Silver Crash,* Harry Hurt III noted that H. L. Hunt was "a man of contradictions and eccentricities . . . but, at heart, he was still a gambler. He still craved new opportunities to make money—not because he wanted possessions per se, but because the gambler in him wanted to see if he could run up the score. Specifically, Hunt wanted to put his profits from East Texas into new drilling ventures, for, as he saw it, 'The more wells you drill, the greater chance you have of finding oil.' "

All the time that Hunt poured money into new wells, he continued to gamble. He considered himself one of the best poker players in America—and not without some justification. The wildcatter once placed a $200,000 bet on a football game that broke all the bookies in Kansas City. Another time he came from $10,000 down to win more than $100,000 from a professional Las Vegas gambler.

H. L. Hunt was a staunch conservative, except when it came to women. He raised six children with his first wife, Lyda Hunt, and had a further eight children with two other women. All of which made for a confusing lineage when the old man died in 1974. Death may have cheated Hunt out of his place on the 400 list, which debuted in 1982. But he was the self-proclaimed richest man in America in his day. And his descendants made a strong showing in that first *Forbes* special issue, with twelve places on the list—outnumbering the Hearsts (five) and Mellons (six) but overshadowed by the Du Ponts (twenty-four).

While Hunt's children, especially Bunker and Herbert, had the luxury of an inheritance to gamble with (and famously went bankrupt in 1980, after trying to corner the world market in silver) most members of the Forbes 400 are self-made: 70 percent in 2006. And so it's all the more noteworthy that so many of them are willing not only to take chances with their fortunes, but also seem to take outsize chances. And often, the deals they sink their money into are exactly the opposite of what conventional wisdom deems a prudent investment.

Jon Huntsman, whom TV talk-show host Larry King once described as "the most remarkable billionaire most of America has never heard of," is one such master risk taker. By his late thirties Huntsman was a multimillionaire, having gone for broke with a $300,000 loan to start the Huntsman Container Corporation in the early 1970s with his brother. Both brothers mortgaged their homes and assets for the loan. Over the following years the brothers diversified into the chemical industry and saw their company bought by a string of firms that finally netted Huntsman $8 million.

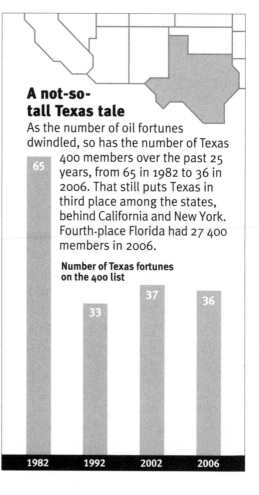

A not-so-tall Texas tale

As the number of oil fortunes dwindled, so has the number of Texas 400 members over the past 25 years, from 65 in 1982 to 36 in 2006. That still puts Texas in third place among the states, behind California and New York. Fourth-place Florida had 27 400 members in 2006.

Number of Texas fortunes on the 400 list

1982	1992	2002	2006
65	33	37	36

In the late 1970s Huntsman, a devout Mormon and father of nine, headed to Washington, D.C., to carry out missionary work. When he returned to Salt Lake City in 1982, at the age of forty-five, he embarked on his riskiest venture yet—the purchase of a $42 million polystyrene plant from Shell Oil. And the methods he employed displayed a mind-boggling mastery of leverage.

It was the depths of the recession, and polystyrene, a kind of plastic used in everything from food packaging to cutlery, was in oversupply. Like many big firms, Shell was desperate to get rid of the plant that it had originally bought for $67 million—so desperate that it was willing to sell the plant for $42 million. But who would want to go against prevailing wisdom and buy it? It turned out that Huntsman would. First he borrowed $500,000 against his house and $1.3 million against assets, including a restaurant. Then he approached petroleum firm ARCO. He asked the company to lend him $10 million. In return, he promised to buy 150 million pounds of raw materials from ARCO every year for the next thirteen years. Finally, he persuaded Shell to guarantee $12 million of a $29 million bank loan and to defer $3 million of the purchase price until later. With that Huntsman bought a $42 million plant.

Although most of the financing came from other people's pockets, as is frequently the case with the biggest risk takers, Huntsman says he could not have convinced any of the other parties to buy in if he hadn't been prepared to put all his possessions on the line: "They want to see some type of equity, and if you don't have a rich uncle, the only equity you can put up is whatever you own—your house and any other assets you may have. They may not amount to much but at least it's everything you've got. Then they can believe you. And that's more important to most people than the equity you put up."

Indeed, the Shell executives were so impressed with Huntsman's risk-taking ability that after the deal they bought him a bronze sculpture inscribed RIVERBOAT GAMBLER. FROM YOUR FRIENDS AT SHELL. The sculpture has pride of place in the lobby of Huntsman's corporate office in Salt Lake City. "I took it as a great compliment," says Huntsman. "Riverboat gamblers were survivors during the 1800s, and I was honored they would characterize me that way. I was their largest single customer for twelve years. I always considered that a badge of honor."

Although Huntsman concedes that he took a risk, he believes there was nothing reckless in his decision. "I thought I had studied my economics well and studied my supply demand curves, and as it turned out I was right," says Huntsman. "Within a few years I broke even, and then the gold hit and I made hundreds of millions of dollars from a very modest investment."

Huntsman makes it sound easy. But a couple of years after he bought the Shell plant, the industry was still in recession and Huntsman was still in financial trouble. Not only did he refuse to give up, but, convinced that the market was about to turn upward, he continued his acquisitions and bought a further three plants from the German chemical firm Hoechst AG for $45 million. This time Huntsman paid nothing up front. The market was so bad, and the cost of closing the plants so high, that Hoechst agreed to defer the cost for five years. Within a month of the deal the market started to make a comeback. And within a year the plants were making enough money to pay for themselves. Ten years later they were worth $200 million.

In the Red

Even the most calculated risk can go horribly wrong. But while many a business owned by the Forbes 400 has plunged into bankruptcy, it is rare that Forbes 400 members have had to file for personal bankruptcy, as did Herbert and Bunker Hunt, following their unsuccessful scheme to corner the silver market in the early 1980s.

One of the unfortunate few, like the Hunts, to file for personal bankruptcy was T. Cullen Davis of Fort Worth, Texas, who, along with his brother Kenneth, inherited a $2 billion oil field supply and production company, Kendavis Industries. The Davis family were pillars of Texas society and power, and the brothers were estimated to have a combined $500 million net worth in 1982. But the firm fell apart during the oil bust of the early 1980s. Cullen embarked on a series of highly leveraged real-estate deals, personally guaranteeing the debt. By 1986, when he filed for personal bankruptcy, he was more than $200 million in the red. His brother lost almost everything, too, though he never personally guaranteed his debts and therefore escaped personal bankruptcy. Cullen emerged with a small oil company, Great Western Drilling, where he employed his brother with an after-tax salary of $25,000. The oil and real-estate collapse of the early 1980s also overwhelmed another Texas oil magnate and member of the Forbes 400, Clint W. Murchison Jr. The founder of the Dallas Cowboys filed for personal bankruptcy in 1985 with debts of more than $500 million, just one year after *Forbes* estimated his net worth to be $250 million.

But personal bankruptcy does not have to mean never making the Forbes 400. William Gordon Bennett filed for personal bankruptcy after his chain of furniture stores went under in the early 1960s. Then age forty-one, Bennett took a job in a Vegas casino. Within ten years he bought the failing Circus Circus Hotel & Casino with a business partner, Bill Pennington, and the pair turned the casino around. Bennett entered the list with a net worth of $215 million in 1985. When he died in 2003, *Forbes* estimated his fortune at $600 million.

If only real-estate and health-care mogul Abraham D. Gosman had been so lucky. During the mid-1990s Gosman had all the trappings of wealth—a plane, a yacht, a multimillion-dollar art collection, and a seven-acre oceanfront property in Palm Beach called Maison de l'Amitie that had once been owned by the Post family. *Forbes* valued his net worth at almost $500 million. But overbuilding and government Medicare cutbacks in the late 1990s drove his businesses—Meditrust, PhyMatrix, and CareMatrix—deep into debt. His personal bankruptcy case in 2001 was one of the largest in Florida history. In 2004 Maison de l'Amitie was sold in an auction at U.S. Bankruptcy Court for $41.25 million. The winning bidder: Donald Trump.

Displaying Huntsman's "riverboat gambler" mentality and his ability to get others to share his risk, fellow 400 member "Red" Emmerson bet his entire business after it was already a success. Emmerson built timber company Sierra Pacific from scratch, starting with a $10,000 loan he and his father took out in 1949. He rode out two recessions between the mid-1970s and the mid-1980s, taking cost-cutting measures such as paving his mill yards so that gravel and mud would not damage the saws. In 1978 and 1979 Emmerson sold two-by-ten white fir at $400 per thousand board feet. By 1981 white fir had fallen to $125 per thousand board feet. He would have gone under were it not for a line of credit from the bank and a resurgence in the market.

But in the late 1980s Emmerson faced an even bigger challenge. Under pressure from environmentalists, the federal government had been implementing measures since the mid-1960s that curtailed logging on public land. Sierra Pacific relied upon these forests for its logging. So in 1987, when the Santa Fe Southern Pacific Corporation put 522,000 acres of Sierra timberland up for sale, Emmerson decided to buy it. He used all ten of his mills as collateral and borrowed $460 million from a syndicate of banks.

Conventional wisdom, of course, held that Emmerson overpaid. But three years later logging on public land was curtailed to save the northern spotted owl, and land prices soared. "Every time I buy something I think I pay too much for it," says Emmerson. "And you look back a few years later and digest it; you think, 'That was a pretty good buy.' " According to *Forbes*, the value of Emmerson's land doubled; Emmerson says the increase was 25 to 30 percent. Either way, it saved his business and made him an even wealthier man. Many sawmills that didn't own enough land were forced to close, and Emmerson was able to expand his holdings even further.

So what is it about risk takers that allows them to pursue one death-defying deal after the next and still sleep at night? It comes down to this: If you're going to take massive risks, you simply can't perceive huge personal debt as the catastrophe that it would be to most people. In fact, the hallmark of risk-taking may well be such an unshakable confidence in success that it overwhelms any concern for failure. Andrew Keyt, executive director of the Chicago Family Business Center at Loyola University, says that although entrepreneurs experience anxiety about their businesses, their fears are overridden by a sense of purpose and a supreme confidence in their ability. And in a 1982 article in *Time* magazine, Jerry White, of the Caruth Institute for Entrepreneurship at Southern Methodist University's Cox School of Business, wrote: "Entrepreneurs have a fundamental need to control their own destiny. Seldom can they find this in someone else's organization."

Huntsman is a classic example of the gambler who is confident because he is in control and has done his homework. In his case he embarked on a highly leveraged acquisition spree only after a careful study of overcapacity and undercapacity in the chemical industry. "I think most of it is sheer hard work and a study of the markets," says Huntsman. "I don't give myself credit for having a golden touch as much as I do for my hard work and understanding of the marketplace. I think that is the definition of an entrepreneur versus the bureaucratic organization."

Such a belief in oneself, combined with careful market analysis, was displayed by Al Lerner when he put his millions on the line in the early 1990s to rescue the troubled Baltimore bank MNC Financial. Lerner had been the largest shareholder in the bank for only nine months, after another bank in which he held a large position was bought by MNC. But in that time he had watched his stock fall to less than one-third its original value. MNC had $27 billion in assets, but almost 20 percent of its loans were non-performing: The borrowers were not making their interest and principal payments. Federal regulators were circling and threatening to seize MNC's biggest asset: MBNA, its credit-card subsidiary.

MNC executives were pessimistic. But Lerner turned them around. He took them into a conference room and announced: "We are not going to fail.

1984

from the pages of *Forbes*

Carl Landegger, heir to pulp and paper mills, is an avid amateur archaeologist; he discovered several pre-Columbian cities, along with a sixteenth-century galleon, the earliest New World salvage vessel on record. (1984 net worth: $150 million)

Philip Knight, CEO of Nike, is a dedicated runner himself, with a four-minute thirteen-second mile. (1984 net worth: $150 million)

Ross Perot, founder of Electronic Data Systems, was the first person to lose $1 billion—on paper, in 1969, when his hot EDS stock plunged. (1984 net worth: $1.4 billion)

August Anheuser Busch Jr., at age eighty-two, was the first American to win the Queen's Cup coaching title in England for precision horse and carriage driving. (1984 net worth: $425 million)

Anybody who believes we are going to fail, I don't want on my team." Lerner called federal regulators' bluff by threatening to declare bankruptcy unless they freed up MBNA for public sale. He even drafted a press release that declared MNC bankrupt to push his point. When regulators backed off, Lerner sold MBNA to the public. And in order to persuade prestigious investment bank Goldman Sachs to lead the deal, he personally bought $100 million worth of shares. In 1991 *Forbes* estimated Lerner's net worth at $290 million. Five years later he was worth $1.4 billion.

Sheldon Adelson, who likewise embodies the self-confidence of a riverboat gambler, has spent the past couple of years jostling for third place on the Forbes 400—the highest spot currently attainable on a list dominated by runaway leaders Buffett and Gates. But if Adelson continues to accumulate wealth at the rate he's been doing for the past few years, *Forbes* estimates he could shoot past both of them by 2012. Between 2004 and 2006, Adelson's wealth increased by a staggering $23.6 million a day. (Or to put it another way: In the time it takes to read a typical paragraph in this book, Adelson's wealth increases by about $16,000.)

Adelson, the son of a Boston taxi driver, made his debut on the Forbes 400 in 1995 with a net worth of $360 million, thanks to his creation of the giant annual Computer Dealer's Exhibition (COMDEX) in Las Vegas. But he owes his multibillion-dollar fortune to the hotel-casino industry. In 1989 Adelson bought his first hotel casino, the Las Vegas Sands, and soon after built the 1.2-million-square-foot Sands Expo Center on the site. But while his COMDEX trade show flourished in the early 1990s, Adelson lost money on the hotel every year for the first five years.

Seated in a conference room at a New York public-relations firm, the pugnacious billionaire claims fearlessness is essential. "I look back now, and I see that if I were to go today and attack any industry, food, furniture, I would find out the way people do things, and I would do it a different way, and I am sure to succeed," Adelson says. "Because I go to somebody and say, 'Why do you do things that way?' and they say, 'Well, we have always done it this way.'

"The reality is a lot of people have good ideas. I am not the only guy in the world with good ideas. But people are afraid to lose, and one of the main characteristics of practicing entrepreneurship is to be unafraid of losing. If you are afraid of losing you will never attack something. It's good to have a risk-taking mentality. Even if I do lose I am not frightened to get up and try again."

Adelson showed no fear in his attack on the Vegas gaming and hotel industry. In 1995 he sold COMDEX to the Japanese firm SoftBank for $862 million (Adelson's stake was worth $510 million). Rather than cash in his chips, he

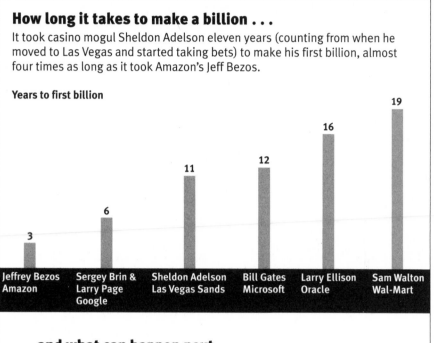

How long it takes to make a billion . . .

It took casino mogul Sheldon Adelson eleven years (counting from when he moved to Las Vegas and started taking bets) to make his first billion, almost four times as long as it took Amazon's Jeff Bezos.

Years to first billion

3	6	11	12	16	19
Jeffrey Bezos Amazon	Sergey Brin & Larry Page Google	Sheldon Adelson Las Vegas Sands	Bill Gates Microsoft	Larry Ellison Oracle	Sam Walton Wal-Mart

. . . and what can happen next

In the two years after Sheldon Adelson took his Las Vegas Sands public, he got rich faster than anyone else in history, according to *Forbes* — making just under $1 million an hour. Here's a rough look at the moneymaking performance of some billionaires during the first two years their companies were publicly owned.

	Millions earned per day	2006 net worth (in billions)
Sheldon Adelson	$23.6	$20.5
Sergey Brin	$13.4	$14.1
Larry Page	$13.3	$14.0
Jeff Bezos	$12.8	$3.6
Bill Gates	$1.8	$53.0
Sam Walton	$0.36	$28.0*
Larry Ellison	$0.31	$19.5

*Net worth at time of death in 1992

plowed them right back into a new venture. He demolished the loss-making Sands hotel and built in its place the four-thousand-room Venetian at a cost of $1.5 billion. Adelson's stake in the venture was almost $450 million in cash and land, with a further $500 million raised in bonds underwritten by Goldman Sachs. Before Adelson, Vegas hotels ignored the midweek convention crowd, who were seen as low spenders. But the opulent Venetian was designed to attract the business visitor. Every room in the hotel is a minimum seven hundred square feet in size. Facilities include faxes, minibars, and food cooked by top chefs. The Vegas Old Guard said it would never work. But it did.

The Venetian, which opened in 1999, is one of the most successful casino hotels on the Las Vegas Strip. Even when first-quarter profits took a hit in 2001—the company blamed a lucky run at the tables—the Venetian still turned a profit, thanks to a 99.6 percent room occupancy, at an average rate of $250 per room. In the first six months of 2006, the Venetian took in revenue of $455 million. But Adelson didn't stop there. In 2004 he opened the Sands Macau in China. A former Portuguese colony that was handed back to the Chinese in 1999, Macau is the only place in China where gambling is legal. As such, it is a new battleground for the gaming industry. Octogenarian Chinese billionaire Stanley Ho monopolized the Macau gaming industry for decades. But in 2002 Macau authorities ended his reign, opening up licenses to outside competitors. Adelson was first through the gates, with his Vegas rival and fellow Forbes 400 member Steve Wynn, owner of the Wynn Las Vegas, not far behind.

While other investors hemmed and hawed over gaming regulations, Adelson threw himself into the fray. He gambled $265 million on the Sands Macau, a casino-only venture that was built in just fourteen months. The Sands Macau raked in $400 million in revenues in its first year. That same year Adelson took Las Vegas Sands public, and his net worth exploded from $3 billion in the fall of 2004 to $11.5 billion in the spring of 2005. When the 2006 Forbes list was published, Adelson's net worth had jumped to $20.5 billion—a gain of $17.5 billion in just two years.

Flush from his Macau triumph and still basking in his extraordinary success, Adelson continues to push his luck. He's built the Palazzo, a $1.8 billion hotel casino, next door to the Venetian. Meanwhile, in Macau, Adelson has embarked on his biggest venture yet—a $6 billion development on the Cotai Strip, a spit of land between Macau's two main islands.

Adelson's vision for the Cotai Strip includes seven hotel casinos, a convention center, and a million-square-foot high-end shopping mall. As with almost every Adelson idea, he's convinced the Cotai Strip will be a great success—yet even here he has insulated himself against risk. Though Adelson will own the centerpiece hotel casino and convention center, the Venetian Macau, the other six hotel casinos will be built and owned by other companies to whom Adelson will pay rent.

Gambling on Vegas

Gambling may be a risky business, but the house always wins in the end. During the past thirty years three men have had more of an impact on, and made more money out of, Las Vegas than just about anyone else. In addition to Sheldon Adelson (see page 56), the current kings of the Strip are Steve Wynn and Kirk Kerkorian. These are the men who made Vegas what it is today, and the men that Vegas made.

Steve Wynn: With a $2.6 billion fortune in 2006, Wynn is credited with leading the resurgence of Las Vegas's fortunes during the 1990s, when he opened the luxury casinos Mirage and Bellagio on the once down-and-dusty Strip. The Mirage featured a "live" volcano, and its Treasure Island lured gamblers with nightly staged pirate battles, while the refined Bellagio offered an indoor lake. Wynn sold the casinos, Mirage Resorts, to fellow 400 member Kirk Kerkorian in 2000 for $6.4 billion, and has since plowed his winnings into the $2.7 billion, sixty-story Wynn Las Vegas. Wynn failed in his bid to secure a gaming license in Singapore—a battle won by Adelson. He also lags behind Adelson in Macau, though he is spearheading a major project there, the $1.2 billion Wynn Macau.

Kirk Kerkorian: He may fill newspaper columns with his backroom brawling at General Motors (after assembling 9.9 percent of the company stock in mid-2005, he unloaded his position in late 2006). But he is also a prince, if not the king, of Vegas, having been around the Strip longer than Adelson and Wynn combined. Kerkorian ran a small air-charter service in the 1950s and 1960s flying gamblers in and out of Vegas. He then went into real estate, leasing a plot of land that sprouted Caesars Palace. Toward the end of the 1960s he bought the Flamingo Hotel and built the International Hotel, where Barbra Streisand and Elvis Presley headlined. He sold both to Hilton Hotels in 1970. After buying the MGM movie studios in the early 1970s, Kerkorian built the MGM Grand, scene of one of the worst Vegas disasters when a fire broke out in 1980 that killed eighty-five people. In 1986 Kerkorian sold the MGM Grand for $590 million to Bally Manufacturing Corporation of Chicago. He then built a bigger, better MGM Grand in 1993 that boasted rivers, waterfalls, five outdoor pools, and five thousand rooms. He increased his stake in Vegas again in 2000, buying Wynn's Mirage Resorts for $6.4 billion. Four years later he bought Mandalay Bay Resorts, including the Mandalay Bay, the Luxor, the Excalibur, and Circus Circus hotels, for $7.9 billion. Kerkorian now owns more than half of the approximately seventy thousand hotel rooms on the Strip and had a net worth in 2006 of $9 billion.

Adelson says he could never have set out on any of his business ventures if he had equivocated. To illustrate the point, he tells a story about a motorist who gets a flat tire and who, on his way to borrow a car jack from a garage, thinks of all the things that could go wrong—the mechanic may be mean, or he may want to charge too much for the repair or loan of the jack. By the time the motorist finds a garage, he is in a foul mood; when the kindly mechanic opens the door, the motorist tells him: "You can take that jack and shove it up your ass." Says Adelson: "If you don't have a conviction about what you are doing, you are never going to make it."

Donald Trump may have as much conviction as Adelson, but he has learned the hard way that, in the casino and real-estate industry, it's best to share the burden among as wide a group of people as possible. One of the highest-profile victims of 1980s overleveraging—and one of the few who lived to fight another day—Trump still emblazons his name on many projects springing up around the country. But it is often other people's money that bears the brunt of the risk.

Trump began building his empire in the early 1970s by buying the railroad yards along the Hudson River of the failed Penn Central Railroad. Then he began investing in land in Atlantic City, eventually buying two hotels, the Trump Plaza and the Trump Castle. Both were described as deteriorating and problematic.

In 1987 Trump added to his Atlantic City gamble by borrowing $80 million to buy a controlling interest in Resorts International, a company that included the Atlantic City Taj Mahal among its properties. The purchase was a first step in wresting control of the company. In addition to wrangling with shareholders, Trump also faced competition from Merv Griffin, the TV tycoon who had recently pocketed $250 million from the sale of his television production company, which had created *Jeopardy!* and *Wheel of Fortune.* Griffin outbid Trump for control of the company, and the two ended up in court. In hindsight, being outbid by Griffin was a godsend, as Trump later admitted to *Forbes.* Resorts was in bad shape. Griffin's company financed the deal using $325 million of junk bonds and went bankrupt a year later when it couldn't handle interest payments. Trump, who had retained only the unfinished Taj Mahal hotel casino (along with a $12 million cash settlement) survived. But then he further added to his debt burden in 1988, when he bought the Plaza Hotel in New York City for $390 million and the Eastern Airlines shuttle, which he renamed the Trump Shuttle, for $305 million.

By 1990 Trump was more than $3 billion in debt. As Mark Singer wrote in

The New Yorker in 1997, Trump's "excessively friendly bankers infected with the promiscuous optimism that made the Eighties so memorable and so forgettable had financed Trump's acquisitive impulses to the tune of three billion seven hundred and fifty million dollars."

Through the early 1990s Trump and his organization went through a debt restructuring. He lost the Plaza Hotel, his Boeing 727, his yacht, and the Trump Shuttle. Worse still, Trump was personally liable for $900 million of the debt and was forced to agree to a personal spending cap of $450,000 a month. In his 1997 book, *Trump: The Art of the Comeback,* Trump recalls walking down Fifth Avenue one December evening with the holiday lights aglow, seeing a homeless bum on a corner, and thinking that this unfortunate man was richer than he was. It would take years for Trump to work his way back.

In the mid-1990s Trump took two of his heavily debt-laden casinos public. The resulting company, Trump Entertainment Resorts, filed for bankruptcy in November 2004 and reemerged the following May with Trump's stake in the company reduced from 47 percent to 31 percent, and with James B. Perry replacing Trump as chief executive. But the Trump Organization survived. Nowadays Trump and his eldest children, Don Jr. and Ivanka, make their fortune overseeing other people's projects and bestowing upon them the Trump name and brand. Trump gets 8 to 15 percent of other developers' condo sales, usually puts up no money, and gets upfront payments of several million dollars. According to *Forbes,* the Trump name can command a premium of 20 to 30 percent in added revenue for any project. And in 2006 the magazine reported no fewer than thirty-three Trump franchise projects under way.

Yet when asked what was the biggest risk he ever took, Trump didn't talk about his brushes with bankruptcy. Instead he replied, "I took a big risk when I decided to star in and coproduce *The Apprentice.* The statistics show that 95 percent of all new shows fail. Those were not great odds, but I had a feeling the show would work. I wasn't expecting the show to become the number one show on television—that was a nice surprise. But I did think the concept had merit and knew we'd encounter some level of success with it."

So how could a man whose businesses were once mired in billions of dollars worth of debt, with $900 million of that owed personally, see his biggest career risk as *The Apprentice?* As weird as it seems, it also speaks to the supreme self-confidence shared by Trump and many others on the Forbes 400. When asked about that time in his life, Trump says, "Pressure can bring out the best and worst in people, and in my case it made me stronger and more determined than ever. I also employed my 'blip versus catastrophe' theory: Yes, I had some financial problems, but it wasn't a war, an earthquake, or something truly horrific. That allowed me to keep my equilibrium and perspective intact, and make my company bigger and better than ever." Then he adds, "I was already planning for the future and what I would be doing, and I just knew that I'd pull through and continue working at what I loved doing."

In case after case, self-confidence and fearlessness save the day for members of the Forbes 400. But it also helps if they are obsessed with their vision. Take, for example, the case of shipping magnate Daniel Ludwig. Born in 1897, Ludwig started out at age nineteen with a $5,000 loan that he used to buy and convert a paddle steamer into a barge. Later he moved on to chartering and eventually building tankers, becoming the owner of the fifth-largest tanker fleet in the United States by the end of World War II.

Ludwig leveraged his tankers to build a fleet that peaked at sixty ships, which he then used as collateral for loans that financed business ventures throughout the world, including real estate and mining. One of America's wealthiest men by the 1960s, Ludwig was convinced that the world was headed for a food and fiber shortage, especially paper, so he embarked on a scheme of enormous ambition: to build a paper mill, a buffalo farm, and a rice plantation in a remote part of the world.

Ludwig focused on Brazil, where he bought more than six thousand square miles of Amazonian rain forest, an area about the size of Connecticut, for $3 million in 1967. The Jari Project, as it was known, was one of the most grandiose and ill-fated schemes the world has ever seen. Ludwig built a port and a twenty-six-mile railroad to transport goods in and out of Jari. He also built three thousand miles of roads, as well as towns and settlements that housed thirty thousand people by 1982. When Ludwig ran into difficulties building a seventeen-story pulp mill and wood-fired power plant in Brazil, he had them built in Japan and towed seventeen thousand miles across the ocean.

But the Amazon was a force Ludwig could not control. The trees he selected for the paper mill either died or grew too slowly in the jungle. The rice plantation failed. As if the Amazon weren't trouble enough, Ludwig came under increasing pressure from Brazilian nationalists who were suspicious of a foreigner's vast acreage and business in the jungle, and by a government bureaucracy that hampered him at every turn.

In 1980 Ludwig delivered an ultimatum to Brazil's military rulers: Either help pay the $5 million annual infrastructure costs of running Jari and ease up on the bureaucratic restrictions, or he would put the place up for sale. Two years later Ludwig gave up, selling Jari to a pool of government-aided Brazilian companies for $280 million. In his prospectus for the sale, Ludwig claimed to have spent more than $850 million on the project, the equivalent of $1.8 billion today. Yet despite his huge losses with Jari, Ludwig still topped that first Forbes 400 in 1982 with a net worth of $2 billion, thanks to his shipping interests and other real estate.

But as the Jari saga illustrates, no risk-taking member of the Forbes 400 is immune to outsize failure. T. Boone Pickens, of Mesa Petroleum, was a larger-than-life success story of the 1980s who led a series of ultimately unsuccessful but highly lucrative takeover bids. Pickens would spot an undervalued company (Gulf Oil, Phillips Petroleum, Unocal) and buy a position. By the time the board woke up to what was going on, they had a battle on their hands to keep control. It often cost Pickens's competitors plenty to keep him from taking over the company—a process referred to as *greenmail*. In the case of the unsuccessful Gulf deal, for example, Mesa made $404 million.

Brilliant as Pickens was—for a decade he financed Mesa's annual $15 million overhead by trading commodities—he was also at risk because of a lack of diversification. Mesa had an 80 percent stake in natural gas. And natural gas was a depressed market from the mid-1980s onward.

Utterly confident that natural gas would bounce back, Pickens borrowed even more money to buy reserves. And he saddled the company with additional debt by insisting on paying shareholders even as the price of gas dropped and Mesa continued to perform badly.

1985
from the pages of *Forbes*

Jane B. Engelhard inherited her money from her husband's mining and minerals empire. Her husband, Charles Engelhard Jr., was the prototype for the horse-loving villain in the Ian Fleming novel (and James Bond movie) *Goldfinger*. (1985 net worth: $365 million)

Sumner Redstone was trapped in a Boston hotel fire in 1979 and hung from a window, with flames licking at his hands, until he was rescued. (1985 net worth: $340 million)

Dorothy Stimson Bullitt, who built a Seattle broadcasting fortune, rafted the Colorado River rapids at age eighty-five. (1985 net worth: $275 million)

Floyd Roger Hardesty, whose fortune comes from concrete and construction, flies his own Boeing 727 and is a big-game hunter. (1985 net worth: $180 million)

Jerry White, of the Caruth Institute for Entrepreneurship, was a minor shareholder in Mesa at the time. Although Pickens's strategies for riding out the storm were excellent, he recalls, "In the end, he was the victim of an unprecedented low in natural gas pricing." By the mid-1990s Mesa, saddled with a billion-dollar debt, was threatened with a hostile takeover; Pickens was forced to sell the company that he had founded in 1956 with $2,500 to Texan investor Richard Rainwater. Pickens walked away with $35 million.

But Pickens's saga did not end there. Since he had proved successful at trading commodities to shore up Mesa, in 1997 he decided to start his own commodities fund, BP Capital Energy Equity, which bet on crude oil and natural gas. It began with $36 million and quickly fell to less than $4 million. Today it's worth billions. During his Mesa days Pickens was never rich enough to make it onto the Forbes 400. Yet BP Capital Management has made him richer than ever. In 2006 *Forbes* estimated his net worth at $2.7 billion.

For many others, failure ends in a slide that takes them off the 400 list, never to return. But there is an upside to even the worst bankruptcies—if not for the individual, then for the larger society, argues George Smith of NYU's Stern School of Business. Smith says it is fortunate that entrepreneurs are willing to stick their necks out, because for every one hundred people who take a risk there is a chance that one will succeed. The United States, he points out, has made it relatively easy for people to fail because of a legal system and bankruptcy laws and protections that give failed entrepreneurs a "soft landing." Unlike in Dickens's day, people aren't thrown in debtors prison. Indeed, the relative ease with which overleveraged entrepreneurs can file for bankruptcy protection led Congress to tighten bankruptcy laws in 2005.

Since the risk gene is so prevalent among successful entrepreneurs, Andrew Keyt of Loyola University says many successful people have been bankrupt before. "Someone once told me that every millionaire has been bankrupt at least once before they have become millionaires," says Keyt. Jon Huntsman, for one, vigorously disagrees. He says it is only when a business is in a tough spot that honorable people figure out how to keep going so they can repay 100 percent of their debt.

"During 2001/2002 we had the perfect storm," says Huntsman, whose Huntsman Corporation found itself in about $2 billion worth of debt. "Everything that could go wrong did go wrong, from the recession to overproduction to the cheap dollar, not to mention extremely high natural gas and oil prices. But those were all vicissitudes an entrepreneur and a self-made person has to endure, and you have to fight through storms and show the banks you are capable of coming out ahead."

However, even in such worst-case scenarios as Huntsman's "perfect storm," bankruptcy is not necessarily as inevitable as it might seem. As many members of the Forbes 400 have found out, the bigger you are, the harder it is to fall: Creditors will sometimes go to great lengths to keep their debtors from going broke. Huntsman's former banker Mark Buchman says that during his forty-four years of banking, he cannot remember a banker ever putting a customer out of business. Buchman says a bank will do whatever it can to keep the business alive, because the alternative means foreclosing on the collateral and trying to release value, usually during a distressed market. According to Buchman, a person's net worth is meaningless. What matters is that they are earning enough money to repay their loan. "There's a saying in banking: A net worth never repaid a loan," says Buchman. "You've got to be working and earning money to pay the loan. So the last thing a bank wants to do is put somebody out of business."

That was precisely the thinking of the banks when Donald Trump ran into financial trouble. As *Forbes* senior editor Alan Farnham put it in *Forbes Great Success Stories: Twelve Tales of Victory Wrested from Defeat*, recounting Trump's near-death experience with debt, "In effect, money center banks like Citibank had to stand by Trump, because if they pulled the rug out from under him, they themselves stood to tumble. Like the Chrysler Corporation of the late 1970s, Trump had grown almost 'too big to fail.' And acting as his own Lee Iacocca, he argued that point persuasively. 'Listen fel-

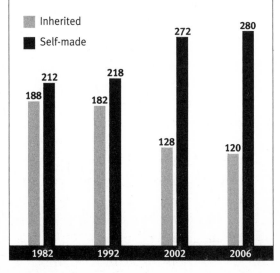

Inherited wealth vs. self-made wealth

Over the last 25 years, the percentage of 400 members who inherited their wealth decreased from 47% on the first list in 1982, to 30% in 2006, while the percentage of self-made fortunes increased correspondingly. Still, the single easiest way to make it onto the list is to inherit a fortune.

Many heirs on the list who inherited fortunes have succeeded in increasing those fortunes many times over and transforming and diversifying family-owned businesses. In a sense, one could argue that they, too, are self-made. For the purpose of these estimates, however, we deemed a fortune "self-made" only if the individual more or less built his fortune from scratch.

■ Inherited
■ Self-made

	1982	1992	2002	2006
Inherited	188	182	128	120
Self-made	212	218	272	280

lows,' Trump recalls saying, 'if I have a problem, then *you* have a problem. We have to find a way out or it's going to be a difficult time for both of us.' " Hundreds of millions of dollars of Trump's debts were written off or put off for a later date.

Indeed, for any rich lister who relies heavily on debt, the bank is a crucial lifeline. Red Emmerson counts himself lucky that he had the support of the banks during his troubles in the early 1980s: "Our bankers believed in us. . . . They thought it will be the survival of the fittest and we were the fittest." During his purchase of the Sierra timberland, Emmerson says his banker told him, "Hang in there, Red; there's no problem."

While an ability to gamble and to get others' financial backing are hugely important, it also bears saying that it is possible to make it onto the list, and remain there, without repeatedly sticking your neck out. Investor Warren Buffett, who has appeared near the very top of the list for more than a decade, has said that most people fail because of "liquor and leverage." Buffett told an audience at Notre Dame in 1991, "I've never borrowed a significant amount of money in my life. You really don't need leverage in this world much. If you're smart, you're going to make a lot of money without borrowing."

Since so few members of the Forbes 400 have ever filed for bankruptcy protection, it's reasonable to surmise that those who do use leverage take very few risks they cannot afford. Jerry White claims that in his thirty years of examining entrepreneurial careers, he has come to the conclusion that entrepreneurs who are successful in the long run are actually moderate risk takers when their leverage is set against the scale of their wealth. Daniel Ludwig lost hundreds of millions of dollars on his failed Jari Project, yet he still had $2 billion the year he sold his ill-fated Brazilian venture. If Warren Buffett gambled $1 billion in 2006 and lost it all, his net worth would still have been $45 billion. And although to an outsider it may seem like the entrepreneur is taking a huge risk—on the order of a fifty-fifty gamble—to the successful entrepreneur, the risk can be as low as 2 or 3 percent: "The thing that drives people on the outside crazy is that no one on the outside has all the information," says White. "People on the outside perceive it to be a big risk. But the long-term successful entrepreneur is always thinking about how to reduce the risk."

White says the media loves the romance of the near-death experience, of the entrepreneur hanging on by his fingernails to the edge of the cliff. But the reality, though no less alluring, is quite different. "If you talk to these people off the record," says White, "then they will tell you that they only lose in proportion to their ability to recover. Now, if I sat there thinking, 'If I don't pull this off, I am going to be wiped out,' then I am in trouble. Long-term successful entrepreneurs wouldn't go there. They would figure out another way of doing it."

Look back at those card games favored by the Forbes 400: poker and bridge. These are games where skill has as much—if not more—to do with winning than luck. "Gamblers are losers and hedgers are winners," says White. "And entrepreneurs instinctively understand that in their gut."

3

Luck—and Timing

If business is a game of risk, then the flip side of the coin, so to speak, is that it is also a game of luck. At the time, the "lucky" break can seem like anything but luck—a bankruptcy, say. Or it might be something as mundane as a chance encounter in the street. But a significant number of the Forbes 400 report that luck has, at some point or another, played a role in their career, whether they see themselves as making their own luck or just catching a wave and being lucky enough to ride it. Whether they would have made it to the top of their industries (or indeed of any other industry) had they not chosen some of the paths they took is another matter. But consider for a moment the lucky breaks in the career of Johnnie Bryan Hunt. By the time of his death at the end of 2006, Hunt could look back with a wry smile on how a series of serendipitous events culminated in his ownership of one of the largest trucking firms in the United States—and a personal net worth of over $300 million.

J. B. Hunt's start in life did not auger well. Unlike H. L. Hunt of Texas (see Chapter 2, Risk), J.B. was no charmed poker player, or wildcatter, or even a distant relative. Hunt was born in 1927 into a poor family of five brothers and one sister. At about age ten, he started working in one of his uncle's sawmills. He left school at age eleven without being able to read or write.

Hunt spent his first twelve years of marriage on the road driving for different trucking firms out of Little Rock and, later, Dallas and St. Louis. One of his regular routes was a 365-mile stretch between Little Rock and St. Louis hauling wood shavings to chicken farmers to be used as poultry litter. There was no CB or radio in the truck, which gave Hunt a lot of time to think as he motored up and down the state.

Hunt had been pondering ways of making money in the poultry litter business since the days of working at his uncle's sawmill. As a boy, he had been paid $4 for a twelve-hour day at the mill where farmers would pick up wood shavings for their poultry litter. The farmers would load the shavings into their truck with a shovel. But Hunt devised a contraption he described as a "playhouse on stilts" that was filled with wood shavings. All the farmers had to do was back their truck up and pull a lever to fill up. The device saved the farmers a lot of time and effort, for which they paid the young boy $4 a load. Pretty soon Hunt was selling four or five loads a day. The lesson: There was good money to be made from poultry litter—if only he could work out how.

In the cabin of his truck, Hunt whiled away the hours devising a way to sell wood shavings to poultry farmers on a large scale. And in the late 1950s he started driving a new two-hundred-mile circular route that took him through Stuttgart, Arkansas, the self-proclaimed rice capital of the world. As Hunt drove, he passed smoke rising from fields where farmers were burning rice hulls—the outer, discarded husks of grain. The unwanted hulls gave Hunt an idea: They would make excellent poultry litter. Better still, he'd be doing the farmers a favor by taking the hulls off their hands. "When I saw those hills of rice as I was driving that truck, that changed my entire life and what I was going to do," says Hunt. All he needed was a process for grinding and packing the hulls. By the time J. B. Hunt Company was born in 1961, Hunt had business notes going back fifteen years.

J. B. Hunt Company was a gamble. Hunt sold his home and borrowed all he could to underwrite the business. He sought help from the soon-to-be governor of Arkansas, Winthrop Rockefeller, with whom he'd had some business dealings. Through his company Winrock Enterprises, Rockefeller helped Hunt put together a brochure for a sale of shares. Hunt took one week off work and went door-to-door selling shares. He raised $120,000 that week (and eventually a total of $135,000, the equivalent of $910,000 today). Rockefeller became one of the major shareholders. In its first year J. B. Hunt Company sustained a $19,000 loss on $50,000 sales, and people advised Hunt to sell out. But Hunt hung on. "Something drove me to it," he says. "I knew I was going to win, but I knew it was going to be a long shot." The following year Hunt reduced the cost of packaging the hulls and profits rose. From that moment on he never looked back.

Had he stayed in the poultry litter business, Hunt could have led a very comfortable life. But there was one more coincidence that would propel him into the ranks of the Forbes 400. In 1969 a manager at pet food manufacturer Ralston Purina complained to Hunt that he was having trouble with one of his haulers. He urged Hunt to buy the hauler out, and in return he guaranteed Hunt trucking business from the firm. Hunt agreed and bought out the hauler. But the Ralston Purina plant closed soon afterward, and Hunt found himself the owner of five old trucks and seven old trailers, with no regular customers.

Throughout the 1970s Hunt struggled to expand his trucking business. He was constrained by the Interstate Commerce Commission's strict trucking regulation. J. B. Hunt Transport Services was a loser. Hunt tried to be as efficient as possible. He employed only nonunion drivers, and he offered bonuses to men who conserved fuel by driving under fifty-five miles per hour. Nevertheless, by the end of the 1970s Hunt was in trouble. For the second time in his life, he almost filed for bankruptcy, even though the rice hulls had been making enough money to keep him afloat. But just as he was on the verge of selling the trucking company, Hunt was advised by Paul Bergant, a Chicago lawyer who later became his general counsel, that trucking deregulation was on the horizon. Deregulation would unleash fierce competition, with an enormous prize for the most efficient service. And Hunt believed that he had that service.

Rather than sell off his trucking business, Hunt applied for new licenses. When deregulation arrived in 1980 it provided just the break he needed. He had decades of experience in the trucking industry on both sides of the steering wheel, as well as decades of experience running his own company. Plus, Hunt was desperate. "We were so fired up hauling cheap stuff and we were so hungry that when the regulations came off, we were like a horse in the fast lane," said Hunt. "Everyone else was not very aggressive, so we ran over them."

Hunt sold the poultry litter business to Eli Lilly for $2.4 million in 1983

1986

from the pages of *Forbes*

Herbert Hunt, of the Texas Hunts, mows his own lawn. (1986 net worth: $350 million)

John Jeffry Louis Jr., heir to the Johnson Wax fortune and former ambassador to Britain, piloted an F-15 fighter jet over Germany for pleasure. (1986 net worth: $400 million)

John Eleuthère Du Pont is the only Forbes 400 member known to be a serious triathlete. (1986 net worth: $200 million) (He was later convicted of murder.)

Retail king **Milton Petrie,** son of a Russian pawnbroker, plays bridge regularly with Laurence Tisch ($950 million) and Alfred Taubman ($800 million) and has spent $2,000 in an afternoon. (1986 net worth: $700 million)

25 years: The founders' club

Only 36 people from the original 1982 list were still alive in 2006 and rich enough to qualify for all 25 years. Even so, only 14 saw their wealth increase more than the annualized return of the S&P 500.

	Gain	Annualized return	Peak value (billions)
Warren Buffett	18,300%	**24.3%**	$46.0
Kirk Kerkorian	6,667%	**19.2%**	$10.0
John Kluge	6,400%	**19.0%**	$13.0
Charles Koch	4,411%	**17.2%**	$12.0
David Koch	4,411%	**17.2%**	$12.0
Leslie Wexner	3,000%	**15.4%**	$3.1
Patrick McGovern	2,900%	**15.2%**	$3.0
Philip Knight	2,773%	**15.0%**	$7.9
Barbara Cox Anthony*	2,420%	**14.4%**	$12.6
Anne Cox Chambers	2,420%	**14.4%**	$12.6
Donald Bren	2,329%	**14.2%**	$8.5
Leonard Lauder	2,220%	**14.0%**	$4.1
Ronald Lauder	2,060%	**13.7%**	$4.0
Herbert Allen Jr.	1,900%	**13.3%**	$2.0
S&P 500	**1,855%**	**13.2%**	
Ray Hunt**	1,650%	**12.7%**	$3.5
Lester Crown**	1,540%	**12.4%**	$4.1
Marc Rich	1,400%	**11.9%**	$1.5
Stephen Bechtel Jr.	1,250%	**11.5%**	$3.5
Ross Perot	1,223%	**11.4%**	$4.3
Hope Van Beuren	1,200%	**11.3%**	$1.7
Donald Newhouse	1,117%	**11.0%**	$7.7
S. I. Newhouse Jr.	1,117%	**11.0%**	$7.7
Dodo Hamilton	1,000%	**10.5%**	$2.0
David Murdock	950%	**10.3%**	$4.2
Frank Batten	900%	**10.1%**	$2.1
Ernest Gallo***	767%	**9.4%**	$1.3
Robert Turner	764%	**9.4%**	$9.1
Roy Disney	700%	**9.1%**	$1.2
Donald Hall	700%	**9.1%**	$1.9
Philip Anschutz	680%	**8.9%**	$18.0
Leonard Stern	640%	**8.7%**	$3.7
Henry Hillman	500%	**7.8%**	$3.0
Sid Bass	200%	**4.7%**	$4.3
David Rockefeller Sr.	160%	**4.1%**	$2.6
Richard Scaife	140%	**3.7%**	$1.2
Gordon Getty	64%	**2.1%**	$4.1

*Died in 2007

**And family

***Died in March 2007

How long can you stay on the list?

Forbes 400 members come and Forbes 400 members go. The average time a member spends on the 400 is 7.7 years. There were 29 first-timers on the 2006 list. Over the 25 years from 1982 through 2006, 1,302 individuals have qualified.

Years on the list	Number of members
25	36
24	20
23	17
22	17
21	20
20	13
19	19
18	20
17	14
16	21
15	29
14	27
13	31
12	41
11	43
10	42
9	49
8	58
7	57
6	49
5	82
4	83
3	146
2	128
1	240

and he took the trucking company public. With J. B. Hunt Transport Services as his main source of wealth, Hunt's net worth climbed from $240 million in 1987 to $415 million in 1993. When many trucking firms were going out of business, Hunt proved flexible, forward thinking, and hard-nosed—a born entrepreneur, in short. But if that manager at Ralston Purina hadn't urged him to take over those five old trucks, Hunt may never have entered the trucking industry at all.

Similar tales can be found among many members of the Forbes 400. Media tycoon John Kluge told *Forbes* that he first became interested in independent television when a friend he bumped into in the street told him about the possibility of buying something called DuMont Broadcasting, two TV stations that were the remnants of the struggling DuMont Television Network. Real estate and publishing tycoon Mortimer "Mort" Zuckerman bailed out of law and into a job at one of Boston's leading real-estate development firms at a spectacularly opportune moment. Microsoft billionaire Paul Allen has been referred to as the "accidental billionaire" for being fortunate enough to have gone to school with Bill Gates. And perhaps the luckiest break of all is inheriting one's wealth.

You would think that something as seemingly random as luck would not incite much controversy. Yet when Harvard sociologist Christopher Jencks published a 1972 study called *Inequality: A Reassessment of the Effect of Family and Schooling in America,* it caused a stir for concluding that luck mattered as much as ability and experience in defining a person's income. Jencks argued that "neither family background, cognitive skill, educational attainment, nor occupational status explains much of the variation in men's incomes." Instead, "luck has at least as much effect as competence on income." The "luck" that Jencks cited ranged from friends and acquaintances helping someone to find work, to being in the right job market at the right time. While Jencks's fellow academics questioned the importance ascribed to luck, many of the Forbes 400 seem to have no trouble crediting luck in getting to the top. Texas oil billionaire Ray Hunt, the son of wildcatting legend H. L. Hunt, liked to say: "Given the choice between luck and intelligence, always take luck."

Ross Perot, one of the many Horatio Alger–like figures found on the 400 list, would agree wholeheartedly that luck matters. "The way the ball bounces has a huge amount to do with what happens," Perot once told an audience at a Columbia Business School alumni dinner. Perot was referring to his decision to join the navy where, in an unlikely setting aboard an aircraft carrier, he met a visiting executive from International Business Machines (IBM) who offered Perot his first big career break. Perot did not know what IBM was. The executive was simply the first man to offer the poor boy from Texas a job. Perot, who went on to become one of IBM's most successful salesmen before striking out on his own—and who has an aphorism for almost every occasion—says today: "Life is not an organization chart. Life is more like a spider's web. Things happen in strange ways."

Mort Zuckerman landed in his chosen industry in a roundabout way, too. A native of Montreal and the son of immigrants who spoke no English, Zuckerman got his BA degree at McGill University, then headed south to Wharton for an MBA. Undecided about what to do next, he returned to McGill for a law degree and then went on to Harvard for a master's degree in law. "I had a very serious problem because I didn't know what the hell to do," he recalls. "I had no great plan. I went to law school because in my family it was not all right to do nothing, but it was all right to go to law school and do nothing. That's how I ended up getting four degrees."

A chance remark by one of his Harvard professors, however, gave him a new idea: "He told us that George Bernard Shaw was a clerk in a dry goods store and decided that he would go to London for three years and write plays, because if that didn't work out, he could always be a clerk in a dry goods store. For me, practicing law was the equivalent of being a clerk in a dry goods store." Zuckerman decided to give himself three years to try out one of his two passions—real estate and journalism. "I couldn't figure out a way to get into journalism, but I knew that I could get a job somewhere in real estate," he says.

And so Zuckerman applied for a job at the prestigious, very white-shoe Boston real-estate development firm of Cabot, Cabot & Forbes (no relation to the publisher). "I was the first person of the Jewish faith to join the firm," he recalls. As luck would have it, the chief financial officer had quit six months before, and the executive vice president for finance twelve months before that; neither had been replaced. Then, five months after his arrival—and after he had proven himself by turning around a big project for the firm in California—Zuckerman's boss, the chief operating officer, also quit. "And so I became responsible for the firm's biggest project, and in effect, the CFO [chief financial officer]," says Zuckerman. He was only twenty-five years old.

"But here's the lucky part," he adds. "The guy who was my counterpart on the construction and management side went to his class reunion at MIT. This was 1963, and a lot of small computer and high-tech companies were being

Age and wealth

The table shows the average net worth (in millions) of Forbes 400 members by different age cohorts. In 1990, 400 members in their forties were the richest (worth an average of $913 million); by 2006, thanks to the Google guys (Sergey Brin and Larry Page, each worth about $14 billion), the wealthiest group was in their thirties (worth: $6.1 billion).

	1990		2000		2006	
	Number of 400 members	Average wealth (in millions)	Number of 400 members	Average wealth (in millions)	Number of 400 members	Average wealth (in millions)
age 90	1	$430	5	$2,352	7	$3,071
80	26	$614	27	$3,362	44	$3,846
70	55	$766	76	$2,814	99	$3,249
60	85	$840	101	$2,339	120	$2,737
50	69	$707	94	$3,051	79	$3,544
40	33	$913	71	$3,868	43	$2,449
30	10	$798	23	$3,418	7	$6,143
20	2	$328	1	$1,300	0	–
unknown	118	$464	2	$1,850	1	$1,100

spun out of MIT. And like the dot-com guys later, they were all getting equity. So he came back and said, 'If I don't get equity, I'm leaving.' And because he and I were on the same level, they offered me equity as well." Not only that: When the equity offered proved too puny for Zuckerman's counterpart, he left—at which point Cabot offered Zuckerman the exiting construction manager's equity interest in addition to his own.

"I still can't believe it," says Zuckerman. "The remarkable thing is that, generally speaking, you learn your craft in your first job but are only able to capitalize on it later, when you strike out in a different direction. But here I was riding in on this guy's coattails and he rides off leaving me with his shares. I was able to learn my craft *and* capitalize on it in my first job. It was absolutely a matter of luck and timing." That hugely lucky break gave Zuckerman not only equity but invaluable knowledge of the field ("Before, I had no idea of real-estate finance"), which put him on track to become a real-estate mogul with a net worth in 2006 of over $2.5 billion. Later, armed with his real-estate riches, he finally found a way into journalism—first buying a group of weekly newspapers on the North Shore of Boston in the 1970s; then *The Atlantic Monthly* and *U.S. News & World Report,* where he regularly pens weekly editorials, in the 1980s; and finally the *New York Daily News* in 1992. He started *Fast Company* magazine in 1995.

Zuckerman's good fortune may well have stemmed from being in the right place at the right time. But Harvard's Jencks notes that every member of the Forbes 400 probably has some such story to tell about incredible luck and timing. In fact, most people, even those without billions in assets, can look back on instances when a chance event altered the course of their life. And the fact that a person can point to one seemingly fortuitous incident, says Jencks, does not mean there were not thirty related occasions over which they had a lot of control and during which they made the right decisions. But as Zuckerman likes to point out, something as elusive as instinct does factor into success. "How do you explain instinct?" says Zuckerman. "I found that I had a great instinct for the real-estate business." Indeed, over the last three decades he has exhibited an uncanny ability to buy properties during market troughs and sell at peaks. In one fabled example, Zuckerman bought *U.S. News & World Report* along with the building in Washington, D.C., in which it was housed, then sold the real estate to Japanese investors at a huge profit just before the collapse of the Japanese economy in the late 1980s. And so the question remains: How much credit should luck, timing, or instinct be given?

Thirty years after the publication of *Inequality*, Jencks, who came out with a later study that put less emphasis on luck, maintains that part of the reason for the antagonism toward his first study was the fact that luck can mean different things to different people and is therefore an extremely difficult factor to define. But he still believes that while a good portion of a person's financial success can be attributed to quantifiable factors such as education, competence, and experience, there is still a large portion, perhaps one-third, that cannot be quantified. One thing is for sure, though: When that piece of luck comes along, members of the Forbes 400 have been smart enough to spot it and leverage it to an exceptional degree.

So where does the ability to spot luck come from? According to Richard Wiseman, a psychologist at the University of Hertfordshire in England who conducted a ten-year study of luck, people's thoughts and behavior are often responsible for their good luck and fortune. Wiseman broke these skills down into four basic principles. Writing in *Skeptical Inquirer* magazine in 2003, he noted that lucky people are "skilled at creating and noticing chance opportunities, make lucky decisions by listening to their intuition, create self-fulfilling prophesies via positive expectations, and adopt a resilient attitude that transforms bad luck into good." In other words, a bad event to someone with bad luck is a disaster—but to a lucky member of the Forbes 400, a bad event could easily have been much worse.

Conversely, Wiseman found that unlucky people are more tense and

The youngest . . . and oldest 400 members

With the notable exceptions of computer maker Michael Dell and Google's Sergey Brin, all the youngest members on the 400 list inherited their fortunes. Abby Rockefeller Simpson's great-grandfather was John D. Rockefeller; Michael S. Currier's great-grandfather was Andrew Mellon, the financier and later U.S. Treasury secretary whose art collection established the National Galley of Art. The oldest 400 members range from Helen Clay Frick, daughter of the industrialist Henry Clay Frick, onetime partner of Andrew Carnegie and art patron, to J. R. Simplot, whose potato company has been the largest supplier of french fries to McDonald's.

Year	Name	Age	Net Worth (millions)	Year	Name	Age	Net Worth (millions)
1982	Abby Rockefeller Simpson	25	$100	1995	Daniel Ziff	23	$666
	Helen Clay Frick	93	$100		Roy Sakioka	96	$350
1983	Abby Rockefeller Simpson	26	$150	1996	Daniel Ziff	24	$1,000
	Helen Clay Frick	94	$125		Claude B. Pennington	96	$550
1984	Abby Rockefeller Simpson	27	$150	1997	Daniel Ziff	25	$1,200
	Helen Clay Frick	95	$150		Irene Pennington	98	$600
1985	Abby Rockefeller Simpson	28	$200	1998	Daniel Ziff	26	$1,200
	Dorothy Bullitt	93	$275		Irene Pennington	99	$600
1986	Michael S. Currier	25	$200	1999	Daniel Ziff	27	$1,200
	Dorothy Bullitt	94	$300		Irene Pennington	100	$975
1987	Lee Bass	31	$1,000	2000	Daniel Ziff	28	$1,300
	Iphigene Ochs Sulzberger	95	$340		Max Fisher	92	$760
1988	Lee Bass	32	$1,000	2001	Daniel Ziff	29	$1,200
	Iphigene Ochs Sulzberger	96	$440		Max Fisher	93	$800
1989	Lee Bass	33	$1,075	2002	Daniel Ziff	30	$1,200
	Daniel Ludwig	92	$550		Max Fisher	94	$750
1990	Michael S. Currier	29	$275	2003	Daniel Ziff	31	$1,200
	Mansfield Freeman	95	$340		Max Fisher	95	$680
1991	Michael Dell	26	$300	2004	Sergey Brin	31	$4,000
	Mansfield Freeman	96	$425		Max Fisher	96	$775
1992	Michael Dell	27	$310	2005	Sergey Brin	32	$11,000
	Mansfield Freeman	97	$400		John Richard Simplot	96	$2,500
1993	Michael S. Currier	32	$300	2006	Sergey Brin	33	$14,100
	Roy Sakioka	94	$350		John Richard Simplot	97	$3,200
1994	Daniel Ziff	22	$500				
	Roy Sakioka	95	$350				

anxious, which means they tend to miss things that are staring them in the face. "Unlucky people miss chance opportunities because they are too focused on looking for something else," he wrote. "They go to parties intent on finding their perfect partner and so miss opportunities to make good friends. They look through newspapers determined to find certain types of job advertisements and as a result miss other types of jobs. Lucky people are more relaxed and open, and therefore see what is there rather than just what they are looking for."

Of course, luck being fickle, it can seemingly run out at the worst of times. Ask Malcolm McLean. McLean, a pioneer of container shipping, entered the Forbes 400 in its first year with the auspicious net worth of $400 million. A couple of years later he bought twelve supertankers for more than $500 million, expecting oil prices to rise. Instead, the market collapsed, and McLean was outmaneuvered by operators of smaller, faster vessels. He plunged into debt to the tune of $1.3 billion and filed for Chapter 11 protection a few years later. Likewise Bunker and Herbert Hunt, who lost billions of dollars trying to corner the silver market in the 1970s. When luck runs out, the results can be disastrous.

But wealth can provide a nice cushion for ill-timed plays and unlucky circumstances. Take Edgar Bronfman Jr., a perfect example of someone *without* the good-timing gene. Through a succession of bad decisions over the course of two decades, he shaved billions off his family's fortune—though his father remains on the Forbes 400 today. (In 2006 Forbes estimated Edgar Bronfman Sr.'s net worth at $3.2 billion.)

Edgar Sr. and Jr. were heirs to the Seagram whiskey fortune. The Seagram empire had been built during the 1920s and 1930s by Edgar Jr.'s grandfather Sam, who never escaped his association with the bootleggers and mobsters of the period. In his youth Edgar Jr. shunned whiskey in favor of chasing a dream as a movie producer and songwriter.* But he eventually succumbed to his fate, joining the family business in 1982. It was an unfortunate time to enter the liquor industry. Liquor sales were down, and whiskey, for which Seagram was famed, was one of the hardest hit. Seagram's profits tripled during the 1980s. But that was due largely to the fact that the company, on the advice of Edgar Sr., had diversified into oil and chemicals, acquiring an almost 25 percent stake in DuPont in 1981.

---

*Bronfman, together with Bruce Roberts, wrote "Whisper in the Dark," which was recorded by Dionne Warwick in 1986.

In his early years Edgar Jr. showed a lot of promise in the family business—so much so that his father passed over his eldest son, Sam, who also worked at the company: He named Edgar Jr. the future head of Seagram. It did not take Edgar long to make his mark. Three months later he had risen to head of European operations. Within three years he was in charge of the company's core distilling and marketing business, House of Seagram, and by the end of the decade he was president of the company.

In 1986 Edgar Jr. was quoted as saying, "I suppose you can always find something better in the way you do things. But any mistakes that I've made I think have been executional in nature, not fundamental." Looking back from the vantage point of today, it's possible that Edgar Jr. might admit that some of his mistakes in timing were pretty fundamental, too.

Like his father, Edgar Jr. began to diversify the company. But unlike his father, his goal was to move into the arena he had been fascinated with since childhood—the entertainment business. Edgar Jr.'s first target was Time Warner. During the early 1990s he acquired a 15 percent stake in Time Warner. But his efforts to amass a controlling interest were unsuccessful. So in 1995, when the Japanese owners of Music Corporation of America (MCA), the parent company of Universal, were looking for a buyer, Edgar Jr. leaped at the chance. He bought an 80 percent stake in MCA for $5.7 billion. In order to finance the deal, Edgar sold Seagram's nearly 25 percent share in DuPont back to DuPont for $8.8 billion. Over the next few years, people would point to this decision as costing the Bronfman family billions.

Although there was little doubt that Edgar Jr. got more than a fair price for Universal (according to *Vanity Fair* magazine, the deal was compared in Hollywood to the Japanese surrender of World War II), the DuPont stock that he sold in 1995 doubled in value over the next few years while entertainment stocks slumped. *Forbes* estimated that the DuPont shares Edgar Jr. sold for $8.8 billion in 1995 would have been worth $17.6 billion two years later. Meanwhile, despite the bull market, Seagram's stock performance lagged.

Scott Black, the founder and president of Delphi Management, said in 1995, "I think the Bronfman kid is making a terrible error," while an unnamed Wall Street executive confided, "This will require a good deal of luck and skill, which Edgar may or may not have." In October 1997 Edgar Jr. sold Universal's cable and domestic television assets to Barry Diller's Home Shopping Network. Of the sale to Diller, an unnamed "Hollywood hand" told *The New Yorker*, "The taking of Edgar is now a cottage industry." Another veteran entertainment executive said, "He's like a piñata. Hit him and money comes out."

"Of course he is going to make mistakes," Edgar Sr. shot back with more than a tinge of impatience. "But the only way to make no mistakes is to do nothing." Never one for doing nothing, Bronfman increased his expansion, snapping up PolyGram Music in 1998 for about $10.4 billion to create industry behemoth Universal Music Group. One year later the music industry went into a nosedive with the emergence of illegal file-sharing Web sites like Napster.

But Edgar Jr.'s biggest mistake was yet to come. In 2000 he executed the biggest deal of his career, selling the family's stake in Seagram to Vivendi for $6.5 billion in Vivendi stock. The Bronfman family was now the single biggest shareholder in the new Universal Vivendi. There were enough skeptics at the time, but no one could have foreseen what was to come. Vivendi CEO Jean-Marie Messier, a flamboyant French businessman who had increased Vivendi's size via a rapid and aggressive acquisition plan, continued the spending spree, plunging Vivendi Universal into massive debt and putting it dangerously close to bankruptcy. In March 2002 Vivendi Universal posted a loss of 13.6 billion euros, about $11.9 billion, for the previous year—a year in which the firm bought fifty-nine other companies. The Universal Vivendi share price slumped, and a power struggle ensued as Edgar Jr. tried to have Messier fired. By the time he succeeded, the damage was done. Two years after the merger, the Bronfman's $6.5 billion stake in Vivendi was worth $2.9 billion.

Bronfman cashed out in 2004, reducing his shares in Vivendi from 8 percent to just under 0.5 percent, to finance a $2.6 billion acquisition of Warner Music Group from Time Warner. That takeover, which included a $1.25 billion cash payment, was launched with the

---

1987

from the pages of *Forbes*

Harvey Roberts "Bum" Bright, whose fortune comes from oil, real estate, trucking, and banking, arranges bills in his wallet by serial number and brushes his teeth a lucky number of times. (1987 net worth: $600 million)

Alexander Gus Spanos, a real-estate magnate, is best known for dancing at selected benefits with his golf buddy Bob Hope. (1987 net worth: $500 million)

Edmund Newton Ansin, who made his money in broadcasting and real estate in Miami, drives a leased Buick and plays racquetball at public courts. (1987 net worth: $280 million)

Edward Perry Bass of the Texas oil clan spent $30 million in 1987 (part of a $150 million multiyear grant) on the Arizona biosphere to see what problems might arise if humans colonized planets or had to live in an artificial environment. (1987 net worth: $725 million) help of a group of private equity backers. Within a few days of the takeover, Bronfman announced that over one thousand jobs—one-fifth of the workforce—had to go, and many top salaries would be drastically cut. Warner's artist roster was reduced by almost one-third. Not that the belt tightening stopped Bronfman and his partners (Bain Capital, Thomas H. Lee Partners, and Providence Equity Partners) from awarding themselves $1 billion in dividends soon afterward.

Experts waited eagerly to see whether Bronfman's poor decision making was continuing in his latest gambit. In October 2004 the *Wall Street Journal* pointed out that if Bronfman had hung on longer, there was a good chance the Vivendi stock price would have recovered. But as it turned out, there was no need to watch Vivendi stock. Warner Music Group was the elusive hit Bronfman had been searching for. In May 2005 he took 23 percent of the company public. The share price rose quickly from $17 to $26, increasing the company's value to $3.9 billion. In 2006 Warner Music was buoyed by rumors of a possible merger with EMI. Those rumors fizzled during that summer, and the long-term effects of Bronfman's music play are still unclear.

Just as easily as a bad deal can shave billions off a Forbes 400 member's net worth, so can a perfectly timed deal add billions. Mark Cuban, the billionaire owner of the Dallas Mavericks, is a textbook case of someone who sold his company, Broadcast.com, at just the right moment. Cuban set up Broadcast.com with Todd Wagner in 1995, at the beginning of the dot-com frenzy. He was already a millionaire in those days, having founded a systems integration firm called MicroSolutions, which he sold very profitably in 1990. But when Wagner and Cuban took Broadcast.com public in July 1998, the success was of a different magnitude: They became centimillionaires overnight. Shares went public at $18 a share and closed at $62.75. At the time, it was the largest one-day rise of a new offering in the history of the stock market. One year later, at the peak of the market, they sold their company to Yahoo for $5.7 billion (Cuban got about $1.2 billion in Yahoo shares). "I had no idea that the Internet stock market would take off like it did," Cuban says.

So was the sale of Broadcast.com at the height of the dot-com boom an example of plain old luck? Not really, claims Cuban. While he attributes the scale of his success to luck, he thinks that selling when he did also has a lot to do with experience. For Yahoo, he says, Broadcast.com was a natural acquisition. It offered market-leading services in 1999 that are still hugely in

One year that shook the 400

When the dot-com bubble burst in 2000 and 2001, the carnage hit the 400 hard. Bill Gates took the biggest dollar hit, losing $11 billion over a year's time, about a fifth of his fortune. But he had plenty of company. On the other hand, Warren Buffett, who shunned tech stocks, did well—up $2.8 billion, or 8.4%. All three of the key stock market indices showed hefty declines.

Biggest losers

	Loss in billions		% change 2001–2002	
Bill Gates	$11.0		-20.4%	
Paul Allen	$7.2		-25.5%	
Larry Ellison	$6.7		-30.6%	
Philip Anschutz	$5.3		-55.2%	
Edgar Bronfman Sr.	$4.6		-67.6%	
Robert Turner	$4.0		-64.5%	
Steven Ballmer	$3.2		-21.2%	
Charles Ergen	$2.7		-38.0%	
Rupert Murdoch	$2.5		-33.3%	
Lee Bass	$2.1		-63.6%	
Dow (price index)			-16.6%	
S&P 500 (price index)			-22.3%	
NASDAQ (price index)			-31.3%	

Biggest winners

	Gain in billions		% change 2001–2002	
Warren Buffett	$2.8		+8.4%	
S. I. Newhouse Jr.	$2.7		+54.0%	
Donald Newhouse	$2.7		+54.0%	
Samuel Johnson	$2.5		+55.6%	
William Cook	$2.1		+190.9%	
Thomas Pritzker	$2.1		+38.2%	
Robert Pritzker	$2.1		+38.2%	
H. Ty Warner	$2.0		+50.0%	
Michael Dell	$1.4		+14.3%	

demand today, including user-generated audio and video content and streaming TV shows. As for his decision to sell as soon as possible—well, he says, that came from his experience of seeing technology companies run up and then collapse.

"From a business perspective, the combination of the two made perfect sense," says Cuban. "Yahoo had an audience. The future of the Net was multimedia, and Broadcast.com was the leader by a long shot in audio and video. It was a great strategic move by both companies. Had the emphasis on multimedia continued for the next six years, Yahoo would now own the rich/multimedia space. From a stock perspective, I had seen multiple 'it's different this time' technologies run up, then collapse. They just weren't as dramatic as the Internet boom. I had zero expectations that the market was efficient or had a clue about what it was doing. So when I had the opportunity to protect myself, I did." Indeed, no sooner was Cuban able to sell his Yahoo shares than he did that as well, telling the *New York Times* in 2002, "I hedged 100 percent of my stock the day I could and since then have shorted more and have made a bunch of money."

Perhaps the most dramatic example in recent years of what happens when you have good instincts—and when you don't—came with the crash of the dot-com economy in 2001, which highlighted the gulf between those who timed their cashing out well and those who didn't. One of the most vocal losers during the crash was Ted Turner. Turner's fortune was wrapped up in Time Warner, which had merged with Turner Broadcasting System in 1996. Following the subsequent merger of Time Warner and America Online (AOL) in 2000, AOL Time Warner stock fell 81 percent, wiping billions off Turner's net worth—from $9.1 billion in 2000 to $2.2 billion in 2002. "I'm the stupidest person in the world not to have sold earlier," Turner said in 2003, shortly after reducing his stake in the company by selling 60 million shares.

Archimedes gave the world new insights into science, mathematics, and engineering. But he also gave mankind a word—*Eureka!*—that sums up the hope of every inventor and entrepreneur who has lived since. (Archimedes is said to have shouted "Eureka!" when he leaped out of the bathtub after realizing that the volume of an object could be measured by the amount of water it displaced when submerged.) More than two thousand years later, human beings still dream of that divine moment when they realize what the world has been missing and how they can deliver it: mass-produced motor cars, computer software, the Beanie Baby.

James "Jim" Clark, who has been on the Forbes 400 list for ten of its twenty-five years, has made billions from a number of eureka moments. He has launched three companies, each with a market capitalization of more than $1 billion. For his first company, Silicon Graphics, he developed a computer chip that created three-dimensional graphics (think *Jurassic Park* and car design). Next he funded somebody else's great idea—marketing the Web browser Netscape.* (See Chapter 6, West Coast Money.)

Clark's third big idea, Healtheon, is less well-known. In 1995, the same year as the Netscape IPO (initial public offering) that made Clark a centi-millionaire—Clark's 20 percent stake in Netscape was worth $663 million on the day of the offering—he was sitting in a hospital waiting to be treated for hemochromotosis, a rare blood disease, when a thought occurred to him. What was it with all the endless forms and bureaucracy of the health-care industry? Rather than filling out so many repetitive forms, what if you could link all of these people—doctors, hospitals, patients, and insurance companies—over the Internet? Clark's idea proved a lot more difficult to effect in practice than in theory, and the company that he gave birth to, Healtheon, now WebMD, has had a rocky history. But to have had a hand in launching three billion-dollar companies shows a rare gift for spotting business potential.

Of course, eureka moments are not just about luck, but the ability to fig-ure out—sometimes to an uncanny degree—where the future is headed. Indeed, many of the Forbes 400 have displayed tremendous vision, which in hindsight seems extraordinarily prescient. One such example is Craig McCaw of Seattle. McCaw's father, John Elroy McCaw, was a highly successful radio entrepreneur. He accumulated all of the accoutrements of success: a mansion with servants, a yacht, and a Learjet. But when he died in 1969, he left behind a good deal of debt. The family had to sell all but one of his businesses, along with the boat and the plane. All that was left was a struggling cable TV com-pany, Twin Cities Cablevision, which his second-eldest son, Craig, helped turn around and grow into a highly successful station. It was sold in 1987 for $755 million.

Craig's greatest success was not in cable TV but in the cellular business. In the early 1980s, the Federal Communications Commission (FCC) began awarding two cellular licenses in each area across the country—one for local

*Clark funded computer genius Marc Andreessen, who had invented a way of accessing words and images on a computer network—the first Web browser. Initially a great success, with 80 percent of market share, Netscape soon ran afoul of Microsoft, which launched its own free Web browser, Internet Explorer, as part of its Windows 95 Plus! Pack. Over the next few years, the two fought for market dominance with a succession of new browser releases. But Netscape could not keep up with Microsoft, which was not only much bigger than Netscape but also had a huge advantage by releasing Internet Explorer with every version of Windows. In 1998, a much-depleted Netscape was acquired by AOL, though Microsoft's hardball tactics would come back to haunt it in a highly publicized antitrust lawsuit.

telephone companies and the other for competitors. The latter were for potential customers, known as "pops." Craig began investing in cellular licenses from the outset, buying pops for as little as $6 each, at a time when the business was so new that few people were thinking about it. But as cellular grew, so did the cost of acquiring the pops. The bill for licenses ran into hundreds of millions of dollars. Throughout the 1980s McCaw bought hundreds of thousands of pops, aided by junk bonds issued by junk-bond king Michael Milken. (See Chapter 8, Beyond Wall Street.)

McCaw began by building a cellular network on the West Coast; but it soon became obvious that he needed a national network. After he sold Twin City Cablevision in 1987, McCaw was free to devote even more time to his cellular plans and to plow ever-greater sums into the acquisition of pops. By 1989 McCaw Cellular Communications controlled licenses for 50 million potential customers. It was the largest cellular operator in the country.

Still, McCaw Cellular's pops did not include such major metropolitan markets in the United States as New York, Los Angeles, Philadelphia, Houston, and Dallas. The licenses for many of these customers were held by a company called LIN Broadcasting. So in 1989 McCaw Cellular Communications paid $3.4 billion for a controlling interest in LIN. That same year the interest on McCaw Cellular Communications' total debt burden of $4.4 billion—about $500 million—exceeded the company's $443 million revenues. By gobbling up cellular licenses across the country, however, McCaw was gambling that one day mobile phones would be as ubiquitous as . . . well, as ubiquitous as they are today. He told *Forbes* in 1989, "In the future telephone numbers will be associated with people, not places. You won't have to be bound by a plug on the wall and a 6-foot cord. People who call your phone number will be connected to you, wherever you happen to be."

The gamble paid off. In 1994 AT&T paid $11.5 billion for McCaw Cellular, of which $2.3 billion was shared among McCaw and his three brothers, Bruce, John, and Keith. No less a visionary than Bill Gates, who predicted the PC boom and spotted the opportunities in the software market while others slugged it out in the computer manufacturing world, recognized McCaw's genius. As Gates said, "Craig is an amazing person. He thinks ahead of the pack and understands the communications business and where it's going better than anyone I know." Not only did McCaw realize early on that success in the cellular business depended on being able to provide a national network, he also realized the importance of an unquantifiable something—the stars aligning just so—in the emergence of a huge new business. During a rare interview with *Fortune* in 1996, McCaw said that neither individuals nor technology were the major drivers of change: "You arrive at moments in time when an entrepreneur, a technology, and the needs of people coincide. You get serendipity every once in a while. You try to be able to accept it when it works on your behalf."

That intersection of entrepreneurship and an emerging technology was a major factor in the success of yet another member of the Forbes 400: Internet loans billionaire Daniel Gilbert, owner of the United States' largest online mortgage lender, Quicken Loans—a company that he sold for $350 million in 1999 and bought back for $64 million three years later. Gilbert showed an entrepreneurial spirit from an early age. Using Chef Boyardee recipes, he started a pizza delivery business in Southfield, Michigan, when he was twelve. His friends delivered the pizzas by bicycle. But following an anonymous tip-off to the health department, which Gilbert believes was made by one of the local pizza parlors, the business was shut down. His drive to make a buck got him into more serious trouble as an undergraduate at Michigan State University, where he was caught running an illegal bookmaking operation. Although Gilbert claimed it was a small-time operation, East Lansing police later said that bets totaled $114,000. Gilbert and three friends were fined and served one hundred hours of community service and three years' probation.

Gilbert started out in real estate while he was in law school at Wayne State University. He would post a For Sale sign outside his parents' house and then take buyers to view other properties. But he soon learned that more money could be made in financing homes than in purchasing them. In the mid-1980s he started his mortgage business, Rock Financial, with a $5,000 investment. By the time he took it public in 1998, it was earning $20 million in profits on $90 million of revenue.

The mortgage business is highly complex, with different regulations governing the fifty states and their approximately three thousand counties. Gilbert says the business requires "intestinal fortitude" to survive. One of his methods has been to break away from the reliance on third-party referrals and appeal directly to consumers. He drummed up business with radio and TV commercials and substituted a central call center for costly satellite offices. The Internet was the perfect medium for Gilbert: He admits that although he could have been very successful pursuing business via 800 numbers and commercials, the Internet—and Rockloans.com—took his vision of appealing directly to consumers to another level.

Better still for Gilbert, Rock Financial and its online operation was the perfect target for bigger companies swept up in the dot-com frenzy. Intuit, the maker of Quicken financial software, was one of those companies looking to expand its online financial services. In 1999 it bought Rock Financial in a stock-for-stock transaction worth $532 million. Gilbert emerged with $350 million and also retained his job as head of the new company, now called Quicken Loans.

Gilbert says his new owners hardly bothered him during the next few years as the business continued to grow. And he claims that although he could have left the company at any time, one of the reasons he stayed—apart from his commitment to the then six hundred employees—was the thought that Intuit might one day want to sell the company back to him: "I did have a sneaky suspicion in the back of my mind." Sure enough, in 2002, just as Gilbert decided it was time to move on (in fact, at his very retirement party), Intuit chief executive Stephen Bennett offered to sell Quicken Loans back to Gilbert for a price that was later set at $64 million.

Although the discrepancy between the 1999 purchase price and the 2002 sale price looks impressive, Gilbert points out that the deal was good for Intuit, too. Quicken Loans kept Intuit afloat during the dot-com crash, when so many other Internet companies were sinking. Even Intuit's Bennett said that Quicken Loans helped it ride out the technology storm. And because Intuit bought Rock Financial with stock, Gilbert says it was able to sell the company back to him using stock for stock. "If you sell for a much lower price there is no markdown on the profit, loss and balance sheet, so they never had to take a write-down," explains Gilbert. "That meant they wanted to make a quick deal, and we were the most logical people to buy it."

In 2006 Gilbert's net worth was $1.1 billion, and Quicken Loans employees numbered four thousand. But does Gilbert believe he was lucky? "Without sounding hokey, I am one of those people that believes that people who are persistent . . . eventually the luck comes your way. Sometimes people don't know it when they are looking at it. The difference is not that some people are more lucky, but who is aware of the threads in front of you. Can you see it?"

4

Winning Is Everything

Millionaires, stretching back to John D. Rockefeller and no doubt farther, have often been portrayed as rapacious, supercompetitive, hyperaggressive, and ruthless—to mention just a few of the more pejorative terms ascribed to the breed. Others see them as foresighted, determined risk takers willing to defy conventional wisdom, and capable of prospering in the often bruisingly tough business world. So which is the more accurate portrait of the Forbes 400? Are they greedy ravagers, or visionary leaders? And are these extremes mutually exclusive?

Long before the advent of the Forbes 400 list, John D. Rockefeller, by most accounts, ruthlessly and relentlessly consolidated the U.S. oil refinery market (only to have it dismantled after the government deemed it a monopoly). Nevertheless, according to biographer Ron Chernow, Rockefeller was outwardly "pious, soft-spoken and almost ministerial." He rarely shouted or lost his temper. Rather, Rockefeller was filled with such an "evangelical certitude about his business plans, such a messianic sense that he represented rationality and order in the oil business and was doing God's work to tame its rough-and-tumble nature, that he disdained those who stood in his way." This sense of destiny, Chernow notes, "is the missionary fervor of the driven entrepreneur that often leads to ruthless behavior. . . . He feels he is relentless in a good cause, rather than ruthless."

Like Rockefeller, fellow industrial giant Andrew Carnegie "survived and triumphed in an environment rife with cronyism and corruption," according to biographer David Nasaw. Carnegie was a master of the game. Unlike Rockefeller, he did not accept the idea of a God who "randomly blessed some with riches on earth." Nor could Carnegie justify the right to his wealth based on his hard work. In fact, from his mid-thirties on, Carnegie "devoted but a few hours to business every morning," delegating what he wanted done to others. While he was on vacation in Scotland, for example, he approved a brutal suppression of the union at one of his steel mills. Indeed, the facts of Carnegie's life, Nasaw says, do not support the telling of "a heroic narrative of an industrialist who brought sanity and rationality to an immature capitalism plagued by runaway competition, ruthless speculation and insider corruption." Nor, on the other hand, adds Nasaw, do they support "the recitation of another muckraking exposé of Gilded Age criminality." The truth, as usual, is more nuanced. Carnegie, who brought state-of-the-art technology and great economies of scale to America's burgeoning steel industry, went on to become one of the greatest philanthropists of his age, endowing, among other things, thousands of public libraries. He "differed from his contemporary Gilded Age industrial barons not in the means with which he accumulated his fortune," Nasaw writes, "but in the success he achieved and the ends to which he put it."

A century after Rockefeller dominated the oil business and Carnegie forged a fortune in steel, the financial success stories of many Forbes 400 members may differ in the details, sometimes dramatically so, but the larger themes remain similar. There are still those who use uncompromisingly hard-nosed business tactics and others who aggressively challenge accepted standards, often engaging in actions that, as the saying goes, push the edge of the envelope. Just as the federal government ultimately broke up Rockefeller's Standard Oil empire in 1911, for example, it tried (albeit unsuccessfully) to do the same in the 1990s with Bill Gates's Microsoft juggernaut. In many cases, companies led by extremely competitive founders—Wal-Mart's Sam Walton, Nike's Phil Knight, as well as Gates—have succeeded in bringing about real industry and consumer benefits, from offering quality products at bargain-basement prices (Wal-Mart) to making innovative and cool sportswear (Nike) to creating an operating system that has revolutionized the workplace, not to mention the home (Microsoft).

And yet, what was the cost? Many of the superrich have a winner-take-all outlook that is integral to their success. They're not afraid to turn convention on its head, destroy an old business model in the interest of a greater good and larger profits, or become powerful agents of change. Yet the rigorous pursuit of their vision doesn't always make them popular, and they can collect a long line of adversaries on the way to the Forbes list—employees, unions, competitors, customers, the media, and, on occasion, the Justice Department and other legal authorities. As a rule, the Forbes 400 is not for the fainthearted.

Take Wal-Mart founder Sam Walton, who cultivated an "aw shucks" image on his way to becoming the world's largest retailer. He drove around Bentonville, Arkansas (where Wal-Mart is headquartered), in a pickup truck and assumed the public persona of a good ol' country boy. It was said that within two minutes of meeting Walton and his wife, Helen, everyone became their best friend. But in accumulating his fortune (which, were he still alive and had it had not been split among his heirs, would have made him richer than Bill Gates), Walton demonstrated considerable tough-mindedness. He paid his hourly employees with small wages—initially below the legal minimum. And he sued the U.S. Department of Labor when the agency advised him to increase their pay in the 1950s.

Walton also demanded a lot from his workers: Sixty-hour weeks were common. According to Bob Ortega, author of *In Sam We Trust: The Untold Story of Sam Walton and Wal-Mart, the World's Most Powerful Retailer,* a book chronicling Wal-Mart's rise, some workers at one distribution center slept in their cars in the parking lot between double shifts. In a move reminiscent of Carnegie's hiring of Pinkerton guards to usher scabs into his steel plants, Walton hired union busters and threatened workers with the loss of their jobs and their profit sharing if they unionized. Although Walton was unusual among retailers in offering profit sharing for the rank and file, and he took pride in giving his workers the chance to buy stock in Wal-Mart at a discount, he also regularly reminded them that they were not so important that they couldn't be replaced. The result: Wal-Mart never unionized and wages remained low.

Even fifteen years after Sam Walton's death, the company's basic formula for success—low prices for customers and a tight lid on all costs, including labor—hasn't changed. One legacy of Walton's approach to labor relations is the dozens of recent lawsuits filed against Wal-Mart for not paying employees for rest breaks taken and overtime worked. In 2006 fines of at least $78 million were levied against Wal-Mart after the company lost its case. A policy of wage caps has also drawn public protests by employees. In addition, the company faces the largest class action suit in history for discriminating against women in pay and promotions. Even now it offers less than half its workers health insurance. And, according to the *New York Times,* while the company is scrupulous about making sure that its employees accept not even a cup of coffee from a potential vendor, it also maintains a large internal security force

In Their Own Words

"Only the little people pay taxes." —**Leona Helmsley**

"Greed is all right, by the way. I want you to know that. I think greed is healthy. You can be greedy and still feel good about yourself." —**Ivan Boesky,** in a 1985 commencement speech at the University of California–Berkeley

"It is a sort of disease when you consider yourself some kind of god, the creator of everything, but I feel comfortable about it now since I began to live it out." —**George Soros**

"For some reason many people think of me as lucky. When I walk down the street people come up and start touching me." —**Donald Trump**

"I felt I had the world by the ass." —**Jack Welch,** former CEO of GE, while gazing out of his apartment in the Trump International Hotel & Tower in Manhattan

"Jeffrey [Katzenberg] was my retriever. . . . He was [the] tip of my pom-pom: I'm the cheerleader." —**Michael Eisner,** on why he didn't promote Katzenberg, chairman of Disney's movie studio, to the presidency of Disney

"All I want in life is an unfair advantage." —**Maurice ("Hank") Greenberg,** former CEO of American Insurance Group (AIG)

that, among other things, ensures that employees follow the company's rules of employee conduct by monitoring phone calls and using other surveillance techniques.

Like Walton, Nike founder and CEO Phil Knight planned to squeeze higher profits out of his athletic shoes by suppressing wages. In the 1990s, he came under fire internationally for human rights violations in his Asian factories. Critics complained that Nike contractors paid below minimum wage in Indonesia, for example—a dollar a day at the time. This, the *Far Eastern Economic Review* wrote in 1992, showed Nike's "rough" side, "the ruthlessness with which Nike pares its costs—the company is forever on the lookout for cheap production costs." At first Nike denied that it exploited Asian workers.

Company spokesmen argued that even a job paying less than a dollar a day was an opportunity for an Asian worker. But after investigations by the Portland *Oregonian,* Nike's hometown paper—as well as by CBS News, the *Multinational Monitor,* and the *Los Angeles Times,* among others—plus threats of boycotts, Nike established a company standard for overseas labor practices that, among other things, outlawed child labor. "The Nike product has become synonymous with slave wages, forced overtime and arbitrary abuse," Knight acknowledged in 1998, when he announced the changes in company policy.

In the world of the Forbes 400, a highly competitive nature can be embraced as a virtue, and few want to be known for their mild-mannered temperament. Bruce Kovner, who heads one of the world's largest hedge funds, Caxton Associates, is known in that high-stress, ego-driven sector for being even-tempered. Yet Kovner is at pains to qualify that reputation. "I might give the impression of being low-key, but I'm very competitive," he says. "It's very important to me to be among the best. I got that from my father. In high school I played basketball, and he was a great coach. He'd say, 'You're letting this guy into the center. That's what elbows are for.'" At the farther extreme, notes historian Chernow, "a reputation for ruthlessness serves the purpose of scaring one's competitors and exaggerating the power of the dominant business." Whether it's Standard Oil or Microsoft, says Chernow, "a sense of omnipresence, of tentacles extending everywhere, certainly enhances the firm's power." A reputation for ruthlessness sends a message of invincibility to rivals, and the "myth can be even more powerful than the actual conduct of the firm," he adds.

Take the legendary battles between Larry Ellison of Oracle and Bill Gates of Microsoft as they tussled to make their respective software companies the world's foremost. As Ellison, paraphrasing Genghis Kahn, once put it: "It's not sufficient that I succeed: everyone else must fail." (Oh no, Ellison later said, laughing, he didn't mean it that way!) But in fact, Ellison's groundbreaking career in computer software has been focused on rolling up his competitors. He grew up impoverished, the illegitimate son of a single mother in Chicago. In the 1980s and 1990s he urged on Oracle's sales force to double sales yearly. The steadily climbing revenue made Oracle a favorite on Wall Street. But then the company started chasing unrealistic expectations. These aggressive tactics led to overstated earnings, which the company had to restate twice in the early 1990s. For fiscal year 1991, the company that had always boasted of record profits had a loss of $12.4 million. As shareholder confidence faded, Oracle stock sank below five dollars a share, from a high of about twenty-five dollars.

Oracle nearly went bankrupt and four hundred workers were laid off. After a 1993 SEC investigation, Oracle paid a $100,000 fine and signed a consent decree promising not to double bill or book premature or nonexisting revenue. "It [overaggressive sales tactics] was an incredible business mistake," Ellison later acknowledged.

Eventually, Ellison admitted that he needed help in running the company and brought in new senior management. With more stability and new financial controls in place, Ellison began trumpeting the Internet. By 2000, the Silicon Valley publication *Red Herring* named Oracle the Comeback Company of the Year. "Ellison, ahead of nearly everyone else, decided that software would trump hardware and, later, that his company's technology must encompass the Internet," wrote one biographer, Karen Southwick. "His weapons are . . . his company's possession of a key technology platform, his willingness to exploit it and his disdain for anyone who gets in his way." Calling him a "modern-day Genghis Khan," Southwick said he "elevated ruthlessness in business to a carefully cultivated art form."

When competitor PeopleSoft proposed a merger with another company that would have displaced Oracle as the second largest in business software, Ellison launched a hostile bid for PeopleSoft. And when the government sued to stop the deal on antitrust grounds, Ellison fought it tooth and nail. Few companies want to engage in a

1988

from the pages of *Forbes*

Winthrop Paul Rockefeller Jr., son of Arkansas governor Winthrop Rockefeller, enjoys cruising with local sheriffs on their rounds. (1988 net worth: $800 million)

Marshall Naify, whose fortune comes from movie theaters and cable TV, was accused by his sister in 1977 of wearing monk's robes and receiving messages from God via FM radio. (1988 net worth: $315 million)

Kenneth Olsen, founder of Digital Equipment Corporation, regularly attends prayer breakfasts and invokes hymns at management meetings. (1988 net worth: $250 million)

Ben Hill Griffin Jr., a Florida citrus grower, was a mule drover in his father's orange grove at age eight and earned money in high school selling grapefruit. (1988 net worth: $300 million)

lengthy court battle with the government, but Ellison did and prevailed. He then sued PeopleSoft to eliminate the takeover defense it had put in place to deter Oracle. As Matthew Symonds, a writer at the *Economist* and author of another Ellison biography put it, "He stalked PeopleSoft a long time until it was weak enough to fall into his hands."

The same winner-take-all philosophy drove Bill Gates and Steve Ballmer, his longtime number two at Microsoft and fellow 400 member. Ballmer had a reputation for being even more competitive than his boss. Once they had defeated such 1980s competitors as Apple, Novell, and Digital Equipment Corporation (DEC), they turned their collective attention to the Internet. That meant capturing control of what was then a new technology, the Internet browser used to access the Web. Their tactics were bare-knuckled. One day in 1995, a team of Microsoft executives showed up at the headquarters of Netscape, the leading Internet browser company, to propose to CEO Jim Barksdale "a special relationship"—an end to competition with Microsoft. The quid pro quo: Netscape would yield them the browser market, stop competing with Microsoft in other areas, allow Microsoft to invest in Netscape, and give Microsoft a seat on its board. "They basically said, 'OK, we have this nice shit sandwich for you,' " Mike Horner, Netscape's marketing chief, later recalled. " 'You can put a little mustard on it if you want. You can put a little ketchup on it. But you're going to eat the f***ing thing or we're going to put you out of business.' "

Instead of accepting the offer, Netscape informed the Department of Justice about Microsoft's move, contending that it was anticompetitive. Other competitors, including Oracle, supported their complaint and even hired private detectives to dig through the Dumpsters at organizations defending Microsoft, looking for dirt on the company. Not surprisingly, Ellison was an outspoken advocate of breaking up Microsoft.

The government's famous 1998 antitrust suit against Microsoft charged the company with predatory pricing, illegally bundling its browser for free with the Windows operating system, and bribing distributors so they would not sell Netscape's browser. Microsoft countered that it had not impeded competitors and that giving away its browser was an innovation that benefited consumers. Netscape lawyer Gary L. Reback saw the situation differently: "The only thing J. D. Rockefeller did that Bill Gates hasn't done is use dynamite against his competitors!" he complained.*

---

*Modern biographers of John D. Rockefeller, such as Ron Chernow, dismiss the tale that Rockefeller ordered a rival refinery blown up, as historian Matthew Josephson recounted in *The Robber Barons: The Great American Capitalists, 1861–1901* (New York: Harcourt Brace, 1934). In *Titan: The Life of John D. Rockefeller, Sr.* (New York: Random House, 1998), Chernow notes that the prosecution never established that an explosion had ever taken place at the Buffalo refinery. He finds knavery aplenty, however, in Rockefeller's scheme to raise the shipping rates on his competitors by colluding with the railroads. As a result most independent refineries were ruined after 1872.

It was a stinging remark, but many others shared his view. Bill Gates had "an incredible desire to win and to beat other people," ex–Microsoft executive Jean Richardson recalled for a PBS documentary, *Triumph of the Nerds.* "At Microsoft, the whole idea was that we would put people under." "My job," said one of Gates's executives in 1991, just as Microsoft Office was being launched, "is to get a fair share of the software applications market. And to me, that's 100 percent."

Microsoft, of course, escaped Standard Oil's fate. Though a federal judge ruled that the company had indeed broken the law by monopolizing PC operating systems and trying to monopolize Internet browsers, the U.S. Court of Appeals for the D.C. Circuit reversed the order to break Microsoft in two (although it upheld the monopoly conviction in part). The Justice Department and the company then negotiated a settlement. As Netscape's cofounder James H. Clark, who was number 354 on the 2006 Forbes 400 list, remarks, "Both Ellison and Gates wanted to kill the competition. They wanted them to go out of business, and that's what they more or less achieved." (In a parallel to Andrew Carnegie before him, Bill Gates is also one of the most storied philanthropists of modern times: The Bill and Melinda Gates Foundation has more than $30 billion in assets.)

This same single-minded focus on a goal and the relentless pursuit of results may not characterize all 400 members, but they certainly are not uncommon attributes. Consider, for example, Rupert Murdoch. He's often portrayed as the impetuous, tyrannical boss of multibillion-dollar News Corporation, his family-controlled company. While there are many tales of his devastating charm, there are also reports of him wielding his power capriciously.

There's nothing hot-tempered, however, about Murdoch's business strategies, which often resemble the campaigns of a brilliant field marshal. When he set out to break the newspaper unions in London in 1985, for example, he planned his move months ahead of time, in total secrecy. His maneuvers showed an acute appreciation of the political environment as well as more basic economic fundamentals. The prime minister at the time, Margaret Thatcher, a Conservative, had cut her political teeth and built her reputation on confronting the coal and steel unions in her effort to remake the sagging British economy. Enter Murdoch, a confirmed Thatcherite, who wanted to apply the same aggressive approach to the newspaper business. The famously independent and vocal unions were the principal reason British papers weren't as profitable as their American counterparts. To eliminate unions at all his London papers, from the tabloids to the august *Times*, Murdoch built an automated printing plant outside London, in the town of Wapping. The first newspaper office in the world to be fully computerized, it rose behind chain-link fences and barbed wire.

Suddenly, in January 1986, Murdoch switched production to Wapping and, with the unions seething outside, calmly went to work. "I saw the plant in Wapping, and it was really ugly—all the unionists and the placards, and the barbed wire—and Rupert's in there, and he's literally working the presses. Sleeves rolled up. Knows everybody by their first names on the floor," recalls one of Murdoch's bankers who requested anonymity. The day he put five thousand or so journalists and unionists out of work, Murdoch was the picture of poise. In the following weeks, as the unions went on strike, trucks making deliveries to the plant were regularly attacked, and unionists and replacement workers fought frequently. The Conservative government sent hundreds of police to defend the plant. After a year, the unions caved, and Murdoch's British papers, without the restrictive union work policies, earned more money for their owner and News Corporation shareholders.

Reflecting upon Murdoch's battles in Britain two decades later, shortly after he made an unsolicited sixty-dollar-a-share offer for Dow Jones Company (publisher of *The Wall Street Journal*) in May 2007, journalist John Heilemann noted that while "the source of the anti-Murdoch sentiment was ostensibly political, in truth the crux of the resentment (in the media Establishment, at least) was primarily cultural." Murdoch, Heilemann wrote, "represented the arrival of market forces"—the notion of giving the audience "what they wanted, not what he thought they needed." The "pooh-bahs" of the British press establishment, Heilemann contended, "may have been politically liberal, but they were institutionally conservative—and they saw Murdoch as a corporate radical. An Australian barbarian at the gate."

Jack Welch was similarly tough-minded. During his twenty-one years at the helm of General Electric, he increased the company's market value by about $400 billion (by his own reckoning) and earned a reputation for superb management. To achieve those results (together with the quarterly increases in earnings that Wall Street analysts yearn for), he earned the nickname Neutron Jack as he systematically closed down factories and divisions that didn't rank number one or two in their industries. During the early 1980s, Welch eliminated 100,000 jobs at GE in the United States; every year he fired the bottom 10 percent of his U.S. workforce. "He wanted to change the nature of the way work at GE was done—break the barriers between departments, and start a new model of management," notes psychoanalyst Michael Maccoby, author of *The Productive Narcissist: The Promise and Perils of Visionary Leadership.* "That included firing a lot of people to increase productivity and putting in place the right people so that GE could deliver a combination of manufacturing and business solutions. . . . [H]e was very, very competitive and a visionary and turned everybody at GE into an instrument of his own vision."

Starting in the mid-1990s, however, some business publications began to question how Welch delivered those twenty years of ever-rising profits, a feat unparalleled in business history. *Barron's,* for example, stated in a 2005 article that GE's reinsurance arm made its parent company's profits look a lot better than they really were. By withholding billions of dollars from its insurance reserves, the company was able to report that its profits per share rose 90 percent between 1996 and 2001. Had the insurance unit been adequately reserved (annual reserve provisions are the largest expense items on the income statements of insurance and reinsurance companies), per-share profits would have increased only 5.6 percent in the five-year period, *Barron's* calculates. That might have cost Welch his place on the Forbes 400, since it was his huge pile of stock options that put him there in 2001, after he retired with $880 million in GE stock.

And that wasn't the only blotch on Welch's managerial record. It was during his tenure that GE refused to clean up all the polychlorinated biphenyls (PCBs) that the company had dumped into the Hudson River before the cancer-causing toxins were outlawed by Congress in 1976. While GE contended for a long time that it was doing what was necessary to mitigate the pollution, it ultimately entered into a consent decree with the Environmental Protection Agency (EPA), agreeing to pay millions for dredging the river, which was declared a Superfund cleanup site.

Another Forbes 400 member, Robert Friedland (2006 net worth: $1 billion), of Vancouver-based Ivanhoe Mines, Ltd. has also had to answer for environmental transgressions. Environmental activists and others in the United States and elsewhere refer to Friedland as "Toxic Bob," partly because of his alleged role in the contamination of a Colorado river in the 1980s and 1990s. Friedland was chairman and CEO of Galactic Resources, Ltd., which was operating a gold mine in the Colorado mountains when, according to the EPA, runoff from the mine carried toxic materials into the Alamosa River, killing fish and other aquatic life along a seventeen-mile stretch. Friedland vigorously contests these allegations, and his lawyers label it an "enviro-myth."

Eventually, after Friedland was no longer head of the operation, Galactic

Resources filed for bankruptcy and pulled out of the mine. Nevertheless, the U.S. government declared the former mine a Superfund site and sued Friedland. The EPA and the state of Colorado have since spent $200 million to clean up the area, and will have to build a water treatment facility on the site to be operated in perpetuity in order to finish the job. In 2000, Friedland, without admitting wrongdoing, paid $20.3 million toward the cleanup to Colorado and the federal government after reaching a voluntary settlement. Friedland contends that previous mining and runoff caused the problem, not the mine's design or operation; U.S. officials now admit that the company was not solely responsible. An attorney for Friedland argued in the *Wall Street Journal* that the EPA used Friedland as a scapegoat, in part because of his wealth.

An obsession with performance was a hallmark of Michael Steinhardt (1993 net worth: $300 million), who ran a pioneer billion-dollar hedge fund from 1967 to 1995. When one of his traders moaned that he was ready to kill himself after mismanaging some bonds, Steinhardt asked if he could watch. In his autobiography, *No Bull: My Life In and Out of Markets,* Steinhardt admitted that he often raged at his employees. He threw out a psychiatrist whom he employed for his traders after he characterized Steinhardt's behavior as "mental abuse" and "rage disorder." As another Wall Street trader recalled about Steinhardt, "If he stopped trusting someone, Michael was ruthless—out to get you." Steinhardt traces part of this monstrousness to his troubled background: His father, who was in New York's Sing Sing prison and was a seller of stolen jewelry and a friend of mobster and Forbes 400 member Meyer Lansky and "Three Finger" Jimmy Aiello, had not only paid for his education, but had staked Steinhardt's hedge fund with illegal winnings.

Or consider the lengths to which Michael Eisner, the strong-willed chief executive of Walt Disney Company who was listed on the Forbes 400 for eleven years, once went to exert his will. Disney was nearly comatose in the mid-1980s when newly appointed CEO Eisner hired Jeffrey Katzenberg, his former head of production at Paramount Pictures, to revive Disney's movie studio. Under Katzenberg's leadership, Disney's great tradition of animation soared again. Katzenberg was deeply involved with every project, nixing characters or styles of drawing, songs, and even entire plots if he believed they'd scare off small children—Disney's target audience. He also hired lyricist Harold Ashman and composer Alan Menken, who created *The Little Mermaid.* With its buoyant calypso tunes and new characters like Ursula, a sea witch modeled on the drag performer Divine, *Mermaid* brought in $110 million at the U.S. box office. Disney's stock soared. Boosted by more runaway hits from Katzenberg, like *Beauty and the Beast*, *Pretty Woman* (starring Julia Roberts and Richard Gere), and *The Lion King*, Eisner earned over $200 million in 1992, making him the highest paid executive in the country.

Katzenberg then asked Eisner for a bonus he'd been promised, and Eisner's inner Lion King emerged. He refused to acknowledge the contract, had his lawyers try to lower the amount of the bonus, and for five years refused to pay out. Enraged and bitter, Katzenberg left Disney and resolved to get some of the money he thought he was owed—as well as a measure of revenge. With friends and Forbes 400 members David Geffen and Steven Spielberg, he started DreamWorks Studio, a rival to Disney. He also sued Eisner. After the trial, during which it was revealed that, among other things, Eisner had dismissed Katzenberg as "a little midget" who was no more important than "the tip of my pom-pom," Eisner relented and paid up—$280 million, more than twice the bonus originally discussed, according to James B. Stewart in his book *Disney War*. With this sum, Katzenberg, too, vaulted onto the Forbes 400 in 1998. Finally, after a shareholder's revolt in 2005, Disney nephew and Forbes 400 member Roy Disney (2006 net worth: $1.2 billion) led the board in ousting Eisner as chairman.

In his 1989 book *The Alexander Complex: The Dreams That Drive the Great Businessmen*, Michael Meyer examined the lives of six empire builders, including five Forbes 400 members—Steve Jobs, Ross Perot, biotech billionaire Robert Swanson, Ted Turner, and the late shipping magnate Daniel Ludwig—to try to divine what drove them to spectacular success. They "live in the grip of a vision," concludes Meyer. "Work and career take on the quality of a mission, a pursuit of some Holy Grail. And because they are talented and convinced they can change the world, they often do."

Meyer refers to Apple founder Steve Jobs, for one, as a "visionary monster," and other accounts seem to bear that out. In *The Silicon Boys*, for example, David Kaplan recounts a telling anecdote about Jobs. Jobs and his buddy Steve Wozniak famously founded Apple Computer in 1976, when both were in their early twenties. As the company grew, stories of Jobs's abrasive personality and propensity for tantrum-throwing swirled around Silicon Valley. Jobs reportedly even cheated his good friend "the Woz" out of his rightful share of fees in an early computer-game venture. ("Oh, he's done it to me again," Wozniak reportedly said when he found out.) Jobs later stated that he didn't recall the exact amount of the fees, but he wasn't blind to his ugly reputation: "People think I'm an asshole, don't they?" he once asked an interviewer.

Sometimes the wealthy simply don't want to accept bad news from subordinates. When the famed Jari Project, Daniel Ludwig's enormous rice and pulp plantation in the Brazilian Amazon, began to hemorrhage money, Ludwig (the richest man in America in 1982, with a net worth of $2 billion) screamed at his managers, "You are cutting my throat with a rusty knife!"

Not surprisingly, a tendency toward bad behavior can intensify to a white heat over the issue of succession. The Forbes 400 list has its share of entrepreneurs who can't appoint successors or who appointed them and then fired them, one after another. Maurice "Hank" Greenberg, the iron-willed chief of AIG, built the company into a worldwide insurance powerhouse, amassing a considerable fortune (2006 net worth: $2.8 billion). Along the way, he earned a reputation as a shrewd negotiator and tough boss. "All I want in life is an unfair advantage" is one of his often-repeated adages. At one point, two of his sons, Jeffrey and Evan, worked for the company and were widely considered to be candidates to succeed their father. Jeffrey, an executive vice president, left first, reportedly after his father screamed at him in public during a dinner with company executives at the "21" Club in New York City. Evan subsequently left as well. Both went on to head other large insurance companies—although Jeff was forced to resign as CEO of Marsh & McLennan, one of AIG's major rivals, after New York State Attorney General Elliot Spitzer filed a suit against a brokerage unit of the company for bid rigging. The senior Greenberg was forced to step down, too, after Spitzer, who has since been elected New York's governor, threatened to indict AIG for accounting irregularities. AIG ended up paying a $1.5 billion fine to settle the charges.

"Why do I have to die?" William S. Paley, founder of CBS and a nine-year member of the Forbes 400 list, asked before his death at age eighty-nine in 1990. Paley famously resisted appointing a successor to his position as chairman; he finally promised Frank Stanton, who had been president of CBS for three decades, that he could succeed him, but then clung to power well past CBS's mandatory retirement age of sixty-five. Then, once he did retire, he engineered a comeback by allying himself with CBS investor Laurence A. Tisch, head of Loews Corporation, a hotel, tobacco, insurance, and investment company, when a hostile tender offer from Ted Turner put CBS in play. After Tisch bought CBS and took over as CEO, Paley returned as chairman. Over time, however, Tisch effectively edged out Paley.

Hand in glove with outsize success can come an almost regal sense of entitlement. Indeed, this may seem endemic to many CEOs, thanks to a few highly publicized cases. Rupert Murdoch, for example, had his company underwrite a temporary apartment, to the tune of $50,000 a month, in 2006 for his family to live in while renovators prepared their new home, the former Upper East Side penthouse of Laurance Rockefeller (which Murdoch had bought for $44 million—at the time the highest price ever paid for a New York City apartment). Only when the expense payments became public and corporate governance gadflies raised eyebrows did Murdoch repay News Corporation. For his part, Jack Welch, upon retirement, wrested millions of dollars in perks from GE's board. They included an $80,000-a-month New York City apartment, a chauffeur, a plane, country club fees, security services, financial planning services, and box seats at Yankee Stadium, Wimbledon, and the Metropolitan Opera—in fact, many of his living costs. He agreed to pay for these himself only after they became public during his subsequent divorce proceedings. The Securities and Exchange Commission admonished GE for failing to describe fully the range of Welch's perks in public filings, perks the SEC said added up to $2.5 million in the first year after Welch's 2001 retirement.

1989

from the pages of *Forbes*

Thomas Stephen Monaghan, founder of Domino's Pizza, was raised in a Catholic orphanage. (1989 net worth: $530 million)

John Willard Marriott Jr., of the hotel fortune, spent two years on the aircraft carrier the USS *Randolph*, where he ran mess operations. (1989 net worth: $466 million)

Jean Paul Getty Jr., son of playboy J. Paul Getty and one of his family's most eccentric heirs, was knighted in 1986 for giving more than $200 million to U.K. charities. (1989 net worth: $300 million)

Fitz Eugene Dixon Jr., heir to a streetcar fortune, wears the opal ring that his grandfather George gave to his grandmother on the deck of the *Titanic* as she stepped into the lifeboat. (1989 net worth: $300 million)

Finally, there is a dark underside to the behavior of some more extreme Forbes 400 members. During his long life, Armand Hammer, the globetrotting CEO of Occidental Petroleum, relentlessly promoted himself as an international statesman, proponent of U.S.-Russian friendship, magnanimous art collector, and oil tycoon. But after his death at age ninety-two in 1990, that myth was exposed by investigative journalist Edward Jay Epstein. Because of a brief meeting with V. I. Lenin, Hammer (the first foreign investor in the Soviet Union in the 1920s and the son of a founder of the

U.S. Communist Party) was granted a monopoly in pencils. Drawing in the 1990s on newly opened files from the Kremlin, the FBI, and the U.S. State Department, Epstein found that Hammer used his profits to launder money to pay for Soviet intelligence in Europe in the 1920s and 1930s, was himself a Soviet agent, and later bribed his way to oil contracts in such places as Libya and Colombia.

Hammer was equally deceptive with his family. One of his mistresses, who expected a marriage proposal when she became pregnant, was instead shipped off to Mexico. He did agree to a quickie marriage and divorce on the condition that the child never learn who her father was. Then he married another woman. He forced another mistress into disguises to conceal her from his third wife, whose fortune he allegedly defrauded in order to buy Occidental. He was equally tough with journalists, deriding any who challenged him as putting him through "the Inquisition." Though the FBI and the State Department tracked him closely, Hammer escaped charges of wrongdoing, aside from an illegal political contribution he made to President Richard Nixon's reelection campaign that resulted in a misdemeanor charge.* President George H. W. Bush later pardoned him.

And then there is the circus-like case of Kenneth Feld, owner of Ringling Bros. and Barnum & Bailey Circus. Feld inherited Ringling Bros. at the age of thirty-six, after his wealthy entrepreneur father died in 1984. As spotlights rotated on trapeze artists in midair and audience members held their breath during a triple flip, Feld, according to an affidavit filed in an employee suit over back pay, was in his office meting out punishment to a freelance journalist who had dared reveal his father's bisexuality in a 1990 magazine article. According to the sworn statement of Clair George, a former Central Intelligence Agency deputy director whom Feld hired to work for him in 1990, Feld was determined to keep the journalist from digging around in his family's past. Measures to accomplish this allegedly included putting the journalist under surveillance, spreading nasty rumors about her, and distracting her from a book she wanted to write about Feld's father by getting another company to hire her to write a different book instead, this one about fellow Forbes 400 members the Mars family.

In another display of aggressive tactics, the circus went after People for the Ethical Treatment of Animals (PETA), which had accused Ringling Bros.

---

*By pleading guilty to a misdemeanor, Hammer escaped more serious felony charges of obstructing justice.

of cruelty to its elephants. When PETA learned that the company had been doing surveillance on it for more than ten years, the organization sued Feld. Court testimony described how Ringling spied on PETA leaders, infiltrated the organization, obtained credit card and other personal data, and stole thousands of pages of the group's documents. PETA eventually lost when a jury found that no harm had been done to them. Even though Ringling spent millions of dollars on its espionage efforts, Feld, who received regular reports from the company's private investigators, claimed he had little or no knowledge of what was taking place.

A three-ring circus, indeed.

Crimes and Punishments

Over the past twenty-five years, at least thirteen members of the Forbes 400 have been convicted of crimes (see table on page 105). Although some of them were incarcerated for acts that were peripheral to the source of their fortunes, the cases reflect a certain disregard for established rules. (Quipped one arbiter of the game, Greek shipping magnate Aristotle Onassis, who later married Jacqueline Kennedy, "The rules are, there are no rules.")

Many of the felons on the Forbes 400 have been financiers: After all, financiers make their living buying and selling risk. As James B. Stewart notes in *Den of Thieves,* his masterly account of the rings of insider trading surrounding Ivan Boesky and Michael Milken during the 1980s, some are more expert than others at calculating the risk of getting caught. "Of course a fair number of financial fortunes are made in the margins," says University of Pennsylvania corporate law professor David Skeel. "Ruthlessness is inevitable in the free market" because the alternative—regulation of every aspect of the markets—is unbearable.

Some Forbes 400 members settled civil cases without admitting guilt. Among them are hedge fund honcho Michael Steinhardt (worth some $300 million in 1993), who was investigated for cornering the Treasury bond market and paid a $52.5 million fine. Similarly, money manager Mario Gabelli (2005 net worth: $1 billion), known as Super Mario for his stock-picking acumen, paid a $130 million fine in 2006 to settle a civil fraud lawsuit that accused him of deceiving the Federal Communications Commission in its auction of cellphone licenses in the late 1990s.

Other 400 members have never been tried or given pardons. Longtime fugitive Robert Vesco, wanted for years for drug trafficking and securities fraud in the United States, is now serving a prison term in Cuba on unrelated fraud charges. (Vesco's last appearance on the Forbes list was in 1984, with a net worth of $150 million.) Commodities trader Marc Rich, worth $1.5 billion in 2006, fled to Switzerland in 1983 to avoid prosecution for illegal trading and tax evasion. Rich, whose ex-wife Denise was a major backer of President Bill Clinton, was given a controversial midnight pardon the night before Clinton's term in office expired. Clinton also pardoned Rich's partner, Pincus Green (2006 net worth: $1.2 billion).

At least one member of the Forbes 400 has the dubious distinction of having amassed his fortune almost entirely illegally. Meyer Lanksy was for decades a key figure in organized crime in the United States. A Polish immigrant, he grew up poor on Manhattan's Lower East Side in the 1910s. But Lansky had a great head for business. He befriended another impoverished street tough, Bugsy Siegel, and ran liquor for gangs in New York during Prohibition, stealing booze from them on the side. He prided himself on not watering down his whiskey; his was good stuff, straight from

Scotland. The economics of bootleg booze during Prohibition were terrific, provided you could stay alive.

During the 1930s, when every state except Nevada outlawed gambling, Lansky switched from booze to illegal casinos in the South. He'd learned how to run hotels and a casino in Saratoga Springs from another mobster, and he bribed the mayor of New Orleans, with an annual deposit of several million dollars into a Swiss bank account, to gain his cooperation in expanding his gambling operations to the Big Easy. Lansky then took his gambling business to Florida, Kansas, and eventually Cuba.

In the 1940s, Cuban dictator Fulgencio Batista asked Lansky for help in running his gambling paradise. American and European tourists then flocking to Havana casinos complained that its houses were crooked. Lansky brought in his own croupiers. Soon the casinos were bringing in and laundering so much money for the Mob that, legend has it, Lansky provided Batista with a sizable kickback. With Siegel, Lansky then helped build Las Vegas into a neon entertainment center.

With his sharp business skills, Lansky could have been chairman of General Motors in another life, an FBI agent once told the New York Times. He was known to keep the numbers for all his businesses in his head. Without a paper trail, the government had a hard time winning cases against him. The federal government convicted him of contempt of court, but the conviction was overturned on appeal; charges of skimming $36 million between 1960 and 1967 from the syndicate casino the Flamingo Hotel in Vegas and of tax evasion were dropped. In the end, Lansky never went to jail. He lived out his days in seclusion in Miami Beach. He was a strong supporter of Israel and of the local public television station. He died peacefully in 1983, a year after the inaugural Forbes 400 tallied his fortune at $300 million, the same as David Rockefeller's.

At the opposite extreme, there is perhaps no better poster boy for white-collar crime than Bernard Ebbers, founder and CEO of WorldCom and one of the most visible examples in the parade of corporate scandals in recent years. Ebbers got into the telecommunications business in the early 1990s, before deregulation. A former milkman and high-school coach, the devoutly Christian Ebbers built the long-distance reseller into the nation's second-largest telecommunications company.

But the government contended that Ebbers had inflated WorldCom's earnings in order to protect his personal fortune ($1.4 billion in 1998) from banks that were calling in their loans after the company's stock took a dive. WorldCom collapsed, shareholders lost $180 billion, 20,000 people lost their jobs, and in 2005 Ebbers was convicted of orchestrating an $11 billion accounting fraud that led to the largest U.S. bankruptcy in history. On the day he entered prison to begin serving a twenty-five-year sentence, Ebbers sold one of his last assets, a 29,000-acre cotton farm, to a company owned by billionaire George Soros. He drove to jail in Louisiana in a white Mercedes.

In trouble with the law

Among the individuals who have appeared on the Forbes 400 list since 1982, at least 13 members have been convicted of crimes or jailed. They include:

	Peak net worth in billions (year)	Source of wealth	What happened
Ivan Boesky	$0.2 ('86)	Arbitrage	Pleaded guilty in 1986 to illegal insider trading. Cooperated with SEC investigation, and received plea bargain of a 3-year sentence, $100 million fine.
John E. Du Pont	$0.2 ('86)	Inheritance	Convicted of 1996 murder of an Olympic wrestler; declared mentally ill. Sentenced to at least 13 years in prison. Settled wrongful death suit for $35 million.
Bernard Ebbers	$1.4 ('99)	Worldcom stock	Convicted in 2005 of fraud and conspiracy in largest accounting scandal in U.S. history. Serving 25-year jail sentence.
Leona Helmsley	$2.5 ('06)	Hotels	Convicted of federal income tax evasion and mail fraud in 1989. Fined $8 million and served 18 months in jail.
Nelson B. Hunt	$0.9 ('85)	Oil	Brothers charged with obstruction of justice in illegal wiretapping in 1970—acquitted.
William H. Hunt	$0.8 ('85)	Oil	Both convicted in 1988 of manipulating the silver market and paid millions in fines.
Michael Milken	$2.0 ('06)	Investments	Pleaded guilty in 1990 to 6 felonies ranging from conspiracy to securities fraud. Paid $900 million settlement and served 22 months of 10-year sentence.
Victor Posner	$0.3 ('84)	Finance, takeovers	Convicted of tax fraud in 1987. Paid $7 million fine, avoided jail by giving Florida homeless $3 million and doing community service.
Leandro P. Rizzuto	$0.8 ('05)	Manufacturing; Conair	Pleaded guilty in 2002 to diverting company income into secret foreign bank accounts. Served 27 months in prison.
Martha Stewart	$1.0 ('00)	Media	Convicted in 2004 of conspiracy, obstruction, and lying to federal investigators in insider trading case. Jailed for 5 months.
Alfred Taubman	$1.4 ('06)	Shopping malls	Former Sotheby's head was found guilty in 2001 of colluding with rival Christie's to fix commissions. Fined $7.5 million and served 9 months in prison.

3 were pardoned:

Pincus Green	$1.2 ('06)	Commodities trading	Indicted for fraud, tax evasion, racketeering in 1983. Partner of Marc Rich, now living in Switzerland. Was pardoned by President Bill Clinton in 2001.
Armand Hammer	$0.2 ('86)	Soviet Union; oil	Convicted of a $54,000 illegal political contribution to Nixon's Campaign to Re-Elect the President (CREEP) in the mid-'70s; later pardoned by George H. W. Bush.
Marc Rich	$1.5 ('06)	Commodities trading	Charged in 1983 with 65 counts of tax evasion, mail and wire fraud. Fled to Switzerland. Pardoned by Bill Clinton in 2001, paid $100 million fine.

2 were charged but acquitted:

Meyer Lansky	$0.1 ('82)	Organized crime	Convicted in 1973 of contempt of court; overturned on appeal. Acquitted of tax evasion the same year; charges of skimming from casinos dropped.
T. Cullen Davis	$0.3 ('84)	Oil	Acquitted of stepdaughter's murder, and attempted murder of judge in divorce case, 1978.

At least 6 others have settled civil charges with the SEC or Department of Justice or signed consent decrees—sometimes paying millions of dollars in fines. Also, Robert Vesco, a fugitive, is in jail in Cuba for medical fraud but wanted in the United States on charges of embezzling $224 million from 4 different mutual funds.

PART TWO

Making It

5

Blue-collar Billionaires

Monaco is one of the world's fairy-tale settings, a blend of natural beauty and man-made glamour. Its sea, sky, and mountains form a backdrop for glittering casinos; megamillion-dollar yachts, more profuse than the principality's brilliant bougainvillea, cluster densely in its harbor. Many of the yachts docked there in early June 2006 were magnificent by any standards. But few could have measured up to a 228-foot floating palace called *The Floridian*, equipped with a swimming pool, alfresco bar, and helicopter pad—one of America's top ten yachts, according to *Power & Motoryacht* magazine. Its owner: H. Wayne Huizenga (pronounced HIGH-zeng-a), a bald, stocky sixty-nine-year-old with eyes so steel blue a rival once described them as "piercing, right to the soul."

Huizenga, with an estimated net worth of $2.1 billion (more than twice the GDP of Monaco), was in town to address the annual Ernst & Young Entrepreneur of the Year World Summit, held that year in Monte Carlo's Grimaldi Forum, a futuristic center built on the sea with expansive harbor views and named after the family that has reigned over the principality for more than seven hundred years.

As winner of the 2005 World Entrepreneur Award and informal king of the conference, Huizenga was invited to deliver the keynote speech, "An Entrepreneurial Journey: The Story of Wayne Huizenga." Even for Monte Carlo, the glitz level was high. In the audience was a pantheon of the world's biggest wealth creators, more than one hundred entrepreneurs from nearly forty countries. It was all the more impressive, then, that Huizenga, a college dropout who started his business with one used garbage truck, was the man standing in front of them.

Think of Forbes 400 members and what comes to mind are tycoons such as computer titan Michael Dell, America Online's Steve Case, eBay's Pierre Omidyar, and Qualcomm's Irwin Jacobs—all former winners of Ernst & Young awards, all high-tech billionaires who made fortunes on flashy, brainy businesses. Then there are the media mavens—Rupert Murdoch, Barry Diller, David Geffen—whose boldface names appear regularly in the papers. Huizenga's fortune, by contrast, derives from a patchwork of low-tech, low-visibility, low-prestige ventures: trash hauling, video rentals, auto sales. What the Wayne Huizenga story really shows is that you don't have to be a high-tech genius or an entertainment mogul to make a mint. Nor do you have to be a Rockefeller, or Wall Street financier, to stake a place on the Forbes 400.

Like Huizenga, a surprising number of Forbes 400 members make bushelloads off basic goods and services—producing plumbing fixtures and used-car parts, for example, or feeding the masses fries, pizza, and subs, or entertaining them at wrestling rings and auto races, or providing workaday services like tree pruning and, yes, trash disposal—practical, down-market, service-oriented niches that keep America humming. These and other "blue-collar" enterprises have helped spawn at least 175 of the fortunes on the Forbes 400 lists over the past twenty-five years. Their aggregate net worth, in any given year, represents roughly 20 percent of the list's total.

What does it take to score big in a low-tech venture? Many of the same characteristics, of course, as in more glamorous industries: discipline, tenacity, and attention to detail, for starters. But there are a few key qualities that set these niche players apart from their more upscale counterparts. One is an intimate, almost in-their-blood familiarity with their business and customers. Many grew up in homes that first exposed them to their future careers. Huizenga's grandfather, for example, was in the garbage business in the late 1800s; during the 1980s more than a dozen Huizenga family members operated their own trash-hauling ventures. S. Truett Cathy, billionaire founder of Chick-fil-A, the fast-food chicken-on-a-bun chain, learned to cook chicken by watching his mother prepare dinner for her boarders. And James Leprino, who made a $1.5 billion fortune in cheese, got his start making homemade ricotta and mozzarella for local stores alongside his Italian immigrant father.

"These folks know and care about their customer, and they know and care about what they are providing their customer," observes Alexander Horniman, professor at the University of Virginia's Darden School of Business.

"They are immersed in their business. Their identities and what they do for their customers are all tied together," he says. You might say that they are so in tune with customer needs that it's a case of "it takes one to know one." Except, as Horniman points out, "You could 'know one' but not give a damn—these folks give a damn."

Many are also self-made successes. Almost everyone, naturally, has some degree of help from family, mentors, and society at large—buttressing forces that Chuck Collins, cofounder of the nonprofit group Responsible Wealth, calls "common" wealth. But even if you define "self-made" in the strictest sense, as Collins does—someone whose parents did not go to college and who did not benefit from family wealth or home equity to start their business—at least 30 percent of the 175 or so blue-collar billionaires are up-by-the-bootstraps successes. A composite of their stories creates a familiar, almost stereotypical profile: They are born poor, have little if any advanced education, start a small business, and then devote their lives to growing it.

Nonagenarian J. R. Simplot typifies the breed. A self-described "old potato farmer" and a legend in his home state of Idaho (his license plate reads MR SPUD), Simplot started trading hogs and growing potatoes as an eighth-grade dropout. During the war years, when fertilizer for his crops was in short supply, Simplot began his own fertilizer plant. Later, he pioneered commercially frozen french fries and supplied the fast-food business with most of its frozen fries. "Nobody ever put a penny in my company," Simplot has said, "not one red cent. I did it by taking care of business. That's what my job was. And it was tough, tough, tough." As a second act in his career, Simplot, at age seventy-one, invested in a small computer-chip venture, Micron Technology, a Boise-based company that has grown into a semiconductor giant. Simplot, whose 2006 net worth came to about $3.2 billion, has offered this advice for financial success: "Work honestly and build, build, build."

Simplot's advice seems to be a kind of mantra for blue-collar business stars. "It's almost a cliché," says Horniman, but there is "a certain entrepreneurial propensity in the personality of these niche players to create, to construct something, or to solve a set of unique problems." Few demonstrate that relentless itch better than Huizenga, as he propelled that one trash truck into an unparalleled series of firsts and mosts: the only person in corporate history to build and float six companies on the New York Stock Exchange (NYSE), three of which (Waste Management; Blockbuster, the video rental company; and AutoNation, possibly the world's largest auto dealership) became multibillion-dollar companies. Huizenga built up those companies through dogged persistence, financial muscle, and hard-nosed deal making, gobbling up mom-and-pop outfits and larger companies that fit into his grand scheme. His underlying strategy: systemize businesses in markets that are fragmented or inefficient. His targets are nearly always service or rental companies—businesses that throw off lots of cash, which can be plowed into

Where the 400 make their money

The ever-changing dynamics of the U.S. economy are reflected in the source of Forbes 400 fortunes. In 1982, 22.8% of 400 fortunes came from oil; by 2006, the number in the oil business slipped to 7.5%. Similarly, manufacturing shows a steep decline as a source of wealth. The sectors that have shown the biggest increases in the past 25 years: finance and technology.

1982

Technology 3%
Service 3.2%
Finance 9%
Food 9.3%
Real Estate 15%
Other 8.5%
Manufacturing 15.3%
Oil 22.8%
Media/Entertainment/
Communications 13.8%

1992

Technology 4.75%
Service 1.75%
Finance 17%
Retail 11%
Real Estate 8%
Food 14%
Other 3.75%
Oil/Gas 8.75%
Manufacturing 14.75%
Media 15.5%

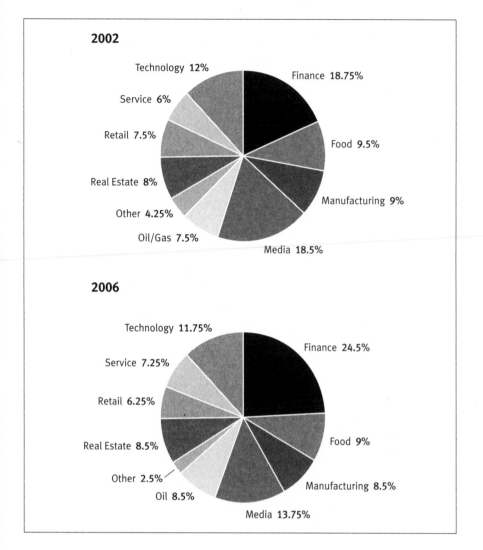

2002

Technology 12%
Service 6%
Retail 7.5%
Real Estate 8%
Other 4.25%
Oil/Gas 7.5%
Media 18.5%
Manufacturing 9%
Food 9.5%
Finance 18.75%

2006

Technology 11.75%
Service 7.25%
Retail 6.25%
Real Estate 8.5%
Other 2.5%
Oil 8.5%
Media 13.75%
Manufacturing 8.5%
Food 9%
Finance 24.5%

continued growth. "I like recurring revenue," says Huizenga. "You sell the customer once and the rest of the time it's just a matter of building the customer relationship." To create Waste Management, for example, he says he bought out about 150 garbage-hauling companies within a one-year period, crisscrossing the country ceaselessly to make his acquisitions.

There can be some seedy consequences associated with running a garbage company, especially one as big as Waste Management. As head of the company Huizenga faced a barrage of media attacks and government investigations (later dropped) claiming that his trash-hauling business had Mob connections. But Huizenga always insisted that he ran a clean shop, and that he purposely stayed out of New York City and New Jersey, where links to

The richest blue-collar billionaires

Big-box retailing, candy bars, toilets and bathtubs, sneakers, chewing gum, potatoes, and the like don't usually come to mind as sources of huge fortunes, yet that is often the case. Blue-collar fortunes accounted for 11% of the aggregate 400 fortunes in 1982; the figure jumped to 24% in 1992, then dropped to 18% in 2006.

		Source of wealth	Peak value (billions)	Peak year
Helen Walton		Retail – Wal-Mart	**$20.5**	2003
Jim C. Walton		Retail – Wal-Mart	**$20.5**	2003
John T. Walton		Retail – Wal-Mart	**$20.5**	2003
S. Robson Walton		Retail – Wal-Mart	**$20.5**	2003
Christy Walton		Retail – Wal-Mart	**$15.7**	2005
Jack Taylor		Retail – auto rental	**$13.9**	2006
Forrest Mars Jr.		Food – candy	**$10.5**	2006
Jacqueline Mars		Food – candy	**$10.5**	2006
John Mars		Food – candy	**$10.5**	2006
Sam Walton		Retail – Wal-Mart	**$8.5**	1987
Philip Knight		Retail – Nike	**$7.9**	2006
H. Ty Warner		Retail – Beanie Babies	**$6.0**	2003
John Menard Jr.		Home improvement stores	**$5.2**	2006
John Simplot		Food – potatoes	**$4.7**	2000
Richard DeVos		Door-to-door sales – Amway	**$4.5**	1994
Jay Van Andel		Door-to-door sales – Amway	**$4.5**	1994
Herbert Kohler		Manufacturing – plumbing	**$4.5**	2006
Bradley Hughes		Public Storage	**$4.1**	2006
William Davidson		Manufacturing – Guardian Industries (glass)	**$4.0**	2006
Forrest Mars Sr.		Food – candy	**$4.0**	1998
William Wrigley Jr.		Food – gum	**$4.0**	2004

% of 400 controlled by blue-collar	1982: **11%**	1992: **24%**	2002: **23%**	2006: **18%**

organized crime were thought to be strongest. In any case, Huizenga stepped down from Waste Management at age forty-seven (he was retired for about "three weeks and twelve minutes," as his wife Marti later recalled), only to embark on more buying sprees. During the following years he bought nearly every type of service and rental business imaginable—laundry, bottled water, lawn care, pest control, portable toilets—and tucked them under the umbrella of Huizenga Holdings.

In the midst of his buying frenzy, a friend took Huizenga to check out a local Blockbuster video store. Huizenga was smitten by the rental aspect of the business and its growth potential as VCRs gained in popularity. The added plus: "I certainly liked the Blockbuster business a lot better than the garbage business because of the image thing," Huizenga has said. He bought the nineteen-store, $7 million business, took it public, and changed the video rental business overnight. Over a six-year span, Blockbuster opened a new store every seventeen hours. By the time Huizenga sold it to Viacom (for $8.4 billion in stock) in 1994, it was a $4 billion video rental and entertainment enterprise, with nearly four thousand stores in eleven countries.

Huizenga's appetite to buy and build continued. He turned his energy partly back to the trash business, transforming another small waste-disposal company, later called Republic Services, into the country's third largest, now competing with the first largest, Waste Management. At the same time, he was making headway toward his next target—the vast, disorganized auto-sales market. In 1998 he named the scattered car franchises he had accumulated AutoNation and turned it into the United States' first nationwide car dealer. (One key investor in the venture was erstwhile Forbes 400 member Jim Moran, himself a titan in the auto-sales business.) By 2006 the company had a network of more than 370 dealerships. What motivates Huizenga? Fulfilling his "long-term strategy," he says. According to his son Wayne Jr., though, it is "the excitement of making the deal. I think that's what drives him." All told, Huizenga has made thousands of deals in an almost manic drive to build, build, build.

One moneymaking maxim that abounds among low-tech entrepreneurs is that you don't have to invent an entirely new contraption; just find a way to make it better, or at least different. David Gold, a sometime member of the Forbes 400 list, illustrates just that point. The son of Russian immigrants and a Los Angeles Community College dropout, Gold tweaked the old five-and-

Rich son, poor dad

Outsize inheritances were out of the question for some erstwhile Forbes 400 members, each a Horatio Alger in his own right. Their fathers came from the humblest of backgrounds.

	Net worth (billions)	Last year on list	Company/ source of wealth	Father's occupation
James L. Clayton	**$0.62**	2002	Mobile homes	Sharecropper
Sidney Frank*	**$1.80**	2005	Liquor distribution	Orchardman
B. Wayne Hughes	**$4.10**	2006	Public storage warehouses	Factory worker
J. B. Hunt*	**$0.34**	1994	Trucking	Sharecropper
Luigino "Jeno" Paulucci	**$0.45**	1991	Chun King and other foods	Iron miner
Marvin Schwan*	**$1.00**	1992	Schwan's ice cream and other foods	Dairy farmer
David Shakarian*	**$0.25**	1984	General Nutrition Corporation; real estate	Armenian yogurt maker
O. Bruton Smith	**$1.40**	2006	Speedway Motorsports	Cotton farmer
Karsten Solheim*	**$0.40**	1994	Golf clubs	Norwegian cobbler
Leonard Stern	**$3.70**	2006	Hartz pet supply; real estate	German bird salesman

*deceased

dime concept twenty-five years ago, when he opened his first 99 Cents Only store. By 2006 Gold had built the company into a network of more than 230 stores, mainly in the Southwest, with more than $1 billion a year in sales. The huge twenty-two-thousand-square-foot stores generate about $250 a square foot, among the highest per-foot performances in the fast-growing deep-discount industry, edging out convenience stores, drugstores, even Wal-Mart, according to market-research firm ACNielsen. In 2003, the last time Gold appeared on the Forbes 400 list, he was worth some $860 million.

But Gold's 99 Cents Only chain almost never happened. As he tells it, his pioneering concept started as a vague notion in the 1960s. He and his wife, Sherry, ran a liquor store in a large indoor market in Los Angeles. They noticed that when they priced a bottle of wine at $.99, it sold better than the same bottle of Chianti or Pinot Noir priced at $.89 or $1.19. "We thought it would be a good idea to have a place that sold everything for ninety-nine cents—quality merchandise all for one low price," says Gold. He was still mulling over the notion twenty years later when a friend exclaimed, "Damn it, why don't you stop talking about it and do it?" That same day, Gold struck a deal for his first 99 Cents Only store near the Los Angeles airport. "We waited so long," says Gold, "we were surprised no one opened up before us!"

At the core of Gold's winning strategy: great bargains on brand-name items, including Coke, Hershey's, and Häagen-Dazs. Many are specially packaged for the store, while others are items that companies want to unload fast in order to empty a warehouse, or because they plan to change the packaging. Knickknacks and useless trinkets, often the mainstay of other dollar-store inventories, are limited to less than 2 percent of stock. Profit margins are hard to squeeze out of $.99 items, so getting great deals from vendors is imperative. Gold says he motivates his dozen buyers with salaries that are double the industry norm, even compared to those at such upscale retailers as Nordstrom. The payoff is that a 99 Cents Only store item often costs the company only about $.60, providing an almost 40 percent gross margin—twice that of many discounters.

Buyers aren't the only ones cashing in at 99 Cents Only. When Gold took the company public a decade ago, he and other top executives, including son-in-law and current CEO Eric Schiffer, son Jeff, who is president, and son Howard, executive vice president, took no stock options. (Family members don't get bonuses, either.) But all workers, including truck drivers, cashiers, and managers, are entitled to options. "We had enough money," says Gold. "We wanted to have them get part of the American pie." By 2006 employees had taken home nearly

1990

from the pages of *Forbes*

Samuel Jayson LeFrak, who made his fortune in Manhattan and New Jersey real estate, has been knighted by the kings of Norway and Sweden. (1990 net worth: $1.6 billion)

Jerry J. Moore, a Texan whose money comes from investments and shopping centers, has 650-plus vintage cars in his collection, which is rated number one in the United States by *Car Collector* magazine. (1990 net worth: $650 million)

Richard Louis Duchossois, an Illinois industrialist and horseracing enthusiast, had a very bad 1989. His farmhouse was torched, and a human skeleton was found on the land. (1990 net worth: $350 million)

John W. Kluge, who built a major media empire, has an eighty-thousand-acre estate—and castle—in Scotland. (1990 net worth: $5.6 billion)

$100 million in profits. Gold claims that many, including some who never finished high school, have used the money to pay in cash for new houses.

Counting pennies helps keep Gold's overhead low. The company operates out of a warehouse in low-income, high-crime City of Commerce, California. Executive perks are nonexistent: no secretaries or special parking spots. "If we operated like everyone else, we couldn't sell things for ninety-nine cents," Gold says. Advertising is done in-house. It often features eye-popping promotions, such as $.99 TVs or iPods for the first nine customers at a new store opening and a $.99 scooter for the next ninety-nine. Gold's frugality spills over to his personal life. He and his wife still live in the house they bought forty-four years ago, shortly after their marriage. They shun the extravagant lifestyle of many fellow centimillionaires. No fancy clothes, jewelry, or cars for them, says Gold. They each drive a fuel-efficient Prius. "More important than being rich," he says, "is family and friends and cleaning up the environment."

Like David Gold, two other members of the Forbes 400—Alex Manoogian, a son of Armenian immigrants who settled in Detroit, and Oregonian Richard Wendt—also found ways to improve on existing models. Manoogian's was a household staple—a perfected, single-handle, washerless faucet—while Wendt, the founder of Jeld-Wen, found his niche in a building basic—diligently crafted windows and doors. Most people have probably never heard of Masco, Manoogian's company, or Jeld-Wen, but their products are found in nearly every American home. Masco makes such nationally known brands as Delta faucets and KraftMaid cabinets, and Jeld-Wen sells more than $2 billion a year worldwide of quality doors and windows. When housing markets boom, the coffers of these companies overflow, adding to the riches of company founders and their offspring.

Manoogian struck gold in 1952 with his redesigned single-handle faucet; within a few years he had sold millions. His plumbing-fixture fortune kept him on the Forbes 400 list for four years before he died in 1996. His son Richard, now Masco Corporation's executive chairman, joined the company in 1958 after graduating from Yale University. He diversified into furniture and other far-flung businesses. Then, in an about-face, he unloaded them to concentrate on the company's plumbing and cabinetry roots. With more than $12 billion in annual sales, Masco is a giant in the consumer durables world. Billionaire Manoogian collects an average annual salary of $9 million. He devotes a good chunk of his riches toward expanding his vast art collection of mainly nineteenth-century American masters.

Penny-pinching, publicity-shy Richard Wendt started Jeld-Wen in 1960, when he rescued an old millwork plant with fifteen employees from foreclosure in his hometown of Klamath Falls, Oregon. (He came up with the odd company name by combining parts of his name with those of his parents and sister.) With a sharp eye on costs and through shrewd acquisitions that consolidated a network of manufacturers and distributors, Wendt and his son Roderick, a Stanford grad and Jeld-Wen's CEO, have quietly turned the company into one of the largest players in the $27 billion windows and doors market.

Wendt, now in his seventies, is notorious for moving below the radar, even in his little town. "Dick can walk the main street of this town, and I guarantee to you that 80 percent of the people will not know who he is," a company employee told *Forbes* a few years back. His parsimonious ways are also legendary. For years, Wendt wore a pair of worn-out loafers on hiking trails, until friends split the cost and bought him a pair of hiking boots. Wendt was worth $700 million in 2003, before newer fortunes pushed him off the Forbes 400 list.

Many self-made entrepreneurs share a deep-seated, almost messianic fervor about how to run a business. Business professor Horniman describes it as a personal and distinct philosophy that permeates their business: "They will say: 'Here's the way we are going to do business.' Often it's a strong religious affiliation, but many times it's not about religion but rather about a strong set of values. They are almost obsessed with it."

In the case of S. Truett Cathy, a devout Southern Baptist who has taught Sunday school for fifty years, it *is* all about religion. He went from an impoverished childhood in Atlanta to amassing a $1.2 billion fortune as founder of Chick-fil-A, the privately owned fast-food chain that sells an annual $2 billion worth of chicken-breast sandwiches and waffle fries. Former president Jimmy Carter, a fellow Georgian, has called Cathy "one of the most remarkable success stories of our time." An energetic octogenarian still known to ride a motorcycle, Cathy remains active in the company; two sons hold top executive positions. The secret to his success, says Cathy, is to put "principles before profits."

That means, for starters, no working on Sundays. Cathy made the decision to shutter his restaurants on Sundays early in his career, even though he says that as much as 20 percent of profits in fast food are made that day. At first, says Cathy, the policy was a hard sell to mall developers as he negotiated

Feeding frenzies

More than 70 Forbes 400 members over the years have made their riches largely by satisfying seemingly insatiable appetites, as this smorgasbord of food and drink fortunes shows.

	Peak net worth in billions (year)	Source of wealth	Comment
S. Daniel Abraham	$1.90 ('06)	Slim-Fast	Brought out Slim-Fast dietary supplement in 1976; sold to Unilever for $2.3 billion in 2000.
John Edward Anderson	$1.90 ('06)	Ace Beverage	Grew Ace largely as a Budweiser distributor. Later diversified into banks and insurance companies.
Harvey Chaplin	$1.20 ('05)	Southern Wine & Spirits	Helped reshape America's tastes from martinis to wine, building up one of the nation's largest liquor distributors.
Bennett Dorrance	$2.10 ('06)	Campbell Soup	Grandson of chemist who invented condensed-soup process. Bennett and other family members own about half the company.
Sidney Frank	$1.80 ('05)	Liquor distributor	Began with low-brow Jägermeister; followed with premium vodka Grey Goose. Sold Grey Goose to Bacardi for $2 billion before he died in 2006.
Ernest Gallo Julio Gallo	$1.30 ('06) $0.30 ('92)	Gallo Wine	Sons of Italian immigrants, the brothers (both deceased) started pressing wine in 1933. A dozen family members now active in Gallo.
Christopher "Kit" Goldsbury	$1.40 ('06)	Pace Picante Sauce	Married daughter of a Louisiana creator of a hot and spicy salsa. Bought him out; sold to Campbell Soup in 1995 for $1.1 billion.
Jess Stonestreet Jackson	$2.20 ('06)	Jackson Wine Estates	Planted vines outside San Francisco; released first Kendall-Jackson wine in early 1980s. Operates dozens of wineries worldwide.
Ray Kroc Joan Beverly Kroc	$0.45 ('83) $1.70 ('03)	McDonald's	Chicago milkshake-machine salesman turned tiny burger joint into the fast-food giant. Married nightclub performer Joan, 26 years his junior. Ray died in 1984; Joan in 2003.
Forrest Mars Jr. Jacqueline Mars John Mars	$10.50 ('06) $10.50 ('06) $10.50 ('06)	Mars Candy	Grandchildren of founders of Milky Way bars. Secretive company's success secrets: quality, cost control, cleanliness.
Wendell H. Murphy	$0.45 ('99)	Murphy Family Farms	Systematized and computerized inefficient hog business; sold to Smithfield Foods in a deal worth $288 million.
Joseph Neubauer	$0.68 ('03)	Aramark	Israeli immigrant grew food preparation unit of Aramark into huge sports concessionaire; food provider for a dozen Olympic games.
Luigino "Jeno" Paulucci	$0.45 ('90)	Chun King, Jeno's Pizza, etc.	Product of Minnesota's iron range; inventive marketer created nearly 70 food brands.
Frank Perdue	$0.454 ('98)	Perdue Farms	Built father's small Maryland egg business into huge poultry producer. Became celebrity via TV and radio ads before his death in 2005.
Robert Rich Sr. Robert Rich Jr.	$2.50 ('05) $1.50 ('06)	Coffee Rich	Robert Sr. created Coffee Rich, a liquid cream substitute; expanded into baked goods. Died in 2006; Robert Jr. is CEO.

	Peak net worth in billions (year)	Source of wealth	Comment
Donald J. Tyson	**$1.00** ('05)	Tyson Foods	Son of founder has grown the poultry company by acquisition and diversifying into pork, fisheries.
William Wrigley William Wrigley Jr.	**$2.70** ('98) **$1.60** ('06)	Wrigley	Fourth-generation William Wrigley, Jr. runs the world's largest gum maker.

leases for his outlets. But eventually landlords obliged. They know that "we do more in six days than the competition does in seven," he claims in his Georgia drawl, "not only because of our food quality but because of the quality of our people." The policy is intended to give employees time to go to church and spend the day with their families. But Cathy says it has an added benefit: It attracts employees and customers who share the same work ethic and religious beliefs.

It also helps instill loyalty among franchisees, employees, and customers. Chick-fil-A franchise operators stay with the company twenty years on average, and employee turnover is 3.5 percent, low by any standards but especially by those within the high-turnover fast-food business. "The more we can foster the feeling that we are a group of people working together, depending on each other, the more likely we are to be loyal to each other," Cathy says. Frederick Reichheld, author of *Loyalty Rules: How Today's Leaders Build Lasting Relationships,* agrees: There is "no clearer case study of the loyalty effect than Chick-fil-A." Such a unifying policy, concurs Horniman, "makes it easier for a business to succeed than to fail."

Cathy learned the rewards of customer loyalty at an early age. His father, an insurance salesman, was a poor provider and an emotionally distant man; his mother ran a boardinghouse to keep the family afloat. He helped out by selling Cokes, magazines, and the *Atlanta Journal-Constitution.* Cathy realized he could get an edge on his competitors, and retain customers, by adding an ice cube to the Coke and delivering a paper closer to a house door. He also filed away lessons learned at his mother's side, watching her cook meals for her seven children and eight boarders. He noticed, for example, that after she seasoned chicken she kept it in the icebox overnight to absorb the spices. The next day she fried it in a huge iron skillet, making sure it was tightly covered to keep the chicken moist. His boyhood observations would help Cathy pioneer the chicken-breast sandwich that made him his riches.

All successful entrepreneurs seem prescient in hindsight. But what some call "vision," others call "determination." What's more, recognizing possibilities, or what former president George H. W. Bush called "the vision thing," is only half the equation: Acting on them is key. To the extent that any single quality determines success, say Warren Bennis and Robert Thomas, authors of *Geeks and Geezers: How Era, Values, and Defining Moments Shape Leaders,* a book that studies the traits that make great leaders, it is the ability "to recognize and seize opportunities." However, given how consumer oriented the blue-collar sector is, and how fickle consumers can be, the ability to recognize opportunity is no easy feat. Who would have predicted the popularity of pizza in 1959, for example? Back then, pizza had made few inroads beyond a smattering of urban Italian restaurants. Yet that year Michael Ilitch, a former marine, and his wife, Marian, mustered up $10,000 and opened a Little Caesars pizzeria in their hometown of Detroit. Four and a half decades later, Little Caesars is a thriving national chain with 2,300 outlets. Ilitch, who is worth about $1.5 billion, also owns the Detroit Tigers baseball team and Red Wings hockey team. And he and his wife of more than fifty years are now placing another big bet by trying to revive casino gambling in Motown. It remains to be seen whether that risky project will, in the future, make the Ilitches look like seers.

Their success with pizza, meanwhile, illustrates another pattern common among many entrepreneurs—the ability to rise above setbacks and obstacles, or what Bennis and Thomas call "crucibles." The son of Macedonian immigrants, Ilitch grew up in a stable, working-class family on Detroit's West Side. He played shortstop on such minor-league teams as the Tampa Smokers, hoping to make it big. But a knee injury forced him to quit. "That destroyed my dreams of playing in the major leagues," he later recalled. But adaptability and necessity—having to provide for his wife and eventually seven children—made him move on.

Pizza parlors were just beginning to pop up, and pizza making intrigued him. When he traveled, he made a point of scouting around for pizza stores to gauge their popularity and the quality of the pizza. To test out the notion's viability, Ilitch also started making pizza behind the counter of a friend's bar. Encouraged by the cash he was taking home at the end of the night, he opened up his own pizza place. Marian named the store Little Caesars after her husband: "Caesar" because she said he resembled the Roman emperor; "Little" because "he hadn't accomplished anything." While he rolled the dough in the kitchen, she ran the register.

The couples' secret recipe for growth combined a laserlike focus on the business, innovations, and more than a few lessons gleaned from observing Ray Kroc, founder of McDonald's and the most legendary of all blue-collar billionaires. "My idol was Ray Kroc," Ilitch explained in a 2006 television interview. "Whenever he spoke I was there. I learned you have to get the food out as fast as you can, and you have to keep the stores immaculate." Growth was sluggish at first. Introducing special ovens outfitted with conveyor belts helped: Pizzas were baked on the belt and moved out every eight minutes.

But by the mid-1980s, competition was intense. Ilitch's crosstown Detroit rival, Thomas Monaghan, founder of Domino's Pizza and a longtime Forbes 400 member as well, stunned the competition by figuring out a profitable way to deliver pizza to homes in thirty minutes or less. Ilitch's marketing response to Domino's threat took the pizza wars to a new level. His "Pizza, pizza" campaign, or two pies for one low price, followed by new products like Crazy Bread, helped secure his niche in the take-out business. By 2006 Little Caesars was one of the country's largest take-out pizza chains, growing at a vigorous 10 to 15 percent rate a year.

Unlike Ilitch, who came from a close-knit family, Monaghan had a troubled childhood. Fatherless at age four, he grew up in orphanages and studied briefly for the priesthood. Then, like Ilitch, he joined the U.S. Marines. Monaghan and his younger brother pulled together $500 and bought a pizza shop in 1960. The following year he traded his Volkswagen for his brother's share of the shop and set about transforming Domino's into a powerhouse. Like Ilitch, he was also a sports fanatic. In 1983 he bought the Detroit Tigers, who won the World Series the following year. But in the late 1990s Monaghan sold Domino's to Bain Capital for $1 billion and vowed to devote his energy to ultraconservative Catholic causes. And when Monaghan was looking to unload the then money-losing Tigers, who should express interest? None other than his old competitor Ilitch, who in the end paid him $85 million in cash for the team.

As many entrepreneurial success stories—blue collar or otherwise—show, vision takes you only so far. You also have to be obsessively focused, a demon for details. Thomas Kinnear, executive director of the Samuel Zell & Robert H. Lurie Institute for Entrepreneurial Studies at the University of Michigan, calls this process "telescoping," or the ability to zero in on the minutiae. Successful entrepreneurs, he says, pay attention to the smallest details because "they want to be sure they're getting it right." Of course, plenty of detail demons don't land on the Forbes 400 list because of that quality alone, but it's also clear that among those who have made it, telescoping is an important factor.

For many blue-collar business models, customer service is the focus, so getting it right with customers is the big challenge. Huizenga likes to say that one unhappy customer would tell ten people, and then you'd have eleven unhappy customers. "If you're going to build a service business, that truck is riding up and down the street and it's got your name on it and that toilet sitting in a yard somewhere's got your name on it," he has said. "If it looks like hell and it's beat-up and it's dirty, that's what people think of your company."

Ray Kroc was notoriously obsessed with details, like the cleanliness of his McDonald's restaurants. The story goes that he used a toothpick to clean the holes in his mop wringer. "It's not a superintellectual thing," says David Gold, whose bottom line for success is as simple as his one-price strategy: "You just treat people like you want to be treated. That means keeping aisles clean, shopping carts available, and making sure that the cashier says 'thank you' clearly, so that the customer can hear it." Gold's 99 Cents Only stores are, in fact, so meticulously laid out and visually stunning that they are practically cultural icons. The Rolling Stones shot a video in one; a photo taken by German photographer Andreas Gursky of the candy aisles in the 99 Cents Only in Hollywood was on display at New York City's Museum of Modern Art in the spring of 2001.

In an industry known for grit, grease, and grime, Roger Penske, the former stock-car driver turned businessman, is a stickler for tidiness. Penske's $16 billion enterprise includes truck-leasing firms, diesel engine manufacturing, auto dealerships, race-car teams that compete in the Indianapolis Motor Speedway, National Association for Stock Car Racing (Nascar), American LeMans, and more. Penske race-car workers wear crisp uniforms and spotless black shoes; they clean and buff the undersides of race cars every day. If Penske spots a dirty rental truck, he is known to pull it off the road. "The real success is in the details," he says.

Business professor Horniman notes that attention to detail is almost a prerequisite for success: "These folks get up in the morning and almost don't go to bed at night because they are driven to excel." Wayne Huizenga often says, "We are never smarter than the competition, so if we want to grow two times as fast, we have to work two times as hard. No one ever drowned in their own sweat." Another Wayneism: "Never fly in daylight," thereby saving precious work hours.

For some ingenious blue-collar entrepreneurs, it was a two-pronged strategy—manufacturing a need and then brilliantly manipulating consumer demand—that earned them their billions. Underlying the success of that strategy, naturally, is an ability to recognize and exploit America's insatiable desire to consume. Witness the case of H. Ty Warner, a Kalamazoo College dropout who single-handedly created a frenetic, nearly decade-long demand for tiny five-dollar stuffed animals. Warner serendipitously hit on the idea after leaving his eighteen-year job as a stuffed-toy salesman to travel around Italy. When Warner returned he designed his own line of malleable little plush animals, inspired by stuffed cats he had seen in Italian stores.

Warner formed Ty Inc. in 1986 and started shipping the toys out of his home. Later he expanded the collection, called it Beanie Babies (each animal got a cutesy name like Cubbie and Punchers), and priced them low enough to appeal to children's wallets. By limiting distribution, Warner cleverly created a collector's market. At the height of the Beanie Baby craze in the late 1990s, some sold on the secondary market for as much as $12,000, many times their original price. "Our name brand will not go away," Warner told *Forbes*. "We want to be the Coke of collectibles."

But by 2000 the Beanie bubble had finally burst, sales fell sharply, and Warner diversified. He bought prime real estate: Chicago office parks, a golf course and country club near Santa Barbara, California, and two Four Seasons hotels. The hotel

1991

from the pages of *Forbes*

Barbara "Basia" Piasecka Johnson, former chambermaid of John Seward Johnson who married him barely a week after he divorced his wife of thirty years (thereby igniting a bitter family feud), bought an eighteenth-century Italian badminton cabinet for a record $15 million. (1991 net worth: $940 million)

Hugh Franklin Culverhouse, investor and owner of the Tampa Bay Buccaneers, went hunting in Tanzania four days after being released from the hospital following surgery for lung tumors, and bagged a kudu from over 250 yards. (1991 net worth: $325 million)

Orvon Gene Autry, known as "the Singing Cowboy," is the only person to have five stars on the Hollywood Walk of Fame—for movies, TV, radio, recordings, and personal appearances. (1991 net worth: $300 million)

J. B. Hunt, who made his fortune off poultry litter and long-distance trucking, favors ten-gallon Stetson hats—and hates ties. (1991 net worth: $295 million) in New York City boasts one of the world's most expensive suites ($30,000 a night), a huge penthouse with onyx walls and sweeping views of Manhattan. By 2006 the dapper, private Warner (his company number is unlisted) was worth $4.5 billion, making him, at age sixty-two and single in 2006, one of the world's most eligible bachelors.

For Clay Mathile (2006 net worth: $2 billion), the challenge was to convince owners of real pets, not stuffed ones, that ordinary chow wasn't good enough for Fido and Fifi. Mathile left a job as a purchasing agent at Campbell Soup to run Iams, a tiny pet-food maker that had been started by self-taught animal nutritionist Paul Iams. At the time, supermarket pet food was cheap but by some assessments low in nutrition. Tapping into pet owners' huge infatuation with their pets, Mathile saw a potentially huge market for premium pet food at a premium price. Mathile bought out Iams in 1982 on the cheap. With no advertising budget, he relied on his wife and children to assemble packets of Iams dog-food samples. On weekends he took the samples directly to potential buyers—kennels, breeders, vets—bypassing traditional outlets like supermarkets. The strategy worked; practically single-handedly, Mathile created the premium pet-food market, in the process turning Iams into one of the world's largest players.

Mathile sold the closely held company to Procter & Gamble in 1999 for $2.3 billion. These days, he spends his time building up Aileron, a center for entrepreneurial education he founded in Dayton, Ohio, that teaches businesses and nonprofits how to think strategically. "We're hoping another Iams comes out of the ground here," he says.

Radical marketers such as Mathile and Warner are pretty much the norm in self-starter, low-tech businesses, where scarce resources make for creative ways to promote products. But it also helps to have a so-called sales personality—the ability to get the message across, persuade, influence, and sell, sell, sell.

For a used-car salesman, Jim Moran had all the raw materials for success: an honest face, velvet voice, and folksy manner. But it was his persuasive personality and creativity that turned him into a billionaire and a semicelebrity. Moran got an early start in business. As a boy he sold sodas at baseball games in Chicago, ran a paper route, and pumped gas to help his widowed mother pay the bills. After high school he put down $360 in savings to buy a Sinclair gas station. But after selling a used car off the apron at the front of the station, he knew he had found his calling. Moran opened a series of auto dealerships that he called Courtesy Motors.

Anything's Possible

It takes a lot of pluck and some scrappy maneuvering to succeed in offbeat and sometimes odd ventures. But as the following examples from *Forbes* show, anything's possible when business ingenuity meets a laissez-faire marketplace.

Junk Man: Bradley Wayne Hughes has amassed some $4.1 billion by storing other people's junk. Hughes began his storage business in the early 1970s, but got off to an inauspicious start. He called it "Private Storage" and wondered why people weren't swarming in. It seems they thought it wasn't open to the public. He changed signs to read PUBLIC STORAGE. The California-based company is now a worldwide operation with more than 2,100 facilities. Hughes gobbled up Seattle-based rival Shurgard in a hostile takeover in 2006, shelling out $5.5 billion and gaining access to its large European holdings.

Dolls with a Difference: During a visit to colonial Williamsburg, Virginia, former schoolteacher Pleasant Rowland was inspired to create historical dolls with their own fictional biographies. She founded the American Girl doll company in 1986, she said, to make history compelling for girls and to emphasize traditional values. The dolls, with names like Samantha, Molly, and Felicity, come with price tags that hover around $100. Twelve years later, Rowland sold the company to Mattel—maker of the impossibly shaped, scantily clad Barbie doll—for $700 million. Rowland's net worth in 1999, the last year she appeared on the Forbes list: nearly $540 million.

A Ping That Went Ka-ching: The son of a Norwegian shoemaker, Karsten Solheim got his start in the golf club business in the mid-1950s by designing and forging putters in his Seattle garage. Solheim used the engineering skills he had acquired during the World War II years, which had also landed him a job at General Electric, to make clubs more efficient. His Ping putter (named for the sound it makes when hitting a ball) became an instant hit. Arizona-based Karsten Manufacturing now makes clubs, golf apparel and accessories, and even parts for the helicopter industry. Solheim's net worth was $400 million in 1994, the last time he was on the Forbes 400. He died in 2000; son John now heads the family-owned business.

A Better Parking Lot: Electrical engineer Monroe Carell decided he knew how to run a better parking lot. The Vanderbilt University grad quit his job at a Tennessee utility in the 1960s to join his father's primitive parking-lot venture. By applying tough business practices, Carell turned Central Parking Corporation into a huge outfit with more than 3,400 garages worldwide. His latest appearance on the Forbes 400 in 1999 put his net worth at $640 million. Part of Carell's winning strategy: Recruit scrappy college grads adept at hustling parking contracts (including those from competitors), and reward strong performers with outsize bonuses.

Matrix Moguls: More than one fortune rests on the back of women's vanity. Take the case of Sydell Miller, who, with her hairdresser husband, Arnold, started an eyelash product company in the basement of their Cleveland hair salon. Later, they created Matrix Essentials, a line of beauty products marketed to professional salons. In 1994 they sold Matrix to Bristol-Myers Squibb for stock. Arnold died two years before the sale, but Sydell was worth some $550 million in 2002, the last year she appeared on the Forbes 400 list.

Not Just Hot Air: Women's eternal quest for beauty also secured Leandro "Lee" Rizzuto a place among the Forbes 400 for four years running. He and his parents founded Conair Corporation in the 1950s with only $100, but powered by his hot-air hair roller. Rizzuto then perfected the pistol-shaped, handheld hair dryer, and sales exploded. He took his company public in 1972, then private again in 1985, before he acquired appliance maker Cuisinart. But Wyoming's richest resident ($925 million in 2005) had a run-in with the feds a few years back, and served twenty-seven months in prison for allegedly diverting income into foreign bank accounts. Meanwhile, Rizzuto put the time to good use. He reportedly developed an electronic way to verify that shipping containers coming into the country have not been tampered with. His next big fortune, perhaps?

But how to get the word out? It was postwar America, and the new medium of television was taking over the land. Television sets were flying off the shelves. "I had a television set," he later recalled. "All I had to do was look at it and say, 'My God, what a great way to advertise cars! And nobody is doing it.'" Moran took to the tube as "Jim Moran the Courtesy Man," delivering pitches not in the guise of a slick, rehearsed salesman, but as an ordinary guy, prone to making a grammatical error or two. He signed off with hand kisses and a "God bless you." His ads were unrelenting; he even taped a few commercials from his hospital bed as he recovered from an appendectomy. Women swooned and dispatched husbands to the nearest Courtesy Motors. In a Chicago poll, Moran proved more popular than national variety-show host and TV icon Ed Sullivan. *Time* magazine, calling him the "man with the magic voice," put Moran on the cover for a 1961 story on the auto industry.

Moran's business was riding high; he was the nation's largest auto dealer and the world's biggest Ford dealer. Then, in 1965, he was diagnosed with melanoma, a deadly skin cancer, and was told he had less than a year to live. He sold the business, retired to Florida, and soon beat the cancer. Once again, he hurled himself into the auto business, acquiring the regional Toyota distributorship. His powers of persuasion extended to the Japanese. As Moran recounted in his 1996 book, *Jim Moran, the Courtesy Man: Inside the Heart of One of the Most Successful Marketers in the Automobile Industry,* the Lexus luxury car was born from a 1984 conversation he had with Eiji Toyoda, then president of Toyota, in which he convinced Toyoda that demand was high for an upscale model. (Moran's powers of persuasion were not as successful with the U.S. Justice Department, however. That same year he pleaded guilty to filing false tax returns, and as part of the settlement he set up a youth auto-repair training center in Broward County, which is still operating today.)

Just as Moran had seen the potential in television advertising many years before, he also foresaw the need to automate the auto business. He was among the first to computerize retail sales reporting and inventory control. The master salesman, as *Forbes* once called him, was, at the time of his death in 2007, honorary chairman of JM Family Enterprises, with $9.4 billion in annual sales. Daughter Pat is on the board. Moran's net worth in 2006: $2.4 billion. "If I hadn't been lucky enough to believe in the importance of two marvels of the twentieth century," Moran once said, "I might still be eking out a living on a Chicago used-car lot. The first was television and the second the computer."

If Moran positioned himself as a man of the people, Vince McMahon's manic antics to promote his pro wrestling company, World Wrestling Entertainment (WWE), brought a whole new in-your-face quality to blue-collar selling. After buying his father's wrestling business in 1982, McMahon took it national and, with a personal net worth of some $1.1 billion, hurled himself onto the Forbes 400 in 2000. Questionable taste was not an impediment to

McMahon's success in promoting a sport that pits huge, spandex-clad men in a ring against each other. That the spectacle is preplanned, and everyone knows it, doesn't faze fans. McMahon, a tough, irascible, sometime wrestler, adds excitement by creating such outlandish fighting personalities as pasty-faced "the Undertaker" and, for a time, "Mr. McMahon," his own strutting, foul-mouthed, on-camera persona.

McMahon turned his company into a Wall Street darling when he took it public in 1999, but he lost his footing on a later venture with NBC, the much-touted XFL pro football league. XFL was a study in macho marketing, featuring teams with names like the Chicago Enforcers and the New Jersey Hitmen, but it never found its audience and met a quick demise. NBC and McMahon lost more than $30 million on the venture. WWE recovered, though, and with McMahon as chairman, wife Linda as CEO, and their two children in top jobs, the company is an entertainment powerhouse that includes TV shows, pay-per-view events, licensing, and home videos.

So have all the lowbrow niches been filled? Not by a long shot, claims octogenarian S. Truett Cathy. "Unexpected opportunities are everywhere," he says—new kinds of foods, for example, or different ways of preparing them. "Everything changes, opening up new opportunities. You just have to be creative and do things better," he says. Megamillionaire trucking titan J. B. Hunt agrees: "The best ideas in the world are still on the shelf," he said shortly before he died in 2006. One wide-open field, many say, is the so-called experience economy, in which value is added to a product or service through customization (think Starbucks, with its myriad coffee choices and clubby atmosphere), a notion popularized by B. J. Pine II and James Gilmore, authors of *The Experience Economy: Work Is Theater and Every Business a Stage*. In this vein, ventures focused on entertainment and relaxation, such as resorts and spas, are said to offer entrepreneurial potential. "There are a lot of little niches to fill in the experience economy," says business professor Horniman. "They may occur below the general radar, but the possibilities are there."

In the end, what begins as a little niche venture can turn into the next Little Caesars Pizza or 99 Cents Only. And although the odds are formidable, one thing's for sure: While public taste may prove fickle, and new goods and services continually spring up to challenge old ones, low-tech billionaires will always be around. After all, you can't eat computer chips or hedge funds, and even media moguls need their trash hauled away.

6

West Coast Money

On a September morning in 1980, a twenty-four-year-old entrepreneur named Bill Gates showed up for the first of a series of business meetings at IBM's offices in Boca Raton, Florida. With Gates was his business partner, Steven Ballmer, who was there to help negotiate a deal to develop an operating system for IBM's first personal computer. Who could have known that Gates, a Harvard dropout dressed in an ill-fitting suit, was about to clinch the deal of the century? Certainly no one that morning, not even Gates, realized the full implications of what was at stake: that his deal with IBM would not only reshape the computer industry and have an impact on billions of consumers around the world, but would help bring about a seismic shift in the accumulation of wealth in America.

The high-tech landscape was changing fast in 1980. Apple Computer, a three-year-old start-up founded by a couple of hippies from northern California, Steve Jobs and Stephen Wozniak, was in the process of racking up $139 million in sales. Later that year, Apple would go public with the most successful stock offering since that of the Ford Motor Company in 1956. An impatient IBM wanted to break into the burgeoning personal-computer market, and it was going into overdrive to take advantage of a new sixteen-bit microprocessor chip developed by Intel, a company founded by Gordon E. Moore (2006 net worth: $3.4 billion) and the now-deceased Robert Noyce (also a member of the Forbes 400 list before his death in 1990). The new 8088 chip made it possible to support 256 times more memory than the previous eight-bit chip. Prior to Apple's astounding success and before the arrival of the 8088 chip, personal computers were viewed as gadgets for hobbyists.

Now, for the first time, the potential existed for the personal computer to have a role in the business world.

Gates and his friend Paul Allen had already established a reputation for themselves as whiz kids in high-tech circles when they developed software to run the first personal computer, the Altair 8800, in 1975. Several years later the two were making a comfortable living with Microsoft, their tiny, Seattle-based software company. Now, suddenly, the industry's Goliath wanted to do business—but only according to IBM's script, and with Gates only playing a minor role in the corporation's plans.

Gates arrived with Ballmer in Miami, Florida, on the red-eye from the West Coast; according to some accounts, they hadn't slept in thirty-six hours. Upon landing, the two realized that Boca Raton was farther away from Miami than they had figured and that they were on the verge of being late. Then Gates discovered he had forgotten to bring a tie, and they lost more time driving around trying to find a store where they could buy one.

When Gates and Ballmer finally showed up in Boca Raton, they were met by about twenty middle-aged men dressed in regulation IBM blue suits who proceeded to grill them. Gates looked young for his age, and his habit of rocking back and forth when he spoke didn't inspire confidence, either, as John Seabrook described in a 1994 piece in *The New Yorker*. The blue suits had years of experience negotiating multimillion-dollar deals and introducing new technology. IBM, which had been founded in 1911 (and originally called Computing-Tabulating-Recording Company), had 340,000 employees and a near monopoly on mainframe computers; they controlled about 80 percent of the market. Based in a suburb of New York City, the company was organized like a typical East Coast corporation: It was hierarchical, it emphasized conformity, and it offered the prospect of lifetime employment. IBM also discouraged risk taking, but in 1980 they did not consider Bill Gates to be a risk.

IBM was betting on something tangible—the machine. But Gates was betting on something else, something seemingly ephemeral: the code—that is, the series of zeros and ones that run the computer. "IBM wanted to bring its personal computer to market in less than a year," Gates later wrote in his memoir *The Road Ahead*, adding, "In order to meet this schedule it had to abandon its traditional course of doing all the hardware and the software itself. So IBM had elected to build its PC mainly from off-the-shelf components available to anyone. This made a platform that was fundamentally open, which made it easy to copy."

Building a device that could be cloned proved to be IBM's first major

Go west, rich man

California (thanks to Silicon Valley) and Washington State (thanks to Microsoft) have seen big increases in 400 members over the last quarter century. New York and Texas have been the biggest losers. In 1982 11 states couldn't claim a 400 member, while 8 couldn't in 2006.

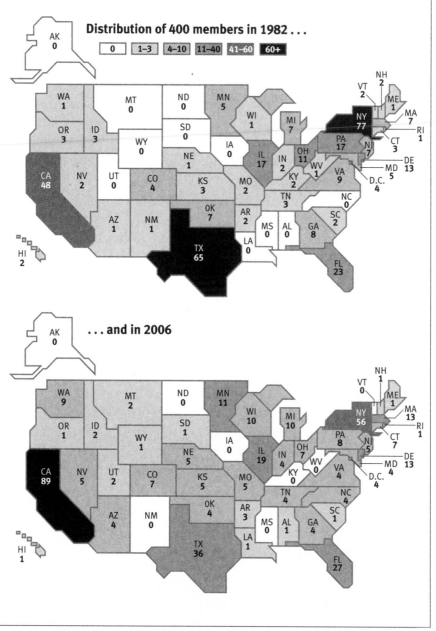

mistake. But the second mistake, allowing Gates to own the rights to the source code for the software that ran the machine, was colossal. Little did IBM suspect that it was Gates's software and not IBM's hardware that would come to dominate the personal computer market in the next few decades. The software operating system not only ran the computer's components but also served as the platform on which software application programs ran. "One of the most important lessons the computer industry learned is that a great deal of a computer's value to its user depends upon the quality and variety of the application software available for it," Gates has written. "All of us in the industry learned that lesson—some happily, some unhappily."

Gates insisted on a license arrangement, which allowed him to make money on each copy of the software that was sold. IBM agreed, but he was given an extremely tight deadline for delivery. So instead of starting from scratch, Gates's partner, Paul Allen, called a small software company named Seattle Computer Products (SCP), which had developed a system known as the Quick and Dirty Operating System (Q-DOS). Gates bought the rights to their software for $75,000 and set about modifying it to fit the specifications of IBM's new computer. Gates gave the result a new, sanitized name: MS-DOS, which stood for Microsoft Disk Operating System.

The rest of the story is now, of course, computer legend. Since IBM's components were made from off-the-shelf components, inexpensive clones manufactured by rivals soon began to gobble up much of IBM's market share. Because Microsoft owned the rights to its operating system, however, it could dominate the software market and also dictate to computer manufacturers. The license agreement that Gates negotiated with IBM reaped Microsoft hundreds of millions of dollars and provided the company with the resources to build its empire. Twenty-seven years after that fateful series of meetings, Microsoft has a market value of $294 billion and IBM, which for decades had ruled the high-tech roost, is now slightly less than half the size of Microsoft, with a market value of $140 billion.

Certainly no one better exemplifies the tectonic shifts in power and fortune from the East Coast to the West Coast over the past twenty-five years than does Bill Gates. He has placed consistently at the top of the Forbes 400 list since 1994. More than a century after New York newspaper publisher Horace Greeley advised young fortune hunters in a now-famous editorial to "Go West, Young Man," his maxim has taken on a fresh resonance with the transformation of the West Coast into a new kind of frontier. Now, instead of prospecting for gold or wildcatting for oil, the would-be billionaires moving out West are making their lucre in industries based on ideas. The West Coast not only has Bill Gates and several other Forbes 400 fortunes generated by Microsoft, including Steve Ballmer (2006 net worth: $13.6 billion), Paul Allen (2006 net worth: $16 billion), and Charles Simonyi (2006 net worth: $1 billion); it also has dozens more billionaires than does the East Coast.

How times have changed. In 1982, when Forbes published its first 400 list, New York State was home to seventy-seven members of the list, and California had only forty-eight. But the West Coast has been gaining ground since 1991, when it overtook the East Coast by gaining eleven new members in just one year. Today California boasts eighty-nine members, who together own 19.8 percent of the total wealth on the Forbes 400 list, compared with fifty-six members who live in New York and who together own 12.9 percent of the total wealth on the Forbes 400 list. And although entertainment still accounts for some of the California wealth, many more fortunes come from computers and high-tech businesses.

The epicenter of burgeoning wealth on the West Coast is not Microsoft's home base of Redmond, Washington (just outside Seattle), but Silicon Valley, which lies along the San Francisco peninsula, sand-

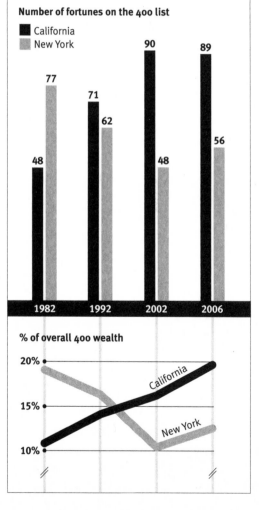

New York's down, California's up

In 1982 New York was at the top of the heap, with more 400 members than any other state. California placed third, behind second-place Texas. But starting in 1991 California took the lead, and it widened until recently, when New York, flush with hedge fund and private equity riches, mounted a small comeback. One consolation for those ever-competitive New York 400 members: The average New York 400 fortune was $2.88 billion in 2006, $91 million more than the average California 400 fortune.

Number of fortunes on the 400 list

■ California
▨ New York

	1982	1992	2002	2006
California	48	71	90	89
New York	77	62	48	56

% of overall 400 wealth

20%
15%
10%

California

New York

wiched between San Francisco Bay and the foothills of the Santa Cruz mountains. In 1999, when David Kaplan published *The Silicon Boys and Their Valley of Dreams*, an account of the astounding accumulation of wealth achieved in the Valley, he calculated that the companies there had a market value of almost $1 trillion, more than either Hollywood or Detroit; and that if the Valley seceded from the United States, it would have the twelfth-largest economy in the world. Venture capitalist John Doerr (2006 net worth: $1 billion) describes the Valley as the site responsible for the "greatest legal accumulation of wealth in the history of the planet."

Aside from its stunning scenery, the Valley does not advertise its riches. With the country's top venture-capital firms and its thriving high-tech companies, Sand Hill Road, the Valley's main strip, is a sort of New Economy version of Wall Street. The four-lane highway runs through a hilly landscape from the town of Menlo Park past the mission-style buildings of Stanford University's campus to the edge of Palo Alto. There are no iconic financial towers dominating the surrounding landscape; nor are there legions of briefcase-toting workers rushing by. Instead, there are views of the mountains and the Horse Park at Woodside, an enormous facility devoted to a variety of equestrian events. Many of the companies are based in anonymous office parks, where the low-rise buildings have oversize picture windows to take in the dramatic vistas.

Instead of paying their dues with years of hard labor at established companies, many members of the West Coast Forbes 400 fraternity were the original pioneers in key New Economy industries and financial services in the Valley, such as high-tech, biotech, discount brokerage, and venture capital. New Economy billionaires often make their fortunes very quickly and at a relatively young age. One of the youngest people ever to make the list was Steve Jobs (number 49 on the 2006 Forbes 400 list), who at age twenty-seven boasted a $100 million fortune, thanks to his success with Apple Computer. Bill Gates was also one of the youngest; in 1986 he joined the list at age thirty, with $315 million. And then came the Google guys: In 1998 Google's founders, Larry Page (number 13 on the 2006 Forbes 400 list) and Sergey Brin (number 12 on the 2006 list), both then just in their mid-twenties, formally incorporated Google and hired their first employee while working on a graduate student project at Stanford University. This became the prototype for the phenomenally successful search engine. In 2004, a year after Google went public, Brin and Page joined the list, each with a fortune of $4 billion that has since ballooned to $14.1 billion and $14 billion, respectively.

At Home in Woodside

Once they make their fortunes, many of the most successful Silicon Valley entrepreneurs head to the historic Silicon Valley town of Woodside. A community of about five thousand people, Woodside is a place of bucolic, two-lane country roads lined with old-fashioned, horseshoe-shaped mailboxes. Looking around, it is difficult to imagine that this town is, in fact, one of the wealthiest in the nation. Although the primary residences of Larry Ellison and Steve Jobs are in nearby Silicon Valley communities, both of which are not more than a twenty-minute drive away, they also maintain estates in Woodside, a town where a billionaire can buy some privacy. Many houses are partly hidden from view, screened by long driveways, stands of redwoods, and dense foliage. The modest town center, which can be accessed by a bridle path, consists of nothing more than a couple of cafés and a grocery store with a billboard of feathered flyers advertising events such as an upcoming arts-and-crafts fair and pony club outings.

Not for Woodside the Manhattan power breakfast: Tech tycoons and venture capitalists such as John Doerr frequent Buck's of Woodside, a funky diner on Woodside Road with kitschy art plastered over the walls and hanging from the ceiling. Even though the latest model sports cars and SUVs are parked outside the restaurant, most of the breakfast entrées are under $10. But although Woodside prides itself on its woodsy rural character, there is no doubt that this is a place where money matters. One class exercise at the local junior high school, designed to help seventh graders sharpen their math skills, is called "How to Be a Millionaire."

West Coast billionaires not only start young; they also tend to be more entrepreneurial and unconventional. The seeds for many of these fortunes are found in eureka moments of scientific discovery—when a new piece of software or hardware is developed, or when someone figures out a process that makes it possible to etch more circuits on a silicon chip or develop mathematical algorithms for a more efficient Web search engine. In fact, many West Coast billionaires did not even begin their careers with the objective of becoming wealthy. Some, such as Jobs and Gates, built their multibillionaire companies on the basis of knowledge they first started acquiring as teenage hobbyists.

West Coast members of the Forbes 400 list have also benefited from distinctive high-tech cultures that developed in the San Francisco Bay Area. In the Pacific Northwest the Microsoft monoculture dates back to the mid-1970s, when Bill Gates and Paul Allen made the arbitrary decision to move back to their home state of Washington after a brief spell in Albuquerque, New Mexico, where they had been working for their first customer, Micro Instrumentation and Telemetry Systems. Microsoft's successful deal with IBM made it possible for Gates to import talented engineers from around the world, such as his top software architect Charles Simonyi, who relocated from Silicon Valley to Microsoft's relatively isolated corporate campus in Redmond. Microsoft's headquarters was a place where employees were not liable to be lured away by job offers from rival software company executives at the local coffee shop, as they could be in Silicon Valley. "Even back in the late seventies," says Charles Simonyi, "Bill anticipated what would happen. In Seattle, there would be stability in the workforce."

In contrast to the one-industry town of Redmond, the story of the Bay Area and Silicon Valley is much more dynamic and colorful. Every few years at least four or five new members from the Bay Area make the Forbes 400 list, while another four or five fall off. Here, strategic steps taken by Stanford University and the nearby University of California–Berkeley set the stage for an explosion of knowledge-based industries that began in the late 1950s and continues to this day. The Valley's relatively contained geography provided more opportunities for people who worked there to form professional and social networks, according to AnnaLee Saxenian, author of *Regional Advantage: Culture and Competition in Silicon Valley and Route 128*. Back on the East Coast, loyalty to the individual firm was more the norm, whereas on the West Coast spin-off companies and job-hopping were standard practice. "From the outset Silicon Valley's pioneers saw themselves as outsiders to the industrial traditions of the East," writes Saxenian. "There was a shared understanding that anyone could become a successful entrepreneur: there were no boundaries of age, status, or social stratum that precluded the possibility of a new beginning; and there was little embarrassment or shame associated with business failure."

If any one person is responsible for the move west, it is Frederick Terman, a Stanford University engineering professor and later its provost. Terman sought to stem the exodus of Stanford engineering graduates, who generally moved East to find jobs. In 1951 Stanford opened an industrial park near the campus for nonpolluting industries, one of the first such parks in the coun-

How the West Coast became the gold coast

Thanks largely to self-made technology fortunes (and perhaps a shot of caffeine from Starbucks), Washington State and California have over the last 25 years become a breeding ground for billionaires.

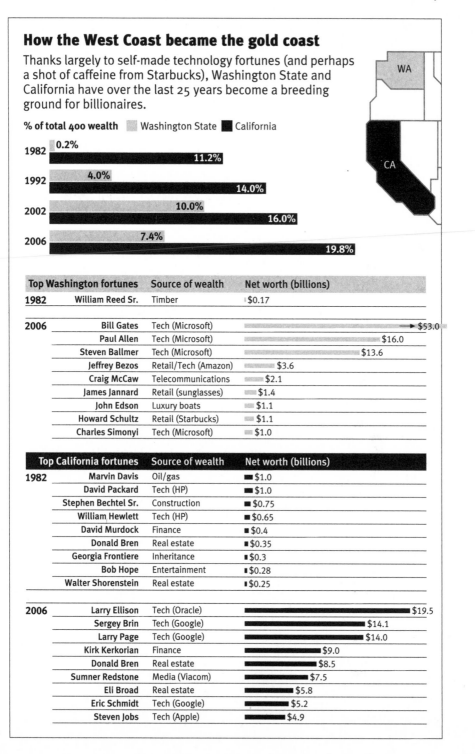

% of total 400 wealth ▓ Washington State ■ California

Year	Washington State	California
1982	0.2%	11.2%
1992	4.0%	14.0%
2002	10.0%	16.0%
2006	7.4%	19.8%

Top Washington fortunes		Source of wealth	Net worth (billions)
1982	William Reed Sr.	Timber	$0.17
2006	Bill Gates	Tech (Microsoft)	$53.0
	Paul Allen	Tech (Microsoft)	$16.0
	Steven Ballmer	Tech (Microsoft)	$13.6
	Jeffrey Bezos	Retail/Tech (Amazon)	$3.6
	Craig McCaw	Telecommunications	$2.1
	James Jannard	Retail (sunglasses)	$1.4
	John Edson	Luxury boats	$1.1
	Howard Schultz	Retail (Starbucks)	$1.1
	Charles Simonyi	Tech (Microsoft)	$1.0

Top California fortunes		Source of wealth	Net worth (billions)
1982	Marvin Davis	Oil/gas	$1.0
	David Packard	Tech (HP)	$1.0
	Stephen Bechtel Sr.	Construction	$0.75
	William Hewlett	Tech (HP)	$0.65
	David Murdock	Finance	$0.4
	Donald Bren	Real estate	$0.35
	Georgia Frontiere	Inheritance	$0.3
	Bob Hope	Entertainment	$0.28
	Walter Shorenstein	Real estate	$0.25
2006	Larry Ellison	Tech (Oracle)	$19.5
	Sergey Brin	Tech (Google)	$14.1
	Larry Page	Tech (Google)	$14.0
	Kirk Kerkorian	Finance	$9.0
	Donald Bren	Real estate	$8.5
	Sumner Redstone	Media (Viacom)	$7.5
	Eli Broad	Real estate	$5.8
	Eric Schmidt	Tech (Google)	$5.2
	Steven Jobs	Tech (Apple)	$4.9

try. Leading technology companies became the first tenants, such as Hewlett-Packard, Eastman Kodak, and Varian Associates, which developed new medical technology, including magnetic resonance imaging. Furthermore, in contrast to MIT (which is located near the Route 128 of Saxenian's book title), Stanford regularly invested in venture capital firms; they, in turn, invested in high-tech start-ups.

Two of Terman's earliest protégés were William Hewlett and David Packard, both of whom were on the Forbes 400 list from its inception in 1982 until their deaths (Packard died in 1996, Hewlett in 2001). They had become friends while undergraduates at Stanford; in typical fashion, both had initially moved to the East after graduation, Hewlett to MIT and Packard to General Electric in New York. Terman lured them back to Stanford for graduate school. Later he encouraged the duo to develop Hewlett's graduate student project on audio oscillators, which measured the intensity of recorded sound, and to form a business to develop and market the device. In 1937, operating out of a garage in Palo Alto with $538 in start-up money lent to them by Terman, the two men formed the Hewlett-Packard Company to produce the oscillators (and later, such innovations as the laser-jet printer). Luckily, they managed to sell the oscillators to the Walt Disney Company. In 1987 the garage became a California State Historical Landmark, and a plaque was erected that identified it as the BIRTHPLACE OF SILICON VALLEY.

Hewlett and Packard are the iconic models for a new kind of Forbes 400 member. They eschewed hierarchies and the perks of position. They were also among the first entrepreneurs to implement profit sharing, and they pioneered what became known as the "walk around" management style, in which managers stroll the floors engaging their employees at their workstations. Hewlett had a professorial air and a casual manner, without a gaggle of assistants and handlers to insulate him from the outside world. One day he answered a call from the then twelve-year-old Steve Jobs, who was calling about getting parts that he needed for a piece of electronic equipment called a frequency counter. Hewlett not only gave Jobs the parts but hired him the next summer in a division of the company that made frequency counters. Jobs later told the *New York Times* that much of what he learned at Hewlett-Packard he subsequently applied to Apple Computer, which he started nine years later.

Terman's influence extended beyond Hewlett and Packard to another notable entrepreneur: William Shockley, a Nobel Prize laureate and a co-inventor of the transistor, the fundamental building block of the modern electrical circuit. Shockley invented the transistor while working on the East Coast at Bell Laboratories, then left in a huff because he was not allowed to share in the profits of his invention. Terman suggested to Shockley that he try making his fortune in the Valley. Following Terman's advice, Shockley assembled an especially talented team for his new company, the Shockley Semiconductor Laboratory. However, his difficult personality drove off many of his most talented engineers. A breakaway group, whom Shockley later referred to as the "Traitorous Eight," left his company to start the Fairchild Semiconductor Company in 1958.* That company was to have a seminal influence on the entrepreneurial culture of the Valley. Fairchild spawned dozens of spin-off companies and begat a culture in which it was common for people to work several years at a place and then go off and start their own company. In fact, today some Valley companies have a genealogical chart hanging in their offices that shows the history of the Valley's various companies and their founders leading back to Fairchild.

Two of the "Traitorous Eight" who went to Fairchild ultimately became members of the Forbes 400: Gordon Moore and Robert Noyce. In contrast to the socially maladroit Shockley, Noyce charmed all who met him. In a 1983 *Esquire* article, "The Tinkerings of Robert Noyce: How the Sun Rose in Silicon Valley," author Tom Wolfe described him as having a "halo effect" and a "Gary Cooper manner." At Fairchild, Noyce designed one of the first integrated circuits, a development that revolutionized the electronics industry. Noyce's invention made it possible to combine multiple transistors by engraving circuits onto a single silicon chip. Before the advent of the integrated circuit, transistors depended upon wires to make electrical connections. As subsequent generations of transistors became ever smaller, however, the mechanical process of stitching transistors together became more labor-intensive, and it became more challenging to produce reliable circuits. Noyce's solution changed all that.

Noyce, along with Moore, a gentle, self-effacing man who had an uncanny knack for backing promising research projects, left Fairchild in 1968 to found the Intel Corporation, one of the leading computer chip manufacturers in the world today. It was at Intel in late 1971 that Noyce and Moore upended the electronic industry once more, when their engineers invented the first micro-

---

*After Shockley's company fizzled, Terman helped him obtain a professorship at Stanford, where he developed further notoriety for his new theory of "retrogressive evolution," which held that blacks were genetically inferior.

processor, an invention that futurist George Gilder has referred to as the most significant product of the second half of the twentieth century. It was the microprocessor, the so-called computer on a chip, which ushered in the age of the personal computer and transformed numerous other industries. Because of its diminutive size and its ability to carry out logic functions, the microprocessor could be used to automate processes in everything from television sets to automobiles.

In contrast to the nurturing environment of Hewlett-Packard, Intel was a pressure cooker, thanks in part to hard-driving CEO Andrew Grove, the first person whom Moore and Noyce hired for their new company. Grove instituted late lists, performance-ratings charts, and mandatory pep rallies, in which he sermonized on the company's core principles. But like Hewlett-Packard, Intel provided a nonhierarchical business culture. In the fast-changing semiconductor industry, the company did not waste time waiting for information to filter up and down chains of command; decisions had to be made fast. The company culture reflected what is known as Moore's Law: Moore's belief that new technology doubles in power every eighteen months and stays at the same price. In the semiconductor industry, a company needed to constantly innovate—or perish.

Not only did high-tech visionaries such as Moore and Noyce invent technology that changed the world, they also played a role in reshaping the way companies were nurtured and financed. In the 1960s Wall Street bankers were not jumping on planes to visit Silicon Valley start-ups. But through contacts, the founders of Fairchild made their way to New York investment banker Arthur Rock (whose first appearance on the Forbes 400 was in 1983, with a net worth of $160 million) and convinced him to take a look at what they were doing. With his first investment, Rock hit pay dirt. He arranged funding for Fairchild Semiconductor and later provided $2.5 million in seed money for Intel. Rock then made what at the time was a radical decision—to leave his job at the prominent investment bank Hayden, Stone and move to California to begin a career as a venture capitalist. "Back in the 1960s, coming out West was a big thing," Rock says. "You had to be adventurous, 'Go West, Young Man,' and all that. It was a different mind-set, and people were willing to take chances and wanted to do great things."

Venture capital was particularly well suited to the start-ups in Silicon Valley. A different breed from conventional investors, venture capitalists typically provide seed money to start-ups in return for a significant stake in the company; they recoup their investment if and when the company goes public.

Many venture capitalists in Silicon Valley had another distinction: Like the entrepreneurs they backed, they had engineering backgrounds, which gave them the expertise to understand and evaluate the technology that a start-up was developing. Perhaps the leading venture capital firm to emerge was Kleiner Perkins Caufield & Byers. Former Forbes 400 member Vinod Khosla joined KPCB after he "retired" at age thirty from Sun Microsystems, an innovative high-tech company that he had cofounded. Another KPCB partner, John Doerr—a current Forbes 400 member and one of the highest-profile VCs in the Valley—previously worked as an engineer at Monsanto, where he had distinguished himself by inventing computer memory devices. The firm played a leading role in the launches of Silicon Valley giants such as Netscape, Compaq Computers, and Sun Microsystems, along with hundreds of others not as well-known. "Kleiner Perkins got fully involved to the point of often getting rid of the management when they came in," says writer David Kaplan. "In other instances they were present at the creation of a firm. The most famous example is Genentech. The one hundred thousand dollars they invested made billions and essentially created the biotech industry."

While venture capitalists were seeding companies all over the Valley, other West Coast entrepreneurs, perhaps inspired by the spirit of innovation that was in the air, were redefining old-line businesses. Consider Charles Schwab, for example, whose Charles Schwab & Co. is one of the nation's largest financial services firms. Schwab (2006 net worth: $4.6 billion) started his firm on Montgomery Street in San Fran-

1992

from the pages of *Forbes*

Milton Petrie, founder and chairman of the eponymous Petrie Stores, has an office full of teddy bears from employees. (1992 net worth: $1 billion)

Raymond J. Noorda, an electrical engineer who pioneered the concept of PCs networked together in offices, drives a pickup to work in Utah and takes advantage of senior discounts. (1992 net worth: $800 million)

Harry Helmsley's wife, **Leona Helmsley,** who helped run her husband's hotel business, offered to turn their New York City hotel properties into housing for the homeless— if she could avoid a four-year prison sentence for tax evasion. (Harry Helmsley's 1992 net worth: $1 billion)

Craig Robert Benson, who made his fortune from technology (Cabletron), has a conference room with no chairs. "When legs get tired, the meeting ends," he says. (1992 net worth: $415 million)

Where sidewalks are paved with gold

The list below shows the top ten cities (including ties) with the most 400 members from 1982 to 2006. New York still has more 400 members than any other U.S. city, just as it did in 1982. Midland, Texas, had 8 members in 1982; by 1992 it had only 3.

1982	1992	2002	2006
① New York 66	① New York 45	① New York 38	① New York 45
② Houston 21	② San Francisco 15	② Los Angeles 22	② Los Angeles 19
③ Dallas 19	③ Los Angeles 12	③ San Francisco 16	③ Chicago 13
④ Los Angeles 10	④ Houston 8	④ Dallas 13	③ Dallas 13
⑤ Beverly Hills 8	⑤ Chicago 7	⑤ Beverly Hills 9	③ San Francisco 13
⑤ Midland 8	⑤ Ft. Worth 7	⑥ Chicago 8	⑥ Houston 9
⑦ Chicago 7	⑦ Atlanta 6	⑥ Ft. Worth 8	⑦ Beverly Hills 8
⑦ San Francisco 7	⑦ Beverly Hills 6	⑥ Palm Beach 8	⑦ Ft. Worth 8
⑨ Baltimore 5	⑦ Dallas 6	⑨ Houston 7	⑦ Palm Beach 8
⑨ Ft. Worth 5	⑩ Palm Beach 5	⑨ Seattle 7	⑩ Atherton 6
⑨ Oklahoma City 5	⑩ Seattle 5		⑩ Boston 6
⑨ Pittsburgh 5			

cisco in 1973 with only four employees. At first it was not clear where the road to fame and riches lay. The financial system was, in effect, rigged against the small-time stockbroker, especially one who worked in San Francisco, three thousand miles away from the Wall Street epicenter. Because of rules of the Securities and Exchange Commission (SEC), which set fixed commissions on stock trades, big firms and rich investors were able to dominate the stock market.

Schwab got his break in 1975, when the Securities and Exchange Commission abolished fixed commissions, or the amounts charged by brokerage houses for trading a share of stock. He realized that large numbers of small investors wanted to play the market but were prevented from doing so by the large commissions that the big brokerage firms were charging. So he began offering discounts of up to 80 percent on trades of less than $2,000. Selling stocks to the general public was a radical enough idea for the buttoned-up brokerage culture of the day, but Schwab's methods were even more radical. He put his picture in advertisements and listed an 800 number. He hired women for top positions before it was usual to do so in other parts of the country—which, he says, gave him a competitive advantage, especially in customer service. And he was quick to take advantage of the technology coming out of nearby Silicon Valley. He installed an online system within his company in the late 1970s, when other firms were still using accounting machines and typewriters.

According to Schwab, growing up on the West Coast gave him a fundamentally different approach to business and entrepreneurship. "I could never have done it in New York," he says. "Everything was so structured there. My observation of people who are brought up on the East Coast is that they have so much pressure to meet the social structure—the expectations are pretty well-defined. The people I know my age who grew up on the East Coast were bracketed—you have to go to Yale, you have to go to Choate, or you are an outcast. Out here there is much more of a sense of entrepreneurial freedom, whether it comes from your academic pursuits or your professional pursuits. I think that on the West Coast there is a tradition of the Wild West."

Other financial service firms in the Bay Area also benefited from Silicon Valley's technological innovations. "With a few PCs and a small clientele in the mid-1980s, you could look as professional and communicate as well as the big firm with the older, antiquated, main computer-based, closed-architecture, dumb-terminal system," says Ken Fisher (2006 net worth: $1.3 billion), who started a financial services firm in Silicon Valley in 1979. "They [the larger firms] took a long time to adapt because they had a big investment in their software and systems."

With high-tech companies and financial service firms moving into Silicon Valley, real-estate prices also soared, as did the fortunes of local developers and real-estate investors such as John Sobrato (2006 net worth: $2.4 billion), Carl Berg (2006 net worth: $1.2 billion), and former longtime members of the Forbes 400 list John Arrillaga and Richard Peery—both of whom, after a nineteen-year stint, fell off the Forbes list in 2006. In 1957 Sobrato began selling residential real estate in a brokerage firm while still a sophomore at Santa Clara University. Once he had made enough capital to start investing on his own, Sobrato teamed up with his mother; together, they erected a new commercial research and development building each year on speculation. Then, in 1963, Sobrato and Berg went into business together as commercial developers (they have since parted ways) and began building industrial buildings and office buildings. Their tenants included companies such as Cisco and Apple. Property values rose so fast that they never had to depend upon investors to realize their gains. Instead, they were able to finance new projects by borrowing against their equity. Without the high-tech boom, Sobrato might have been just another prosperous businessman. "A lot of it is focus," he says. "I have always worked hard at whatever I did. But I was certainly in the right place at the right time."

By the mid-1970s, California, fueled by Silicon Valley development and the new start-up capital pouring in, had become a magnet for entrepreneurs and iconoclasts of all stripes. Before he started Apple Computer, Steve Jobs had dropped out of college, tried LSD, lived in a commune, and traveled to India on a spiritual quest. But while experimenting with a hippie lifestyle, Jobs was also experimenting with computers. He was a member of the Homebrew Club, a cultlike group of computer zealots who held regular meetings at the Stanford Linear Accelerator Center (SLAC). At one club meeting Jobs met fellow hobbyist Steven Wozniak, who had recently designed a prototype of one of the first personal computers. The twenty-one-year-old Jobs had a premonition that what appealed to the Homebrew zealots would also appeal to households all over America and, together with Wozniak, formed Apple Computer in 1977. It was an extremely modest beginning: Jobs sold his minivan to finance the new company. The first Apple computers retailed for $666.66, and the company sold about 175 of them.

Buoyed by their success, the duo set out to raise more money for mass production. Had he had been living on the East Coast, the notoriously unkempt Jobs probably wouldn't have stood a chance. But this being Silicon Valley, Jobs was able to get in to see top executives at Intel and Hewlett-Packard, as well as venture capitalists. Still, most Silicon Valley executives were not impressed with Jobs or with his gadget. "Why did you send me this renegade from the human race," Don Valentine, a prominent venture capitalist, remarked to a public relations person whom Jobs had persuaded to represent him. But the Valley's tech community was favorably disposed toward the undynamic duo. Jobs was introduced to A. C. Markkula, a thirty-four-year-old engineer who became a member of the 1982 Forbes 400 list (his last appearance on it was in 1992). Markkula, who had recently retired from Intel, bought a third of Apple for just $91,000 and helped Jobs raise additional funds.

The don't-look-back attitude of the West Coast also appealed to Larry Ellison (2006 net worth: $19.5 billion), who was as iconoclastic as Jobs and "the Woz." In 1966, after dropping out of two universities, Ellison showed up in Berkeley, California, in a secondhand Ford Thunderbird. A self-taught computer programmer, he did not have any serious career plans. He was more focused on outdoor sports, such as rock climbing and hiking. He bounced around the Bay Area from one high-tech company to another before founding, with two partners, a software company in 1977. "Basically, programming gave me the freedom to screw around through my twenties," he told his biographer, Matthew Symonds.

The company would eventually become Oracle and make Ellison the richest man in California. "He had to be rich," recalled Stuart Fagin, an engineer who worked at Oracle with Ellison in the early days. "He always lived better than he could afford. He had to have a Mercedes, even if it was so rusty it was held together by paint. He could barely make the payments on his house: Whenever I heard him on the phone, he always seemed to be talking to builders and bankers at the same time. I always felt that I needed three years' salary in the bank. Larry didn't have three days.' "

In Silicon Valley, Ellison didn't need the pedigree of a top-notch university or even funding. "The weird thing about software is that it is really creating something out of nothing," he told *Forbes* in 1992. "A couple of programmers really can start in their garage. In fact you don't even need a garage." Ellison and his partners combed research papers and technical journals in search of a way to wealth, eventually turning up an IBM paper that contained the specifications for SQL (short for Structured Query Language), which would allow the creation of relational databases. SQL held out the promise of creating databases that could be queried, manipulated, and cross-referenced. While IBM sat on a very profitable database market oriented toward mainframe computers, it hadn't taken the trouble to develop SQL. Just as Bill Gates foresaw the potential of personal computers, Ellison and his partners foresaw the tremendous potential of SQL—again at IBM's expense.

And in Silicon Valley, there existed the reservoir of technical know-how to turn an idea into an empire. "In terms of the availability of talent, money, and companies—both rivals and potential partners—it was all there," says Matthew Symonds. Ellison quickly learned to market himself and his company. In the early days Oracle was especially notorious for advertising software before it was even developed. And as Oracle grew, Ellison became the object of much bitterness as he waited until his rivals were weak enough to succumb to a buyout, a strategy he continues to practice. In the past few years Oracle has acquired two of its leading competitors, both located in the Bay Area—Siebel Systems and PeopleSoft.

Siebel Systems, a leading developer of sales automation software, was founded by former Oracle salesperson Thomas Siebel (tied for number 242 on the 2006 Forbes 400 list). The company had attempted to define itself as a kind of anti-Oracle before Oracle finally swallowed it in January 2006. "Too many companies here have an arrogant self-image," Siebel told author Symonds several years before selling out. "Their attitude is 'We are geniuses and visionaries who make insanely great technology.' And there is the cult of the software CEO, where it's all about 'me, me, me' and my transitory fulfillments." There's little doubt that he was referring to Ellison. David Duffield (2006 net worth: $1.2 billion), founder of PeopleSoft, which Oracle gobbled up in a hostile takeover in 2005, also views his company as having had a fundamentally different approach to business than does Oracle. "PeopleSoft prided itself on customer relations that was at the heart of our body, whereas the heart of Oracle is technology and competitiveness," says Duffield.

Duffield began his career on the East Coast as an engineer and salesperson at IBM, where he had to wear suits at business meetings and was discouraged from socializing with customers. While still at IBM, Duffield cofounded Integral, a company that specialized in human-resources software. On weekends and during his vacations, Duffield would travel all over the country to sell his software. Several years after he started Integral, he sold a human-resources software system to University of California–Berkeley and had to spend time there to install it. Duffield fell in love with northern California's moderate weather and its more relaxed lifestyle, and decided to relocate his business to Walnut Creek, near Berkeley. He started a new company, PeopleSoft, which grew to be the second-largest database company in the world before Oracle acquired it. Duffield says that he also found the West Coast liberating. It was "Try something different, it is okay to be different, and take risks," he says.

The Valley has always been a turbulent place that thrives on creative destruction of a kind not found on the East Coast. Multibillion-dollar companies suddenly appear as a result of some seemingly esoteric research project—and then just as quickly are destroyed within a few years by a new development. Only half of the top forty high-tech firms of 1982 were still in business in 2002; more than half of the Valley's present top forty high-tech firms hadn't even been founded in 1982. One entrepreneur who epitomizes the Valley's extreme vicissitudes of fortune is James "Jim" Clark (number 354 on the 2006 Forbes 400 list), a former Stanford University computer science professor who formed two multibillion-dollar companies, Silicon Graphics and Netscape—both of which faded into irrelevance within a decade of their founding.

Clark's first billion-dollar idea was to build a computer that could produce three-dimensional images in real time. Amazingly, when Clark tried in the early 1980s to sell the license for his idea to companies such as Hewlett-Packard, IBM, and computer-manufacturing company DEC, no one saw the potential of producing pictures on computer screens. Undeterred, Clark left Stanford in 1982 with a half dozen graduate students to form Silicon Graphics, which began to produce high-end terminals. The sophisticated terminals were a big hit in Hollywood, where they were used to produce special effects. George Lucas (2006 net worth: $3.6 billion) and Steven Spielberg (2006 net worth: $2.9 billion), both of whom were pioneers in marrying computer technology with film technology, were early customers. Soon Silicon Graphics was earning billions and was one of the most successful companies in the Valley. But as the personal computer grew more powerful, it became apparent that it would soon be feasible for a relatively inexpensive PC to produce the same images that Silicon Graphic's more expensive machines did. Clark also foresaw that a wave of Microsoft software coming down the pike was about to wipe out his company. Silicon Graphics entered into a long period of decline and even filed for Chapter 11 bankruptcy for a brief period in 2006.

With Silicon Graphics sinking into irrelevancy, Clark set out in a new direction. At first he tried to design an all-in-one device, the telecomputer, through which all media and communications could be transmitted. Almost immediately, Microsoft and other high-tech heavyweights also began researching the possibilities of such a device. But after a brief infatuation with the telecomputer, Clark abandoned it and set about teaching himself computer programming. He wanted to create software that could transmit images and messages between computers over the Internet. At the time, most computer and software companies were focused on closed-terminal systems, in which only a specified network of computers could communicate with one another. Clark's vision of the future would probably have been dismissed as just another far-fetched idea had he not already had his Silicon Graphics success. Clark's quest led him to a software program called Mosaic, written by a twenty-two-year-old student at the University of Illinois, Marc Andreessen. In the early 1990s Clark and Andreessen developed the Web-browsing software that became Netscape and begat the Internet craze. Once again, Clark had come up with another blockbuster. "Bill Gates sent a memo to his employees saying that the Internet now posed the greatest threat to Microsoft's control of the computer industry," writes Michael Lewis in *The New New Thing: A Silicon Valley Story,* an entertaining account of the life and times of Jim Clark. "The one thousand Microsoft employees dedicated to building a telecomputer were reassigned to compete with Jim Clark's startup. Thousands of others at Oracle and Sun and even Time Warner were similarly redirected."

Microsoft was ultimately able to outmaneuver Netscape and leave the company, which AOL bought in 1998, a shadow of its former self. But the browser battle became the basis for the U.S. Justice Department's 1998 antitrust suit against the software giant. Meanwhile, Netscape had made Clark a billionaire within two years of its going public. Despite the fact that it was hemorrhaging money, investors expected that the company responsible for the Internet revolution would somehow become profitable. Netscape's phenomenal IPO also ushered in the age of shoot-from-the-lip investing, where the buzz became more important than the business plan. "The speed with which Clark had made himself and a lot of other engineers rich created new forces of fear and greed in the Valley," writes Lewis. "Up until then the typical engineer's decision about where to work turned on old-fashioned considerations like salary and benefits and the inherent technical interest of the work. Suddenly, all of these were overshadowed by stock options."

The dot-com crash of 2000 is the ultimate morality tale of just how changeable high-tech fortunes can be. Throughout the 1990s the Internet bubble grew and grew, and kids just out of college earned fortunes in stock options. When the bubble burst, however, the tech-heavy National Association of Securities Dealers Automated Quotation System (NASDAQ) stock index fell 37 percent over a ten-week period, losing $2.3 trillion in market value. Many West Coast fortunes on the Forbes 400 list simply vanished. California was especially hard hit: In 2000 the state boasted a record 107 members on the list; six years later, it had yet to climb back over 89 members. Many fortunes were made and lost within a year or two. Michael Robertson made it onto the Forbes 400 list in 1999 (net worth: $1 billion) with his start-up, MP3.com, which at the time was the most popular music site on the Internet. In 2000 Robertson was off the list, having lost $1.4 billion after a flurry of copyright infringement lawsuits from the music industry. Scott Blum, the founder of Buy.com, an online retailer that sold below-cost goods, became a billionaire for a few months in 2000, only to lose most of his $1.5 billion fortune by the end of the year. Even the richest techies took a huge hit: Bill Gates lost $11 billion between 2000 and 2001, and Larry Ellison recorded a net loss of $6.7 billion between 2000 and 2001, over 30 percent of his net worth. "A great many fortunes in these areas are inherently very, very vulnerable," says money manager Ken Fisher.

But then, just to remind everyone how quickly a huge Forbes 400 fortune can be made, along came Google. When Larry Page and Sergey Brin, two brainy twentysomethings, were building Google in Brin's dormitory room at Stanford, it seemed inconceivable that they could establish a multibillion-dollar company based on a search engine alone. Huge Internet portals and browsers such as Yahoo, Microsoft's MSN, and Netscape already dominated the search-engine market. The emphasis had been on keeping people on the host site, where they could be bombarded with banner advertisements while they surfed weather forecasts, news stories, and personal listings. Even if Brin and Page could come up with a better search engine, how could they deploy it? And how could they outflank Yahoo, also founded by a couple of former Stanford students, David Filo (2006 net worth: $2.5 billion) and Jerry Yang (2006 net worth: $2.2 billion), and which already had hundreds of millions in cash in its war chest?

As with all technologies, however, there is always room for something faster, better, and more powerful. Before Google, searching the Internet was a crude and unsatisfactory business. Search results were calibrated by the frequency of the appearance of a key word or phrase on a Web page. Often, businesses would finesse the search engine by figuring out the most-used search terms and then inserting them into Web pages so that their site would show up at the top of the result list. The challenge was to make the process more intuitive and provide more accurate results for what people actually were searching for.

Brin and Page developed a new way to rank Web pages by using special algorithms called PageRank that determined a Web page's relevance to a particular search. Their software calibrated that ranking by counting the number of pages linked to a particular Web page and then, in turn, counting the amount of links the linking pages had. Thus, if one were trying to find a professor Tom Smith at Stanford, and there also happened to be a student Tom Smith at Stanford, the professor's name would normally pop up first since there would be more searches for him.

Because they were working on a graduate student project at Stanford's

1993
from the pages of *Forbes*

Aaron Spelling, TV producer extraordinaire (*Dallas; Dynasty; Beverly Hills, 90210*), spent a year in bed at age eight because of a nervous breakdown. (1993 net worth: $300 million)

Doris Duke, sole heir to a tobacco fortune, has a character as outsize as her art collection. She plays jazz piano; two of her favorite causes are historic preservation and animal rights. (1993 net worth: $750 million)

Roy Park, a media executive and entrepreneur, raises peacocks with his wife: "They make terrific watchdogs." (1993 net worth: $550 million)

Melvin Simon, who made his fortune malling America, is known as "Meshuggener Mel" because of his colorful clothing and exuberant manner. (1993 net worth: $300 million)

The boy billionaires club

Making the Forbes 400 list at any age is accomplishment enough, but becoming a self-made multimillionaire before age 30 and then turning it into a billion in fairly short order takes it to a wholly different level. Below are five— all from west of the Mississippi—who made the big bucks early on.

	Date of Birth	Source of Wealth	Year Became a Billionaire	Comment
Bill Gates	October 28, 1955	Microsoft	1987	Gates first made the Forbes list in 1986, when he was 30 years old and worth an estimated $315 million. A year later, he became a billionaire. By the time he was 35, he was worth $4.8 billion. And at the ripe old age of 45, his fortune had ballooned to $54 billion.
Michael Dell	February 23, 1965	Dell Computer	1996	Dell first hit the list when he was 26; by the time he was 30, he was worth $740 million. A year later he was a billionaire. He was worth $16 billion at age 35. Five years later his fortune was pegged at $18 billion.
Steven Jobs	February 24, 1955	Apple, Pixar	1998	Jobs was on the first Forbes 400 list in 1982, when he was 27 years old. But he only crossed the billion-dollar threshold 16 years later, when he was 43. He was worth $1.6 billion at age 45. Four years later, his fortune had increased to $4.9 billion.
Sergey Brin Larry Page	August 1, 1973 December 1, 1972	Google	2004	The Google guys weren't rich enough to make the Forbes list when they were 30, but at 31 and 32, respectively, they were each worth $4 billion. In 2006, Brin, 33, and Page, 34, were each worth $14.1 billion.

Computer Science Department, Brin and Page had an advantage not available to high-tech entrepreneurs working out of, say, a basement in Kansas: They were able to access expensive, state-of-the-art computers with bigger disk space than ordinary PCs provided. At one point, their student search-engine project was using almost half of the university's bandwidth.

Before long, everyone at Stanford was Googling. And it was not much longer before the venture capitalists, many of whom were headquartered just a few miles up the road from Stanford on Sand Hill Road, came knocking with proposals in hand. One of them, Vinod Khosla of Kleiner Perkins Caufield & Byers, showed up with an offer from Excite, a company in which he was invested, to buy Google for $750,000. But Brin and Page held out for $1.6 million, and the deal fell through. In 1998, however, they got $100,000 in start-up capital from another Silicon Valley investor, Andreas von Bechtolsheim, a cofounder of Sun Microsystems, and moved their company from Brin's dorm room into a bedroom that they rented in a friend's house.

A year later, even though they didn't have a business plan showing how they were going to make a profit, Brin and Page picked up $25 million in seed money from other Valley venture capitalists and industry insiders, including former Netscape executives Kavitark Ram Shriram (number 242 on the 2006 Forbes 400 list) and Omid Kordestani (number 189 on the 2006 list). Von Bechtolsheim's initial $100,000 investment in Google in 1998 eventually earned him hundreds of millions of dollars and landed him on the Forbes 400 list in 2004, the only year he made the list. Initially, Brin and Page even affected disinterest in making their search engine commercial; they were loath to clutter up their Web pages with the banner advertising that the browsers and portals depended on for revenue. They also rejected attempts to market or advertise Google, preferring to get their message out "virally"— tech-speak for word of mouth. However, their unconventional approach ultimately proved to be savvy business strategy, garnering them glowing press reviews and a cult following. "It wasn't clear that it was a great business when we started it," Brin told *The New Yorker* journalist Jeffrey Toobin in 2007. "In fact, the companies that were doing search were moving away from it. But we thought it was important, and we thought that where there was a will, there would be a way."

In 2001 Silicon Valley veteran Eric Schmidt (2006 net worth: $5.2 billion) was hired away from Sun Microsystems to provide some adult supervision as CEO and chairman. It was also the year in which Brin and Page finally hit on a way to make money without corrupting their ideal of a pure search. They established AdWords, which consists of paid text advertisements that appear in a separate column alongside the column containing the pure search results. AdWords has proved to be catnip for advertisers because the advertisements, which are programmed to complement the pure search results, target the interests and tastes of the person doing the search.

Today the Silicon Valley–based Google is a behemoth that is gobbling up companies and threatening not only Microsoft but traditional media conglomerates. It is doing an end run around advertising companies by signing agreements directly with newspaper chains, which have watched with dismay as their ad revenues migrate to Google and various other Web sites. Microsoft and Yahoo are scrambling to catch up, investing tremendous sums of money buying gigantic computer servers so they can archive more Web pages and media content and also deliver search results more rapidly. Because software entrepreneurs are now designing programs to run off Google's Web-based software instead of Windows, Google also has the potential to supplant

Microsoft as a platform. "Microsoft's dominance comes from a monopoly of an operating system," says David Kaplan. "But what if they don't have that anymore—that is why you see them talking about coming up with their own search engine and diversifying into other areas where people are making money, whether it is iTunes or search engines."

So is the future of Silicon Valley, and the high-tech dominance of the West Coast, assured? Will new generations of Brins and Pages appear to replace Hewlett, Packard, and the other pioneering high-tech members of the Forbes 400? The prognosis appears mixed. Despite Google's amazing success, the possibility exists that it could be toppled someday by savvy entrepreneurs from a new generation of Stanford graduate students or by new search-engine technology. After all, Google's market value in November 2006 was $156 billion, only slightly higher than the $150 billion market value former media darling Yahoo enjoyed in January 2000. The newer high-tech fortunes appear to be inherently more volatile than those based on the older Valley industries such as chip manufacturing or software companies. "In the age of the Net, most of these things are marketing creations," says Kaplan.

The Valley's culture has also changed significantly over the years. In the 1980s and 1990s, although the corporate headquarters stayed, much of the semiconductor industry moved abroad, where chips could be manufactured more cheaply. Software companies and later Internet start-ups moved in. Some observers say that, in general, the emphasis in the Valley today is less oriented toward developing a business than it is toward developing a technology or a network site to the point where it can be sold. "The spirit before was one of self-funding—you had a good idea, and you invested your own money before you took anyone else's money," says David Duffield. "You bootstrapped your way to success. But the idea of the venture capital approach today is that you find a good idea, give the guy $10 million, and go exploit it." As a result, it's hard to retain enough of a company to become a member of the Forbes 400. "When you look at the West Coast today," says Ken Fisher, "it is really rare to make a billion bucks in a venture-capital-backed deal."

Nor is it clear whether Silicon Valley will continue to be the world's leading incubator of new companies. The technologies and innovative business practices developed there have by now spread throughout the United States and the world. "We kind of had it all in the nineteen seventies," says John Sobrato, adding, "but now it is not just Boston; there are high-tech clusters in

Austin, Texas, and there is a huge effort to emulate Silicon Valley in China." Arthur Rock also sees a threat from the Far East. "The world is tilted to the East—to India and China," he says. "I think that's where the world is going. I think our educational system is so bad that we're not going to be able to produce people who will be able to do the things that are necessary to do. They'll all be done in the Far East."

Still, don't count the Valley out yet. Companies there account for one-third of all venture capital invested in the United States today—more than twice the amount invested in the country's second-highest-ranked region, New England. Moreover, many of the most successful high-tech entrepreneurs in places like India were educated in the Valley and maintain links to companies there. The flexible approach to partnering and outsourcing has actually enabled the Valley to benefit from the growth of high-tech sectors in places like China and India.

And despite the rise of high-tech sectors in other parts of the world, no place overseas has yet been able to re-create the dynamic and innovative culture of the Valley. "If we were just holding steady with technology the way it is, I think that we would lose everything to India and China," says David Duffield. "But I don't think that is the way things are going. There are problems that we cannot even describe today that are going to get solved five years from now. And the Indians and Chinese are not going to solve them—it is going to be the folks around here that have that mentality of creativity."

Ironically, there is always the possibility that the biggest threat to the creation of new fortunes in Silicon Valley will come from within. Google currently appears to be buying all the promising start-ups and all the promising engineers. As Reid Hoffman, the founder of LinkedIn, a business networking Web site popular among Silicon Valley's digerati, told the *New York Times* in 2005: "Google is doing more damage to innovation in the Valley right now than Microsoft ever did. It's largely that they're hiring so many talented people, and the fact they're working on so many different things. It's harder for start-ups to do interesting stuff right now."

7

Entertainment and Media

The year was 1982. Steven Spielberg wanted to preview his new baby at his "lucky" theater in Dallas, where *Jaws* had premiered. Universal's movie studio was ascendant in Hollywood, and Spielberg was its cosseted prodigal son, having just returned from making *Raiders of the Lost Ark* for rival Paramount Pictures. MCA/Universal chairman Lew Wasserman leased a corporate jet and flew to Houston because the lucky Dallas theater was not available; he sat in the theater with other executives as the credits rolled. Several hours later, Wasserman was sobbing in his seat. The audience was standing, cheering joyously. *E.T.: The Extra-Terrestrial* had transported Hollywood's glacial, domineering king and was about to transport a nation.

Not so long ago, Hollywood was the undisputed center of the big entertainment fortunes in this country. Its stars and starlets were larger than life. So were its handful of moguls, including the six entertainers, filmmakers, and Hollywood studio heads who made the first Forbes 400 list in 1982—among them Wasserman, Bob Hope, and director George Lucas. Twenty-five years later, Hollywood is still represented on the Forbes 400, and an even greater number of 400 members have dabbled in financing the odd movie or making a splash on the pumped-up LA social scene. But the excitement has shifted away from Hollywood's content producers—the filmmakers, studio chiefs, and even the stars, like Tom Hanks and Nicole Kidman, who can command as much as $50 million a picture—to entrepreneurs who invent new forms of entertainment and new means of reaching audiences.

Ted Turner, John Malone, Stanley Hubbard, and a dozen others on the Forbes 400 fueled the surge of cable and satellite TV over the past twenty-five years, and prospered as leisure time and disposable income increased. Steve Jobs championed such entertainment-oriented icons of the Internet age as the Mac, the iPod, and the iPhone, accelerating a fundamental shift in the pricing of entertainment and its distribution to handheld devices. More recently, Google founders Larry Page and Sergey Brin created new means of sharing information and selling advertising. At the same time, a few entertainment empire builders like Rupert Murdoch and Sumner Redstone raged through the landscape, swallowing newspapers, magazines, TV and cable stations, record companies, Hollywood studios, theme parks, Web sites: any form of entertainment, in short, that they could get their hands on to feed every new form of distribution.

Today, no other industry is in such upheaval, with its future so unclear. Digital entertainment is challenging old Hollywood and old media ferociously: Practically every day their titanic clashes make headlines. A fickle field, entertainment devours egos and fortunes in the blink of a misjudgment. Witness AOL's Steve Case (sidelined after a boardroom clash), Edgar Bronfman Jr. (mocked for buying record companies high and selling movie studios low), and Disney's Michael Eisner (stripped of his power after a triumphant but tyrannical reign), to name just three. Even so, the smart money is betting that in the end, as the entertainment business becomes transformed by mass audiences making their own hits and distributing them on the Web via services like YouTube and MySpace, there will always be a healthy crop of new billionaires—though fewer and fewer may work in Hollywood itself.

When the Forbes list was first published, power in Hollywood was concentrated in the hands of a small coterie of men. Of the six listed in 1982, entertainer Bob Hope was the richest, with a $280 million fortune seeded by his long entertainment career; but most of his money was actually made investing in California real estate and oil wells. George Lucas, wealthy from *Star Wars* and other hits, was the only bona fide filmmaker then on the list. Columbia Pictures producer Ray Stark, a pillar of Old Hollywood who signed Barbra Streisand to reprise Fanny Brice in *Funny Girl*, had $110 million. Roy E. Disney, Walt's mild-mannered nephew and a major shareholder in the company his uncle founded, had $150 million, as did Doris Stein, the widow of Music Corporation of America (MCA) founder Jules Stein.

Of all of them, Lew Wasserman, with a net worth of $115 million, was the most influential. Wasserman ruled Hollywood for forty years until 1990, when he sold MCA/Universal to a Japanese conglomerate. He'd helped build MCA into the United States' most important talent agency, even as it was dogged by allegations of Mob connections. He also shifted power away from the studios by negotiating higher pay for stars, especially after the government busted the studios' monopoly on entertainment in 1948 by forcing the sale of their chains of movie theaters. Wasserman profited hugely from increasing actors' pay, taking a percentage as their agent. "I run all the studios," the thirty-eight-year-old Wasserman famously boasted in 1951, turning down an offer to run MGM. With his firm grip on many of the stars, he was not exaggerating.

After engineering MCA's purchase of Universal in 1958 and becoming president of the combined studio after the 1962 merger, Wasserman threw open Universal's fabled back lots to television production, and Universal became primarily a TV studio. Selling reruns of old TV series to independent TV stations was the most lucrative part of the television business. The geyser of cash from syndication offset Hollywood's rising production costs and made fortunes for many of its top studios and independent producers, such as Norman Lear, who created *All in the Family* and *Maude,* and his partner: another ex-MCA agent, Jerry Perenchio. The sale of their Embassy Productions to Columbia Pictures landed them on the Forbes 400 in 1985, with $175 million apiece. Aaron Spelling, one of Hollywood's most prolific and most successful TV producers (including *Charlie's Angels, Dynasty,* and *Beverly Hills, 90210*), arrived on the Forbes list in 1989 with $345 million, several years after his production company went public. Spelling was well-known for opulent gestures both on and off the small screen. The sets of *Dynasty* were luxuriously furnished, and so was his own home, one of Hollywood's largest. Once he had a ton of snow trucked to his 123-room home so his family could enjoy a white Christmas.

When, in 1983, the Federal Communications Commission (FCC), Justice, and Commerce Departments under then president Ronald Reagan decided to rescind the regulations regarding the sale of syndication rights, a move that would hurt the Hollywood studios but help the Big Three TV networks, Wasserman lobbied hard to maintain the status quo. Among other things, he visited President Reagan, his former client, in the Oval Office, and the decision was eventually reversed. Not until a decade later were the rules finally changed, giving the syndication rights to the networks. The stakes were plenty high: U.S. and foreign syndication of even one hit series such as *The Cosby Show* raked in millions. Journalist Edward Jay Epstein, author of *The*

Big Picture: The New Logic of Money and Power in Hollywood, reports that the show, which starred comedian-writer-producer Bill Cosby (the first actor to break the color barrier as a leading man in a dramatic series on television), earned over $500 million from syndication. As part owner of the show, Cosby received hundreds of millions from its reruns and a place on the 400 list (1994 net worth: $325 million).

Today, the richest producer in Hollywood is power broker David Geffen. In many ways, Geffen is a throwback to Wasserman. His sixth sense for pop-culture trends and great timing in selling three companies have made him a multibillionaire ($4.6 billion in 2006). Only a few entertainment moguls are wealthier than Geffen today: Rupert Murdoch, Sumner Redstone, and Steve Jobs (worth $7.7 billion, $7.5 billion, and $4.9 billion, respectively, in 2006). All, like Geffen, have extensive histories and interests in the movies. Murdoch-controlled News Corporation owns Twentieth Century Fox and the Fox TV network, among its vast global portfolio; Redstone's Viacom and CBS Corporation own Paramount Pictures, CBS television, MTV Networks, and many cable systems; and Jobs, besides running Apple, developed Pixar, the computer animation pioneer and maker of *Toy Story,* which he sold to the Walt Disney Company for $7.4 billion in 2006. But none are Hollywood insiders like Geffen, who has, over the last thirty years, made himself part of the warp and woof of the town.

Geffen's first millions were made from records. He grew up poor in Brooklyn, the son of a Russian immigrant mother who supported her family making brassieres and corsets. Smitten with the movie business, Geffen decamped to Los Angeles immediately after graduating from high school and then returned to New York, where he talked his way into becoming an agent at talent agency William Morris. Although he had flunked out of two colleges, he lied on his application for a job in William Morris's mail room, saying that he had graduated from UCLA. But the company never caught the misrepresentation. Geffen intercepted the university's reply to the agency's request for verification, steamed open the envelope, and copied UCLA's letterhead onto a new letter confirming his credentials. He left William Morris after a year to sign up young artists whom he liked: Laura Nyro and Jackson Browne, for example. When he sold Laura Nyro's song catalog for $4 million, he got to keep half. "I felt sure I would never be poor again," he told an interviewer. "I could genuinely be fearless about the future." At age twenty-seven, Geffen started Asylum Records, and signed Joni Mitchell, the Eagles, and Linda Ronstadt, among others. He quickly sold Asylum to Warner Communications for

$7 million. Still, money didn't make him happy, and he sought psychoanalysis. "When I had all this money and still didn't feel quite right, I crashed," he told *Playboy* in a 1994 interview. "I thought, 'Oh shit. Money isn't the answer.' This, of course, is a revelation when you grow up poor and assume that money will solve everything." A broken love affair with Cher caused more heartbreak.*

Geffen, said Sandy Gallin, a well-known Hollywood talent manager, "knew from very early on that he should not be only in a service business: He should have assets to accumulate and sell." And he knew, too, that his greatest assets were his performers. From disco queen Donna Summer to Guns N' Roses, Geffen was in the forefront of practically every pop music trend. John Lennon recorded his last album with Yoko Ono for Geffen Records, his second record company. Geffen went on to discover XTC, Nirvana, and dozens of other pop acts. Many of the artists broke through and sold more than fifty gold record albums, making Geffen Records perhaps the most influential label of the 1980s. Profits largely settled in Geffen's pocket, since under the terms of the deal he had made with Warner's chairman, Steve Ross, his friend and benefactor who staked him for the company, he got half the profits and was responsible for none of its losses. On Broadway Geffen produced *Cats* and *Dreamgirls,* and in the process reinvented the cast album. *Risky Business,* the movie that launched Tom Cruise, was yet another Geffen hit.

Then, in 1990, Geffen sold out again, this time to MCA/Universal for stock worth $545 million, hoping that Wasserman would appoint him his successor. Instead, Wasserman, then seventy-seven, sold MCA/Universal to Matsushita Electric, the owner of Panasonic. But while his ambition to run Universal was thwarted, Geffen hardly faltered. He proved as canny in picking an investment advisor as he was in scouting talent. He cashed out his MCA stock for $710 million, post-tax. Some he put into bonds, and he invested $200 million with hedge fund manager Edward Lampert. By 2006 that nest egg had turned into $1 billion. He also requited his longing for a studio by joining Hollywood pals Jeffrey Katzenberg (who had just been fired from Disney by Michael Eisner) and Steven Spielberg to start one of their own, DreamWorks SKG, in the mid-1990s. The three each invested $33 million in the venture, while Microsoft cofounder Paul Allen anted up $550 million.

The timing for DreamWorks hardly seemed propitious. "The movie business was shrinking," notes Jonathan Taplin, an adjunct professor at the

---

*In the early 1990s, he came out as gay at a benefit for AIDS Project Los Angeles.

Annenberg School for Communication at the University of Southern California and a veteran movie and television producer. "A library is what sustains these companies, and DreamWorks didn't have that, so it rose or fell based on what it made that year. Not a sustainable business." But if you were writing the script a little over a decade later, when DreamWorks SKG was sold for $1.6 billion to Paramount, a subsidiary of Viacom, it might have been called "Gimme Satisfaction." Geffen netted at least $300 million, ten times his original investment, on the sale and a public offering of shares in the animation studio several years earlier. Besides, Geffen, Paul Allen, and Katzenberg (peak net worth: $820 million in 2001, the last time he appeared on the Forbes 400 list) still control DreamWorks Animation, the computer animator that is a distant second to Pixar.

These days, Geffen is a mogul without much of a portfolio—but with a massive pile of money. In 2006 he announced that he was quitting show business. "He is bored with the movie business, and he is restless," said a Hollywood executive who has known him for decades.

Today, as always, would-be movie moguls are as plentiful as the palm trees in Beverly Hills, continually plastered over the trade press and the glossy magazines. But anyone following where the really big money has been made in entertainment over the last twenty-five years would leave Hollywood far behind and head out into the hinterlands. More new fortunes on the Forbes 400 list have come from cable television than anywhere else in the entertainment spectrum between 1982 and 2006. And despite the symbiotic relationship that exists between cable television and the big screen, the movie big shots (and their posses) and the cable entrepreneurs inhabit totally different worlds.

Wasserman and Geffen got enormously rich from their uncanny ability to pick American (and world) idols among the tens of thousands who wanted to see their names in lights. Cable rewarded a completely different crowd—local entrepreneurs, a hodgepodge of visionaries and hardscrabble men. They stuck with the new technology while Hollywood tried to kill it off in the 1970s and 1980s and, in time, were richly rewarded.

Cable TV hasn't exactly been a democratic engine of wealth: It required not only large capital expenditures to lay the cable originally but was, and still is, a highly regulated business, dependent on being granted a local monopoly. But a prerequisite for success was a gut for gambling. Alan Gerry, a high-school dropout, started Cablevision Industries from the back of a Long Island appliance store. Roustabout Bob Magness mortgaged his Texas cattle ranch to start Tele-Communications Inc. (TCI). Charles Dolan laid cable for the future Home Box Office (HBO) under New York City streets when broadcast TV seemed invincible, reaching over 90 percent of American homes.

Unlike the old Hollywood movie moguls, who tried to quash television in its infancy, CBS, NBC, and ABC initially ignored cable, believing that a pay service that screened old Hollywood movies, TV reruns, and sports couldn't compete with free TV. But the landscape shifted dramatically when a gutsy entrepreneur and millionaire's son named Robert Edward "Ted" Turner launched his "superstation," offering his local, over-the-air Atlanta TV station via satellite to cable systems nationwide. Then, several years later, in 1980, he started Cable News Network. It was a wild bet: Turner was worth approximately $100 million at the time, and he plowed most of that into CNN, barely staying one step ahead of his creditors. In fact, Turner wasn't the first to distribute television programming by satellite: That distinction goes to Charles Dolan's HBO. But Turner was determined to prove the "nitworks," as he called the Big Three networks, wrong: The public would pay for television. He denounced CBS's programming as "a whorehouse." In 1982 he began a second network, Headline News, followed by many others. Turner even launched a hostile takeover of CBS in 1985. Though Turner failed, William Paley, the patrician and brilliant patriarch of CBS, then eighty-four years old, allied himself with Laurence Tisch, head of Loews Corporation (and a member of the Forbes 400 from the first year), who initially bought a piece of CBS and later the entire company. Paley (peak net worth: $530 million in 1989) was then edged out.

Captain Outrageous, as Turner was sometimes known, also got into dire financial straits in 1986, when he overpaid Kirk Kerkovian for MGM/UA Entertainment, whose library of classic movies he wanted for Turner Broadcasting System (TBS). He was bailed out by a group of cable operators led by John Malone, a Yale graduate with two MBAs and a PhD who was then CEO of TCI, the cable system founded by cable pioneer Bob Magness.

Turner was vindicated in his failed bid for CBS and its vaunted news division after CNN's twenty-four-hour coverage of the Gulf War in 1990 made it the world's most important news channel. "You rarely find people like Turner," says David Waterman, author of *Hollywood's Road to Riches* and a telecommunications professor at Indiana University in Bloomington. "He innovated lots of things: He came up with many programming ideas, he

Old media vs. new media

Once upon a time, Hollywood was the undisputed center of big entertainment fortunes in the United States. No longer. Today, digital entertainment is mounting a challenge, and the surge in cable and satellite TV has brought vast new wealth. A look at the "old media" players of the past 25 years, versus the new names:

Old Media Moguls (Movies and More)

	Source of wealth	Peak net worth in billions (year)	Comment
Philip Anschutz	Investments, oil, movie theaters, newspapers, movies	**$18.00** ('00)	Fiber optic cable made his fortune, but bringing C. S. Lewis's *Narnia* to the silver screen gave him greater public prominence. "My friends think I'm a candidate for a lobotomy" for producing movies, he says.
Bill Cosby	Television	**$0.33** ('94)	Revived the family sitcom with gentle humor
Michael Eisner	Walt Disney Company stock	**$0.80** ('00)	Fired Jeffrey Katzenberg in 1995 after his animated features (*The Little Mermaid*, *Beauty and The Beast*, *The Lion King*) helped turn Disney around
Roy Disney	Walt Disney Company stock	**$1.20** ('06)	Hired Michael Eisner as CEO in 1984; spearheaded his ouster in 2005
David Geffen	Records, movies	**$4.60** ('06)	Landed his first job at William Morris by claiming he was a graduate of UCLA—then intercepting the university's reply to the agency's request for verification and copying the UCLA letterhead onto a letter confirming his credentials
Bob Hope	California real estate; television	**$0.28** ('82)	"Mr. Entertainment" worked in every form of the business for five decades
Jeffrey Katzenberg	Hollywood animation	**$0.82** ('01)	Best known for *Shrek* and *The Lion King*
George Lucas	Movies	**$3.60** ('06)	Obtained sequel and merchandizing rights for five sequels to *Star Wars*
William Paley	CBS-TV	**$0.53** ('89)	A radio man who resisted TV, he eventually built CBS and then, Lear-like, drove out Frank Stanton and his successors
Jerry Perenchio	Television	**$3.10** ('00)	Sold Spanish-language broadcaster Univision for $13 billion in 2006
Sumner Redstone	Media, Viacom and CBS	**$7.50** ('06)	Won Paramount in 1994 and Viacom in 1986
Haim Saban	Mighty Morphin' Power Rangers	**$2.80** ('06)	Made billions from the cartoon TV series
Aaron Spelling	Television	**$0.35** ('89)	The man behind *Charlie's Angels*, *Dallas*, and *Dynasty*
Steven Spielberg	Movies	**$2.90** ('06)	"E.T. phone home"
Martha Stewart	Publishing	**$1.00** ('00)	Served a stint in prison for insider trading. Author of *The Martha Rules*, a book on business management, among many others
Lew Wasserman	MCA/Universal stock	**$0.32** ('89)	The big, tough, King of Hollywood who saved TV syndication for Tinseltown
Oprah Winfrey	Television; magazines	**$1.50** ('06)	Her nod makes a book a best seller. Started a $40 million leadership school for poor African girls in 2007

New Media Moguls (Cable, Internet, Digital)

	Source of wealth	Peak net worth in billions (year)	Comment
Sergey Brin	Google	**$14.10** ('06)	Built a better search engine
Mark Cuban	dot-coms; sports	**$2.30** ('06)	Signed up Dan Rather as the face of hard news on his HDNet channel on satellite television
Barry Diller	InterActive Corp., a Web holding company	**$1.60** ('03)	One of the highest compensated CEOs in the U.S. with a $457 million pay package in 2005 and $232 million in 2006
Charles Dolan	Cablevision Systems	**$3.20** ('00)	Declared a special dividend in 2006, netting $580 million. In 2007, took his company private
Stanley Hubbard	Satellite TV	**$1.80** ('96)	Pioneered first satellite TV in 1993
Steve Jobs	Apple Computer; animated movies	**$4.90** ('06)	The man behind Apple, the Mac, iPod, iPhone, Pixar. Highest paid CEO in U.S. in 2006 with $647 million pay package
John Malone	Cable TV	**$3.40** ('99)	Monster cable TV deal maker now pushing satellite TV
Craig McCaw	McCaw Cellular	**$7.70** ('00)	Cellular pioneer trying for a comeback with wireless access after 2000 telecom wipeout
Rupert Murdoch	Media/Internet	**$11.00** ('00)	"I just want to live forever—I enjoy myself too much."
Larry Page	Google	**$14.00** ('06)	Helped make "the world's information universally accessible and useful"
Ted Turner	Cable television	**$9.10** ('00)	Imagined multichannel television in 1980; once known as the "Mouth of the South"; now selling bison burgers at his Ted's Montana Grill restaurants

developed superstations and a substantial number of the leading cable networks, and he did a lot of it very early, before hardly anyone believed that cable would be successful."

Eventually, Turner scored a brilliant coup, selling Turner Broadcasting for $7.5 billion to Time Warner in 1995. Two years later he famously pledged $1 billion to the United Nations. After Time Warner merged with America Online, Turner, then vice chairman of the world's largest media company, saw his net worth balloon to $9.1 billion in 2000, only to see it plummet again when the Internet bubble burst. By 2006, his fortune much diminished to $1.9 billion, he was out of the media business, tending to his philanthropic interests and his many herds of bison on his extensive land holdings in the West.

As Turner was transforming TV, cable was transforming communications. Turner's good friend and deal maker John Malone turned TCI into the country's number one cable operator with such hardball tactics as turning off its signal in towns that didn't renew contracts. Malone first appeared on the

Forbes list in 1993 with a fortune of $450 million. Then, after Brian Roberts, president of Comcast in Philadelphia (Roberts's father, Ralph, had founded the cable company), persuaded Bill Gates to invest $1 billion in his company, cable stocks soared. (Both Robertses, father and son, are on the Forbes list.) Many cable pioneers decided to cash out. Malone sold TCI's cable systems to AT&T in 1999 for $54 billion, but had Liberty Media, another company he controlled, hold on to TCI's programming assets. Leonard Tow sold his Century Communications cable group for $5.2 billion in 1999 to Adelphia Communications. Viacom paid $3 billion for Black Entertainment Television (BET) in 2000, catapulting founder Robert Johnson onto the Forbes 400 with $1.3 billion, one of the few African Americans to make the list. (Johnson subsequently fell off the list after a divorce.) "The cable TV business was essentially a compulsory savings system," says Malone, who is still in the media business. "It wasn't a bonanza where you got in and automatically got lucky. It was a story that went on for forty years. There were bodies along the road, but those who managed properly turned out very wealthy."

At the same time that cable was exploding, second-generation Minnesota broadcaster Stanley Hubbard was mounting a lonely challenge to it and broadcast TV by way of digital TV. "I lived on the road for eleven years trying to raise money," says Hubbard. "People in the cable industry laughed and said DBS [direct broadcast satellite] stood for 'Don't be stupid.' The networks went out of their way to prevent digital satellite TV from happening—telling investors it won't work."

Eventually, after making more than a thousand presentations over a

1994

from the pages of *Forbes*

Larry Ellison, Oracle founder and daredevil driver, spun out his Acura NSX in front of company headquarters while turning at such a speed that "it took four months for the tire skid marks to wash away." (1994 net worth: $2.9 billion)

Leslie Gonda, who made his fortune in the airline leasing business, escaped from a forced-labor camp in Hungary in 1944, changed his name, and settled first in Venezuela, then in the United States. (1994 net worth: $340 million)

Gordon Getty, heir to the Getty Oil fortune, is a conservatory-trained composer and pianist who would "rather be on the music pages." (1994 net worth: $1.5 billion)

Edmund Wattis Littlefield, who made his fortune in mining and land development, can shoot his age (80) in golf. (1994 net worth: $360 million) twelve-year period, Hubbard and his family were able to come up with the $30 million needed to partner with Hughes Aerospace for the launch of a satellite. The first high-powered direct broadcast satellite soared aloft in 1993, and the system succeeded spectacularly, sending back a crisp and high-quality image. The low cost of the eighteen-inch satellite dishes and receivers needed to capture the signal of U.S. Satellite Broadcasting enabled subscribers nation-wide to receive one-hundred-some channels of television and cable program-ming. By 1998 Hubbard was worth $825 million on the Forbes 400. He merged his U.S. Satellite Broadcasting into Hughes DirecTV a year later and left the field. "I hated to do it," he says, "but it made business sense. We owned the satellite together but we were competing for customers."

In the "what goes around, comes around" media business, John Malone's Liberty Media is now DirecTV's biggest shareholder. Malone, who gained control from Rupert Murdoch in a 2006 stock swap, has now set his sights on the cable industry he helped create. DirecTV plans to launch two new satel-lites and add one hundred new high-definition channels in 2007. Malone has hinted that he might urge DirecTV to ally with the number two satellite player, Dish Network, owned by 400 member Charles Ergen (2006 net worth: $7.6 billion), or possibly compete with Hollywood and television networks and produce its own high-definition (HD) shows. HD appears poised to be one of the next big gushers. Mark Cuban (2006 net worth: $2.3 billion) and his partner, Todd Wagner (2006 net worth: $1.4 billion), who sold Broadcast.com to Yahoo at the height of the Internet boom, now control HDNet, the high-definition television network available on DirecTV and Dish. Meanwhile, Stanley Hubbard (2006 net worth: $1.4 billion) also has new partners: movie producers Bob and Harvey Weinstein, founders of Miramax Films. They co-own tiny arts channel Ovation TV, which DirecTV will also broadcast.

As media morphs from one format to another, as analog moves to digital and old technologies drop into the computer trash bin at warp speed, only a very few entrepreneurs have managed to keep their bearings. Fewer still have managed to build new empires that blend traditional and digital media and entertainment. Four who have—and who have succeeded brilliantly at the game—are Rupert Murdoch, Sumner Redstone, Barry Diller, and Michael Bloomberg.

Murdoch and Redstone have much in common. Murdoch, age seventy-six in 2007, has been on the Forbes 400 list for twenty-two years, just one year less than Redstone, age eighty-four. Their wealth peaked (so far) in 2000, when Murdoch was worth an estimated $11 billion, Redstone $14 billion. In 2006 Forbes estimated their wealth at $7.7 billion for Murdoch, $7.5 billion for Redstone. Both have recently divorced and remarried. Both have fractious families who have skirmished over succession and family assets. And both have well-earned reputations as tough bosses. "I am Viacom," Redstone once said, echoing Louis XIV's "L'État c'est moi."

Unlike Redstone, however, Murdoch has seemed destined since childhood to be a press lord. Born into a wealthy family, Murdoch inherited a newspaper in Adelaide, Australia. Then he maneuvered his way around the world with a fistful of loans and a remarkable ability to seize opportunities and build major media properties from scratch. Every acquisition Murdoch made was financed by mortgaging his properties to buy new ones. He started with newspapers: the *News of the World* and the *Sun,* two British tabloids best known for their outrageous headlines and seminude photos; and, in the United States, the *San Antonio Express-News* and *New York Post.* In every market he entered he was feared for his ruthless charm and for bullying his editors and local politicians.

After sweeping up more newspapers, including the buttoned-up *Times* of London, Murdoch moved on to magazines (*Seventeen, TV Guide,* the *Daily Racing Form*). In 1990, however, News Corporation owed $7.6 billion to more than one hundred banks and struggled to stay afloat. After renegotiating its debt, it bought television, movie, satellite TV, and now Internet companies. Murdoch has, along the way, arguably created more billionaires than anyone else through his over-the-top prices for acquisitions. In 1988 he paid $3 billion to Walter Annenberg (peak net worth: $4.2 billion in 1998) for Triangle Publications, then $2 billion to Forbes 400 member John Kluge for his Metromedia TV stations.* Then, after creating the Fox Network, a fourth TV network in the United States, something few thought he could do, Murdoch partnered with Haim Saban, an Egyptian-born music promoter who grew up in Israel and emigrated to the United States. Each owned 49 percent of the Family Channel, for which Saban (2006 net worth: $2.8 billion) created *Mighty Morphin' Power Rangers,* the preteen cartoon megahit in the mid-1990s.

Like Murdoch, Redstone also inherited his first media properties: a chain of Boston drive-in movie theaters called National Amusements. Several years

---

*Kluge's peak net worth was $13 billion in 2000; he's been on the Forbes list for twenty-five years. In 1987 he was first on the list, worth $3 billion.

after narrowly escaping death in a hotel fire in Boston, he had a change of ambition at age sixty-three, and decided to enter the national media fray. His hostile tender in 1986 for cable company Viacom, owner of MTV Networks, was followed by a bid for Paramount in 1994, which he won against Barry Diller. He merged Viacom with CBS in 2000 and six years later split them apart again, into CBS Corporation and Viacom.

As wealth creators, both Murdoch and Redstone sit atop gangly empires of mostly old media and entertainment (Murdoch in newspapers, TV, movies, and book publishing; Redstone in TV, radio, publishing, and movies) and new media such as cable, with just a smattering of Internet assets. Murdoch's News Corporation recently spent more for Internet portals and businesses such as MySpace ($580 million) than any entertainment conglomerate before it, as Murdoch declared that the explosion of video sharing, social networking, blogging, and downloading music and movies around the world is creating a historic watershed. Redstone tried to buy MySpace, too, but Murdoch swept in and outbid him. Losing MySpace, Redstone admitted on national TV, was "humiliating." Since then Redstone hasn't embraced the Internet as exuberantly as has his rival.

"To find something comparable, you have to go back 500 years to the printing press, the birth of mass media, which incidentally is what destroyed the old world of kings and aristocracies," Murdoch told *Wired* magazine in an interview at his New York headquarters in 2006, speaking of his view of the tectonic shift created by the Internet. "Technology is shifting power away from the editors, the publishers, the establishment, the media elite. Now it's the people taking control." His goal, Murdoch says now, is to sell data mined from MySpace users' profiles to advertisers, and turn MySpace into a giant

---

1995

from the pages of *Forbes*

Paul Mellon, the banker and scion of the Mellon family, donated half of the philosopher John Locke's library to Oxford. (1995 net worth: $1.1 billion)

Michael Dell of Dell Computers has no chair in his office: "I've discovered that I think faster on my feet." (1995 net worth: $740 million)

James LeVoy Sorenson, inventor and producer of cutting-edge medical devices, including the computerized heart monitor, believes that sign language will become a global second language. (1995 net worth: $1.2 billion)

LBO king and Revlon boss **Ronald Perelman** smokes five cigars a day. (1995 net worth: $4.2 billion)

Internet marketer. He's already made deals that, analysts say, value MySpace at a multiple of several times what he paid for it. Adds Professor Jonathan Taplin, "If he can keep MySpace together—keep it hip, keep it modern—that's the big question." It's the same question for Redstone, too, who is also trying to find a way to grow online, especially in the exploding video- and movie-download market.

Compared to the sprawling colossi of News Corporation, Viacom, and CBS, Michael Bloomberg's and Barry Diller's creations seem like all-digital niche players—yet they more likely represent the way media fortunes will be made in the future. Bloomberg is now arguably better known as mayor of New York City than as a media mogul. His wealth ($5.3 billion in 2006) comes from his 68 percent share in the online news company he started in 1981, the eponymous Bloomberg LP. Its sophisticated computer terminals deliver real-time, twenty-four-hour market data to Wall Street and businesses worldwide, along with news and analysis. The syndicated news service competes with Reuters, Dow Jones, and the *New York Times*. From the start, Bloomberg had a fairy-tale success as an investment banker turned media entrepreneur. Selling blocks of stock at Salomon Brothers in the early 1970s, Bloomberg was a partner, but not a star; in an office shake-up he was shunted from the front lines to run the company's back-office computers. Then, when the firm was acquired, Bloomberg was fired and cashed out his partnership, pocketing about $10 million. He realized from his exposure to computers and his years as a trader that Wall Street needed a computer able to display every publicly traded stock so traders could compare prices and other characteristics, and he bluffed his way into a contract with Merrill Lynch, the largest security firm in the world, before he had even begun building such a machine.

Luckily, in six months he and a team of former Salomon colleagues delivered a terminal that gave traders a competitive edge. Merrill Lynch was thrilled and bought 30 percent of the company. (It now owns 20 percent.) Today Bloomberg continues to dominate the market, in part because his terminals allow traders to be in constant communication with one another while watching real-time financial data, and also because Bloomberg's news analysis from journalists around the world is available only to subscribers who rent the terminals by the month. Not coincidentally, the company is a gigantic moneymaker. In 2006 its operating profits totaled $1.5 billion, according to published estimates, ten times the profits of Dow Jones, its chief rival.

Barry Diller (2006 net worth: $1.3 billion), head of Interactive Corporation (IAC) in Manhattan, is one of the only entertainment executives to forsake Hollywood for the Web, but he came to the decision opportunistically after a failed bid to run a movie studio. A college dropout like David Geffen, Diller also started in the mail room at William Morris. He was head of Paramount Pictures for ten years, but then lost a power struggle for the top job at its parent, Gulf & Western. (At Paramount Diller mentored future Walt Disney Company chairman Michael Eisner and Disney's future animation wunderkind, Jeffrey Katzenberg—two of a group of big-time media executives who became known as "the killer Dillers.") Murdoch hired Diller to create the Fox TV network, but Diller eventually left when Murdoch refused to make him a principal.

Murdoch, however, gave Diller a hefty severance, enough so that he appeared on the Forbes 400 list in 1993 with an estimated net worth of $345 million. With it, he bought a $25 million stake in QVC, the home shopping network, then resigned from it in 1995. He made another fortune buying the USA cable television network cheaply (from Seagram heir Edgar Bronfman Jr.) and selling it expensively (to Vivendi, the French water company that tried to become an entertainment company before crashing spectacularly). Throughout much of the 1990s, Diller was on-again, off-again about the Internet, depending on his mood. But since the late 1990s Diller has bought dozens of interactive businesses, including Expedia.com, LendingTree.com, Match.com, and most recently Ask.com, creating an interactive commerce conglomerate. (He also paid himself handsomely, more than any executive in the country in 2005.)

Only two traditional movie directors have made enough money by their extraordinary talent, outsize visions, pioneering work in digitized filmmaking, and shrewd business moves to make it onto the Forbes 400 list. Steven Spielberg made his fortune (2006 net worth: $2.8 billion) largely within the Hollywood system, rolling out one blockbuster after another, while George Lucas earned his by bucking the system.

Lucas enrolled in the University of Southern California's prestigious film school after a drag-racing crash in high school cured him of wanting to become a race-car driver. Very quickly, he showed the vision and desire for creative control that has made him a fortune. Executives under Lew Wasserman at MCA/Universal forced him to make several cuts in his second film, *American Graffiti*. From then on, Lucas hated Hollywood: For his third film he made a deal that allowed him to break away. Several studios rejected his script for *Star Wars,* including Universal, but Twentieth Century Fox liked it. Lucas's lawyer, Tom Pollock, who later became chairman of Universal and is now co-owner of an independent production company in Hollywood, remembers that above all Lucas wanted to make the *Star Wars* series his way: without interference from studio executives. Lucas asked for a modest writer's and director's fee. In exchange, he retained sequel rights, TV serial rights, music publishing rights, and soundtrack album rights—but not merchandising rights. "Those were not a big deal then," Pollock says. "Merchandising was basically Bugs Bunny and Mickey Mouse."

Once *Star Wars* became an unprecedented hit, however, it was clear that merchandising money would be huge; so as part of the deal on the sequels, Lucas insisted on retaining merchandising rights as well. In return, he took no salary. "In terms of wealth creation, George's decision to bet on himself and sacrifice the up-front money for back-end control was the key," says Pollack. "This was not a decision for George based on money or how much wealth he thought it would create for himself," he adds. "His rationale was he'd had a bad experience with Universal and he'd watched [his friend] Francis Ford Coppola [director of *The Godfather*] have a bad experience with Warner Bros. and Paramount, and he was very worried about whether something he created would be taken away from him. Some have called this paranoia. It was a reasonable fear. He was never a studio person: He's always been an outsider—and still is."

Lucas, only thirty-two at the time of the negotiation, went on to make five more *Star Wars* movies between 1980 and 2005, all of which he financed himself. He kept the bulk of the income from *The Empire Strikes Back* and all the subsequent sequels, and the money made from merchandising *Star Wars* characters. Movie merchandising—toys, Franklin Mint statues, video games—is a multibillion-dollar industry today largely because of *Star Wars.* As film historian David Thomson points out in *The Whole Equation: A History of Hollywood,* the *Star Wars* deal was "the most decisive negotiation ever carried out in Hollywood." No director financed by a studio ever again got all the sequel and merchandising rights, because the studios did not want to make the same mistake twice. For Lucas, it's immaterial whether Darth Vader tries to kill Luke Skywalker on a cell-phone screen or in a digitized theater: He still gets all the action. According to Forbes.com, total revenues from the *Star Wars* franchise reached $20 billion by 2005, and in 2006 Lucas's fortune stood at $3.6 billion. "I've earned enough," Lucas told a television interviewer recently. "I've worked enough to be able to fail the rest of my life."

"What's great about George is that he's always had a vision for what he needed for himself to make films," says Janet Healy, former head of computer graphics at Disney, who worked on *Star Wars.* "George pushed digital effects in a huge way. He and Steven Spielberg and James Cameron [the Academy Award–winning director of *Titanic*]—you can't underestimate the amount of risk they assumed in the service of their vision. They all shared in common an ability to see what the computer-graphics technology could do before anyone else, and before the technology could do it. For instance, Steven said, 'I'm going to make digital dinosaurs for *Jurassic Park.* No one has ever done a digital character in a movie, much less with a moving camera, but I believe you all will do it.' " Healy, visual-effects producer on the 1993 film, recalls that with new moving cameras from George Lucas's special-effects house, which revolved repeatedly around life-size models, digital dinosaurs were born: "It was a huge paradigm shift." It's estimated that, on *Jurassic Park* alone, Spielberg earned $294 million of the $951 million gross from his director's fee, his percentage of the box office, and sales in ancillary markets such as merchandising and foreign markets.

A talent in front of the camera propelled two others onto the Forbes 400 list: Oprah Winfrey and Martha Stewart. Two of the few self-made women to make the 400, they had a knack for turning themselves into eponymous brands. (The only male member of the 400 to achieve that kind of recognition is Donald Trump.) Until the mid-1990s, Forbes 400 women in media and entertainment had inherited their empires. They included the octogenarian Cox sisters, Barbara Cox Anthony* and Anne Cox Chambers (2006 net worth: $12.6 billion each), who own $12 billion Cox Enterprises in Atlanta, Georgia, plus its seventeen daily newspapers, multiple cable systems, radio and TV stations; and publisher Katharine Graham (peak net worth: $875 million in 1987), who rose to national prominence when she took over the Washington Post Company after her husband's death. In contrast, Oprah was the first to arrive on her own merits in 1996. Owning her fabulously popular TV talk show made her a billionaire (2006 net worth: $1.5 billion).

Then came Martha. Born into a middle-class family in New Jersey, Stewart learned her homemaking skills from her grandparents, who taught her to can fruits, and her parents, who taught her to sew and garden. After stints as a model and a stockbroker, she opened a catering outfit in Westport, Connecticut, an upscale suburb near New York City.

Stewart pitched herself at women who were interested in high-end

*Barbara Cox Anthony died in 2007.

Making It the Oprah Way

After twenty-one years—a record in the industry—millions in the United States and in 132 other countries tune in daily to watch Oprah Winfrey for her unique empathy with the controversies of the day and with the abused and the neglected, her delight in luxury, and her belief that you can change your life, no matter how rough you've had it.

Oprah Inc. includes *The Oprah Winfrey Show;* two slick glossies, *O, The Oprah Magazine* and *O at Home;* a Web site; a production unit for movies and TV specials; a guru business; a stake in the women's cable channel Oxygen Network; the charities Oprah's Angel Network and the Oprah Winfrey Foundation; Oprah's Book Club; and XM Radio's new channel Oprah & Friends. Along the way, Oprah, who shattered the color barrier in TV news, has become the richest African American in the country—and one of the few working women on the Forbes 400 list—with a net worth estimated at $1.5 billion in 2006.

How ironic, given that in the mid-1970s Oprah was told that she was not attractive or talented enough to be a star and was fired as the coanchor of an evening TV news show in Baltimore. She moved to Chicago and found her groove there hosting a third-ranked morning talk show, an ideal spot for showing off her sympathetic interviewing style. Soon she was outdrawing Phil Donahue.

Her salary as Chicago's most popular TV talk host ran to $230,000 in 1984. Enter Chicago lawyer Jeff Jacobs. Oprah hired Jacobs to negotiate a new contract with the local ABC station that was producing her show. In 1985 Jacobs got the station to rename the program *The Oprah Winfrey Show* and sell it outside Chicago. ABC allowed the sale so long as its affiliates got first crack. Since by law ABC couldn't syndicate the show itself in the 1980s, the deal was good for them, too. Jacobs then brought in King World Productions to distribute it nationally.

After giving an Oscar-nominated performance in *The Color Purple* in 1985, Oprah went back on the air as a celebrity. Ratings climbed rapidly, and her show brought in $115 million in revenues during its first two seasons. Then Jacobs moved in for the kill. He negotiated for ownership to return to Oprah, and gradually cut the amount of revenues King could take in return for distribution, increasing Oprah's share. As long as local affiliates bought her show every year, Oprah grew richer. She also received big stock options in King World each year she renewed her contract. "I had to get rid of that slave mentality," Oprah has said. "That's where Jeff came in. He took the ceiling off my brain."

In 1994 Jacobs negotiated a nine-figure annual salary, and Winfrey became the top-earning female performer in the country. She already owned her production company, Harpo (Oprah spelled backward), which holds her magazines, online media, and television interests. She also owns the film studios where her talk show is taped in Chicago. Her far-flung real-estate holdings include a chunk of prime coastline in Hawaii, as well as an extravagant 1920s Spanish Colonial mansion that she and partner Stedman Graham share in exclusive Montecito, California.

Off camera, Oprah is a generous woman and one of the top givers in showbiz. In 2005 alone, she gave nearly $52 million to help others, according to the *Chronicle of Philanthropy*. In 2007 she opened a $40 million Oprah Winfrey Leadership Academy in South Africa for young girls whose families, many devastated by AIDS, are unable to pay their school fees. Oprah, teary-eyed with pride at the opening ceremonies, may have flashed back to her own dirt-poor and abused Mississippi girlhood as the 150 students filed by in beautiful new uniforms.

Selling shares in her company, however, is anathema to her: "If I lost control of the business, I'd lose myself—or at least the ability to be myself."

homemaking—an ever-larger group as more and more middle-class women made their way into the workforce. She wrote a best-selling cookbook, then started a TV show based on her decorating magazine, *Martha Stewart Living*, and not long after that, a line of houseware items at Kmart. In 1997 she consolidated her publishing, TV, and merchandising ventures into Martha Stewart Living Omnimedia. When it went public in 1999, Stewart climbed onto the Forbes 400 with a fortune estimated in 2000 at $1 billion.

Four years later she served a jail sentence for lying to investigators and obstructing justice in an insider-trading case. Her fall was harsh: Stewart cannot assume control of her company again until 2011, when an SEC ban on her serving as an officer or employee of a public company is lifted. But she has hardly let the episode be her undoing. Since her 2005 release from jail, among other things she's returned to host *The Martha Stewart Show* on TV; licensed her name to a line of midpriced homes modeled on her own dwellings in New York and Mount Desert Island, Maine; and tried a weekly call-in radio show on Sirius Radio. But while the value of shares in her publicly owned company have risen, she has fallen off the Forbes 400 list.

With change constantly roiling the entertainment industry, it's difficult to predict where the next media fortunes will be made. Nevertheless, there's no shortage of prognosticators, including current Forbes 400 members themselves. "TV on the Web, TV on your cell phone," says tycoon John Malone. "There will be a lot of wealth created in that space." New York entertainment lawyer George Cooke agrees: "The next wealth accumulator is the provider of the search engine in the interactive Web TV world. Everyone wants to be the controller of your at-home information interface." The media pundits come at the question from a slightly different slant. Says author Edward Jay Epstein, "Hollywood is not going to collapse, because it is in the business not of making movies but of creating and acquiring intellectual properties, and those become more and more valuable over time—in any new format." *The New Yorker's* media critic, Ken Auletta, isn't so sanguine. "Everyone is in a panic," he says, because no one knows how to make money year after year in digital markets. "Opposite things are happening simultaneously," Auletta continues. "On the one hand, the Internet is ushering in a whole new world of more choices and democratization of the media. People can publish their books, you can go online and publish videos, TV shows, and be in touch with anyone you want in the world—that's democratization. But companies are also buying up other companies: Google and YouTube. So at the same time that these big companies are being threatened by the Web, they are threatening. That's one of the great paradoxes of the era we live in: We see more decentralization and democratization of the media, and at the same time we see more concentration." In such an uncertain environment, there's perhaps only one certainty: Whoever figures out the next wave first is bound to make a lot of money.

8

Beyond Wall Street

O ne by one, the line of cars filed through the entrance to the grounds of the great house overlooking Long Island Sound, on a promontory across from the yacht club in Greenwich, Connecticut. Allowed in once a year at Christmas, the sightseers, waved on by police, had come to view the mansion's spectacular Christmas lights and gossip about its underground parking garage for twenty-five cars and famous holiday parties featuring the Rockettes. And who could resist? With its Monticello-like central dome and enormous classical portico framing the offshore islands in the distance, the $50 million home of hedge fund manager Paul T. Jones II is not only an emblem of elite wealth few can aspire to; it attests to the arrival of a new crowd of superrich.

Greenwich, a suburb near New York City known over the years for its wealthy CEOs, entertainers, newscasters, and the old rich, could now fairly be called Hedge Fund Acres. So many hedge fund managers have arrived from Wall Street over the past decade that one little Versailles follows another in some parts of town. The new crowd is dropping alleys of trees via cranes to frame thirty-thousand-square-foot homes in which nannies keep order and butlers oversee six-thousand-bottle wine cellars, world-class art collections, outdoor skating rinks, private cinemas, and bowling alleys.

The mansion building in Greenwich follows an extraordinary surge in the wealth of hedge fund managers in this country. Since the turn of the twenty-first century, they have outearned everyone on Wall Street. Seventeen of the eighty-three financiers on the 2006 Forbes 400 list founded hedge funds, compared to just five in 2001. According to *Alpha* magazine, the highest paid,

James H. Simons, earned $1.7 billion in 2006 running his Renaissance Technologies corporation from his office on Third Avenue in New York City. But he's hardly the only manager of a hedge fund to pay himself a billion-dollar salary: Ken Griffin and Edward Lampert also made over a billion in 2006. And others, like Steven Cohen, George Soros, and Stanley Druckenmiller, regularly take home hundreds of millions a year. In an age when the salaries of baseball players and movie stars are common knowledge, there's hardly a household name among the moneymen, who are the best-paid professionals of them all.

Hedge fund managers have not just raised the bar on Wall Street; they're also changing the U.S. economy. Money invested in hedge funds amounts to $1 trillion in a $13.2 trillion economy—a considerable sum. But perhaps more important, hedge funds both individually and collectively can be the largest investors in a company's stocks—sometimes determining, with a flick of a computer key, whether a takeover attempt will succeed or fail. Hedge funds now control an estimated 20 to 55 percent of trading on most major markets. And increasingly, federal and state regulators are attempting to track their trading activities for evidence of illegal market manipulations. In early 2007, for example, it was reported that the SEC was conducting an investigation into whether Wall Street bank employees are tipping off hedge fund traders, their best customers, to major deals.

Since ancient times, financiers have been regarded by their critics with suspicion and dislike: They don't produce anything useful, so the thinking goes, and there is the constant maneuvering and manipulating to extract as much as they can get from every deal. The counterargument is that financiers create value and that the U.S. economy—or any economy, for that matter—couldn't grow as fast without the financial innovations that have rooted out the inefficient and incompetent and provided capital for business, albeit with the occasional scandal and crimes. "Only the final conflagration will put an end to Wall Street speculation and Wall Street swindles," one commentator observed—160 years ago.

In part, the dislike of financiers may stem from a lack of understanding of what they do—what's a derivative, anyway? You can still make a princely fortune on Wall Street—like Henry Paulson, who took in $38 million as head of Goldman Sachs before becoming Treasury secretary in 2006—or like some of the traders at his former company, who reportedly pulled in $90 million apiece in 2006. But even those unprecedented sums are nothing compared to what those who have left top Wall Street firms, like Goldman Sachs and Merrill Lynch, now command. How have the new elite been able to generate sums

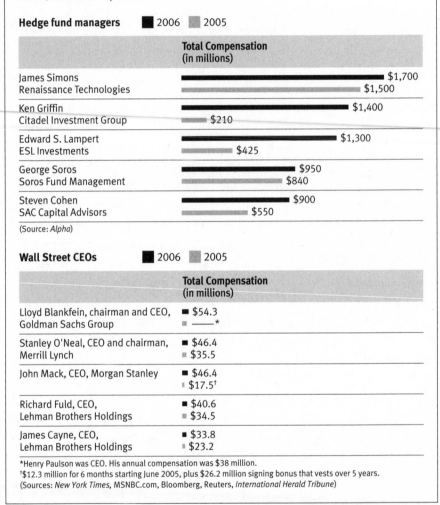

Hedge fund managers vs. Wall Street CEOs

The paychecks of the biggest Wall Street CEOs look like peanuts when compared to the amounts the top hedge fund managers are putting in their pockets. The figures for the Wall Street CEOs include cash, salary, restricted stock, and stock options.

Hedge fund managers   ■ 2006   ▨ 2005

	Total Compensation (in millions)
James Simons Renaissance Technologies	$1,700 $1,500
Ken Griffin Citadel Investment Group	$1,400 $210
Edward S. Lampert ESL Investments	$1,300 $425
George Soros Soros Fund Management	$950 $840
Steven Cohen SAC Capital Advisors	$900 $550

(Source: *Alpha*)

Wall Street CEOs   ■ 2006   ▨ 2005

	Total Compensation (in millions)
Lloyd Blankfein, chairman and CEO, Goldman Sachs Group	$54.3 ——*
Stanley O'Neal, CEO and chairman, Merrill Lynch	$46.4 $35.5
John Mack, CEO, Morgan Stanley	$46.4 $17.5†
Richard Fuld, CEO, Lehman Brothers Holdings	$40.6 $34.5
James Cayne, CEO, Lehman Brothers Holdings	$33.8 $23.2

*Henry Paulson was CEO. His annual compensation was $38 million.
†$12.3 million for 6 months starting June 2005, plus $26.2 million signing bonus that vests over 5 years.
(Sources: *New York Times*, MSNBC.com, Bloomberg, Reuters, *International Herald Tribune*)

that make their counterparts in major Wall Street firms seem like paupers by comparison? What is it that separates the astronomically wealthy from the merely rich in the world of finance?

For starters, being in the right place during two great bull markets—when falling interest rates made borrowed money cheap—profoundly helped the financiers who have landed on the Forbes 400 list. In addition, all had the financial acumen, analytical skills, old-fashioned salesmanship, relentlessness, and know-how to knock down a deal. But above all, those who have made phenomenal sums in the financial sector since the first Forbes 400 list appeared in 1982 share the ability to create a new wrinkle in finance—whether it be hedge funds, venture capital, junk bonds, or private equity—and exploit it amid the cutthroat environment of Wall Street. In doing so, they have changed the financial landscape almost as dramatically as Silicon Valley transformed the dissemination of knowledge via the PC and individual software.

Back in 1982, it was the masters of leveraged buyouts who were coming into their own. Kohlberg Kravis Roberts & Company was the first to raise pools of blind capital from limited and general partners to invest in leveraged buyouts, or private equity deals—a novel idea. (The capital was considered "blind" in the sense that the investors handed it over to the firm to invest as it wished, within relatively broad parameters.)

Although there had been a few limited partnerships put together earlier by investment banks, the classic LBO was largely the brainchild of KKR's founding partner, Jerome Kohlberg (2006 net worth: $1.2 billion). A crusty but likable man of few words, Kohlberg, cohead of investment banking at Bear Stearns on Wall Street in the mid-1970s, had been tinkering with buying companies mostly for debt, taking them private, and streamlining them for resale five or six years later. Buying and selling companies, of course, was nothing new; but buying them with 90 percent plus debt was. Only if the target companies' cash flow gushed sufficiently to meet that mountainous debt could a leveraged buyout turn a profit. At the time, burdening a company with 90 percent debt was viewed by many as financially unsound.

After fifteen deals at Bear Stearns (only a few of which returned any money), Kohlberg, then age fifty but already a multimillionaire, left to perfect his idea with two younger colleagues, Henry Kravis and George Roberts. Finding companies that might benefit from an LBO, as well as lenders and investors for KKR, was initially a slow process. His innovation, Kohlberg says, was "the equity piece," insisting that "management of the company we were buying put their own money on the line. So instead of huge salaries and lots of perks, they had ownership of the company, too, and were on the same side of the table as us" (since KKR usually bought 10 percent of the company). That way, when KKR urged management on to greater efficiency, including firing workers and selling divisions to repay debt, the bosses usually obliged because they, too, could get rich when the company was resold.

To lure lenders, KKR gave insurance companies and banks "who usually loan money just on the basis of an interest rate, an interest in the ownership," says Kohlberg. "That was attractive enough to overcome their reluctance." Along with Kohlberg, Henry Kravis (2006 net worth: $2.6 billion), a smooth, charming, ambitious investment banker from a wealthy Oklahoma family, wooed investors—as did his more introverted cousin, George Roberts, who was based in San Francisco. "They went out to the state pension funds and big endowments before anyone else," says a Wall Street insider, "and said, 'We can get you outsize returns.'" Rather than 8 percent from blue-chip stocks and 3 to 4 percent from bonds (pension funds' usual returns), Kohlberg, Kravis, and Roberts had a track record of 30 to 40 percent returns by the early 1980s.

At first KKR had ground out small margins with gritty manufacturing companies. But in 1979, after its first LBO of New York Stock Exchange company Houdaille Industries, a tool- and die-maker, Wall Street took notice. By 1983 KKR claimed an astonishing average annual return of 62.7 percent for its investors before fees. Kohlberg, an uncommon combination of rectitude and cunning, rapidly increased his fortune. He and his two partners took a fee of 1 percent of the assets the firm managed each year and divided 20 percent of their profits when they eventually resold the companies. Soon their fees grew: 1.6 percent of assets plus multimillion-dollar advisory fees from the companies and their buyers. By 1986 Kohlberg, Kravis, and Roberts were each worth $180 million and on the Forbes 400 list.

Others also got the LBO bug. William Simon, a former Treasury secretary during the Nixon and Ford administrations, and his private investor group, Wesray Capital, made a great splash in 1982 with an LBO of card company Gibson Greetings. They took Gibson private for $80 million, with just a sliver of equity. When they sold it to the public eighteen months later for $290 million, Simons's $330,000 investment turned into a profit of $66 million in cash and securities. The "obscene profits" in LBOs, Bryan Burrough and John Helyar noted in *Barbarians at the Gate: The Fall of RJR Nabisco,* their best-selling book about KKR and the takeover of Nabisco and RJR Tobacco in 1988, brought competitors. Theodore Forstmann and his brother, Nicholas, started the buyout firm Forstmann Little & Company in 1978. Peter G. Peterson, commerce secretary in the Nixon administration, and Stephen A. Schwarzman (like Peterson, an alumnus of Lehman Brothers, an old-line Wall Street firm) started Blackstone Group in 1985. Forstmann's niche was friendly buyouts; Blackstone, buttressed by Peterson's connections and Schwarzman's deal-making drive, became more of a small investment bank. But by getting

The really big money men (and one woman) . . .

The financial business has been minting money since the Forbes list began in 1982. In the tables below are the men—and one lone woman—who make money investing and deploying capital, grouped by how they made their fortunes. In recent years, hedge fund and private equity managers have raked in the biggest bucks.

Hedge Fund Founders	Years on list	Peak year	Peak value (billions)
Louis Bacon	3	2006	$1.0
Steven A. Cohen	4	2006	$3.0
Stanley Druckenmiller	12	2006	$2.0
Israel Englander	1	2006	$1.2
Ken Griffin	4	2006	$1.7
Paul Tudor Jones II	4	2006	$2.5
Bruce Kovner	15	2006	$3.0
Edward S. Lampert	5	2006	$3.8
T. Boone Pickens Jr.	3	2006	$2.7
Julian H. Robertson Jr.	10	1999	$1.7
David E. Shaw	1	2006	$1.0
James H. Simons	3	2006	$4.0
George Soros	21	2006	$8.5
David Tepper	2	2006	$1.5
Daniel Ziff	13	2006	$1.5
Dirk Ziff	13	2006	$1.5
Robert Ziff	13	2006	$1.5

Venture Capitalists	Years on list	Peak year	Peak value (billions)
John L. Doerr	6	2006	$1.0
Vinod Khosla	5	2001	$1.0
Arthur Rock	11	2000	$2.0

Private Equity Managers	Years on list	Peak year	Peak value (billions)
Leon Black	1	2006	$2.0
Alec Gores	5	2003	$1.6
Tom T. Gores	6	2006	$2.0
Carl Icahn	20	2006	$9.7
Jerome S. Kohlberg Jr.	21	2006	$1.2
Henry R. Kravis	21	2006	$2.6
Thomas H. Lee	14	2006	$1.4
Nelson Z. Peltz	18	2006	$1.3
Ronald Perelman	20	2006	$7.0
George R. Roberts	21	2006	$2.6
Stephen A. Schwarzman	3	2006	$3.5

Mutual Fund Founders	Years on list	Peak year	Peak value (billions)
Thomas Bailey	7	2006	$1.2
John P. F. Calamos	3	2005	$2.1
Edward Crosby Johnson III	22	2006	$7.5
Rupert Johnson Jr.	15	2006	$3.7
Jonathan Lovelace Jr.	1	2006	$1.1
Elizabeth S. Wiskemann	3	2005	$1.4

. . . and their rising riches

Over the last 25 years, the percentage of overall wealth of the 400 controlled by financiers has increased from 0.1% ($160 million in 1983) to 7.5% ($93.5 billion in 2006).

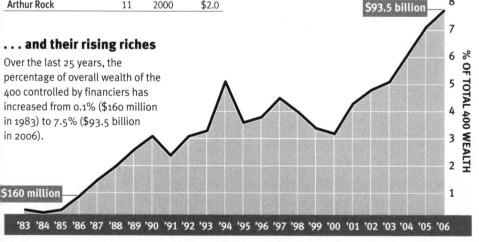

in early on the LBO craze, they also became renowned, and Forstmann and Schwarzman landed on the Forbes 400 list, as well.

Leveraged buyouts are "a way of buying what you otherwise couldn't afford," notes David Skeel, professor of corporate law at the University of Pennsylvania Law School and author of *Icarus in the Boardroom: The Fundamental Flaws in Corporate America and Where They Came From.* "It wasn't an obvious idea, but it was extremely successful," he adds, because it made the founders of the company being bought out rich, as well as the managers who stayed on to run it. As for the LBO financiers themselves, they got even richer, with little of their own cash up front and relatively little effort—but with a lot of smarts about how to break up companies and sell off the pieces.

Several other factors also favored the rise of LBOs in the 1970s and 1980s. In order to buy low and sell high, as KKR and other private equity firms did, stock prices had to be depressed: "After a period of great inflation in the early 1970s and 1980s, a lot of companies were still being valued at preinflation prices," notes Charles Geisst, a historian of Wall Street and prolific author. Additionally, the government permitted interest on debt to be charged against income, fattening the bottom line for taking companies private, while, at the same time, long-term capital gains were taxed at a lower rate, meaning that when partners took their profits from the deals, more ended up in their pockets. Pretty soon, the megabucks were piling up faster than pancakes on a Sunday morning.

"In the eighties, you had a bunch of newcomers doing LBOs who structured deals that used a postage stamp for equity and just barely covered interest payments," notes one Wall Street insider. "Their view was if the deal worked, they made oodles of money. If not, it was a wipeout with someone else's money. KKR's genius was recognizing that they couldn't lose money, or they wouldn't be able to raise [money for] another fund. They made handsome returns and rarely lost money." Kravis and Roberts took over KKR in 1987, after they and Kohlberg disagreed about several policy issues and Kohlberg, also beset by a benign brain tumor, resigned. Kravis, particularly, was also "insightful" with his institutional investors, the same insider notes: "His returns made them look very smart. He treated them well, wined and dined them, sent them to ski conferences and to his box at the opera and ball games. The perception was that Kravis was the gold standard and that they had a personal relationship with him. He was safe, and others less certain. He wrote the book on how to make investors happy."

In the ensuing LBO frenzy of the 1980s, KKR's hallmark became deals too big for others: Duracell and Motel 6; then $6.2 billion Beatrice Companies, its first hostile buyout; $4.4 billion for Safeway Stores; and then the famous megabillion-dollar battle for RJR Nabisco. By 1986 mergers and acquisition activity on Wall Street had hit record levels. It was a "casino society," remarked investment banker Felix Rohatyn of Lazard Frères, then one of Wall Street's celebrated private firms, with outposts in London and Paris.

Another new wrinkle—junk bonds—helped LBO returns soar, though Ted Forstmann, who claimed returns equal to or better than KKR, derided them as "wampum." The junk bond market was promoted by a then-unknown investment banker, Michael Milken, at Drexel Burnham Lambert, a second-tier investment bank that, because of Milken, would soon outperform many of its white-shoe competitors. Milken's key insight was that the low-grade debt of many companies with poor credit ratings was a good deal. He based his conclusion on an academic study of thousands of companies, which showed that firms with low-rated debt had gone into default only slightly more often than those with stronger balance sheets and rock-solid debt ratings.

Milken, who first made the Forbes 400 list in 1986 with $500 million, took this arcane form of financing and made it user-friendly. He stripped it of the usual covenants attached by insurance company lenders and sold the bonds to new buyers, such as newly deregulated savings and loan associations and high-flying investors. The appeal was obvious, so long as you could stomach the risk. Junk bond yields were 3 to 5 percent above Treasury and higher-rated corporate bonds.

At first Milken underwrote new junk bonds for companies too minor or unproven to issue investment-grade bonds,* such as the young telecommunications companies that were just starting to challenge AT&T's government-backed monopoly, and entrepreneurs shunned by Wall Street, including insurance company CEO Carl Lindner, the target of an SEC investigation in Cincinnati, and Victor Posner, a conglomerator with an unsavory reputation.†

---

*Typically, credit-rating agencies like Standard & Poor's (S&P) and Moody's assessed the financial strength of a company issuing debt. The debt of companies with the strongest financial position would be granted the highest credit rating—AA or AAA. In turn, the company would pay investors who bought the notes a lesser interest rate than on debt issued by companies with a lower credit rating.

†Carl Lindner signed consent decrees with the SEC for securities fraud and manipulation in 1976 and 1979. Victor Posner was convicted of tax fraud in 1987. He signed an SEC consent decree in the mid-1970s over charges that he looted the pension funds of Sharon Steel, a company he controlled.

Then, in 1984, Milken began using junk bonds to finance takeover bids. Until that time, the only way to get the funds for a takeover bid was to borrow. But banks did not lend quickly. LBOs weren't a good weapon, either, because the insurance companies and banks that lent for them were also slow to sign. Milken realized that he could replace the insurance companies' slice of funding in an LBO with junk bonds, which he could raise at a moment's notice from his investors. Much of the 1980s bull market is attributed to the Milken machine that bought and sold junk bonds for corporate takeovers. Without the hundreds of billions of dollars in these low-grade bonds that he and Drexel raised, the takeover boom might have been far smaller, and his raider clients such as Ronald Perelman, T. Boone Pickens, and Carl Icahn might never have landed on the Forbes 400.

"There was fear everywhere," remembers Leon Black, cohead of corporate finance at Drexel in the 1980s and now head of a major New York private equity firm (and number 160 on the Forbes 400 in 2006). "Every CEO was worried. They'd read the *Wall Street Journal* in the morning and learn that their company was under attack by some guy we'd financed for $10 billion that morning. Nobody felt safe." Black famously conceived the "highly confident" letter that Drexel gave raiders, essentially a pirate flag that told takeover targets the fearsome bank was backing them.

Carl Icahn, for example, a secretive former Wall Street stock arbitrageur and fiendish poker player, came out of nowhere to earn over $100 million from hostile purchases of stock in companies like Marshall Field's and over $500 million from Texaco, whose corporate boards paid him to go away—the greenmailing strategy. Not all of his deals prospered: His purchase of Trans World Airlines (TWA) in 1985 with excessive junk debt caused the airline to go bankrupt after he busted its union. Icahn landed on the Forbes 400 list in 1987 (net worth: $525 million).

Dallas-based oil tycoon T. Boone Pickens, another Drexel client, also came home rich from raiding. Arguing that he was increasing shareholders' value, he bought stock in Cities Services (Citgo). Then he earned $30 million selling his shares back after losing a hostile bid to buy the company, which was twenty times the size of his own Mesa Petroleum. Later he earned $760 million pre-tax for himself and his investors when his partial tender offer for Gulf Oil scared the company into the arms of Standard Oil of California.

By financing the takeover boom, Milken became the top banker in the country, and one of the richest. "Did you ever go to a specialist doctor who has ten cubicles and patients waiting in each? That was what it was like in Los

Angeles at Milken's office," says one Wall Street billionaire. "But in each cubicle, you had John Kluge, you had Rupert Murdoch, you had Ted Turner, you had Carl Icahn. Milken knew their companies as well as they did and had great ideas for them—that's why they were willing to be there at five a.m.! Then he'd go run a bond desk, where he sat in the middle of this *X* in a huge trading room, trading hundreds of billions of dollars. They went to him because he was creative, and he had the muscle in the financial markets to make things happen for them, which no one else was able to devise." As Milken once bragged to a colleague, "We're going to tee up GM, Ford, and IBM, and make them cringe."

However, even as Milken helped unleash a phenomenal restructuring of American business, all the LBO activity had a not-so-hidden downside. In a 1987 speech to KKR investors, the same year he resigned from the firm he founded, Kohlberg excoriated the "overweening, overpowering greed that pervades our business life. . . . We must all insist on ethical behavior, or we will kill the golden goose." Others in Congress, the SEC, and the business community, including investor Warren Buffett, were also sounding the alarm about the rising debt in corporate America from LBOs. Undeterred, Kravis and Roberts, using a mountain of junk bonds, offered $25 billion in 1988 for the Georgia-based food and tobacco giant RJR Nabisco. Wall Street rushed to finance the deal—the biggest in history. Drexel Burnham Lambert arranged a bridge loan for KKR after the SEC accused Drexel and Michael Milken of insider trading, stock manipulation, fraud, and other violations of the securities laws during previous takeover battles.

It was a surreal juncture, vividly recounted in *Barbarians at the Gate*. With the fate of the country's top banker the talk of the Street, four hundred revelers in evening dress gathered in the grand ballroom of the Pierre Hotel in New York City to celebrate the closing of the RJR Nabisco deal. Hosted by Kravis and Roberts, the party feted lawyers, investment bankers, accountants, the cream of Wall Street, who together had orchestrated the buyout with KKR. Dom Perignon champagne corks flew. A banquet of lobster, followed by veal with morel sauce, was crowned by an elaborate cake studded with candy replicas of Nabisco products like Oreo cookies. Opening the speeches, a lawyer exclaimed, "To think it only took a billion in fees to get us all together!" The ballroom roared: As was well-known on the Street, KKR alone earned $75 million for its investors from merger and acquisition fees. A group of banks that put together some of the financing divided $325 million.

In fact, the RJR deal turned out to be a near fiasco for KKR. During the fierce bidding war, they didn't examine RJR's books and overpaid. In 1990 KKR had to refinance the junk bonds in the LBO, and several years later spun off RJR's tobacco interest to shareholders. The iconic tale of 1980s greed finally ended in 2000, when Philip Morris bought Nabisco Holdings. Carl Icahn laughed loudest: After making his third unsuccessful bid for RJR Holdings, the company that owned 80 percent of the food group, he earned a $590 million profit selling his stock when Philip Morris bought the food group. "It's a pleasant way to lose," he said.

Milken pleaded guilty to six felonies in 1990, including conspiracy with Wall Street arbitrageur Ivan Boesky and numerous violations of securities laws. By the time he paid over $900 million in fines and entered federal prison in 1991, the junk bond market had collapsed and so had Drexel, undone by the damage to its reputation and capital. Milken was released on probation after serving twenty-two months in jail.

By then, some major LBOs, like UAL Corporation, the parent company of United Airlines, and West Point–Pepperell, funded with insupportable levels of junk bonds, also failed. The savings and loans industry, the principal buyers of junk, nearly crashed before a federal bailout cost taxpayers billions, and the country headed into a recession. About the only private equity funds able to raise new capital in the early 1990s were bankruptcy funds and junk bond critic Ted Forstmann.

Today Milken's spokesperson still tells journalists that he did nothing wrong in the 1980s; it's people's perceptions of him that are wrong. Certainly, without his financial skill, young companies—including many in telecommunications, such as MCI and McCaw, and cable television—might have had great difficulty raising the capital to survive and grow. But millions of small investors lost savings when other of his clients, such as Integrated Resources, which

---

1996

from the pages of *Forbes*

Larry Ellison of Oracle is buying a supersonic jet fighter: "Maybe I should fire a few Maverick missiles into [Bill Gates's] living room." (1996 net worth: $6 billion)

Ebullient **Steven Ballmer,** Bill Gates's right-hand man at Microsoft, blew out his vocal chords at a company meeting in 1991. (1996 net worth: $3.7 billion)

Theodore Waitt once appeared in one of his Gateway company ads as a ponytailed janitor. (1996 net worth: $1.7 billion)

Stuart Robert Levine, whose fortune comes from technology, was voted least likely to succeed in high school. (1996 net worth: $830 million)

The Greatest Investor of All Time

He's the most storied investor in the world—someone who did not make or sell anything, but instead got rich solely by buying stocks. To some, Warren Edward Buffett is the greatest investor in history.

Modest and arrogant at once, Buffett has made immense wealth for many, mainly the hundreds of thousands of shareholders of his conglomerate, $82 billion Berkshire Hathaway of Omaha, Nebraska. A number of early investors in Berkshire Hathaway are also on the Forbes 400 list (see "The Berkshire Hathaway Bunch," page 196). Ten thousand dollars invested in Berkshire Hathaway about thirty years ago would be worth $15.9 million in early 2007. The same amount invested in the S&P, with dividends reinvested, would have netted only $328,400. "If I wanted to," he once said, "I could hire 10,000 people to do nothing but paint my picture every day for the rest of my life. And the GNP would go up."

Buffett bought his first stock at age eleven. In the 1950s, after graduating from the University of Nebraska, he studied under investment guru Benjamin Graham, the father of value investing, at Columbia University. Graham's basic argument was that you could get wealthy if you studied companies exhaustively, because some were bound to be trading at prices below their real value.

Buffett started out in 1965 buying his first dog—a textile company with two mills that made the linings of men's suits and handkerchiefs in New Bedford, Massachusetts. It had not showed a profit in a decade. But it had major tax-loss carryforwards. Buffett sold most of its assets; in 1967 he merged it with two insurance companies in his native Nebraska. Why? He was after the float from the sale every year of new insurance policies. He invested most of that float—the reserve insurance companies must keep on hand to meet future liabilities—of $20 million in several stocks to hold indefinitely. Buffett didn't borrow against the float for acquisitions; instead, he searched the market for reputable, underpriced companies and used it to buy them outright or take controlling positions in their stocks when they were very cheap.

A few brand-name, consumer-product companies with good records, such as American Express, Gillette, and Coca-Cola (the biggest earner in his portfolio for many years), caught Buffett's eye. He held these through bull and bear markets. But he also keeps a portfolio of disparate, more prosaic companies, including candy, jewelry, and underwear manufacturers. He trades commodities and arbitrages takeover deals, too.

His commodity trading and arbitrage deals became more prominent after 1996, when he bought 100 percent of car insurer Geico and loaded up on commodities such as crude oil and silver. He added many more companies (some private, including Executive Jet, which he bought in 1998 for $725 million) and rode the fad among the rich to own private planes. By 2005 Berkshire Hathaway owned more than sixty-five businesses, but still was mostly an insurer, with a $49 billion float to invest. Its book value has grown 21.5 percent a year, compounded, since 1965.

Not that Buffett doesn't have his share of horror stories. Three episodes might have hurt him badly. The first came in 1954, when his net worth was about $54,000, and he was nailed in a short squeeze, an unexpected surge in the price of a stock he'd shorted that could have cost him all his money. He escaped—barely. Then he discovered a huge fraud in his insurance operations in the early 1970s. Fortunately, it wasn't as bad as it first looked. Most recently, in 2005, his largest insurance business, General Re, which insures other insurers, was devastated by claims from three hurricanes and was also hurt by continuing fallout from investigations into fraudulent sales of insurance to American Insurance Group (AIG).

Throughout it all, the Oracle of Omaha stayed cool, avoided companies that he didn't understand, and paid a dividend only once. Derided in the late 1990s for not buying dot-coms and tech companies, he was then canonized when many crashed in 2000. Wall Street is home to shysters and advisors who distract investors from the real gems in the market, Buffett believes. He sees himself instead as the honest investor: plain-spoken, thrifty, and witty, an American everyman who drives his own car (his license plate: THRIFTY). Except, of course, that his every utterance makes news and he is the second-richest person in the country (2006 net worth: $46 billion), almost all of that money from Berkshire Hathaway stock. He has beaten the S&P index every year except six.

Interestingly, Buffett champions inheritance taxes. The gap between people like him and the average Joe pains him: "There is class war all right, but it's my class, the rich class, that's making war, and we're winning," he has said. Perhaps to balance this social inequality, Buffett, like Andrew Carnegie before him, is giving away almost all his fortune.

sold tax-shelter partnerships, and Columbia Savings and Loan, folded or went into receivership. Some in the financial world still regard him as a genius; John Steel Gordon, a prominent business historian and author of a book on Wall Street, for example, suggests that government prosecutors were overzealous in prosecuting Milken. Milken has been barred from the securities business for life, but still wields influence. Number 153 on the Forbes 400 list with a $2.1 billion fortune (as of 2006), he funds an economic think tank as well as research about prostate cancer, the disease he was diagnosed with in 1993 just before his prison term ended.

Certainly, Jerome Kohlberg, the man who let loose the LBO genie, did not foresee that it would become one of the great engines of wealth creation in the last quarter of the twentieth century. LBOs lost favor in the 1990s, during the wave of mergers between tech companies for stock, but roared back after 2000. Kohlberg now admits he "used to feel a little guilty" at how his idea, which he saw as a service to family companies whose owners needed cash, helped drive the roaring 1980s bull market.

While LBOs and junk bonds created many of the vast Forbes 400 financial fortunes of the last quarter century, another way of financing companies— venture capital—also flourished. But with venture capital, which also originated on Wall Street but was mostly practiced elsewhere, the story is quite different. Only a few VCs have amassed enough wealth to find a spot on the Forbes 400 list. Arguably, however, their national influence has been disproportionate to their numbers: They have underwritten the development of giant new sectors in the economy, expanded employment by the tens of millions, and made their investors and themselves rich, albeit sometimes more slowly.

As general partners of a venture capital fund, VCs take about 1.4 percent of committed capital a year as a salary but often wait a decade to share in the profits, until one of the companies they have seeded has an initial public offering of stock. At that point, 20 to 30 percent of any profit is theirs, slightly more than that claimed by private equity firms. However, by the nature of the business, venture capitalists are wrong more often than right. Most of the companies they finance fail, and when that happens, the founders wind up with empty pockets and employees lose their jobs. Or companies that survive long enough to go public often see huge run-ups in their stocks in initial public offerings only to suffer later, as happened so dramatically in 2000, when tech stocks crashed. Since 1986 the average return in venture capital has been slightly higher than LBOs, about 15 to 20 percent a year. It's the few companies that go like gangbusters that create great wealth.

The early venture capitalists were mostly private East Coast financiers, such as John "Jock" Hay Whitney, the publisher of the *New York Herald Tribune;* the Rockefeller family; and a Harvard business school professor, General Georges Doriot, who earned a 101 percent annualized return on investment when his company took Digital Equipment Corporation public in 1968. These men bankrolled new companies like Eastern Airlines and Minute Maid. But the term *VC* didn't exist until it was invented by Wall Street investment banker Arthur Rock. His instincts for picking creative people who could turn brilliant ideas into businesses led to an extraordinary string of hits, such as Scientific Data Systems, Teledyne, Intel, and Apple Computer.

Rock, now an octogenarian (2005 net worth: $1 billion), says Intel, the semiconductor manufacturer, was the only company he was 100 percent sure would make it. Gordon Moore and Robert Noyce, also members of the Forbes 400, had founded an earlier company, Fairchild Semiconductor, which was the birthplace of the integrated circuit, with venture capital Rock arranged while he was employed by a Wall Street firm. Moore and Noyce's work in silicon transistors at Fairchild impressed Rock so much that when the pair decided to go into business for themselves in 1967, he raised $2.5 million in an afternoon. He put in $10,000 of his own funds and received founder's stock as Intel's first investor. He also wrote its first business plan, chaired its board, and batted around all the early decisions with Noyce and Moore, as well as invested another $300,000 in an early financing. In 2001 his Intel stake was worth more than $500 million.

Both Intel and Apple were huge winners for Rock, but Intel is "where Arthur made much of his money," says Dick Kramlich, Rock's former partner, who runs New Enterprise Associates and is a former president of the National Venture Capital Association. "It sort of dwarfed everything else, no matter how good they were." Rock had the VC gene, Kramlich adds: "Instinct, the ability to work with people to achieve unusual goals, and knowledge of developments converging in a field, and the timing of those trends. And how to build markets. They don't exist when a company starts out." And, he might have added, discretion. A shy and intimidatingly quiet man, Rock typically did just three or four deals a year. He had only two general partners in his business career.

As with LBOs, success bred imitation. The boom years in the 1980s for

venture capital attracted a host of new firms in the 1990s, which in turn fun-
neled hundreds of millions of dollars into start-ups that capitalized on new
technology, everything from biotech to the Internet. Lured by the prospect of
huge returns, many young dot-coms went public before achieving any profits. Nevertheless, their stocks soared. Venture capitalists, whose returns are
calculated based on the stock price rather than on operating profits, were
earning returns of 20 percent or more in less than a year. And as long as the
market went up, they got very rich.

One who promoted the Internet and scored big is John Doerr (2006 net
worth: $1 billion), a partner in the Silicon Valley VC powerhouse Kleiner
Perkins Caufield & Byers. Cofounded by Forbes 400 member Eugene Kleiner,
one of the scientists Arthur Rock funded to create Fairchild Semiconductor,
the private partnership dominates its field. Doerr, an electrical engineer from
St. Louis, has been lauded for backing Netscape, Excite, and that onetime darling of the Internet revolution, Amazon.com. KPCB was a founding investor
in Amazon and reaped a return of 55,000 percent at the stock's peak in
December 1999. It is the great Google growth machine, however, that has
made Doerr's fortune. KPCB's original $12.5 million investment in the Inter-
net search giant was worth $1.6 billion in 2006.

But why rest on past laurels? Today Doerr has raised funds to invest heavily in the areas of the economy most affected by the weather—companies and
industries that account for one-third of the U.S. gross domestic product.
With worldwide growth increasing demand for raw materials and energy, the
race is on for new forms of fuel that will reduce global warming. Doerr is
championing green fuels and "clean" technology, such as solar cells and air
and water purification, presently a field all the rage in venture capital. "Green
tech," he believes, "could be the largest economic opportunity of the twenty-
first century."

Doerr has plenty of company. Vinod Khosla, another Fortune 400 member, cofounder of Sun Microsystems and a KPCB alum, is investing tens of
millions of dollars from his private fortune in the new field. "Energy is
subject to the same sort of scientific breakthroughs, innovation, and entrepreneurial efforts that have characterized Silicon Valley's impact in micro-
processors, PCs, biotechnology, telecommunications, and the Internet," he
told *Time* magazine. "There is zero question in my mind we can replace all
the petroleum used in cars." Khosla, Bill Gates, and Sir Richard Branson of
Virgin Airways are building refineries to wring oil from corn. Khosla's portfolio of twenty-four clean tech start-ups also includes companies experiment-

ing with fuel from waste cellulose and electricity from solar thermal sources: For example, Range Fuels of Colorado, which he founded, plans to turn wood chips, agricultural waste, municipal sewage, and pig manure into ethanol. "I'm going after green and 'cheaper than fossil' technologies," Khosla argues from his Menlo Park, California, office, "because it's the only way to solve the scale problem and to attract the hundreds of billions—or even trillions—of dollars necessary to make a difference in global warming." Biofuels could be a $50 billion market by 2015 and could retool Detroit, some predict. In 2006 VCs poured $727 million into thirty-nine alternative energy start-ups, according to the National Venture Capital Association. Optimism, every VCs's fuel, is never in short supply.

But of all the Forbes 400 financial fortunes minted in the past quarter century, hedge funds have created the largest ones the fastest. These vast pools of unregulated capital are open only to investors worth $2.5 million and up. In 2006 more than eight thousand funds managed $1 trillion in assets—and they bore little resemblance to the original concept of a hedge fund, a conservative investment vehicle intended to protect investors from the ups and downs of the stock market. Indeed, one of the ironies of hedge funds these days is that few are actually involved in hedging at all. Compared with either LBOs or venture capital, which usually invests in companies for at least six months, the hedge fund impulse is more ruthless: Fast in, fast out, make a killing.

Throughout history, most investors have held investments such as objects or paintings or financial instruments long-term while they appreciated in value. In 1949 *Fortune* editor and sociologist Alfred Winslow Jones wrote a story setting forth his idea that investors could achieve higher returns if they hedged their positions. Jones bought undervalued stocks to hold until they rose (going long) and overvalued stocks to hold until they declined (going short). The hedge was covering his long positions with his shorts: In other words, he was insulating himself against the market's ups and downs because he profited no matter which direction it went. For his investment efforts and expertise, he paid himself a small management fee, typically 1 percent of the fund's assets, and 20 percent of profits every year.

Jones's idea proved to be brilliant. Between 1962 and 1966 he outperformed the top mutual funds by over 85 percent after fees. Investors plunged into hedge funds, and investment managers were only too happy to oblige: With the incentive fees, they could earn ten to twenty times more than they could running a mutual fund. Investors didn't balk as long as they earned outsize returns. But by the late 1960s many hedge funds collapsed, the victims of strategies that didn't work, and the idea lost favor.

Until, that is, George Soros appeared on the scene. Eerily analytical and detached, and imperious in personality, Soros (2006 estimated net worth: $8.5 billion) was a natural global speculator who scoured the world for opportunities, placing enormous bets—the largest of their kind—on where currencies and interest rates were headed, seeking to outperform the markets and win fantastic sums. In 1969, at age thirty-nine, he opened a secretive off-shore hedge fund called Quantum with then partner Jim Rogers.* By 1986 Soros had accumulated a large enough fortune ($200 million) to appear on the Forbes 400 list.

Soros's investment strategy was based on acceptance of chaos in the markets and their inefficiency, a contrarian thesis. Since the markets constantly misvalued securities, smart investors just had to find the errors. Soros made his investment judgments without any analytical materials from Wall Street. Instead, he relied on his own investment savvy, garnered from newspapers and an army of paid informants around the globe who worked in central banks and on trading desks. Charges of insider trading have dogged him.† In 1992 he became infamous when he shorted the British pound, betting that its value would drop. The pound was part of the European currency peg, which obliged Common Market countries to value their currencies within close reach of one another. The British government tried to prop up the pound to keep it near the stronger German mark, buying it heavily and raising interest rates despite high unemployment—to no avail. Britain was forced to withdraw from the European Exchange Rate Mechanism (ERM), the pound plunged, and Soros's $20 billion hedge—the idea of his chief investment officer, Stanley Druckenmiller—made him $1 to $2 billion. But it also earned Soros notoriety for "breaking the Bank of England." He sometimes couldn't walk from the stress such huge and highly leveraged risks caused, Soros confessed to *The New Yorker* in 2004.

In another gamble, he lost $2 billion in equity investments in Russia when the ruble unexpectedly collapsed in August 1998. Nonetheless, though similar losses in Russia's long-term debt crash bankrupted a famous rival, Long-Term

---

*Rogers, who went on to establish the Rogers International Commodity Index (RICI)—one of the best-performing indexes worldwide—left in 1980.

†In 1977 he signed a consent decree, neither admitting nor denying SEC charges of stock manipulation. He is appealing a conviction in France on insider-trading charges.

194 All the Money in the World

Capital Management (whose two Nobel Prize–winning economists believed they had a foolproof way to make money), Russian bear Soros managed to finish the year up 12 percent for his investors. "I don't play the game by a particular set of rules; I look for changes in the rules of the game," Soros once said. "If you are right in a position, you can never be big enough."

But in 2000 Soros's dazzling run ended, broken by Druckenmiller's decision to buy tech stocks the year before. Soros Fund Management lost $600 million when the tech bubble burst. It was Soros's second down year since 1969—an incredible record. Closing his Quantum Fund, Soros wrote investors: "During its 31½-year history, Quantum provided its shareholders with an annual return in excess of 30 percent. An investment of $100,000 in the fund at its inception would be worth $420 million today." Today Soros's two sons from his first marriage run his new funds, while Soros himself concentrates on influencing international political and environmental issues. With an estimated $8.5 billion, Soros ranked twenty-seventh on the Forbes 400 list in 2006. Stanley Druckenmiller now runs his own fund; his net worth is estimated at $2 billion on the 2006 list.

Julian Robertson's (net worth: $1.7 billion at his peak in 1998 and 1999) road to riches was similarly rooted in global opportunities. But while Soros placed bets on currencies and interest rates, Robertson searched the globe for undervalued companies and for years had a Midas touch in finding them. His mantra was simple enough: "Long the best stocks and short the worst," meaning he would invest in tried-and-true companies and stay away from ones he judged too risky, often new technologies.

A North Carolina native with a military bearing and a short fuse, Robertson founded Tiger Management in 1980 after bailing from Wall Street investment bank Kidder Peabody. The "hedge fund setup" appealed to him, he says, because "it is the best way to compensate a manager for his expertise." A contrarian, Robertson invested early in Japan and Korea in the 1980s. He scored big betting on a fall in the stocks of the Japanese banks before the Nikkei index crashed in 1990. Later he bobbed in and out of Asian currencies, shorting the yen (and sometimes losing a ton on dollar-yen trades) and going long in the Korean and Hong Kong stock markets. Citibank was another signature trade. He bought at $10 in 1990, when the bank looked like it would go under. The stock rose to $20, and his traders wanted out. Robertson instead doubled up, saying that at $20 it was cheaper than at $10. Citibank, he reckoned, had resolved the problems it had in real estate when he first bought in. As the stock climbed, his analysts again begged him to sell. He kept buying, past $60. It finally reached $100 a share after splits, according to *Inside the House of Money: Top Hedge Fund Traders on Profiting in the Global Markets*, Steven Drobny's insightful book of interviews with hedge fund managers. A huge bet on United Airlines was another winner, yielding "tens of millions" in profits, Robertson recalls.

At Tiger, Robertson alone decided positions: Everyone else was an analyst. He started trading commodities in the early 1990s, making a long bet on palladium, used in jewelry and in catalytic converters on combustion engines. "Are we right about this situation? If so, we should be bigger," he'd demand. He sent one trader to the northern Siberian mines, which produce most of the world's supply, to determine the extent of the chronic global shortage of the metal. The trader returned convinced the shortage was real, and Robertson's fund maintained its position through several years of losses. "He had a high tolerance for pain," a former trader remembers. When palladium soared from $180 to $800 an ounce between January 1995 and April 2000, Tiger reaped a windfall. But after a twenty-year magic-carpet ride, Robertson, like Soros, crashed in the 2000 tech carnage. Shorting the new economy during the Internet boom was a "recipe for bankruptcy, because the worst stocks were rising," he has said ruefully. "I should have stopped earlier." He started closing his funds in 2000. "Some investors probably got 1,000 to 1. Others got a loss," he says. Even so, he ended up with plenty in his own bank account. In 2007, in his mid-seventies, he manages only his own money, an estimated $1 billion. He's seeded twenty-five new hedge funds, which he says manage $13 billion in assets and are headquartered in his glass-walled Park Avenue offices. Still an investing legend, he helps underwrite public policy forays, such as Clinton's Global Warming Initiative and the campaign for California's 2002 zero emission laws. He also imports wines from his estates in New Zealand, where he lives four months of the year.

If nothing else, financiers are ingenious at recycling capital. Out of the busts of the early twenty-first century, even greater Forbes 400 fortunes have arisen. The successors to Soros and Robertson are a close-knit, secretive group of men in their thirties, forties, and fifties who often run funds half the size of their predecessors, but with more diverse strategies that also get outsize returns. These days most of the largest hedge funds are operated by Wall Street investment banks like Goldman Sachs and JPMorgan Chase & Company: 80 percent of the over $1 trillion under management is invested in the

The Berkshire Hathaway Bunch

If only you had invested in Berkshire Hathaway when Warren Buffett was starting out. Among those who did buy in early and stuck with him along the way, earning themselves a place on the 400 list:

Charles T. Munger: Omaha native and Buffett's alter ego, Munger has been with Buffett for forty years. Vice chairman of Berkshire Hathaway, Munger is an acerbic lawyer who graduated from Harvard Law School without a bachelor's degree. His $1.6 billion fortune is mostly in Berkshire stock. "We tap dance to work," Buffett says.

Alfond family: Harold Alfond and family sold Dexter Shoe Company to Berkshire in the early 1990s for 25,203 shares of Berkshire Hathaway. The family was worth $632 million in 1992, according to *Forbes*.

Franklin Otis Booth Jr.: A meeting with Warren Buffett in 1963 set up by Charles Munger produced a $1 million investment in Berkshire Hathaway that was worth $1.6 billion in 2006. Booth is the great-grandson of *Los Angeles Times Mirror* founder Harrison Gray Otis.

Chace family: Founders of the Berkshire textile mill in Providence, Rhode Island, in 1806. Their descendants sold to Buffett in the 1960s, but Malcolm G. Chace, the chairman, held on to his shares—making his children very wealthy. His heir, Malcolm "Kim" Chace III, and family, ranked 209 on the Forbes 400 in 2002, with $1 billion in assets.

David Gottesman: Ranking 117 on the Forbes 400 in 2006 (net worth: $2.5 billion), Gottesman was an early investor in Berkshire Hathaway because he was a believer in Benjamin Graham, Buffett's investing mentor. He founded the investment advisory firm First Manhattan Company in New York.

Albert Lee Ueltschi: A pilot and associate of Charles Lindbergh, he ranked 258 on the Forbes 400 in 2005 with $1.3 billion. He received 16,256 shares in Berkshire Hathaway in exchange for his pilot training school, Flight Safety International.

top one hundred funds. Still, Soros's and Robertson's successors have had some of the most spectacular returns of them all.

Consider, for example, Edward S. Lampert, a dapper forty-five-year-old based in Greenwich, Connecticut, who runs one of the biggest hedge funds outside of Wall Street. Lampert is frequently compared to Warren Buffett, his investing model. Since forming ESL Investments in 1988, after leaving Goldman Sachs at the youthful age of twenty-six, Lampert has largely traded undervalued stocks, such as IBM and Wells Fargo. The rise in value of Auto-Nation, a national car dealership, and AutoZone, a car-parts retailer, which tripled and quadrupled, respectively, after he bought big stakes in them, made him a billionaire.

"For Lampert, investing is all about figuring out the way the world works," says Michael Peltz, executive editor of *Institutional Investor*. "An avid reader of nonfiction, he likes companies that have long histories, because with those histories comes the ability to see how businesses have performed in good times and bad. Like Buffett, Lampert looks for undervalued companies with strong potential cash flow whose businesses can be improved. Studying history helps him identify them."

Recently, as hedge funds, private equity, and venture capital have all begun to invest in companies and lend money to start-up companies, thereby coming closer and closer together, Lampert has changed his strategy. In 2003 he shocked the Street by buying Sears for $11 billion and merging it with another tired retailer, Kmart, which he'd recapitalized and taken public. Where other investors saw nothing but down-at-the-heels merchants far behind the fashion curve, Lampert saw stores sitting on valuable real estate. Now he chairs Sears Holdings and helps make its marketing decisions, too. But does the improved profitability of Sears reflect Lampert's success as a retailer? Not at all, argues *Washington Post* business columnist Steven Pearlstein. "Eddie Lampert has not turned around Sears and Kmart, just as he did not turn around AutoZone for the long run," Pearlstein writes. "He cut costs, reduced service, disinvested and got a few good years of operating results out of it. And why should we be surprised? He is not an experienced operator—he's a financial engineer, and a damn good one. Eddie Lampert may fancy himself as the next Warren Buffett, but he's got a long way to go to prove it. . . . So far, all he is is a Wall Street sharpie along the lines of Carl Icahn."

Maybe so, but a very rich one. Lampert (number 67 on the 2006 Forbes list, with a net worth of $3.8 billion) earned $1.3 billion in 2006 and claims a

28 percent average return, compounded since 1988, according to *Institutional Investor,* which is slightly more than Buffett's in Berkshire Hathaway.

Paul Tudor Jones II (or PTJ, as he is known in financial circles) operates another of the largest hedge funds outside Wall Street, also located in Greenwich. The son of a Memphis lawyer, Jones made his first fortune trading cotton on Wall Street. In his second career, running the hedge funds managed by Tudor Investment Corporation—the TBBI Global Fund and the Tudor Futures Fund—Jones has never had a down year. His best years have been in bear markets. In 1987, for example, when the market crashed, he pulled out a 200 percent return. On average, his TBBI Global Fund has returned 24 percent compounded since 1986 to investors, mostly because "he avoids the train wreck," notes Tiger Williams of Williams Trading, a financial services company that trades for a select group of hedge funds. "He's willing to incur lots of itsy, bitty little losses. Soros was very good at admitting when he was wrong, but Jones was probably quicker to say, 'Let's get out before we have a big loss.'"

"Thrashing through a lot of trades and taking tiny margins is not unusual," says the head of a company with whom Jones does business, "but it's hard to be very good at, which he is. If you are taking small losses and small wins, you have to be right more often than wrong, and because the markets are very efficient, that's difficult." Jones used to do big trades wearing Bruce Willis's red sneakers from *Die Hard;* now he mostly concentrates on management. (His funds charge hefty management fees—4 percent plus 22 percent of profits over certain benchmarks for one fund, for example.) He avoids interviews and the limelight, though he does allow that neighborly peek at the Christmas lights on his mansion each year. He cofounded the Robin Hood Foundation, one of the hedge funders' charities of choice, which supports innovative schools in New York City's poorest neighborhoods.

1997

from the pages of *Forbes*

Warren Buffett, fabled investor, completes his own tax returns. (1997 net worth: $21 billion)

David Duffield is a member of his PeopleSoft company's rock band, the Raving Daves. (1997 net worth: $1.7 billion)

Charles Wang of Computer Associates wrote a cookbook entitled *Wok Like a Man.* (1997 net worth: $1.1 billion)

Charles Butt, a historic preservationist whose money comes from high-end grocery stores, set up his company headquarters in a restored Civil War–era arsenal in San Antonio. (1997 family net worth: $900 million)

Down the seemingly gold-paved streets of Greenwich, neighbor Steven A. Cohen charges the biggest fees in the business: up to 50 percent of the profits from his fund, SAC Capital Advisors, along with a 1 to 3 percent management fee. A tape trader, he trades three hundred stocks a day, glued to the screen of his twenty-thousand-square-foot trading room in nearby Stamford, watching for anomalies in stock prices or mispricings between stocks. He's the best on earth at tape trading, some say. He learned it as a teenager, chilling out at a local brokerage firm on Long Island after school, watching the ticker tape for hours to discern patterns. Cohen also owns large stakes in public companies. On the Street, he's often been accused of "front-running," buying big blocks of stock that traders whisper his rivals or mutual funds are about to buy and then selling them back at higher prices. In 2006 a Canadian drugmaker, Biovail Corporation, sued Cohen and his hedge fund for orchestrating a massive "bear raid" on its stock to benefit his short position—that is, trying to depress its share price through market manipulation. In the case of Biovail, Cohen was accused of paying stock analysts in Arizona to write negative reports on the company. He denies the charges.

His strategies and tactics have, however, netted Cohen some mammoth rewards. *Forbes* estimated his fortune at $1 billion in 2003, his first year on the list. Last year it stood at $3 billion. He throws a lot of these winnings at art: $137.5 million for *Woman III* by Willem de Kooning, for example. His collection, whose value is estimated at $700 million, boasts an Édouard Manet and a Jackson Pollock, as well as Damien Hirst's famous shark pickled in formaldehyde, which he won at an auction in 2005 for $12 million. Apparently, Cohen's artistic tastes are as catholic as his appetite for stocks. His home is a fourteen-acre walled estate, for which he paid $15 million in cash. It has an outdoor ice-skating rink, a basketball court, an indoor pool, a twenty-seat movie theater, a two-hole golf course, and formal gardens.

With many hedge fund fees sometimes exceeding returns to investors, controversy about the power, secrecy, and reputed insider trading of the funds is increasing. Because most no longer just take long and short positions in stocks, but invest in anything and everything—real estate, private equity, Hollywood movies, corporate lending, distressed corporate debt, derivatives in energy, shipping, or the weather, "they are having an impact all over the U.S. economy," notes John Coffee, a professor at Columbia University Law School and an expert on white-collar crime. "They're probably the principal short-sellers and activists operating in the markets today." Their dominance means that they can have a powerful impact on the daily price movements of stock. "Hedge funds are capable of trying to manipulate a stock because they are usually ahead of the market, and they are interested in pushing stocks up or down," Coffee continues. "Is that illegal? Maybe—if you can prove that what they are doing is manipulative, but that's very hard to prove." While recognizing the benefits of hedge funds, corporate law professor David Skeel is also worried: "Hedge funds have done fabulously well for their investors by manipulating shareholder votes, cornering the market for U.S. Treasury notes, controlling the debt of companies in bankruptcies, or illegally buying and selling stakes inside the cover of mutual funds after the close of trading. But they have been cheating the rest of us, and it could get worse," he says.

There are also pressures from within. Once, says Bruce Kovner, who runs Caxton Associates—which, with a value of $15 billion, is one of the biggest hedge funds—annual gross returns ran as high as 40 percent. Now Caxton's performance results are lower than half of that. "We had so few rivals," says Kovner. "Now we have eight thousand rivals, and we have to reinvent ourselves." Average returns in the field are now often no better than the S&P 500. Still, money from pension funds, university endowments, and wealthy investors continues to pour into the crowded field. McKinsey & Company, the consulting firm, predicted in an influential 2006 report that investors' dissatisfaction with high fees for mediocre returns will stop the funds' proliferation and force mediocre managers to seek the next big thing.

Indeed, the ground is already shifting—providing fertile fields, perhaps, for another bumper crop of Forbes 400 fortunes. Wall Street is witnessing another boom in private equity. Veteran buyout companies such as Kohlberg Kravis Roberts & Company, the Blackstone Group, and Apollo Management are enjoying unprecedented liquidity. Private equity firms can afford to spend $1.6 trillion on acquisitions in the next several years, according to one published calculation, taking into account the money raised and the amount of debt that can be leveraged against it. The 1980s are no longer the golden age of the LBO; in fact, fifteen of the world's twenty largest leveraged buyouts occurred in an eighteen-month period beginning in the second half of 2005. And the new private equity boom is fattening the pockets of many of its veteran practitioners: The fortune of Blackstone's Stephen Schwarzman, for example, increased by $1 billion from 2005 to 2006, and is likely to soar much higher after a planned public offering in 2007.

"Private equity is a huge force—nothing is out of range for it. *Nothing,*" says venture capitalist Dick Kramlich. But the newly minted financiers, ensconced in their Park Avenue triplexes and Greenwich mansions, would do well to bear in mind the admonition of Henry Kravis, delivered in an early 2007 interview with the *Wall Street Journal:* "Any fool can buy a company," he says. "You should only be congratulated when you sell."

Kravis, who engineered the RJR Nabisco debacle, should know.

PART THREE

Spending It

9

Conspicuous Consumption

The Hamptons, particularly Southampton and East Hampton, on New York's Long Island have long been summer refuges for the elite, who vacation among the farmers' fields and pine forests that lie just a stone's throw from idyllic white sandy beaches (and within a couple hours' drive, traffic permitting, of Manhattan). Formerly a center of potato farming, the area is among America's richest, attracting temporary residents that include Forbes 400 members Ronald Lauder, Steven Spielberg, Ronald Perelman, David Geffen, Mort Zuckerman, Carl Icahn, and Leon Black, to name but a few. The average cost of a home in the Hamptons in 2005 was $1 million, more than three times the national average of $300,000. In 2005 pharmaceuticals tycoon Stewart Rahr bought a twenty-five-room mansion in East Hampton for $45 million. That same year, Seagram heir Edgar Bronfman Jr. bought an estate and adjacent grounds in Bridgehampton for $31 million. With the popularity of the area soaring, its permanent and seasonal inhabitants have grown used to the massive mansions that sprout up beside roadside farm stands. But nothing prepared the residents of the hamlet of Sagaponack, between Bridgehampton and East Hampton, for billionaire industrialist Ira Rennert's enormous home—the incongruously named Fair Field.

The drive to Sagaponack (population about five hundred) takes the visitor past the manicured homes and lawns of Bridgehampton and out among gently rolling hillsides. The first hint of Rennert's home comes about a half mile away, as a cluster of chimney stacks that rise among the low-lying hills. Rennert made his fortune with polluting steel mills, lead mines, coal mines, and a plant that extracts magnesium from Utah's Great Salt Lake. In the mid-1990s this plant, the Magnesium Corporation of America, was the single biggest polluter in the state. Employees were bused to work because chlorine fumes from the plant stripped the paint from vehicles left in the parking lot. In 1992 Rennert bought then bankrupt AM General, the maker of the Humvee, and transformed a troop carrier into the Hummer—the macho vehicle of choice for Arnold Schwarzenegger and other boldface names of the 1990s.

In many ways, Fair Field is the Humvee home of the Hamptons. The centerpiece of the five-building compound, which sits on sixty-three acres of beachfront property, is a sixty-six-thousand-square-foot Italianate mansion with twenty-nine bedrooms, whose interior is said to be decorated in Italian marble, murals, and gold. The estate is supplied with energy from its own on-site power plant. One side of the compound is visible from a bumpy, pothole-strewn access road called Peter's Pond Lane, which leads to a local beach. From here, the neoclassical buildings, with their stucco walls and regal balconies, are visible in all their imposing glory. It's as if a gargantuan villa had been ripped from an Amalfi Coast hillside and plunked down in the Hamptons. Rennert's compound includes three swimming pools, a two-lane bowling alley, and a 164-seat movie theater. The estate is valued at $185 million.

Fair Field did not rise without a protest. In 1998 Rennert tried to push the plans past his well-heeled neighbors by filing them in the dead of winter, when most of the area's summer residents are living in the city. A group of neighbors raised the alarm, and then a fighting fund, to halt the plans. They filed a lawsuit to stop the town from issuing a building permit, but the suit failed. Neighbors have called the house "arrogant" and "an elephant in our living room." The writer Kurt Vonnegut even threatened to move out of his nearby home if Fair Field was built.

As Ira Rennert's villa by the sea signals, the past two decades have been an era of

1998

from the pages of *Forbes*

Kirk Kekorian, whose fortune comes from investments and casinos, made $660 million in 6.5 hours on May 6, the day Chrysler announced plans to merge with Daimler-Benz. (1998 net worth: $5 billion)

Investor and art lover **Eli Broad** bought a Roy Lichtenstein painting for $2.5 million—with his American Express card. (1998 net worth: $2.7 billion)

Bernard Marcus, cofounder of Home Depot, keeps a framed copy of an early, skeptical *Forbes* story as a memento on his bathroom wall. (1998 net worth: $1.8 billion)

Carl Icahn, one of the toughest of all Wall Street raiders, started his career with $4,000 in army poker winnings. (1998 net worth: $2.6 billion)

The high (and low) cost of living well

Since the 1970s, Forbes has been calculating what it calls the CLEWI — the Cost of Living Extremely Well Index. While the consumer price index (CPI), which roughly measures the increase in the cost of living for more average Americans, has doubled since 1982, the CLEWI has almost quadrupled. But have the wallets of the rich been hurt? Hardly. As the dotted line indicates, the very rich have gotten much, much richer over the same period—by a factor of ten, in fact. So these days the 400 are spending a much smaller percentage of their wealth living extremely well than a quarter of a century ago.

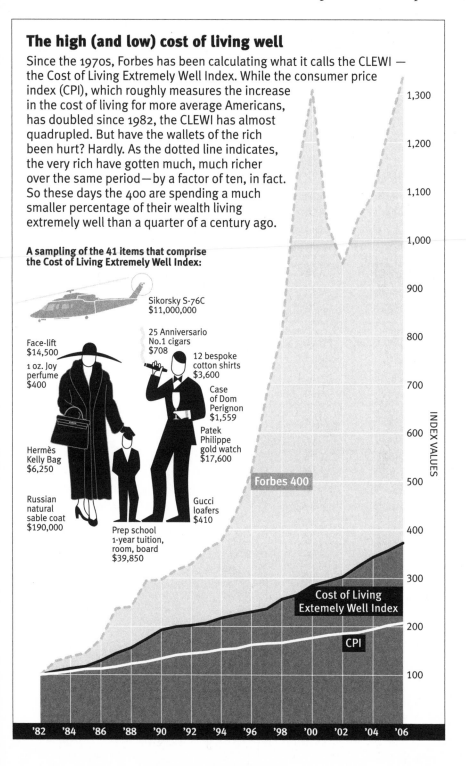

A sampling of the 41 items that comprise the Cost of Living Extremely Well Index:

Sikorsky S-76C
$11,000,000

Face-lift
$14,500

1 oz. Joy
perfume
$400

25 Anniversario
No.1 cigars
$708

12 bespoke
cotton shirts
$3,600

Case
of Dom
Perignon
$1,559

Patek
Philippe
gold watch
$17,600

Hermès
Kelly Bag
$6,250

Russian
natural
sable coat
$190,000

Gucci
loafers
$410

Prep school
1-year tuition,
room, board
$39,850

Forbes 400

Cost of Living
Extemely Well Index

CPI

INDEX VALUES

1,300
1,200
1,100
1,000
900
800
700
600
500
400
300
200
100

'82 '84 '86 '88 '90 '92 '94 '96 '98 '00 '02 '04 '06

Everyday essentials for the modern billionaire

How much does it take for modern multimillionaires to keep up their lifestyle? To find out, Forbes compiles its annual Cost of Living Extremely Well Index (CLEWI). Listed here are items and prices from 2006. To see how the CLEWI compares to the increases in the Consumer Price Index (CPI) and the overall total wealth of the Forbes 400, see the chart on page 207.

Coat: Natural Russian sable, Maximilian at Bloomingdale's	$190,000
Silk dress: Bill Blass Ltd., classic	$1,875
Loafers: Gucci	$410
Shirts: 1 dozen cotton, bespoke, Turnbull & Asser, London	$3,600
Shoes: Men's black calf wing tip, custom-made, John Lobb, London	$4,128
School: Preparatory, Groton, 1-year tuition, room, board	$39,850
University: Harvard, 1-year tuition, room, board, insurance	$43,655
Catered dinner: For 40, Ridgewell's, Bethesda, MD	$7,469
Opera: 2 tickets, 8 performances, Metropolitan Opera, Saturday night, parterre box	$5,440
Caviar: Tsar imperial beluga, 1 kilo, Petrossian, Los Angeles, CA	$7,600
Champagne: Dom Perignon, case, Sherry-Lehmann, NY	$1,559
Filet mignon: 7 pounds, Lobel's, NY	$231
Dinner at La Tour d'Argent: Paris, estimated per person (including wine and tip)	$402
Piano: Steinway & Sons, concert grand, Model D, ebonized	$103,400
Flowers in season: Arrangements for 6 rooms, changed weekly, Christatos & Koster, NY, per month	$8,175
Sheets: Set of linen lace Figna, Pratesi, queen-size	$3,940
Silverware: Lenox, Williamsburg Shell pattern, 4-piece place setting for 12	$5,424
Hotel: 2-bedroom suite, Four Seasons, NY	$3,450
Face-lift: American Academy of Facial Plastic & Reconstructive Surgery	$14,500
Hospital: VIP, Washington Hospital Center, Washington, D.C., 1 day, concierge, security, gourmet meals	$1,315
Psychiatrist: Upper East Side, NY, 45 minutes, standard fee	$300
Lawyer: Established NY firm, Schlesinger, Gannon & Lazettra, average hourly fee for estate planning by partner	$750
Spa: The Golden Door, California, basic weekly unit	$7,500
Perfume: 1 oz. Joy, by Jean Patou	$400
Sauna: Finnleo Sauna and Steam, 8-by-10-by-7 feet, 8-person, Nordic Spruce/Abachi	$14,580
Motor yacht: Hatteras 80 (with 1550-HP CAT C-30s)	$4,870,000
Sailing yacht: Nautor's Swan 70	$4,070,661
Shotguns: Pair of James Purdey & Sons (12 gauge Side-by-Side), Griffin & Howe, Bernardsville, NJ, & Greenwich, CT	$185,655
Thoroughbred: Yearling, average price, Fasig-Tipton Saratoga summer select sale	$323,731

Swimming pool: Olympic (50 meters) Mission Pools, Escondido, CA	$1,312,500
Tennis court: Clay, Putnam Tennis and Recreation, Harwinton, CT	$55,000
Train set: Christmas Passenger starter set, LGB, at Miller's Toys, NY	$400
Airplane: Learjet 40XR, standard equipment, certified, 7 passengers	$8,750,000
Helicopter: Sikorsky S-76C++, VIP options	$11,000,000
Automobile: Rolls-Royce Phantom	$333,350
Telephone call (without calling plan): 10 minutes, AT&T, NY–London	$30
Cigars: Aniversario No. 1, Dominican Republic, 25 cigars, Davidoff, NY	$708
Magazine: *Forbes*, 1-year subscription	$60
Duffel bag: Louis Vuitton, Keepall Bandouliere, 55 centimeters	$1,060
Watch: Patek Philippe classic men's gold, leather strap (Ref#3520 yellow gold on leather strap)	$17,600
Purse: Hermès, Kelly Bag, calfskin, rigid, 28 centimeters	$6,250

extravagant spending by certain members of America's superrich, a period that mimics earlier epochs of flamboyant wealth in American history. The economist and sociologist Thorstein Veblen coined the phrase *conspicuous consumption* to describe this type of spending. As he wrote in his 1899 book, *The Theory of the Leisure Class,* "To gain and to hold the esteem of men it is not sufficient merely to hold wealth and power. The wealth and power must be put into evidence." Then, as now, houses were one common extravagance. Evidence of vast wealth might also be a mega-yacht, a private jet, a string of beautiful wives, parties, art, or anything else that strikes the fancy.

In Veblen's day, when the Vanderbilt family was at the pinnacle of New York society, perhaps the most visible sign of wealth and power was the handful of enormous mansions built by the family along New York's prestigious Fifth Avenue, as well as a half dozen spectacular holiday homes in the countryside, plus a private railroad car for travel. Showiest of all was the house at 660 Fifth Avenue occupied by Alva Vanderbilt, the queen of New York society and daughter-in-law of William H. Vanderbilt, who was then the richest man in the world. Modeled on a sixteenth-century French château, it took one thousand workmen three years to build. The main hall, sixty feet long and twenty feet wide, resembled the interior of a Gothic cathedral with its arches and vaulted, sixteen-foot-high ceilings. Magnificent Italian tapestries hung above the carved stone walls.

Nowadays you don't have to look far to find similar indulgence, not to say excess. In 2007 timber baron Tim Blixseth advertised a 53,000-square-foot stone-and-wood mansion at his exclusive Yellowstone Club near Bozeman, Montana (where Bill Gates is a member) for a record-breaking $155 million. Blixseth said that the property, set among 160 acres and equipped with its own chairlift, is already drawing interest from a number of Forbes 400 members. And Blixseth should know what they want. Before his 2007 divorce from his wife Edra (see Chapter 11, Family Feuds), the two owned a number of stunning properties around the United States, including the 420-acre Porcupine Creek near Palm Springs worth an estimated $200 million.

The rise of the billionaires has had a dramatic effect on a number of monied enclaves across the country, not least Palm Beach, Florida, where mansions regularly change hands for $20 million and up. Media mogul John Kluge owns a 21,000-square-foot mansion there, valued at $28 million. Financier Stephen Schwarzman paid $20.5 million for his 13,000-square-foot Palm Beach mansion in 2003, while Revlon billionaire Ronald Perelman sold his 33,000-square-foot Palm Beach mansion, set on six beachfront acres, for a record-breaking $70 million in 2004. On the West Coast, the tech boom has fueled conspicuous construction in Medina, Washington, near Microsoft's Redmond headquarters, where Microsoft programmer Charles Simonyi built a 22,000-square-foot lakeside home close to Paul Allen's 74,000-square-foot, Scandinavian-inspired compound. Multimillion-dollar homes have also invaded small but notably affluent towns in Silicon Valley, such as Woodside, which is home to Larry Ellison, Gordon Moore, and software tycoon Thomas M. Siebel.

Few areas of America have been so transformed by the Forbes 400 in the past decade, however, as Greenwich, Connecticut. By the end of 2006, Green-

1999

from the pages of *Forbes*

Charles Simonyi, Microsoft tech wizard, lives in a twenty-two-thousand-square-foot, totally wired, glass and steel house, complete with heliport and revolving bed. (1999 net worth: $1.5 billion)

Nathan Myhrvold, also a Microsoft alumnus, studied at Cambridge University with Stephen Hawking and spends up to $10,000 a month on books. (1999 net worth: $650 million)

Frank Lyon Jr., who made his fortune in Coca-Cola bottling and banks, is often seen on his tractor farming rice and soybeans. (1999 net worth: $700 million)

Jerry Yang and **David Filo** of Yahoo fly coach, park their own cars, and eschew offices for cubicles. (1999 net worth: $3.7 billion each) wich (population 63,000) was home to between 6 and 10 percent of the world's $1.2 trillion hedge fund industry, including Paul Tudor Jones in his $50 million home and Steven Cohen, with his fourteen-acre estate that includes a nearly seven-thousand-square-foot ice rink. According to *Vanity Fair* magazine, between 2000 and 2005 there was a threefold increase in demolitions in Greenwich as these moneymen flooded the area, acquiring old properties and replacing discreet estates with oversize mansions often positioned conspicuously within sight of passersby. By 2005 the average price of a Greenwich home was $2.5 million, with only seven homes selling for less than $500,000 that year; sixteen homes sold for more than $10 million. After speaking with Greenwich interior designers, *Vanity Fair* writer Nina Munk estimated that curtains for just one room in a Greenwich mansion cost in the region of $30,000 to $35,000, and a lighting system and light fittings for a home costs upward of $500,000. "The people who count now in Greenwich and everywhere else in America, it seems, are no longer Mrs. Astor's 400, but the Forbes Four Hundred," she wrote.

While huge spenders are by their very nature highly visible, they seem to be in the minority among the Forbes 400, most of whom wish to remain anonymous. But there are the colorful few who, for whatever reason, choose to live a life that others can only imagine. As Malcolm Forbes, inventor of the Forbes 400 list and a man who believed in the good life, once said, "I'm just doing with my money what anybody with this much money would do."

Software tycoon Larry Ellison is as competitive about acquiring the accoutrements of the good life as he is in his corporate life. Ellison has spent years comparing himself to his Microsoft nemeses, Bill Gates and Paul Allen. For a few heady months in 2000, when Bill Gates's net worth took a hammering after the tech bubble burst, Ellison squeezed ahead of Gates with a net worth estimated at $53 billion, compared to Gates's $51.75 billion. But apart from that brief period, Ellison has had to content himself with besting his rivals in other ways. Gates may be known for having one of the largest and most technologically advanced homes in the world, but it's not worth as much as Ellison's home in Woodside, California. In 2007 the online real-estate Web site Zillow.com* valued Ellison's home at $170 million, while Gates's home was valued at a slightly more modest $136 million. Ellison's home is hidden in the

---

*Zillow.com was started by two former Microsoft executives, Richard Barton and Lloyd Frink, who also created Expedia.com.

A House Fit for a Tech Titan

Looking out toward Seattle from Medina, Washington, Bill Gates's house is the testing ground for his dreams about the home of the future. The building is about as ecologically friendly as they come. Made largely of Douglas fir timber rescued from an abandoned lumber mill, the house is powered by one hundred microcomputers that raise and dim lighting according to outdoor light, and control heating as people enter and leave rooms or fall asleep. The Gates residence is a living, breathing organism. Guests are issued electronic pins that track the wearers as they move throughout the building. Tell the computer your favorite music, television shows, and your preferred temperature, and that is exactly what you will get when you enter a room. The computer will even control lighting behind and ahead of you and display your favorite works of art on digital screens in each room. If your mom calls, only the phone nearest you will ring. In the 2,300-square-foot reception hall, a video wall of twenty-four rear-projection television monitors show individual images, or combine to form one giant display.

The Gates compound, which covers five acres, is valued by real-estate Web site Zillow.com at $136 million. Much of the compound, including the 45,000-square-foot house, is made of timber, sandstone, and granite, buried in a hillside, and obscured from view by native alder, maple, and Douglas fir trees. The family has a relatively modest 11,500-square-foot living area, with four bedrooms and a room for a nanny. The compound's enormous guest wing has two further bedrooms, a twenty-seat art deco movie theater, and a massive, 2,100-square-foot library that holds ten thousand rare hardbacks as well as Leonardo da Vinci's notebook, the Codex Leicester, which Gates bought in 1994 for just under $31 million. There's also a separate two-thousand-square-foot, one-bedroom guesthouse buried underground, a trampoline room, an eighteen-hole miniature golf course, a 1,000-square-foot formal dining room, and vast business and reception facilities. In short, a home fit for a technology titan and the richest man on the planet.

midst of a tranquil, twenty-three-acre estate modeled on a sixteenth-century Kyoto palace and gardens. The main house is an actual Japanese villa—a cluster of small wooden houses that were constructed in Japan and transported to Woodside. There they sit, dwarfed by giant redwood trees, beside a man-made, earthquake-proof lake, surrounded by boulders from the Sierra

Nevadas. The estate even has its own waterfall powered by an underground filtration system.

Ellison is one of the Forbes 400's most prodigious spenders. In 2002 his financial advisor warned that his runaway spending on yachts and homes had pushed him into more than $1 billion in debt. "I'm worried, Larry," his advisor, Philip Simon, wrote in an e-mail, later quoted in the *San Francisco Chronicle*. "I think it's imperative we start to budget and plan." The following year Ellison purchased the longest yacht in the world, the *Rising Sun*. About ninety feet longer than a football field, the 453-foot boat includes a basketball court and two upper decks made entirely of glass. *Vanity Fair* described the interior as "opulent," though not gaudy. It's rumored that Ellison specified the length of the *Rising Sun* in order to beat the 414-foot yacht *Octopus* of Microsoft's Paul Allen, which was under construction at the same time and which briefly occupied the world's number one spot when it launched before Ellison's in 2003. (Allen's boat is noted for its James Bond–like gadgets: It is equipped with two helicopter pads and a 118-foot marina that can hold a 59-foot boat and a 39-foot, ten-man submarine.)

And Ellison's conspicuous spending—and his adventurous streak—are not confined to land and sea; during the 1990s he tried to buy a Russian MiG fighter jet for $20 million, but was prevented by U.S. customs authorities. So he had to make do with an Italian fighter jet instead. In recent years he has bought swaths of real estate in Malibu, California, valued at over $150 million.* As for women, the thrice-divorced Ellison courted a string of beautiful girls until he fell for and married romance novelist Melanie Craft (more than twenty years his junior) in 2003, when Ellison was fifty-nine.

Ellison is indisputably a conspicuous consumer par excellence. But he has never captured the public's imagination with his spending. Donald Trump has. Trump's outsize persona extends across every part of his life, beginning with his highly publicized marriages and divorces.

During the 1980s Trump bought the 110,000-square-foot Mar-A-Lago mansion and estate in Palm Beach, Florida, turning it into one of the country's premier country clubs. It costs $150,000 to join and $7,500 in annual dues. He also bought *Nabila*, the 282-foot yacht that formerly belonged to high-living arms dealer Adnan Khashoggi, and renamed it the *Trump*

---

*Oprah Winfrey is another big buyer of real estate along the California coast, with a forty-two-acre estate in Montecito that she bought for $50 million in 2001. She also owns 102 acres of waterfront property in Maui and a $6 million co-op and $800,000 condo in Chicago, the home of her Harpo television studios, plus a ten-thousand-square-foot house in Greenwich and condos in Atlanta, Milwaukee, Nashville, Fisher Island, Florida, and Franklin, Tennessee.

Princess. For a few brief seasons, Trump was the owner of the New Jersey Generals football team. He has impressed clients and journalists with a private plane, Trump One, which is bedecked with gilt fixtures and impressionist paintings. And in 2004, as an investment, he bought the 43,000-square-foot Palm Beach mansion Maison de L'Amitie for $41.5 million; assigned Kendra Todd, the winner on his hit prime-time TV show, *The Apprentice*, to renovate it; and put it back on the market the following year for a then record $125 million.

Trump does not believe in the maxim "Less is more." He has brought personal brand awareness to new heights by emblazoning his name across the landscape and gilding every conceivable surface. As Todd Millay, the executive director of Wharton Global Family Alliance, which researches family wealth, says, Trump's business is all about marketing. "He has the image: the exotic supermodels [Trump owns the Miss Universe franchise in partnership with NBC] and fancy homes and gold-plated stuff." Or, as Stephane Fitch noted in a 2006 *Forbes* cover story on Trump, "Through it all [his 'tempest-tossed business career'] Trump has nurtured a valuable brand name that has withstood the scorn of his many critics." In New York alone, there's Trump Tower on Fifth Avenue (the top three floors of which are occupied by Trump's thirty-thousand-square-foot penthouse), Trump World Tower, which literally towers over the United Nations, and Trump International Hotel and Tower on the edge of Central Park. In Vegas there's the Trump Las Vegas, and in Atlantic City it's the Trump Plaza Hotel and Casino, the Trump Taj Mahal, and the Trump Marina. In addition to Trump's *The Apprentice*, Trump is online via Trump University and the Trump blog. There are Trump books: The latest, coauthored with *Rich Dad, Poor Dad* author Robert Kiyosaki, is *Why We Want You to Be Rich: Two Men—One Message*. There is Trump the Fragrance, the Donald J. Trump Signature Collection of menswear, and even his own bottled water, Trump Ice.

The very name *Trump* carries with it the connotations of unapologetic extravagance. But whatever his net worth (languishing at a reported minus $900 million, as it was in the early 1990s, or soaring to $2.9 billion as it did in 2006, according to *Forbes*), Trump's billionaire lifestyle is great for business. A 2000 Gallup poll ranked Trump the most famous businessperson in America: 98 percent of respondents recognized his name—not bad, considering that the only two other members of the Forbes 400 who scored in the ninetieth percentile were the world's richest man, Bill Gates, and two-time presidential hopeful Ross Perot.

In the late nineteenth century, proper millionaires strove to imitate the trappings of wealth they had seen during their European tours of English country estates, châteaus on the Loire, and opulent palaces in Russia. Maroon-liveried footmen with white silk stockings and gilt buckles on their shoes were the order of the day. Today, there is no end of Forbes 400 members chafing to put on the biggest, most lavish parties. When Saul Steinberg's twenty-five-year-old daughter, Laura, married thirty-four-year-old Loews scion Jonathan Tisch in 1988,* they threw a $3 million wedding replete with searchlights shining out of the stained-glass windows of the Central Synagogue on Lexington Avenue in Manhattan; the Steinbergs' antiques decorated the inside of the house of worship. After the service, guests assembled at the Metropolitan Museum of Art, where a reception was held at the Egyptian Temple of Dendur. Wedding guests such as Norman Mailer and Barbara Walters were entertained by a Brazilian band on stilts; the wedding cake soared ten feet into the air. The following year, when Steinberg turned fifty, his third wife, Gayfryd (one of the most slavishly covered socialites of the 1980s and early 1990s), threw a million-dollar party at which models, one of them nude, posed as figures from Steinberg's favorite old-master paintings.

Malcolm Forbes understood the appeal of an opulent party (as well as the related power of publicity). He threw one of the parties of the century in 1989 to celebrate his seventieth birthday, at his Moroccan castle Palais Mendoub in Tangiers. Forbes flew in the approximately eight hundred guests, including Elizabeth Taylor and Henry Kissinger, on three airplanes—a 747, a DC-8, and the Concorde—for the three days of celebrating. The almost $2.5 million tab for the party included paying more than three hundred horsemen in Moroccan costume and six hundred drummers, belly dancers, and jugglers. More recently, financier Stephen Schwarzman spent more than $3 million on his sixtieth birthday party at the Park Avenue Armory. The party, for about six hundred guests, included performances by rock crooner Rod Stewart and soul singer Patti LaBelle. It was as much the talk of the town as Alva Vanderbilt's lavish parties had been in the 1890s. (Her most famous party reputedly cost as much as $250,000, or around $5.5 million today.) Paparazzi jostled to snap photographs of the star-studded guest list, which included former secretary of state Colin Powell, New York's Cardinal Edward Egan, and fellow

---

*The couple divorced in 2000.

The State-of-the-Art Trophy Wife

In every era a handful of women personify the trophy wife—beautiful, and often much younger than her tycoon husband. The Trump women have gotten steadily younger over the years: Ivana (born 1949), Marla (born 1963), and Melania (born 1970). (The Donald, of course, has also gotten older: he's now sixty-one.) And who could forget former Playmate Anna Nicole Smith, who, when she was all of age twenty-six, married the elderly J. Howard Marshall, who was more than triple her age? But these days the ultimate trophy wife is more than young and beautiful; she is a leader of society. She sits on the board of venerable institutions, throws lavish parties—often for a worthy cause—and is endlessly pictured on the society pages of newspapers and magazines in a parade of couture fashion.

During the 1980s, Gayfryd Steinberg, third wife of Saul Steinberg, personified the trophy wife. The daughter of a Canadian clerk, Gayfryd had already been married twice—first to an engineer and later to a Texas oilman. She met Saul at a dinner party in 1982, as her second marriage was crumbling. The two left the table halfway through the meal, never to return. Within a couple of years they were married, and Gayfryd had embarked upon her mission to capture New York society. She joined the prestigious board of the New York Public Library, threw charity galas for the literary group PEN, and arranged dinner parties for the city's movers and shakers at the couple's spectacular 740 Park Avenue apartment. In the 1990s, the Steinbergs' world came crashing down; Saul had a stroke and business reverses. Gayfryd memorably stood by her man, nursing him and arranging for the discreet sale of his beloved apartment (and thereby proving that not all trophy wives are hit and run). They moved to a nearby town house and are still together.

The 1990s ushered in a new generation of socialites. Mercedes Bass married oil tycoon Sid Bass in the late 1980s, shortly after his divorce from the popular balletomane Anne Bass; Mercedes promptly set about creating an empire fit for the queen of society. She masterminded the building of the Basses' palatial Georgian home on Fort Worth's tony Crestline Road, and the redecoration of Sid's eighteen-room Fifth Avenue apartment in New York with lashings of gold and French art and antiques. Mercedes is famed for her generosity toward the arts (as well as her penchant for lecturing about her interests), particularly the Fort Worth Symphony Orchestra and the Metropolitan Opera, which received a $25 million pledge from the Basses in 2006—the largest donation in its history. Articles about Mercedes often comment on her wardrobe, which leans heavily toward Oscar de la Renta. Not all of the coverage is kind. New York socialite Nan Kempner, who died in 2006, labeled Mercedes the "Duchess of Bass" in a 2005 *Vanity Fair* interview.

Capturing a wealthy husband is not always easy, especially as society frowns upon infidelity or bachelors dating a string of different women. Therefore, the future wife will often pursue a discreet introduction with the mogul through friends, as did Jane Beasley, second wife of GE chairman Jack Welch (sixteen years her senior), who was introduced by former Citibank chief executive Walter Wriston's wife, Kathryn. Of course, Welch would famously run off a decade later with yet another woman, Suzy Wetlaufer: They met when she was interviewing him for the *Harvard Business Review*. Trophy wives must often pursue their target relentlessly. Georgette Mosbacher told *Texas Monthly* magazine that when Houston oilman Robert Mosbacher, twenty-one years her senior, tried to cancel their dates, she intimidated him until he relented.

Finally, there's the "working rich," glamorous women who have a serious résumé of their own. Fashion designer Carolyne Roehm, the second wife of financier Henry Kravis, is one such example. The couple divorced in 1993. But Kravis continued the trend toward accomplished partners: His current wife is economist Marie-Josée Kravis, née Drouin, a fellow at the Council on Foreign Relations and a senior fellow at the Hudson Institute.

Forbes 400 members Jack Welch and Donald Trump. As if to drive home the extent of Schwarzman's wealth, the venue, lit by chandeliers and embellished with orchids, was hung with a fifty-foot silk-screen re-creation of his $30 million apartment three blocks away at 740 Park Avenue—the most prestigious address in New York City.

If the Forbes 400 had an address, in fact, it would be 740 Park Avenue. The building has been home to the city's richest inhabitants ever since it opened its doors in October 1930, sheltering Rockefellers and Vanderbilts as well as the modern-day rich such as David Koch, Ronald Perelman, Edgar Bronfman, and Henry Kravis. Apartments cost between $20 million and $30 million. Schwarzman's apartment, 15/16B, is the largest in the building and one of the largest in Manhattan, with thirty-four rooms covering nineteen thousand square feet. It was previously owned by Steinberg, who bought it from

John D. Rockefeller Jr. Steinberg's second wife, Laura, told *New York* magazine that the apartment "meant he was going up in life. It was a status symbol, just big enough for his ego."* The average monthly maintenance cost of an apartment in the building is $10,000, according to Michael Gross's recently published and exhaustive history, *740 Park: The Story of the World's Richest Apartment Building.* In order to be admitted by this, the choosiest co-op board in the city (which has turned down Neil Sedaka and Barbra Streisand without giving a reason), the owner reportedly must have a minimum $100 million in liquid assets. As Gross writes, "A co-op at 740 Park, then, is the ultimate sign of arrival. . . . It's as refined a form of ostentation as buying a van Gogh at auction, guaranteed to enhance one's brand and ensure it never loses its desirability." Indeed, it is one of the paradoxes of 740 Park Avenue's inhabitants that many of its residents profess the desire for anonymity while residing in one of the city's most talked-about buildings.

Displays of wealth have not always been popular in America. In his 1983 book *Notes on Class: A Guide Through the American Status System,* the historian Paul Fussell noted that the Great Depression taught many of America's superrich to be cautious about flaunting their wealth, especially in big cities where they could be viewed daily (and dangerously) by the hoi polloi. Indeed, the Vanderbilt family and their peers suffered a great deal of vitriol during the Depression, when millions scraped by as high society continued to spend hundreds of thousands of dollars a year on clothes alone. "Showing off used to be the main satisfaction of being very rich in America," wrote Fussell. "Now the rich must skulk and hide. It's a pity." According to Fussell, after the Depression the very rich concealed their displays of wealth in holiday homes around the country and abroad. As it turned out, however, Fussell's *Notes on Class* was almost immediately outdated, at least in its depiction of wealth. Instead, the 1980s set new standards for displays of wealth. It was a decade when people clamored for Calvin Klein and Chanel, and the newly wealthy—particularly the masters of the Wall Street universe—made headlines by competing with old-money art collectors.

Not surprisingly, yachts—the epitome of the rich man's toy—were part of the splurge. According to the American novelist Alison Lurie, "A high status sport, by definition, is one that requires a great deal of expensive equip-

---

*His fortune now depleted (he last appeared on the 400 list in 1995), Steinberg, sixty-eight, has had health problems since suffering a stroke in 1995. He now walks with a cane and lives in a more modest town house two blocks away.

The Man Who Brought Old-Money Style to the (Upper-Middle-Class) Masses

For generations, the American public has marveled at an old-money vision of the good life, best exemplified, perhaps, by the British in India and Africa and by WASPs in Newport or the great American West—a vision replete with lavish mansions, shingled holiday homes by the sea, tennis whites, buttery leather armchairs, Indian blankets. The spectators knew they could never afford to live this way. But Ralph Lauren, a former tie salesman from the Bronx, persuaded them that they could, at the very least, have some of the accoutrements.

Lauren started his multibillion-dollar empire in the 1960s with a vision of how he could reinterpret American nostalgia for a bygone era. His English country style became popular in the 1970s, after he designed costumes for a movie version of F. Scott Fitzgerald's novel *The Great Gatsby,* about a previous golden age in America. He built collections around the perfect summer cottage, the grand Adirondack lodge, and the like, and expanded into perfume, shoes, and luxury homeware. Advertisements for his products are drenched with the feeling of a tennis-playing, yacht-sailing, WASPy world. And what better logo to symbolize that class than the mallet-swinging polo player?

Though Lauren brought the old-money sensibility to the masses, Polo is not especially affordable. Sure, you can pick up reduced items at factory outlets and on sale, but an original item of old-money chic like the classic Polo shirt costs $75. Not in the same price bracket as a Van Gogh, to be sure. But it is a symbol that the wearer recognizes class when he or she sees it. Meanwhile, faux old money has helped propel Lauren from a net worth of $300 million in 1986 to $3.9 billion in 2006.

ment or an expensive setting or both." This, of course, is infinitely true of yachting. Or as Fussell observed, "Knowing how to sail a boat well is so indispensable to upper-middle-class status that it can almost serve as a class division in itself. And of course racing a boat is higher than just tooling about in one."

Commodore Vanderbilt was the first American to commission a private yacht. Costing $500,000 (the equivalent of $11.5 million now) and powered

Masters and Commanders

When Larry Ellison sailed into the industrial port of Valencia, Spain, in 2005 to kick off the city's multiyear America's Cup preparations, his *Rising Sun* yacht was too big for a jetty that had been specially built to dock the expected megayachts. Instead, Ellison had to berth his 453-foot boat on the far side of the harbor next to the container cranes. In an effort to prevent similar embarrassment, marinas around the world are scrambling to accommodate the surge in giant yachts that has taken place in the past five or ten years. Yacht Haven Grande in U.S. Virgin Islands' St. Thomas, for example, was recently upgraded at a cost of $200 million. The benefits of luring billionaires to a marina are obvious. The question is: With so many luxuries on board, why would anyone want to go ashore?

A yacht is more than the world's most expensive toy. It's a private floating island over which billionaires have complete power and control, making it perfect for meetings and private holidays. Though yachts are a conspicuous bauble for many, for others they are a secret hideaway; for that reason, some sales are kept private, and crews are sworn to secrecy. Of the ten biggest yachts in the United States, at least eight are known to be owned by members of the Forbes 400. The other two? No one is sure. But with upkeep running into tens of millions of dollars each year, you pretty much have to be a billionaire to afford one.

The Top Ten U.S.-Owned Yachts

1. Larry Ellison, *Rising Sun* (452'8")
2. Paul Allen, *Octopus* (414')
3. Leslie Wexner, *Limitless* (315'8")
4. Paul Allen, *Tatoosh* (301'8")
5. Peter Lewis, *Lone Ranger* (255')
6. Getty family, *Talitha* (247'4")
7. Anonymous, *Laurel* (240')
8. Charles Simonyi, *Skat* (233')
9. Unknown (charter yacht), *Reverie* (229'7")
10. Wayne Huizenga, *Floridian* (228')

Source: *Power & Motoryacht* magazine

by four coal-fed boilers, the *North Star* was 270 feet long and took its owner on a grandiose tour of Europe.* A century later, when the International Superyacht Society was founded in 1990, only 2,500 boats passed the eighty-foot benchmark. But by 2005 there were 6,000. Paul Allen, for one, owns not only the second-largest yacht in the United States, *Octopus*, but he also owns the fourth-largest: the 302-foot *Tatoosh*, formerly the property of communications mogul Craig McCaw. Such boats sell for up to $200 million and cost about 10 percent of the purchase price each year in running expenses and maintenance. In a world where even islands are a dime a dozen, these floating palaces separate the haves from the have-mores.

Taking sailing to the next level, the Vanderbilts also led the way in racing, winning the most prestigious sailing prize, the America's Cup, several times. But competing for the America's Cup is not cheap: J. P. Morgan spent $175,000 in 1903, the equivalent of $3.9 million in 2007, to bankroll America's Cup winner *Reliance*. Nowadays billionaires are prepared to spend $15 million on research and development alone for a race in which victory can turn on a fraction of a knot. Salaries for tacticians and crew run in the hundreds of thousands of dollars. Plus there's the cost of feeding and housing a team of one hundred or more and accommodating their families in nearby hotels.

It's a costly and occasionally dangerous obsession, as Larry Ellison found out after being caught in a storm during the Sydney-Hobart Race in 1998, during which six men died. Ellison spent $194 million on his yacht over three years, and a further $80 million on the America's Cup, according to an accounting document from 2000. Ted Turner was the first of the Forbes 400 to win the America's Cup, skippering the *Courageous* in 1977 and famously turning up drunk at the postrace press conference. When Koch Industries heir Bill Koch attempted the race in 1992, he was the laughingstock of the sailing world, with bookies giving his team odds of 100-1. But with the help of sailing legend Harry "Buddy" Melges—and an investment of $68 million—he soon wiped the smile off of everyone's face.

---

*According to Arthur T. Vanderbilt II, who wrote a book about the family entitled *Fortune's Children: The Fall of the House of Vanderbilt*, the yacht "had a satinwood-lined grand saloon, rosewood furniture carved in the style of Louis XV and covered with green velvet plush, positioned around a circular crimson-plush sofa that could seat twenty. The walls of the dining saloon were of highly polished marble that glistened like a mirror. Its white ceiling was covered with scrollwork of purple, light green, and gold surrounding medallion paintings of famous Americans: Webster, Clay, Calhoun, Washington, and Franklin."

On dry land, Forbes 400 members have taken an interest in other sports such as horse racing and polo. Texas billionaire Bunker Hunt owned a world-renowned stable of racehorses before he lost his fortune in the silver crash. Professional sports have also caught the fancy of the 400. Bunker's brother Lamar, a sports entrepreneur, changed the face of tennis by pioneering the first major professional tennis tournament—World Championship Tennis—that forced previously amateur competitions such as Wimbledon and the French Open to accept professional players. Lamar was also heavily involved in soccer as an early member of the North American Soccer League and owner of the Dallas Tornados. But he is best known for his involvement in football. When the National Football League (NFL) refused Lamar a license to establish a Dallas football team in the late 1950s, he founded the American Football League. He owned the Dallas Texans, later renamed the Kansas City Chiefs, until his death in 2006. The breakaway league lasted for almost ten years; when it finally merged with the NFL, Lamar came up with the name for a new championship showdown: the Super Bowl (named after his daughter's red, white, and blue SuperBall). Although brothers Bunker and Herbert were the wheeler-dealers of the family, it was Lamar, with his sporting connections, who stole the limelight. "All through our school years, everybody knew Lamar as my younger brother," remarked Herbert Hunt once. "Now that he's involved in the sports world, every time I meet somebody, they say, 'Oh, you're Lamar's brother.' "

Over the past twenty-five years, more than eighty members of the Forbes 400 have owned sports teams and seen their status rise as a result. As Warren Buffett wrote in his 2006 annual letter to Berkshire Hathaway investors, "Ownership of a city's paper, like ownership of a sports team, still produces instant prominence." (Buffett should know: He himself is a minority owner of the Omaha Royals minor league baseball team, as well as having a significant interest in the Washington Post Company.) And then there is the value of sports-team ownership in clinching business deals and impressing people. Ross Perot Jr. convinced the city of Dallas to contribute public funds to a downtown redevelopment project after he bought the Dallas Mavericks. And at a match between soccer teams Los Angeles Galaxy and the San Jose Earthquakes in 2005, John Prescott, the British deputy prime minister, was no doubt impressed when he asked his host, Philip Anschutz (2005 net worth: $7.8 billion), which team he was cheering for. The legendary investor replied that it didn't matter, because he owned them both.

Loans tycoon Daniel Gilbert, who bought the Cleveland Cavaliers NBA team in 2005 for $375 million, says part of the appeal was the raft of

Buy Me Some Peanuts, Cracker Jacks . . . and a Sports Team

It's almost impossible to buy a sports team and not be conspicuous about it. By a conservative count, almost ninety of the Forbes 400 either have owned a sports team or had an interest in one over the past twenty-five years. Most have gotten not only great perks—beginning with the best seats—but a healthy return on their investment as well. Among them:

Mark Cuban
Dallas Mavericks, National Basketball Association (NBA)

Cuban bought the Mavericks from Ross Perot Jr. in 2000 for $280 million. Perhaps one of the most outspoken franchise owners in the country, his courtside outbursts have cost him more than $1 million in fines. In 2002 he said the NBA league's director of officials wasn't good enough to work at a Dairy Queen. That cost him $500,000 and a day serving cones behind a Dairy Queen counter. In 2007 *Forbes* estimated the Mavericks to be worth $463 million.

Stan Kroenke
Owns a franchise for every occasion: St. Louis Rams, National Football League (NFL); Denver Nuggets (NBA); Colorado Avalanche, National Hockey League (NHL); Colorado Rapids, Major League Soccer (MLS); Colorado Mammoth, National Lacrosse League (NLL)

Kroenke, who made a fortune in real estate himself, is the husband of Wal-Mart heir Anne Walton. As head of Kroenke Sports Enterprises, he owns five teams—one in each major sport. Kroenke paid $219 million for an ever-increasing stake in the Rams between 1972 and 1995. (In 2006 they were worth $841 million.) In 2000 he bought the Nuggets, the Avalanche, and their Pepsi Center home for $450 million.

Micky Arison
Miami Heat (NBA)

Carnival Cruise Line heir Arison inherited the team from his father, Ted, who bought the team in 1987 for $32 million. In 2004 Arison hired Shaquille O'Neal from the Los Angeles Lakers and in 2007, fresh from their NBA finals victory, *Forbes* estimated the team to be worth $409 million.

Michael Ilitch
Detroit Tigers (MLB); Detroit Red Wings (NHL)

Ilitch played shortstop for the Tigers' feeder team in his youth, but an injury cut short his career. So he struck out for the pizza business, making a fortune with Little Caesars pizza. He bought the Tigers franchise in 1992 from rival pizza tycoon Thomas

Monaghan for about $92 million. In 2006 the franchise was valued at an estimated $365 million.

Malcolm Glazer
Tampa Bay Buccaneers (NFL); Manchester United (soccer, United Kingdom)

Glazer borrowed almost all of the staggering $1.4 billion price tag for Manchester United, the world's richest football club, in May 2005. Meanwhile, the Buccaneers, which Glazer bought in 1995 for $192 million, were worth almost $1 billion by 2006. Glazer suffered strokes in April and May 2006.

Arthur Blank
Atlanta Falcons (NFL); Georgia Force, Arena Football League (AFL)

The Home Depot cofounder bought the Falcons for $545 million in 2002. Four years later *Forbes* estimated their value at $730 million, thanks in part to the team's success and forty-thousand-person waiting list for season tickets. Blank bought Georgia Force in 2004 and narrowly lost out on an Atlanta triple when the Time Warner–owned Atlanta Braves major league baseball team was bought by John Malone's Liberty Media in 2007.

Robert Kraft
New England Patriots (NFL); New England Revolution (MLS)

Kraft paid a then record $172 million for the New England Patriots in 1994. Twelve years later, after their third Super Bowl, *Forbes* estimated the franchise to be worth $1.2 billion, the second most expensive NFL team after the $1.4 billion Washington Redskins— which is owned by Daniel Snyder, the chairman of theme park operation Six Flags.

Jerral Jones
Dallas Cowboys (NFL); Dallas Desperados (AFL)

Oil billionaire Jones captained the University of Arkansas Razorbacks football team to victory in the 1964 Cotton Bowl. An avid football fan, he bought the Dallas Cowboys in 1989 for $150 million; during the 1990s the team won three Super Bowls. *Forbes* estimated the team to be worth $1.2 billion in 2006, not including debt from a giant $650,000 stadium.

Paul Allen
Portland Trailblazers (NBA); Seattle Seahawks (NFL)

Allen has not had equal luck with his sports toys. The Microsoft billionaire bought the Portland Trailblazers for $70 million in 1988 and put the team up for sale in 2006 for $300 million, but called it off about a month later. A year after that *Forbes* estimated the team to be worth $230 million. Allen has had more success with his Seahawks team, which he bought in 1997 for $194 million. Nine years later *Forbes* estimated its value at $888 million.

opportunities ownership presented—such as renaming the stadium Quicken Loans Arena and having the financial incentives of merchandising and additional business opportunities.* But for Gilbert, as for most members of the Forbes 400, a major factor when it comes to owning a team is a passion for sports. The current owner of the Mavericks, Mark Cuban, has a higher profile than many of his peers as the billionaire who has been fined more than a million dollars for his unruly (but passionate) courtside behavior. Says Cuban: "I like the competitive aspect of it, but I love the games. I love the fans and the guys. It's fun." Gilbert, a basketball fanatic, says one of the main reasons he bought the Cavaliers was the old cliché that if you cannot play pro sports, then owning a team is the next-best thing. "Even pro athletes want to own teams," says Gilbert, who at five feet six was never going to make it as a pro basketball player. (Despite his height disadvantage, however, the ultracompetitive Gilbert still plays weekly pickup games.)

Although most investors make money when they sell their team, profit does not seem to be the overriding factor behind a purchase. "People buy these teams because if you are a sports enthusiast, let alone a fanatic, there is a very, very limited supply," says Steve Greenberg, managing director of investment banking company Allen & Company, which helped Gilbert buy the Cavaliers. "And it's the ultimate fantasy for any American boy growing up to either play for or own a major league team, sort of a dream come true." Consider, for example, Carl Lindner, who bought the Cincinnati Reds in 1999 after they had fallen on hard times. "There was the prospect of the team being thrown out of baseball, and there was no one in the city prepared to step in and take over the reins of the team and do what was required," says Greenberg. "Carl Lindner stepped up and put up the money. He was already king of Cincinnati and a very behind-the-scenes kind of guy, so there was no need for him to make a vanity play. He went to every home game. He built a new stadium."

The line between conspicuous consumer and passionate fan also blurs in the world of art. It is said that hedge fund head Steve Cohen led a somewhat inconspicuous lifestyle until he splurged on his Greenwich mansion and needed something to put on the walls. Cohen's art collection could soon be worth $1 billion, with works by Vincent van Gogh, Paul Gauguin, Andy Warhol, and Roy Lichtenstein. He has even found room for a fourteen-foot tiger shark in formaldehyde, the work of controversial British artist Damien Hirst.

---

*In 2006 Gilbert added to his sports franchise by buying an NHL team, the Utah Grizzlies, for an undisclosed sum that he described as "a few million dollars."

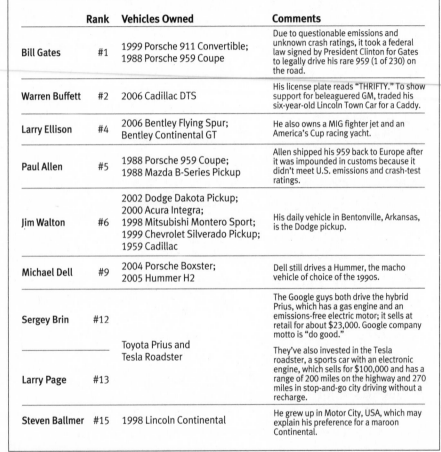

Wheels of fortune

Stretch limos may be the vehicles of choice for rappers and rock stars, but while some 400 members have a taste for luxury and speed, others shun flashy and super-expensive roadsters. Here's what some (listed in order of their ranking on the 2006 400 list) were driving in 2005 and 2006, according to state department of motor vehicle records.

	Rank	Vehicles Owned	Comments
Bill Gates	#1	1999 Porsche 911 Convertible; 1988 Porsche 959 Coupe	Due to questionable emissions and unknown crash ratings, it took a federal law signed by President Clinton for Gates to legally drive his rare 959 (1 of 230) on the road.
Warren Buffett	#2	2006 Cadillac DTS	His license plate reads "THRIFTY." To show support for beleaguered GM, traded his six-year-old Lincoln Town Car for a Caddy.
Larry Ellison	#4	2006 Bentley Flying Spur; Bentley Continental GT	He also owns a MIG fighter jet and an America's Cup racing yacht.
Paul Allen	#5	1988 Porsche 959 Coupe; 1988 Mazda B-Series Pickup	Allen shipped his 959 back to Europe after it was impounded in customs because it didn't meet U.S. emissions and crash-test ratings.
Jim Walton	#6	2002 Dodge Dakota Pickup; 2000 Acura Integra; 1998 Mitsubishi Montero Sport; 1999 Chevrolet Silverado Pickup; 1959 Cadillac	His daily vehicle in Bentonville, Arkansas, is the Dodge pickup.
Michael Dell	#9	2004 Porsche Boxster; 2005 Hummer H2	Dell still drives a Hummer, the macho vehicle of choice of the 1990s.
Sergey Brin	#12	Toyota Prius and Tesla Roadster	The Google guys both drive the hybrid Prius, which has a gas engine and an emissions-free electric motor; it sells at retail for about $23,000. Google company motto is "do good."
Larry Page	#13		They've also invested in the Tesla roadster, a sports car with an electronic engine, which sells for $100,000 and has a range of 200 miles on the highway and 270 miles in stop-and-go city driving without a recharge.
Steven Ballmer	#15	1998 Lincoln Continental	He grew up in Motor City, USA, which may explain his preference for a maroon Continental.

It goes without saying that art isn't just a status symbol or an expensive hobby; it can also be a great investment. A study by NYU's Jianping Mei and Michael Moses showed that between 1996 and 2006 postwar and contemporary art performed better than the S&P 500 Total Return Index. Art can also have tax benefits. Banking tycoon Andrew Mellon saved on his enormous estate tax bill by donating his art collection to the nation just before his death;

The A-Listers of the Art World

Every year *ARTnews* publishes a list of the top two hundred art collectors around the world, based on the most active acquirers that year. In 2006, more than twenty places were taken by members of the Forbes 400 and their keen-eyed wives—including, significantly, seven places in the top ten (the three remaining places were occupied by foreign tycoons such as British advertising mogul Charles Saatchi). The top-ten contingent: Leon and Debra Black, Eli and Edythe Broad, Steve Cohen, Ronald Lauder, Mitchell Rales, Leslie and Abigail Wexner, and Stephen and Elaine Wynn.

Meanwhile, one Forbes 400 member, David Geffen, made huge headlines in 2006 for selling art. Between October and November 2006, Geffen, who was included in *ARTnews*'s list, raised more than $400 million in four private sales. The music tycoon sold a number of valuable works from his considerable collection of abstract expressionists, including two de Koonings: *Woman III*, which he had acquired from a Tehran museum in 1994 in exchange for a sixteenth-century Persian manuscript, and *Police Gazette* (previously owned by Steve Wynn)—both to Steve Cohen. Geffen also shattered records with a $140 million sale of Jackson Pollock's *No. 5, 1948* (previously owned by 400 member S. I. Newhouse Jr.) to Mexican financier David Martinez. He also unloaded a Jasper Johns painting, *False Start* (also previously owned by S. I. Newhouse Jr.), for a further $80 million. His selling spree sparked rumors that he was raising capital for the purchase of the *Los Angeles Times,* which was in play at the time.

Other members of the 400 who spent their way onto *ARTnews*'s 2006 list were Paul Allen, Donald and Doris Fisher, Henry Kravis, Leonard Lauder, S. I. Newhouse Jr., John Pritzker, Steven Rales, Jay Rockefeller, Fayez Sarofim, Charles Schwab, Michael Steinhardt, Alice Walton, and Steve Wynn.

it would become the National Gallery in Washington, D.C. Many other Forbes 400 members have, of course, also made major philanthropic gifts to art museums and other institutions, with similarly advantageous tax write-offs. But rare is the case in which a billionaire keeps his treasures, displays them conspicuously—and still gets a tax break. Yet that's just what casino mogul Steve Wynn has managed to do. Wynn persuaded the Nevada legislature to exempt his art collection from sales tax by arguing that because it was on view in his Bellagio Hotel, it served an educational purpose to local people—never mind that Wynn was charging admission to see the artworks. When the apparent double standard was brought to light, Wynn offered locals a reduced entrance fee, and the tax exemption was allowed to stand.* Some collectors may sail very close to the wind when it comes to tax savings on their art purchases, but all will no doubt have one eye on the fate of fellow 400 member Leona Helmsley, who served eighteen months in prison during the late 1980s for tax evasion on her art purchases.

As much as the Steinbergs, Schwarzmans, and Trumps of the world may wish to trumpet their success, a substantial number of the Forbes 400 would rather do just the opposite. When the *Kilgore News Herald* in Texas asked Ross Perot to comment after he was included on the first Forbes 400 in 1982, the former IBM salesman called *Forbes* "the *National Enquirer* of the business world." Perot, whose net worth *Forbes* estimated that year at $325 million, added: "Nobody lucky enough to make a little money wants to have it put up on a billboard." (This was, of course, ten years before Perot spent millions of his own money running for president. Even—or especially—the rich have the prerogative to change their minds.) Indeed, the letters of denial and protest sent to *Forbes* by centimillionaires, billionaires, and their lawyers over the years attest to how many of America's wealthiest dislike being fingered as fabulously rich (partly due to their ongoing fears of kidnapping).

Many members of the 400 have an almost moralistic aversion to flaunting wealth. Warren Buffett, the nation's second-richest man, famously remains in the Omaha, Nebraska, home that he bought in 1958 for $31,500 (in 2003 it was valued at $700,000). Likewise, the recluse Richard Wendt, who made a fortune in building products and real estate, was still living in a four-bedroom house valued at $440,000 in 2000, the year Forbes estimated his net worth to be $750 million. When Sam Walton topped the rich list for four years—1985, 1986, 1988, and 1999—he stubbornly continued to drive an old red-and-white Ford pickup and live in a large but unassuming four-

---

*Wynn, who suffers from a rare disease called retinitis pigmentosa that has left him with poor peripheral vision, accidentally put his elbow through his most prized possession, Picasso's *La Reve*, in 2006, shortly before it was due to be sold to Steve Cohen for what would have been a record at the time: $139 million. Wynn said that the painting could be repaired, but the sale was called off shortly afterward. Wynn later announced that he had changed his mind about the sale anyway.

thousand-square-foot ranch house in Bentonville, Arkansas. And David Filo of Yahoo, whose personal wealth was valued at $2.5 billion in 2006, continued to live in his small apartment in Mountain View, California.

In the late 1990s, with the stock market setting historic highs, *Forbes* was reporting a "wave of extravagant consumption," with a marked increase in demand for customized homes and exclusive resorts. But the hunger for extravagant goods was counterbalanced by a desire in many quarters to hold back from ostentatious display. Monster homes were submerged below ground, and flashy clothes were stuffed to the back of the wardrobe in favor of Ralph Lauren's old-money chic or the odd sight of a CEO in flip-flops—a trend that continues today in the person of YouTube CEO Chad Hurley.

At the end of the millennium, conservative author and commentator Dinesh D'Souza argued that the middle-class yearnings of the new rich were more than just a social pose—that they reflected a genuine conflict in their psyche. "Theirs is not old wealth that has marinated over the generations and has come to seem natural and inevitable to its possessors," he wrote in *Forbes*. "Many like Gates, [Jeff] Bezos [founder of online retailer Amazon] and [Eric] Schmidt [CEO of Google], grew up in the middle class. Applying bourgeois values like ambition and hard work, they became wealthy. They want to enjoy their wealth, but they don't want to lose their middle-class self-image. The new rich know they're doing well, but they also want to feel like they're doing good . . . and they desperately want to raise their children with the values that helped them get where they are." In that vein, Beverly Hills psychologist Lee Hausner notes that one of the main worries afflicting the new rich is that they will fail to pass on middle-class values to their children. Not for them the over-the-top spending of Larry Ellison or of Bill Koch, who built his son a two-acre playground complete with a dozen jungle gyms.

Writer and *New York Times* columnist David Brooks christened this new affluent class—children of the 1960s who have melded capitalist success virtues with countercultural values—*bourgeois bohemians,* or *Bobos* for short. According to Brooks, in his tongue-in-cheek sociological study *Bobos in Paradise: The New Upper Class and How They Got There,* while these new billionaires have no problem spending their hard-earned dollars on beautiful homes and yachts, woe betide anyone who flaunts his riches egregiously. "Earlier this century social climbers built ornate castles, aping the manners of the European aristocracy," Brooks writes. "Today a vice president at Microsoft might build a huge modern mansion, but if he built a house like J. P. Morgan's, he'd be regarded as a pompous crank."

10

Heirs

Huntington Hartford II lost it all: tens of millions of dollars, a vast collection of art, and four beautiful wives. When *Forbes* tracked Hartford down in 1985, he was reclining on a bed in a dank room on the third floor of his four-story Manhattan town house, his $90 million inheritance reduced to an $8 million trust he had resolved to give to charity. Seven years later he filed for bankruptcy to fend off a pending foreclosure on the house.

Hartford was an heir to the great Atlantic and Pacific Tea Company fortune. In the first half of the last century, his family ranked among the wealthiest in America, alongside the Du Ponts, the Rockefellers, and the Mellons. He was groomed for society by his mother, Henrietta (his father died when he was young), who would walk the porch with the young boy, a croquet mallet pressed to the small of his back to ensure good posture. When he started out on his business career, he hadn't a care in the world. "I was in my 20s, and I had $1.5 million in income a year—all the money I needed. I never thought about how I would get a return on my investments," he told *Forbes* magazine.

Hartford's daughter Juliet says her mother believed Hartford would have been a very simple man if he had not inherited the money. But a succession of bad luck, poor business skills, and a dependence on drugs later on reduced him to one of the most prominent inheritance cautionary tales of the twentieth century. Hartford's first job out of Harvard, working as a clerk for A&P, was a harbinger of things to come. He was often seen arriving late, leaving early, and sometimes sleeping at his desk. A succession of business and philanthropic failures followed. He secured a job as a reporter on the New York

Tough times for "old money"

What's happened to America's "old money" over the last 25 years? We looked at 12 families and how they fared. It's a complicated story. As the graph at the bottom of the page shows, the percentage of total 400 wealth held by these 12 families has slipped dramatically. Yet some old families, like the Hearsts, Rockefellers, and Fords, still have plenty of money. There were 24 members of the Du Pont family on the list in 1982; by 1998, no Du Ponts were rich enough to be on the list. The Rockefellers had 14 on the list in 1982, just one in 2006. But the remaining Rockefeller—David Sr.—has seen his wealth increase from $1 billion to $2.6 billion. That's only an annualized return of 4.1%, however.

Number of family members on the list

	'82	'83	'84	'85	'86	'87	'88	'89	'90	'91	'92	'93	'94	'95	'96	'97	'98	'99	'00	'01	'02	'03	'04	'05	'06
Du Pont	24	20	14	27	18	13	4	11	12	11	11	11	7	9	6	5	3	0	0	0	0	0	0	0	0
Duke	2	2	2	2	2	2	2	2	2	2	2	2	0	0	0	0	0	0	0	0	0	0	0	0	0
Field	3	3	3	3	3	3	3	3	3	3	3	2	2	2	2	2	2	2	2	2	2	2	2	0	0
Ford	3	5	5	4	5	2	3	2	2	2	2	2	2	2	2	2	2	2	1	2	2	2	2	2	2
Frick	1	1	1	0	0	0	0	0	0	0	0	0	0	0	0	0	0	0	0	0	0	0	0	0	0
Getty	1	1	1	2	2	1	1	5	5	5	5	5	6	5	5	5	4	4	4	4	4	4	4	1	1
Harriman	1	1	1	0	0	0	0	0	0	0	0	0	0	0	0	0	0	0	0	0	0	0	0	0	0
Hearst	5	5	3	5	5	5	5	5	5	5	5	6	5	6	6	6	6	6	6	6	5	5	5	5	5
Hunt	11	11	10	10	10	3	3	3	3	3	3	3	3	3	2	2	2	1	1	1	1	1	1	1	1
Mellon	6	9	9	9	9	6	6	4	9	6	9	8	3	3	3	3	3	2	2	2	2	2	2	1	1
Rockefeller	14	14	13	9	8	3	3	3	3	3	3	3	3	3	3	3	3	3	3	3	3	3	3	2	1
Whitney	1	1	1	1	1	1	1	1	1	1	1	1	1	1	1	1	0	0	0	0	0	0	0	0	0

The percentage of the total wealth of the 400 held by the 12 families fell from 21.4% in 1982 to 1.7% in 2006. Also shown is the Du Pont family decline in wealth.

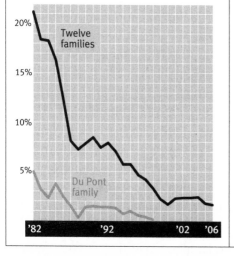

Over the last 25 years, the wealth of many of the 12 families, as measured by the 400 list, has sharply declined. But not in every case. The big winner: the Hearst family. In 1982 its family fortune was $800 million; in 2006 it was $10.1 billion—an annualized increase of 11.1%.

	Peak value in billions	Year
Du Pont	$4.61	1982
Duke	$0.88	1987
Field	$1.20	2003
Ford	$2.60	2005
Frick	$0.15	1984
Getty	$4.91	1997
Harriman	$0.15	1984
Hearst	$10.10	2006
Hunt	$6.60	1982–1984
Mellon	$4.14	1992
Rockefeller	$5.20	1999–2003
Whitney	$0.78	1991

newspaper *PM* following a $100,000 investment in the business. The job lasted six months, and the paper eventually folded. Afterward Hartford set up a modeling agency and then an institute for handwriting analysis, both of which failed. The more Hartford put in, the more he lost. In the 1960s he spent $30 million buying and developing an island in the Bahamas he called Paradise, only to sell it for $1.5 million seven years later. His philanthropic ventures were no more successful, the most spectacular failure being Hartford's multimillion-dollar flop: the Gallery of Modern Art in New York.

Every culture has its version of the saying "Shirtsleeves to shirtsleeves in three generations" (in China it's "Rice paddies to rice paddies," in Holland it's "Clogs to clogs"). Often the combined effect of never having seen their parents struggle and the knowledge that they need never work saps the character, drive, and business skills needed for a successful career. In his book *Old Money: The Mythology of Wealth in America,* Nelson W. Aldrich Jr. (himself a Rockefeller relative) quotes an anonymous inheritor as saying: "The older I get, the more I see how pervasively money has influenced me. . . . I've always been proud of being very laid-back. I don't get hot under the collar at meetings. I don't usually get embroiled in office politics, and so on. But now I see that a lot of that comes from the expectation that I'll always get my way because I can buy it. A rich person doesn't need to be a scrappy infighter . . . you don't learn those skills in rich families." Aldrich writes firsthand of the detachment an inheritor can feel from his own abilities and success: "To the self who inherits it, his money remains adventitious, wholly other, like a chauffeur in a limousine. Thus, intermittently, it is believed that 'legacies' do not get to Harvard on their own two feet: The chauffeur got them there, the Mercedes, their grandparents, the honest gains of two great-grandparents, the ill-gotten ones of two others. And the legacy intermittently thinks so too. It would be the same if the legacy were beautiful: Everything he or she did or was could be accounted for by his or her beauty."

People are fascinated by America's great fortunes: the Carnegies, the Vanderbilts, the Du Ponts, the Mellons. And those fortunes are still very much in existence today. In 2000 *Forbes* estimated the Du Pont family's total net worth at $14 billion, the Mellons' at $10 billion, and the Rockefellers' at $8.5 billion. Yet in 1999 barely any individual family members made it onto the Forbes 400: three Rockefellers and not a single Du Pont, who in 1982 made up close to 4 percent of the total wealth of the 400, with twenty-four family members on the list. Over the past fifteen years the number of self-made fortunes has increased from 218 in 1992 to 280 in 2006. Meanwhile, the number of inherited fortunes has fallen correspondingly. Look at the very top of the list and you will see a succession of self-made men: eighth-grade dropout Daniel Ludwig, JCPenney management trainee Sam Walton, German immigrant John Kluge, and the privileged but by no means dynastic Bill Gates. To locate the only inheritor ever to top the list, one must go back more than twenty years to Gordon Getty, the son of oilman Jean Paul Getty, who had a net worth of $2.2 billion in 1983 and $4.1 billion in 1984—the year after he sold Getty Oil to Texaco for $125 a share.

What are the reasons for the great families' decline? And what problems lie ahead for the newest American dynasties such as the Walton family, which, since Sam's death in 1992, has dominated the top of the list? In 2006 Sam's widow, Helen, his children, and daughter-in-law, Christy, occupied positions six, seven (a tie), nine, and eleven on the list, with a combined net worth of $77.7 billion. (Helen Walton died in 2007.) That's $6.5 billion more than second-place Warren Buffett and just $4.5 billion short of Bill Gates, the richest man in the world. But the Waltons face a string of obstacles in maintaining that wealth. For starters, the sheer size of a rapidly expanding family so dilutes the wealth that the rising benchmark for entry onto the list (from $90 million in 1982 to an eye-catching billion in 2006) simply becomes too high. But dissipation of wealth is just one of several problems that face the Forbes 400. There's the burden of inheriting an enormous sum of money that can destroy an heir's ambition, the pressure of emulating a father's or grandfather's success, the difficulties of running a large corporation, the intricacies of establishing consensus between an ever-growing network of cousins, and the ominous reach of the tax man's outstretched palm at the grave. It's hardly surprising that the number of American fortunes of staggering magnitude

---

2000

from the pages of *Forbes*

Ted Turner, founder of CNN, advocates prairie dog rights and tours his extensive land holdings out West in a Chevy Suburban emblazoned with a SAVE THE HUMANS bumper sticker. (2000 net worth: $9.1 billion)

Amazon's **Jeff Bezos** reads the Declaration of Independence to himself every Fourth of July. (2000 net worth: $4.7 billion)

William Cook, who made his fortune from medical devices such as catheters and stents, is a former Chicago cabbie and onetime tour-bus driver for John Mellencamp. (2000 net worth: $1.1 billion)

Ernest Gallo of Gallo wine kayaked on a trip to Turkey with his family—at age ninety. (2000 net worth: $800 million) that have been diluted in the past twenty-five years far exceeds those whose heirs are still on the Forbes 400 list.

Perhaps the most immediate question facing second and third generations of inherited wealth is this: How does an heir who will inherit such a vast sum of money keep his or her feet on the ground? A century before Warren Buffett disavowed dynastic wealth, Andrew Carnegie was sounding the warning bell: "The parent who leaves his son enormous wealth generally deadens the talents and energies of the son and tempts him to lead a less useful and less worthy life than he otherwise would," Carnegie wrote.

As is true of any parenting, one of the keys to producing a successful heir is not to spoil one's children. Given the sheer magnitude of many of today's fortunes, however, that's often difficult to do. Todd Millay, executive director of Wharton Global Family Alliance, says that while it may seem obvious, it bears repeating that parents of a child who is going to inherit a large sum of money face bigger challenges than regular parents in making sure their kids turn out well: "If you never have to work and everything is provided for you, it has a very toxic effect on people." Psychologist Dr. Lee Hausner, of the family-wealth consulting firm IFF Advisors in Irvine, California, says wealthy children are susceptible to two problems in particular: "entitleitis" and "affluenza." Following a talk in Beverly Hills about not spoiling children, Hausner says one woman told her she was building an eight-thousand-square-foot playhouse for her daughter. Another said that she dressed her three-year-old daughter in designer clothes because the little girl "loved fashion." This kind of behavior, in Hausner's view, is mostly found in newly affluent parents trying to give their kids everything they never had as a child. "You wouldn't find old money spending seventeen thousand dollars on a birthday party," Hausner says.

David Rockefeller Sr., the grandson of John D. Rockefeller and as old money as they come, is a case in point. He went on to have a distinguished career as head of Chase Bank and a world statesman. But as a child, he earned his 25¢ allowance by raking leaves for eight hours a week. In his PhD thesis for the University of Chicago, *Unused Resources and Economic Waste*, Rockefeller wrote: "From our earliest days we are told not to leave food on our plates, not to allow electric lights to remain burning when we are not using them, and not to squander our money thoughtlessly, because these things are wasteful ... of all forms of waste, however, that which is most abhorrent is idleness." This from a man whose father inherited $450 million.

Creative Heirs

Warren Buffett has devoted his life to looking for stocks and companies to invest in. But like every good father, he told his children they should pursue whatever profession they loved. Howard decided to run his own farm, Susie works at the family foundation, and Peter composes music. The Buffett kids are not the only ones to strike out in surprising directions from their father: Wal-Mart heir John Walton volunteered to serve in Vietnam in the 1960s, where he was a medic and was awarded the Silver Star. After returning to Arkansas, he rejected a career at the family company, turning instead to building his own motorcycles, boats, and airplanes. Similarly, the oil business proved of little interest to Gordon Getty, who sold the family's Getty Oil in the mid-1980s. Getty spent the following twenty years composing classical music. He also invested in wine, backing the PlumpJack wine business of friend and former San Francisco mayor Gavin Newsom, which includes a forty-eight-acre vineyard, café, and inn. And Getty's nephew Mark Getty has carved his own niche in the media industry by cofounding a successful stock photo business, Getty Images. Edgar Bronfman Jr. tried his hand at the music industry, cowriting a number of songs including Dionne Warwick's "Whisper in the Dark" before steering the family wealth out of whiskey and into the media business. And then there's filmmaker and Johnson & Johnson heir Jamie Johnson, who has made his career studying his fellow rich in the documentaries *Born Rich* and *The One Percent*.

In fact, Rockefeller is a product of a different tradition—wealthy parents who apply too much pressure or are overly parsimonious with their children. In David Rockefeller Sr.'s *Memoirs,* he says that his grandfather drove his two eldest children very hard. John D. Rockefeller Jr. dropped out of the family firm, Standard Oil, under the pressure, and his sister Abby became a recluse. Likewise, legendary Texas oilman H. L. Hunt set exacting standards for his children. His wife, Lyda Hunt, is said to have blamed her husband for putting their son Hassie under such enormous pressure that he had a nervous breakdown. (Hassie would eventually have a lobotomy and, not surprisingly, was never the same again.)

"Give them enough to do anything but not enough to do nothing": that's Warren Buffett's motto. Buffett, of course, made headlines worldwide in 2006 by pledging to give away virtually all of his money, most of it to the foundation of number one billionaire Bill Gates and his wife, Melinda. Whatever Buffett, in the end, leaves to his children, he has been keen to instill in them a strong sense of the value of money. Each of the children was given a $10 million charitable foundation as a Christmas present at the end of the 1990s, and before that a joint charity called the Sherwood Foundation. His son Peter Buffett says the idea was "to prime the pump for us to think what it's going to be like if we have to give some money away."

Possibly as a result of Buffett's strategy, his children have all pursued their own independent lives, and they show no signs of desperately trying to get on the Forbes 400 list. Susie worked as an assistant to the publisher at *The New Republic* and at *U.S. News & World Report*. Peter has had a successful career as a composer and musician, and Howard runs a farm near Decatur, Illinois (although Peter jokes that Howard's farm would make a lot more money if Howard didn't buy so many huge agricultural machines). All three Buffetts are now in charge of billion-dollar foundations, which is in itself a full-time job.

Ivanka Trump and her older brother, Donald Jr., claim not to have been particularly spoiled as children. Although Ivanka went to Choate Rosemary Hall, a boarding school whose alumni include John and Bobby Kennedy, she says she and her brothers were raised to appreciate everything they were given. She says the stories of her mother paying only her tuition and that she had to work for anything else she wanted are untrue ("They gave us what every parent would want to give their kids"), but Ivanka did turn to modeling at age fourteen to supplement her income. "Our parents were very careful not to bestow us with a sense of entitlement," Ivanka says. "And I think that is key when you are surrounded by a tremendous amount of money. Everything we have got, my brothers and I have worked for."

The Trump children were still able to live a life most young people can only dream about: attending the best schools, traveling all over the world, and making important contacts. But Ivanka points out that her mother, Ivana, having grown up in Communist Czechoslovakia, knew the meaning of austerity. And Ivanka's father had very strong, frugal parents: Donald's father, Fred Trump, built more than twenty-seven thousand apartments and row houses in Brooklyn and Queens. He amassed a fortune estimated at more than $250 million, yet even at the height of his career would pick up spare nails at his construction sites to be used the following day.

According to *Forbes*, Donald—whose own father bailed him out once or twice in his checkered career—has been an exacting tutor to his children,

Heirs, heirs and more heirs

The average number of children produced by a 400 member is three. But some have been much more productive—and a few much, much more so.

= # of Kids   # of 400 Members

14 | William Pulte | | | 1

12 | Leonard Shoen | | | 1

11 | Alan Ashton | | | 1

10

August Busch Jr.	Nelson Peltz	Frederick Smith
George Mitchell	Richard Schulze	

5

9

David Duffield	Jon Huntsman	Robert Shelton
Kingdon Gould Jr.	John MacMillan III	

5

8

Frederick Field	Charles Munger	James Sorenson
William Hilton	Winthrop Rockefeller	Edwin Whitehead

6

7

Robert Anderson	Christopher Hemmeter	James McGlothlin
Edgar Bronfman Sr.	Kenneth Hendricks	Diane Miller
Steven Cohen	Michael Ilitch	Roy Richards
Lester Crown	James Jannard	William Simon
Henri Du Pont	Jane MacElree	Steven Spielberg
Mary Du Pont Faulkner	Alfred Mann	Peter Wege
Gordon Getty		

19

6

S. Daniel Abraham	Barry Gordy	Abby O'Neill
Terence Adderley	Helen Hendrix	Ronald Perelman
Sheldon Adelson	Thomas Hicks	Generoso Pope Jr.
Arthur Appleton	Jeremy Jacobs Sr.	David Rockefeller Sr.
Louis Bacon	Charles Johnson	Shapman Root
Arthur Blank	James Johnson	Roy Sakioka
Franklin Booth Jr.	John Johnson	Walter Scott Jr.
Octavia Du Pont Bredin	Howard Kaskel	Mariana Du Pont Silliman
Donald Bren	William Koch	Harold Simmons
Oliver Carr Jr.	Donald Koll	Herbert Simon
William Connell	Carl Landegger	Saul Steinberg
Fred Crow	Robert Lurie	Glen Taylor
Roy Cullen	John Menard Jr.	Gary Tharaldson
John Dempsey	Sy Merns	William Turner
Charles Dolan	Gerrish Milliken	Samuel Wyly
Stanley Durwood	Rupert Murdoch	
Malcolm Glazer	Robert Naify	

51

The New-Style Socialite

William Barron Hilton can't be overly pleased with his two infamous grand-daughters, Paris and Nicky. The Hilton sisters embody the image of the vacuous heiress, staggering from nightspots into the camera flashes of the paparazzi and serving as a mother lode of material for gossip columnists.

But Hilton can take heart in one respect: Neither of the girls need survive on her inheritance alone. They command five-figure fees just to appear at Vegas nightclubs. And they don't just make their money from late-night appearances.

Nicky has her own clothing label and ambitions to strike out in the family business with a range of hotels, Nicky O (although both are in the infant stage, and the clothing line has yet to make a splash). Meanwhile, Paris remains one of the most recognizable faces of her generation, with a reality TV show, a perfume line, clothing lines, a recording contract (and a stint in jail). "Paris Hilton" was one of the most Googled phrases of 2006, helped no doubt by the notoriety of an illicit sex tape, *One Night in Paris,* that shot around the Internet. Paris is also one of the few people in the world who can trade on a single name.

Not so long ago, heiresses (and parvenus alike) aspired to be a grande dame, as personified by Brooke Astor. Vincent Astor, Brooke's husband, was the grandson of the original New York socialite, Caroline Astor, who invented the idea of the "400" based on the number of people she could entertain in the ballroom of her Fifth Avenue mansion. This 400, most of them fabulously wealthy, were also the most socially prominent New Yorkers of the late nineteenth century. And true to form, Brooke Astor presided for a generation over New York's social and philanthropic life.

Now, however, the new goal of the very rich and socially ambitious is to be a *celebutante*—those socialites and entertainers who are known for the places they hang out, the people they hang out (and often sleep) with, and the column inches they provide, rather than the opulence of their mansions or their fancy dress balls.

Though most heiresses need never work, many take positions at their families' firms or strike out on their own, continuing their careers at the same time as they raise their families. Ronald Lauder's daughter, Aerin Lauder Zinterhofer, a mother of two, is on the board of the family business, the Estée Lauder cosmetics empire. Lauder joined the firm in 1992 and worked her way up through marketing, product development, and advertising, and is now in charge of the image of the Estée Lauder brand. Her involvement in fashion circles helped her lure friend and former Gucci designer Tom Ford to the firm in 2005, as well as attracting Gwyneth Paltrow to be the new face of the brand the same year. And former model Ivanka Trump, of course, oversees a part of her father's business empire.

Other heiresses have found a niche in the fashion world, as socialites increasingly take the place of supermodels. Cousins and Hearst heiresses Lydia Hearst-Shaw and Amanda Hearst appear in ads for Prada and Louis Vuitton. Meanwhile, designers Diane von Furstenberg (now married to Forbes 400 member Barry Diller), Carolina Herrera, and Carolyne Roehm, second wife of 400 member Henry Kravis, have parlayed their talent, money, and connections into their own labels.

Another working girl/socialite is Ralph Lauren's daughter Dylan; while in her midtwenties, she founded a chain of candy stores, Dylan's Candy Bar, helped by a loan from her parents. Her business includes a flagship ten-thousand-square-foot store on Third Avenue in Manhattan as well as four satellite stores nationwide. Her father told the *New York Times* in 2006, "If she can't pay me back, I know whatever she did she's done because she believes in it and was honest about it and works hard. I'm glad she had a chance to use her creativity and express herself."

schooling them in all aspects of the Trump business empire, from marketing the Trump brand to mixing concrete. By all accounts, Ivanka and Donald Jr. make a great team. Donald Jr. is the hard-driving details guy who spends long hours at the office poring over the more than three hundred proposals that cross his desk each year. Meanwhile, Ivanka, vice president of development, is in charge of putting the chosen projects in motion. (Their younger brother, Eric, two years Ivanka's junior, joined the business in August 2006.) "They work well together and finish each other's sentences," reported one *Forbes* article. Both kids are in the process of completing an on-the-job apprenticeship with Donald after finishing their formal education at their father's alma mater, the Wharton School.

Ivanka thinks that stories like hers and her brother's—heirs who go into the family business and work extremely hard—are not uncommon. "A lot is made of the devastating effects wealth has on the second generation, possibly because there are so many horror stories, and people like to hear about it," Trump says. "There is a little bit of enjoyment that a child of wealthy people didn't turn out well because people like to think that not everybody is perfect. But I have a lot of very close friends who come from very privileged upbringings who turned out just fine."

With or without the billions in inheritance, there's an awful lot of pressure that comes simply from the weight of the celebrated surname. John D. Rockefeller Jr. was plagued by feelings of inadequacy in the shadow of a self-made man who amassed a fortune worth, in 2006 dollars, $305 billion. His children and other Rockefeller descendants have had to wrestle with the complicated Rockefeller legacy. John D. Rockefeller Sr. may have been the richest man in America and a figure now accorded legendary stature, but in his day he was considered, by some, one of the most infamous of industrialists. David Rockefeller's daughter Abby was a supporter of Fidel Castro and an ardent feminist. And his daughter Peggy distanced herself from her parents for many years and worked with the poor in the favelas of Rio. In turn, Abby Rockefeller's daughter, Sandra, dropped the family name in favor of a surname from her mother's side of the family so she would not be identified as a Rockefeller heir. Though the individual Rockefeller wealth is dwindling, the family name will continue to be associated with money and power for generations to come, even if Rockefeller descendants have little of either.

And so it is with all other great names. Can a Vanderbilt or a Whitney, a Gates or a Buffett ever escape the baggage of the surname? And what of all the Forbes 400 Juniors out there, made in their father's image? Just as John D. Rockefeller Jr. struggled to emerge from his father's shadow, so Herbert V. Kohler Jr., heir to the bathroom and plumbing fortune, struggled with his own identity. Of his rebellious teenage years, Kohler says: "I was fundamentally trying to find myself. Who is this person called Herbert V. Kohler Junior? And that 'Junior' is a tough part because you have the same name as your father, and your father happens to be famous. Here is this big shot," he says, describing an overarching mushroom shape with his hands. "And here I am," he continues, pinching his upturned finger and thumb together. "Who is this person? What are his capabilities? What are his limits?"

The downside of having a prominent family name is well known. Jamie Johnson, heir to the Johnson & Johnson fortune and a budding filmmaker, has produced two documentaries examining the subject of wealth. In his

Wayward Heirs

Huntington Hartford was not the first heir to squander his inheritance. A century after Cornelius Vanderbilt's death in 1877, not a single one of his more than seven hundred descendants was wealthy enough to be counted among the Forbes 400. Many were the victims of an ever-growing family tree. But others found much more enjoyable ways of lightening their pockets.

Commodore Vanderbilt's son Corneel was the first in a line of profligate Vanderbilt heirs. He frittered his fortune away running a money-losing farm and paying frequent visits to New York gambling dens and brothels, finally declaring bankruptcy in 1868. The Commodore's grandson George Washington Vanderbilt II lost his fortune on bad investments and one of the biggest white elephants of all time, the gigantic Biltmore estate in Asheville, North Carolina. The centerpiece is the 175,000-square-foot Biltmore mansion, the largest private home ever built in America. His widow had to sell Biltmore in order to repay his debts. The Commodore's great-grandson Reginald Claypoole Vanderbilt squandered his fortune on women, gambling, and booze. And the Commodore's great-great-grandson Cornelius Vanderbilt IV went broke during the 1920s launching a newspaper empire that failed.

Other heirs have taken a more circuitous route to ignominy. During the 1980s E. Newbold Smith and his wife, Margaret Du Pont Smith, were so worried that their son Lewis Du Pont Smith had fallen under the sway of fanatic Lyndon LaRouche that they placed him under the control of a financial guardian to stop him from squandering a $10 million inheritance on the extremist group. The worried parents claimed that their son, then in his thirties, was neither sane nor competent, charges that Lewis denied.* Another Du Pont heir, John E. Du Pont, was found to be mentally ill after he shot Olympic wrestler David Schultz at point-blank range on his estate in 1997. Du Pont was sentenced to between thirteen and thirty years in jail.

*The guardianship was subsequently reversed in 1994.

2003 film, *Born Rich*, made when he was twenty-one years old and on the verge of inheriting a vast fortune, he asked peers such as Georgina Bloomberg (daughter of New York mayor and multibillionaire Michael Bloomberg) and S. I. Newhouse IV (an heir to the vast Newhouse publishing fortune) what problems they faced as the children of America's wealthiest men. Almost universally there was a sense of guilt and a struggle to find the person behind the name. Josiah Hornblower, heir to the Vanderbilt and Whitney fortunes, tells Johnson he became so depressed at college that he had to take a couple of years off, traveling to Texas where he did manual labor for an oil field services company. S. I. Newhouse IV said fellow pupils at a Quaker school beat him up when they found out how rich he was.

Of course, as many children of the rich soon find out, their name can also be a big help. Ivanka says the Trump name has created many opportunities. "It's not a bad shadow to be under," she says of growing up with her famous father. While Susan and Peter Buffett have no doubt that their surname helps when they are raising money for their foundations, Peter says that his famous name had virtually no effect on his life in Milwaukee, where he spent fifteen low-key years, composing and producing music for commercials, films, and TV. But when he moved to New York in his late forties, his father was regarded as a Wall Street rock star and the Buffett name opened many doors. He says it was easy to cope with the attention as long as he remembered that many people were interested in him because of his name.

Whatever the luster and access provided by a name that is synonymous with a fortune, it's interesting that very few heirs of the Forbes 400 have matched the success of their parents. While second- and third-generation Tisches, Pritzkers, and MacMillans (of the Cargill agricultural fortune) are doing fine, over the twenty-five-year history of the Forbes 400 list it is difficult to pinpoint a single heir who managed to outperform his or her parents. One of the few heirs poised to build on the success of his father (and, possibly, rival him in wealth one day) is Ross Perot Jr. He stands to share his inheritance with four sisters—but he turns fifty in 2008 with a string of his own successes behind him.

"It all goes back to creativity," says Ross Perot Sr. from his offices in Dallas, Texas. "As a child we encouraged him to create his own toys. He was always doing really interesting things. I would ask him how he did it, and he would say, 'I thinked it out.' " One of Perot Sr.'s favorite anecdotes about his son is of paying him 75¢ for each bush he planted outside the headquarters of Electronic Data Systems, Perot Sr.'s company, when he was fourteen years old. Perot Jr. struck rock a few inches down and had to take out a pickax to complete the work. "I will never forget that right after the company [EDS] started getting successful, a reporter from New York was interviewing me in the house, and Ross walked in the door, and the reporter turned to Ross and says, 'What does it feel like to be the son of a wealthy man?' " recalls Perot Sr. "And he said, 'Mister, all I know is I get fifty cents a week, and if I want any more, I have to work for it.' "

Like many second-generation (as opposed to third-generation) heirs, Ross Perot Jr. has memories of humble beginnings. He remembers his mother having to drop his father off at IBM so that she could use the family's only car to run errands. And he also remembers his father working into the night in the family's living room to set up Electronic Data Systems. Yet by the time he was a teenager, his father was one of the wealthiest men in America. He accompanied his father on trips to Vietnam and Laos to search for MIAs and on a trip to the Middle East, where Perot Sr. says he was both amused and taken aback to see his son questioning General Ariel Sharon about his recent victory in the Six Days' War. Perot Jr. grew up in a household where Lord Mountbatten once stayed during a visit to the United States and where astronauts such as John Glenn and Frank Borman were not uncommon guests around the dinner table. And of course, there were always plenty of Vietnam War veterans whom Perot Sr. hired to work at EDS. "All of these experiences had a big impact on a little boy's life," says Perot Sr. "He really learned a lot from these experiences, and he went on to follow his own path."

It is startling how similar the two men's lives have been. Just as Perot Sr. went riding with his own father every day after school in Texarkana, Texas, so Perot Jr. went riding with his father every day. Perot Sr. entered the navy. His son joined the air force and served in the reserves for eight and a half years. The pair has worked together for more than twenty years at Perot Investments and Perot Systems.

Perot Jr.'s choice of a career in real estate came about largely because of his father's decision to sell the family business to General Motors for $2.5 billion in 1984. When Perot Sr. acrimoniously parted ways with GM two years later, he signed a noncompete agreement that effectively barred him from setting up a similar data company for the following three years. So father and son decided to focus on their real-estate holdings and possibilities for expansion. According to Perot Sr., his son walked into his office one day with a map of the Dallas–Fort Worth area, pointed to an area to the north, and suggested that it was ripe for development. His father agreed, and they instantly began buying land. Before long Perot Jr. was well on his way to building America's first dedicated cargo-handling airport, the Fort Worth Alliance Airport. The airport was a great success and has been described as Perot Jr.'s EDS. It is now home to more than one hundred companies and a Nascar Speedway. But what impressed Perot Jr.'s father the most was his son's ability to turn around a project that should have taken up to ten years in just three. "People say, what makes your son so decisive? Well, when you are flying faster than the speed of sound, you don't call a committee meeting," says Perot Sr.

While the Perots have had extraordinary business success, even they have hit a few bumps along the way. Perot Jr. took over Perot Systems from his father in 2000, at a time when the computer outsourcing company was struggling. The company continued its weak performance until 2004, when Perot Jr. reduced his role, moving from CEO to chairman as his father slipped into the role of chairman emeritus.

Perot Jr. has also come in for some criticism over his method of using public funds for private projects. Perot Jr.'s Alliance Airport was partly financed with more than $200 million in cash and tax breaks. And when Perot Jr. wanted to develop a swath of downtown Dallas a few years ago, he bought a 67 percent stake in the Dallas Mavericks for $125 million and used the promise of a new arena as leverage for public funds. The city put up $125 million (to be raised via car-rental and hotel taxes) for that project, and Perot Jr. sold the team a couple of years later for $280 million.

Perot Jr. says he wants his own children—the ones at risk of falling foul of the "shirtsleeves to shirtsleeves" jinx—to have the same opportunities he had, but at the end of the day, whether they succeed or fail will be up to them. He believes in children being allowed to decide for themselves what they want to be; the important thing to remember is that it is incumbent upon each one of them to work hard.

"If every generation doesn't work hard, it's going to fall apart," Perot Jr. says. "Every generation has to pull its own weight and add to the family. You are always going to have some families that work well and some families that don't. It's life. It's human nature. And I am not sure if you are ever going to change it. You will have people with very little money who will squander their money, and you will have people with a little family business who will be ruined. The money just magnifies what is already there. If you are good, you can look really good; and if you are bad, you can look really bad."

Todd Millay claims it's even more complicated for future generations. While the wealth creator became a success through a combination of luck, timing, skill, and perseverance, inheritors need all those qualities and more: "Sustaining wealth takes as much effort and perseverance and tough decisions as building it. But you have to have a totally different mind-set. You have to think about diversification and about managing risk and about protecting against the downside."

However successful heirs are at guarding against the downside, they will always be faced with the biggest problem of all for those who inherit money—the dilution of wealth. H. L. Hunt's estimated $2 billion fortune was divided, albeit unequally, among fourteen children and forty-plus grandchildren. By 1995 there were 110 direct descendants of John D. Rockefeller, but only three, David Jr. and Laurance from the third generation and Winthrop Paul Rockefeller from the fourth generation, made it onto the Forbes 400. Sara Hamilton of Family Office Exchange, which advises some of America's wealthiest families, including the Sulzbergers (publishing) and the Weyerhausers (lumber), tells of a Rockefeller family member who turned twenty-one and went along to the family office, only to discover that his inheritance was a mere $2 million. "He's fifth or sixth generation, but everybody expects because his name is Rockefeller there's a lot more there," Hamilton says. "People expect these household names to have a tremendous amount of wealth when, in fact, they may not. You could say it's amazing any fourth or fifth generation shows up on the list, because the numbers alone—the taxes, inflation, and spending—make it very difficult." In that case, the Pritzker family is doing extraordinarily well: The fourth-generation Pritzkers occupy almost one dozen places on the list. But their success is qualified by the fact that it was the second and third generations that built up the family firm to 400-type proportions; and the stability of the dynasty is already in doubt. Meanwhile, the third generation of other great families, such as the Hearsts and the Gettys, barely makes the cutoff mark for inclusion, with about $2 billion apiece. The fourth generation might make it onto the Forbes 400, but they will have to work for it.

Just because individual family members are not represented on the list does not mean their families have failed completely in preserving their worth. The Du Pont family still has a considerable net worth, and two hundred years after the founding of the DuPont company—then a gunpowder manufacturer—by Éleuthère Irénée Du Pont, the firm is still at the top of its game. Unlike Huntington Hartford, whose decline into poverty was aided by the mismanagement of the A&P board (which presided over a stock slump from $70 a share in 1960 to $8 a share by the late 1970s), the Du Pont heirs were luckier: The company, which like all chemical companies was hit hard by a recession in the early 1970s, was radically overhauled. About one-third of the workforce was laid off; the remainder, from executives to janitors, was offered company stock to generate a sense of ownership. Lammot Du Pont Copeland was the last family member to run the company, retiring as chairman in 1971, so credit for the overhaul goes to nonfamily members. But over the past thirty-five years a number of Du Ponts have taken an interest in the firm, including Thère Du Pont, who joined the board of directors in January 2006, and H. Rodney Sharp III, who has been on the board since 1981.

Although the Du Ponts no longer make the list, their influence in the state of Delaware, site of the company headquarters, continues to be huge. There's the imposing Winterthur Museum and Garden, and the Longwood Gardens nearby in Kennett Square, Pennsylvania, whose 350 acres and twenty indoor gardens are widely regarded as some of the best in the United States. In fact, the Du Pont family has such green thumbs that in 1990 the American Horticultural Society granted the entire family a National Achievement Award, only one of five such awards it has ever presented.

Meanwhile, Todd Millay believes that the Rockefellers have succeeded dynastically where such families as the Vanderbilts have failed. "If the goal was to have the name Vanderbilt mean you are rich, then they blew it," says Millay, who blames a combination of conspicuous consumption, mismanagement, bad investment advice, and an inability of heirs to cope with their fortune. Millay points to white elephants that sucked up cash, including the Breakers, the Vanderbilts' Newport summer home, which was sold to the Preservation Society of Newport County in 1973, and the magnificent Biltmore mansion, originally built on 125,000 acres in North Carolina by George Washington Vanderbilt, which survives today as a tourist attraction (albeit a lucrative one) for his heirs. In contrast, Pocantico Hills, the Rockefeller estate in Westchester County, New York, is a mere 3,400 acres—but it remains in the family.

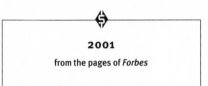

2001

from the pages of *Forbes*

Pierre Omidyar allegedly created eBay in 1995 so his girlfriend could trade Pez dispensers—a story subsequently revealed as a publicity ploy. (2001 net worth: $4.6 billion)

Joseph Ricketts of discount brokerage Ameritrade makes annual pilgrimages to the famed Sturgis, South Dakota, motorcycle rally. (2001 net worth: $850 million)

Jerral Wayne Jones, Texas oilman and owner of the Dallas Cowboys, claims to have lost fifty-five pounds just by giving up cheeseburgers and beer. (2001 net worth: $850 million)

William Morean, whose fortune comes from computer outsourcing, was briefly a bush pilot in Alaska and also swept floors for his dad. (1999 net worth: $1 billion)

The Eyrie "Folly"

Every summer for decades, the Rockefeller family would gather at the Eyrie, their hundred-room mansion on Mount Desert Island, Maine, less than ten miles from New England's fashionable Bar Harbor resort and the stunningly gorgeous Acadia National Park, which an ancestor helped create. After the death of John D. Rockefeller Jr. in 1960, the children decided to demolish the outdated house, which had become something of an architectural folly. But before the wreckers moved in, they resolved to restore it to its former glory one last time. Their mother, Abby Rockefeller, a lover of Eastern art, had filled the house with Asian paintings and ceramics, many of which were removed when their father remarried following her death in 1948. With the help of people who had visited the Eyrie over the decades, the children re-created their childhood retreat, reinstalling paintings and Oriental objects, even decorating the house with flowers and lighting fires. Once the house was returned to its former resplendent state, they called in architectural photographer Ezra Stoller, who documented the rooms. After Stoller was finished, the siblings divided up their parents' possessions, and the building was torn down.

As for the Rockefellers, Millay concedes that before long they, too, will disappear completely from the Forbes 400 as their wealth dissipates further. In 2006 only David Rockefeller Sr. remained on the list with a $2.6 billion fortune. But he says that the family's success rests in their wise use of philanthropy, which has been organized and passed down through the generations, and for which the Rockefeller name is renowned. "If you want to be one of the four hundred wealthiest people, that's one thing," says Millay. "But the Rockefellers are not worrying where the next meal is coming from. If the definition of wealthy is having enough independent means to do what you want and having the resources to make a difference, and you have, say, fifty million or sixty million dollars, I would say you were definitely a wealthy person."

In the case of old families such as the Rockefellers, the greatest threat for the first couple of generations is the burden of inheriting so much money. When John D. Rockefeller Jr. established trusts for his six children in 1932, his biggest concern was not the dissipation of the Rockefeller wealth but the effect vast wealth could have on his sons and daughter. As he wrote in a note to the trustees: "The Grantor is more concerned as to the harmful effect upon his children and their descendants of having more money than they can wisely use and unselfishly administer than of their having less."

John D. Rockefeller Jr. established a second set of trusts in 1952 to pass a further fortune on to his grandchildren. But as the Rockefellers married, divorced, remarried, and died, their children and their children's children placed increasing strain on resources. Even the original 1932 trusts, which upon the death of John D. Rockefeller Jr.'s children were passed to their beneficiaries, proved insufficient for the next generation.

By the 1970s and 1980s the third generation of Rockefellers, among them Nelson Rockefeller and David Rockefeller Sr., were vastly outnumbered by a fourth generation of Rockefellers known collectively as "the Cousins," plus a fifth generation, both of which had their own ideas, needs, and desires. In his memoirs, David Rockefeller Sr. notes that he and his brothers were at loggerheads over the future of their philanthropic arm—the Rockefeller Brothers Fund—as well as over the family office (known as room 5600 in Rockefeller Center) and the family's Pocantico Hills Estate. "Our debates and disagreements over these family institutions were affected by the attitudes and actions of the 'Cousins' during this time—so much so that a divisive intergenerational struggle briefly threatened the cohesion and continuity of the family itself," he wrote.

The Rockefeller disagreements were complex and made even more so by the family trusts, which wielded enormous power over Rockefeller family business. But even when trusts are not involved, heirs can face problems with cousins who are more concerned with cashing out than with the family staying in control.

Herbert V. Kohler Jr. faced a similar problem in the 1990s, when a couple of cousins started selling rare and highly sought-after shares of the Kohler company for what were described as "eye-popping prices." "You always get to a point where a block of them wants to liquidate," says Kohler. "They are not satisfied with the income, and so they see a big juicy plum up there and they attack it."

Kohler was an unlikely savior for the family firm. An ebullient man who, by his own admission, was a scofflaw and a rebel in his youth, he was more interested in poetry and theater than in business. When he assumed control of Kohler Company in 1972 as chairman and chief executive, and finally in

1974 as president, he was faced with a company that had sixty thousand shares spread among four hundred shareholders. Many of the shareholders were nonfamily members who had bought shares that had filtered out during the 1960s and 1970s because of sales and loans by two of Kohler's cousins.

But Kohler proved adept at reinstating tight family control. He announced a one-for-twenty reverse stock split, which forced anyone with fewer than twenty shares in the company either to buy enough shares at $8,200 per share to make the twenty needed for one new share, or to sell the shares back to Kohler. By the end of the process the number of Kohler shareholders was reduced to 250, and the Kohler family owned 96 percent of Kohler stock. The drastic move caused some friction within the family. But throughout, Kohler said his aim was to avoid his two biggest fears—having the number of shareholders exceed 500, which in turn would have forced the company to make its financial information public, and being at the mercy of cash-hungry cousins. It's for this reason that Andrew Keyt of Loyola University says it's important that a successor have a strong sense of self. "Cousins have less in common than siblings," says Keyt. "One generation will face challenges that a generation ahead will not face. They also need the social skills to build a consensus among the family so there doesn't have to be a family fight."

Kohler is of the third generation of family money, and should, by rights, be in his shirtsleeves. Instead, he is planning the succession line of the future: All three of his children work at Kohler Company. Laura is director of the Kohler Foundation, Rachel is president of Kohler Interiors, and David is president of Kohler's Kitchen & Bath Group. Natalie A. Black, Kohler's wife since 1988 and the company's vice president, says the legal, management, and business structure is in place for Kohler's children to take the company forward. But the deciding factor will be whether they can work together successfully. "We have given them the framework to manage the company for generations to come as a privately held business, so it's really up to them to make the human element work," Black says. "That's something you can't dictate. But I think they are very well on the way to getting that done."

The twenty-fifth anniversary of the Forbes 400 list coincides with a period that is witnessing the largest transfer of wealth in history—trillions of dollars, according to Andrew Keyt. And some families are eager to stop the federal government from gobbling up their fortunes when they die. A concerted effort by opponents of the federal estate tax, many of them members of the Forbes 400, is pushing for a repeal; other members of the 400, including Warren Buffet and George Soros, rush to its defense.

A century ago the most popular insurance for future generations was the trust company. A wealth creator who established a trust could apply strict rules pertaining to when and how heirs would gain access to their inheritance. At its most benign, a trust might dictate that the heirs get an education or a job. But the rules might even dictate that an heir attend a particular college or score above a minimum grade point average. The trust was seen as a surefire way of maintaining control from the grave and of avoiding estate taxes. It also helped heirs to manage the family's assets, such as investments and estates.

Many trusts have been so successful that they have opened up to other clients. Wilmington Trust, for example, which originally was set up for the Du Pont family, now maintains more than twelve thousand accounts, totaling more than $30 billion, many of them multiple accounts for other clients and families. But as time-honored as they have become, trusts have their critics. Rod Wood, of Wilmington Trust, says that wealth creators who lay down rules that are too strict for future generations can run into trouble. "The more restrictive the request," Wood says, "the worse they become."

Sara Hamilton says the force wielded by trusts leaves many heirs powerless to determine their own fate, much as David Rockefeller found in the family struggles of the 1980s. "Trustees were told to sit in the corner and keep quiet and take the income," Hamilton says. "They were essentially disempowered by the system put in place to protect them from their wealth." She says that a further criticism of trusts is the conservative approach they have taken with funds—much of it imposed by law—which led many heirs during the 1980s to fear that, in the long run, they might not outlast the dissipation of their wealth.

But for all their rigidity, trusts remain the best bet for protecting against creditors, divorce, and bad investments, as well as for avoiding the estate tax. At the same time, more and more superwealthy families are also employing family offices to steer them in the right direction. Hamilton estimates there are about four thousand family offices in the United States today, an increase of about one thousand in less than ten years. The offices are customized, offering a range of services from investment decisions and tax advice to philanthropic research, prenuptial agreements, and help with heirs' education. Some family members may not be wealthy enough to afford all of these services on their own, but as a combined force they have powerful advice at their fingertips. What the family offices excel at, says Todd Millay, is keeping the dividends rolling in. "The best way to make a small fortune is to start with a large one," he says. "Hanging on to what you've got is an overriding goal for many families."

Huntington Hartford, of course, failed miserably at keeping the wealth going. His downfall may carry with it all of the delicious satisfaction of seeing a man who should have had everything end his life in failure. But what it really shows is that Hartford's start in life was not nearly as easy as it seemed. Being an heir is often a mixed blessing. For each generation, the game is different. The second and third generations typically must work through the pressures of inheriting an enormous sum of money, and in many cases trying to make it grow. Subsequent generations must often cope with the fact that the family name carries an aura of wealth that in reality is lacking. And all of their actions will be scrutinized beneath the magnifying glass that wealth creates.

Sam Walton's heirs may have dominated the Forbes 400 for fifteen years, but the experience of generations of wealthy families before them dictates that their reign will by no means be indefinite. If mismanagement, stupidity, and conspicuous consumption don't get them, then the expansion of the family will. The bar for entry to the list will continue to rise. And the Walton wealth will continue to trickle down through the family tree. If they are not careful, they could end up like the Vanderbilts—whose name is now synonymous only with a bygone age.

11

Family Feuds

"All happy families are happy alike, all unhappy families are unhappy in their own way," Leo Tolstoy wrote in *Anna Karenina*. But when it comes to unhappy superrich families, there seems to be a familiar sameness to their unhappiness. Not surprisingly, it tends to revolve around feuding over the family fortune. There is, in fact, no greater threat to a fortune than a family feud, whether it results from sibling avarice, succession struggles within the family business, haggling over a will, or a marriage that ends in a take-no-prisoners divorce. And the corollary seems equally true: There is no greater threat to a family than a fortune. True, masses of money can often bind a family together, as can the legacy of an admired wealth creator. But vast riches can also be a gargantuan inducement for envious siblings, jilted spouses, or subsequent generations of cousins to tear one another apart, often in a highly public battle.

"When you have a family that is very wealthy, all of the emotional and social dynamics are amplified, and that is how these feuds get so intense," says Thayer Willis, an heiress to the Georgia Pacific paper-company fortune and author of *Navigating the Dark Side of Wealth: A Life Guide for Inheritors*. It's a matter of scope, agrees Joseph Astrachan, management professor at Kennesaw State University in Georgia. "It's like a Shakespearean definition of tragedy—that a tragedy is only a tragedy if it involves people of note and worth."

Admittedly, arguments among families of all income brackets can be brutal. But when one of America's richest families is at war, the whole country often takes note. Few family feuds have been as protracted and acrimonious as the one that raged among the Koch brothers of Kansas, sparking fifteen years of litigation and more than twenty years of mudslinging and bad blood. In a parody of Charles Dickens's *A Christmas Carol,* with its moral of love beginning anew on Christmas Day, the long-simmering feud erupted dramatically over Christmas 1979. The four Koch "boys"—Fred, Charles, and twins David and William (known as Bill), all in their late thirties and early forties—had gathered to celebrate with matriarch Mary Koch, widow of oil tycoon Fred C. Koch, at her home overlooking the exclusive Wichita Country Club. In the dining room Mary reigned elegantly as her sons sat around the dinner table. But the picture-perfect scene shattered that day into what has been called "perhaps the nastiest family feud in American business history." According to Mary, Bill started making such "unkind remarks" about Charles that "I got up and left the table crying." From that point on, the only room Mary would share with all her sons would be a courtroom.

The stage for the feuding among one of Kansas's richest families had been set long before. Patriarch Fred Koch, a formal, distant man, had shown little warmth toward his shy and sensitive eldest son, Fred, whom he considered self-indulgent because he preferred art and theater to the family's Wichita-based oil firm. But although Fred was a disappointment, it was the virulent antagonism between second son, Charles, and his little brother Bill that caused the family's unraveling. Over the decades Bill has characterized Charles as a bully. For his part, Charles has accused Bill, who has had bouts of depression in his life, of distorting their childhood history as a result of his many years in therapy. "I know he feels we had bad relations as children. I don't think we did," Charles later said. "We had fights, I think. But we were boys."

By his own admission, the tall, rakish Bill could be something of a hot-head. During his youth he often fought with his twin, David, who sided with elder brother Charles, a pattern that would continue into adulthood. But a huge part of the brothers' strained relations came as they struggled to run the family firm following their father's death. Oldest brother Fred had long given up on playing a role at Koch Industries to pursue his passion for art collecting. (His disappointed father had disinherited him in his will, although Fred lived nicely off his trust fund.) Favorite son Charles went to Koch Industries in 1960, after his father issued an ultimatum: Either Charles would join the family business or he would sell it. When his father died seven years later, Charles took over as president of the then $177 million firm. Twin brothers David and Bill joined the company a few years later. By the late 1970s annual sales had grown to $11 billion, thanks largely to modernization and expansion undertaken by Charles, a stolid and demanding leader.*

But the company kept dividend payments low, and that irked Bill. (To this day Charles is proud to say that Koch Industries plows 90 percent of earnings back into the company, rather than having a shortsighted focus on quarterly earnings, as do many public companies.) For Bill, a 20 percent shareholder, the measly $5 million or so that Koch Industries paid out each year was peanuts. He was also irritated by some of the causes Charles supported. In the late 1970s and early 1980s, Charles was pouring large sums of money into the Washington, D.C.–based libertarian think tank the Cato Institute, as well as into the coffers of the Libertarian Party, on whose ticket David ran as vice president in the 1980 election. "Here I am, one of the wealthiest men in America," Bill complained to the New York Times, "and I had to borrow money to buy a house. What's the point of building a company if you are not able to take out the assets and do what you want with them?"

Bill's frustration came to a head in 1980, when he staged a classic boardroom coup, rallying a group comprising 51 percent of Koch shareholders. He called for a special meeting to install new directors who would strip Charles of some of his powers and who would vote for more generous dividends. A small yet vital cog in Bill's plan was allying J. Howard Marshall III, who held a small percentage of Koch stock. But just before the crucial board meeting could take place, Bill's plan was foiled. Charles hopped on a plane with Marshall's father, J. Howard Marshall II, who in the 1950s had gained a 16 percent share of the company. Together they flew to his son's Los Angeles home, demanding that he sell back his shares. The younger Marshall complied; with majority control now in Charles's hands, Bill was fired. (The elder Marshall never forgave his son for siding with Bill, and cut him out of his will. That same document would later be hotly contested by his third wife, Anna Nicole Smith.)

---

*Koch expounds his management theories in *The Science of Success: How Market-based Management Built the World's Largest Private Company* (Hoboken, N.J.: John Wiley & Sons, 2007). In reviewing the book, Forbes.com commented: "Before diving into Charles Koch's *The Science of Success,* you must understand two things: Koch is an engineer, born and raised in the Midwest, and he's an autodidact, with a passion for the free market theories of Austrian economist Ludwig von Mises. Combine the two and you get a management philosophy book long on hard-edged statements where the author professes an almost Marxist faith in the 'fixed laws' that 'govern human well-being.' . . . The book is especially obtuse when Koch describes his system for grading employees, a four-box 'virtue and talents matrix' that balances 'values and beliefs' against the skills needed to run the business."

Over the next few years bitterness ensued as Charles and David fought to buy out the rebel block, while Bill tried to muscle up the price. Mary was drawn in to induce a little motherly guilt. "It was an emotionally wrenching time," Bill told the *New York Times*. "Even our mother would call and say she would die unless I sold my stock at the cheap price." In 1982, the battle still unresolved (and with the Koch brothers—apart from Fred, who had been disinherited—named to the first Forbes 400 list with $266 million each), Bill sued the company, alleging corporate mismanagement. His brothers fired back with a $167 million libel countersuit. A temporary truce was signed in 1983, when Charles and David agreed to buy out the dissident shareholders for $1.1 billion.

But hostilities flared again two years later, when Bill and Fred launched a lawsuit accusing Charles and David of hiding assets and using misleading accounting practices that had lowered the buyout price. At one point in 1986 David prematurely announced a victory for all: "They wanted a lot of cash and they got it. But we got the company. I guess we both got what we wanted." If only. The intrafamily Koch battles would continue for another twelve years and involve at least nine lawsuits.

Kicked out of Koch Industries, Bill had gone off on his own in 1983, forming Oxbow Corporation, a Florida-based holding company for a raft of businesses from real estate to commodities and offshore oil. But so distrustful was he of his brothers that he feared they were spying on him. "When people are spreading things about you, out to kill you, you get paranoid as hell," Bill later said. He hired Marc Nezer, an Israeli-trained former marine, to hunt for moles, sweep for bugs in his offices, and target possible traitors within Oxbow. Bill also went on the offense, hiring detectives to investigate claims that Koch Industries had stolen oil from Native American lands. In 1989 he passed on his evidence to a Senate committee, which decided that Koch Industries had indeed taken $31 million worth of oil over a period of three years. But the case was later dropped for insufficient evidence.

The legal wrangling over the shareholder buyout finally came to an end in 1998, as the two sets of brothers walked silently past each other in a courtroom. Bill lost; but he wouldn't let the accusations of stolen oil die. He sued his brothers in federal court the following year, accusing Koch Industries of underreporting the amount and quality of oil purchased from federal and Native American leases. This time he won. Under the nation's whistle-blower laws, Bill was entitled to 30 percent of the penalties, or about $120 million. Two years later the brothers agreed, for an undisclosed amount, to end all litigation. They issued a joint statement describing the litigation of the past two decades as "a painful experience for the employees of both companies."

For all its rancor the Koch feud did not end badly, at least financially. In 2006 Forbes estimated Bill Koch's net worth to be $1.3 billion, ranking him 297th on the list. Sales at his Oxbow Corporation came to some $1.5 billion. Meanwhile, Koch Industries, after buying paper firm Georgia Pacific in 2005 for $21 billion in cash, became the country's largest privately held firm, with annual sales of $80 billion. Charles's and David's 2006 net worth: $12 billion apiece, leaving them tied for thirty-third place on the list.

Things can get even messier and more complex as the family business and fortune pass down through subsequent generations. "In the early years all the money can be kept in the business because there is only one person who has to be pleased, and he is running it," says Joseph Astrachan. "But in later years, as you move to cousins and greater extended family, more of the wealth needs to be distributed." Indeed, the longer a fortune exists, the greater the threat to its survival, as brothers and sisters give way to grandchildren and cousins who have weaker bonds with one another and who inherit a smaller and smaller part of the spoils. According to the U.S. Small Business Administration (SBA), 90 percent of businesses are family-owned, yet only 30 percent survive into the second generation and an even smaller 15 percent into the third. Aside from cases in which heirs simply do not want to continue the business, the SBA also blames this low survival rate on a lack of succession planning and the ensuing conflict among future generations.

While survival rates among Forbes 400 family businesses are lacking, there is plenty

2002

from the pages of *Forbes*

Mark Cuban, cofounder of Broadcast.com and owner of the Dallas Mavericks basketball team, has been fined a record $1.5 million over the last two seasons, mostly for verbally abusing game officials. (2002 net worth: $1.3 billion)

Marvin "Buzz" Oates, who made his money in real estate, earned two Distinguished Flying Crosses as a World War II bombardier. (2002 net worth: $800 million)

Thomas Friedkin (Toyota dealerships) is a Hollywood stunt pilot and a big-game hunter on his preserve in Tanzania. (2002 net worth: $650 million)

Robert Galvin of Motorola and his wife are the founding patrons of the Stradivari Society, which buys violins crafted by the great master and lends them to budding virtuosos. (2002 net worth: $675 million) of anecdotal evidence that shows the ever-diminishing fortunes of subsequent heirs. In fact, only a few old-money families remain on the Forbes 400 list. Although the Du Ponts were the richest family in America in 2004, for example, with a combined net worth of $15 billion, the fortune is shared today by more than three hundred cousins and accounts for only 15 percent of the company. Sure, two Du Pont relatives sit on the company's board; yet more than thirty years have passed since a Du Pont has guided the firm, and eight years since an individual Du Pont earned a place on the Forbes 400.

Often the dissolution of family dynasties is helped by messy successions and eccentric (or egocentric) personalities. Such was the fate of the Getty Oil family business. Suspicion, envy, and bitterness racked the dysfunctional Gettys for generations. Millionaire oilman George Getty so mistrusted his playboy son, Jean Paul, known as J. Paul, that when George died in 1930, he left the bulk of his $10 million fortune to his own wife, Sarah. That didn't stop J. Paul from trying to wrest a share of the money. In the first of many Getty lawsuits, he sued his mother; in an attempt to shield the fortune, she retaliated by creating the Sarah C. Getty Trust in 1934. According to its terms, the trust's assets would not be released until after the death of J. Paul and his sons. But George and Sarah Getty's fears about their son's business judgment were unfounded. J. Paul took a multimillion-dollar firm and turned it into a multibillion-dollar behemoth, far surpassing his father in ambition and wealth.

Meanwhile, J. Paul's family expanded as fast as his business. He wedded and divorced a succession of five women, who bore him five sons. (True to his playboy reputation, he also carried on numerous extramarital affairs; upon his death he left a token bequest to eleven different women.) Though he was interested in oil and women, he was not much taken with his offspring. An uncaring and cold husband and father, he is said to have changed his will twenty-one times in order to exert control over his progeny. When his son Timmy died of a brain tumor in 1958 at age twelve, Getty, who was abroad at the time, did not return for the funeral. The surviving four sons didn't expect much affection from their father, and they weren't disappointed. In 1959, at the age of sixty-six, J. Paul bought Sutton Place, an English estate with a seventy-two-room mansion, where he spent much of the rest of his life away from them all.

The principal financial problem for the Getty heirs was that the Sarah C. Getty Trust's only asset, Getty Oil stock, did not pay cash dividends. For those who worked at the firm and drew a salary, such as sons George and Jean Paul

Jr. (who was born Eugene Paul but changed his name in 1958), the situation was tolerable. But for J. Paul's other son, Gordon, who had failed at the firm and was merely a consultant, it presented a problem. J. Paul appeased Gordon in 1962 by paying him a small dividend of about $50,000 a year from Getty Oil stock. But at the same time he punished Gordon by removing him from the list of sons eligible to become a future trustee of the Sarah C. Getty Trust. A few years later Gordon sued, claiming he was entitled to much more. Gordon lost the suit, which dragged on for six years. "Your lawyers are killing my husband," Gordon's wife, Ann, beseeched J. Paul over the phone, according to the *Wall Street Journal*. "Keep killing my son," J. Paul was later heard instructing his lawyers.

Though Gordon was publicly cast aside, his brothers Ronald and Jean Paul Jr. did not fare much better. Ronald failed in the family business and was disowned by his father as a result of a nasty divorce between J. Paul and Ronald's German mother, Adolphine Helmle. Jean Paul Jr. dropped out of the family business and became addicted to heroin. The only son to remain at the firm was J. Paul's eldest, George, though he, too, suffered a tragic fate. Routinely humiliated by his venomous father, George killed himself in 1973 by taking an overdose of prescription drugs and stabbing himself in the stomach. As with Timmy, J. Paul did not attend the funeral. With no one left to turn to, J. Paul grudgingly lined up Gordon as future trustee of the Sarah C. Getty Trust. Three years later J. Paul died with an estimated net worth of $2 billion. The bulk of his estate went to the J. Paul Getty Museum, now composed of the main Getty Center in west Los Angeles and the original, recently renovated Getty Villa near Malibu, which houses a stellar collection of Greek, Roman, and Etruscan art.

It wasn't long before ferocious fighting broke out within the extended family. Gordon, although a talented composer, had a reputation within the upper echelons of Getty Oil, and throughout the family, as a second-rate businessman. As sole trustee of the Sarah C. Getty Trust, which controlled 40 percent of Getty Oil stock, he had a seat on the company's board. When, during the early 1980s, the company's stock fell from $110 to $50 within two years, Gordon scouted around for a quick fix. His search for a solution fueled speculation that Getty Oil was on the block. Company management was irate, as were family members such as Jean Paul Jr., who sued on behalf of his fifteen-year-old son, Tara Gabriel Galaxy Gramophone Getty, for the right to be made cotrustee of the Sarah C. Getty Trust.

The legal battles raged until 1984, when Texaco offered to pay more than

$10 billion for Getty Oil—$125 a share—an offer too good to refuse. Gordon Getty helped push through the sale, which yielded the trust $3 billion after taxes, a masterly display of timing considering that the price of oil plummeted in subsequent years. Yet despite Gordon's colossal success, Getty heirs persisted in trying to get him to appoint another trustee or to remove him as trustee entirely. Eventually, Gordon laid the feud to rest by parceling out the money among the four branches of the family, thereby greatly diluting the family fortune. While once there were seven members of the Getty family on the Forbes 400 list, today only Gordon qualifies, with a 2006 net worth of $2.3 billion.

As *Forbes* makes clear each year in computing the wealth of the 400, it does not have access to private balance sheets, and many families find ever more ingenious ways of hiding their wealth. But for the many Forbes 400 families who revel in their relative anonymity, there's nothing like a family squabble to propel them and their private empires against their will into the public eye—especially battles that end up in the courts, where filings, depositions, testimony, and the like become public information. That was the case with Chicago's preeminent but intensely private Pritzker family, whose members for decades sat quietly on prestigious Chicago boards, gave generously to civic and artistic city causes, but kept the extent of their wealth hidden from public view in a vast network of private entities. After the death of wealth creator Jay Pritzker in 1999, however, infighting enveloped the fourth generation of Pritzkers. A lawsuit from Jay's niece Liesel, then eighteen years old, alleging mismanagement on the part of Robert, her billionaire father, dragged the family into court and exposed the unrest that roiled beneath the family's united front.

The Pritzker family first became prominent in the nineteenth century, when Ukrainian immigrant Nicholas Pritzker founded the law firm of Pritzker and Pritzker in Chicago. His son, A. N. Pritzker, took the business into real estate and manufacturing. And A.N.'s sons Jay and Robert, helped at first by their brother Donald, who died of a heart attack at age thirty-nine, presided in turn over decades of expansion that swelled the family coffers. Jay, in particular, led the Pritzker family's acquisitions for fifty years, including the 1957 purchase of a small Los Angeles airport motel that grew into the worldwide Hyatt chain, with more than two hundred hotels. By the end of the 1990s the empire encompassed a diverse portfolio of assets, including

Hyatt and Royal Caribbean cruise lines, as well as the multibillion-dollar industrial conglomerate Marmon, and companies that sold everything from credit checks to chewing tobacco. The combined family wealth was an estimated $15 billion, secured within a complex network of twenty-five hundred domestic and offshore trusts. At the empire's core lay Pritzker and Pritzker, the family law firm that effectively acted as an investment bank managing the family trusts.

"If we are going to have a problem, it's probably going to be a ne'er-do-well," Jay Pritzker said in 1988. But the challenge, when it came, was hardly from someone without accomplishment. Liesel Pritzker was a budding actress who starred in *A Little Princess* (1995) and *Air Force One* (1997) when barely into her teens. During the 1990s she fell out with her father in a battle over whether she could adopt her stepfather's surname and be called Liesel Pritzker-Bagley. (In protest she adopted the stage name Liesel Matthews, after her brother, Matthew.)

The roots of the feud that erupted at the start of the millennium, however, lay not with Liesel but in a memo that Jay dictated in 1995. Jay's son Tom was the heir apparent, so it seemed fitting that the cousins gather at his Chicago apartment to hear Jay lay out the framework for handling the family fortune. All of the adult cousins were there, but Liesel, who was nine or ten at the time, along with her brother and their young cousins, were left out of the meeting—and the succession plan.

The eleven assembled cousins heard how they would share in the Pritzker wealth, whatever their chosen career. The memo outlined how the Pritzker empire would be led by a triumvirate of cousins, with Tom at its head and Penny and Nicholas second in command. Jay guaranteed the older cousins, most of them in their thirties, a cash payout of $25 million before each of them turned forty. But a slightly larger share, he warned, would go to family members who worked at the family firm and therefore deserved extra compensation in the form of salaries and equity. "I expect our modus operandi will continue harmoniously through this next generation," Jay instructed in the memo.

Within months of Jay's death, however, the fourth generation's mutual mistrust had bubbled up. In 2000 Tom's brothers John and Dan headed a small group of inquisitive cousins who hired lawyers to examine the family's books. The investigation discovered that through a series of deals, Tom, Nick, and Penny had awarded themselves some $500 million over the previous few years. The cousins were outraged; but as an intensely private family, the

Pritzkers settled the matter quietly as best they could. They agreed in 2001 to carve up the $15 billion empire over the next ten years, with each of the eleven cousins getting $1.4 billion. And everything would be kept under wraps.

Liesel's lawsuit the following year shattered the family's private plan. Liesel was of the same generation as Tom and the more powerful cousins. But at age eighteen in 2002, she was thirty-four years younger than Tom and had considerably less money. In her lawsuit she claimed her father and her cousins had raided trusts that belonged to her and her brother, selling assets to family members at below-market prices and moving some funds into family philanthropies. The family protested that Liesel and her brother each had $160 million in the bank. Liesel claimed that the family owed her $1 billion plus $5 billion in punitive damages.

The case was a massive embarrassment to the Pritzker clan as it dragged through the courts for more than two years. When the family finally settled, Liesel and her brother got just under $500 million each; in return, they gave up all future claims to the Pritzker assets. As planned, the empire will be divvied up by 2011; but as more young family members come of age, and with suspicion still lingering over the troika's $500 million rewards to themselves, few would be surprised to see another feud erupt in future years. "It's classic fourth-generation stuff," a banker who had dealings with the family told the *Financial Times*. "Many mouths to feed, a lot of them just want their share of the fortune, to get on with their lives and party. They don't want to get involved in running anything." For now, though, the Pritzker fortune seems safe: All eleven cousins had a spot on the 2006 Forbes 400 list, with fortunes ranging from $1.6 billion to $2.3 billion.

Many family dynasties fall apart as a result of high-stakes, no-love-lost marital tussles. A messy divorce in a Forbes 400 family can tear it apart just as violently as a long-simmering multigenerational feud and undo even the most carefully cultivated public persona. And because of the wealth involved, divorce battles among the supperrich tend to get magnified in the public eye.

The statistics are all too familiar: Half of all marriages will end in divorce. Surprisingly, however, Forbes statistics show that among members of the 2006 Forbes 400 known to have been divorced at least once, the divorce rate hovers at around 30 percent. That's about a 10 percent increase from the 1982 list, but still below that of the average American marriage. The statistics hold yet another surprise. According to a 2005 study published in the *Journal of*

Sociology, "Marriage and Divorce's Impact on Wealth," divorced people in the general population see an average drop in net worth of 77 percent, a figure that might well encourage some couples contemplating divorce to work harder on their marriage. Yet Forbes 400 members known to have been divorced at least once showed a slightly higher average net worth than those who were married but had never been divorced: $3.3 billion in 2006, versus $3.1 billion.

Still, when the superrich do decide to call it quits, money makes the decision easier. As William Zabel, a New York lawyer who handled the 2004 divorce case of George Soros (from his second wife, Susan, after twenty-five years of marriage) and that of former GE chief executive Jack Welch and his second wife, Jane Beasley Welch, says: "It seems that the more money people have, the easier and more likely it is for them to get divorced." Judith Stern Peck, a therapist and director at New York's Ackerman Institute for the Family who has counseled Forbes 400 families, agrees: "When people are unhappy and they think that breaking up their marriage would make them happier and that their lifestyles would not suffer, then they are more apt to say, 'Let's get divorced,'" she says.

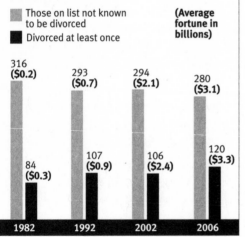

The marrying kind

About half of all U.S. marriages end in divorce. But for the Forbes 400, only 20% to 30% do, though the percentage has been increasing over the last 25 years. Interestingly, those who divorce are, on average, richer than those who don't. The divorce premium in 2006: about $200 million.

- Those on list not known to be divorced
- Divorced at least once

(Average fortune in billions)

	1982	1992	2002	2006
Not divorced	316 ($0.2)	293 ($0.7)	294 ($2.1)	280 ($3.1)
Divorced	84 ($0.3)	107 ($0.9)	106 ($2.4)	120 ($3.3)

The increased use of well-crafted prenuptial agreements, which limit payouts to ex-spouses, may be a factor contributing to what Zabel calls "recidivist divorcés" among the superrich. He believes the percentage of premarital agreements among the Forbes 400 is way up compared to people of lesser means. The agreements can cover it all—from divorce or the death of the rich party to who gets the dog or the box seat at the stadium. To be sure, all those mundane calculations can take some of the romance out of a new marriage, but prenuptials also come with a huge benefit: They can help provide a shield of confidentiality, as such serial divorcés among the Forbes 400 as Larry Ellison and Ronald Perelman have discovered.

Larry Ellison was divorced three times by the time he was forty-two. Before marrying third wife, Barbara, a former Oracle employee, he presented her with a prenuptial agreement that capped her entitlement at $1 million. As the story goes, the couple's lawyers, her father, and his brother-in-law kept wedding guests waiting as they negotiated the final details of the agreement. Three years later the marriage was over. Whether Barbara's lawyers were able to get more than $1 million out of Ellison is unknown, although she did get enough to keep up their luxurious Tara estate in Woodside, California, and fifteen horses. Larry got his freedom and in 2003 married wife number four, novelist Melanie Craft.

When Revlon billionaire Ronald Perelman (number 40 on the 2006 Forbes list, with a net worth of $7 billion) filed for divorce in 2006 from his fourth wife, the actress Ellen Barkin, the process went quickly, thanks in part to their prenup (see box, page 264). Barkin got a reported $20 million, and then collected another $20 million by selling off the fabulous jewelry that Perelman had given her during their six-year marriage. Before consigning all of the baubles to auction, she said that she wanted absolutely nothing that reminded her of that period in her life. "As exquisite as the collection is," Barkin told *Vogue* magazine, "they're just not memories I want to wear out every day. For other people, they're pieces of jewelry; for me, they have a history. . . . I'll take a break from the jeweled trophy-wife look."

These days the vast majority of divorce cases (80 to 90 percent, according to Zabel) are settled before they reach the glare of a public trial, and settlements among the very rich are usually kept confidential. But there are bruising exceptions. Take the case of Ronald Burkle (2006 net worth: $2.5 billion). A former grocery store bag boy who later made a fortune in the supermarket business and who now heads a California private equity firm, Burkle is a close pal of former president Bill Clinton. During a messy divorce from wife Janet, from whom he had been estranged since 1992, Burkle asked the California Supreme Court to keep the divorce papers sealed. The court turned down the request in 2006 (although it did agree to keep his financial records private), leaving the press free to dig through more than one thousand pages of documents. Among the items found by reporters: Janet's $10,000-plus-a-month tab for clothing. More damaging to Burkle's image was a declaration from his adult daughter that her father had told her he had videos of Janet and her boyfriend, an ex-convict, having sex. Burkle publicly denied that the tapes existed and blamed his daughter for having misconstrued their conversation. Fifteen years after the marriage ended,

The Merry Exes of Ronald Perelman

Some 120 members of the 2006 Forbes 400 list had been divorced at least once. But then there are those who can't seem to stop marrying—and divorcing. A famous case in point: Ronald Perelman. The Revlon billionaire has wooed, wedded, and dumped four women—at a cost of some $180 million.

1. Faith Golding
Married: 1965–1984   Children: 4 (3 adopted)   **Settlement: $8 million**
Real-estate heiress Golding met Perelman on a cruise to Israel when she was seventeen years old. Once married, he reportedly borrowed $1.7 million from her—seed money for his future leveraged buyout empire. In the early 1980s Golding hired detectives to trail Perelman. They reported that he was having an affair with a New York florist.

2. Claudia Cohen
Married: 1985–1994   Children: 1   **Settlement: $80 million**
New York gossip columnist Cohen met Perelman over lunch at the tony Le Cirque restaurant. During a Paris vacation the couple was introduced to socialite Patricia Duff, who would become Perelman's wife No. 3.

3. Patricia Duff
Married: 1994–1996   Children: 1   **Settlement: $30 million**
Duff was reportedly handed a prenup agreement while she was in the hospital delivering Caleigh, Perelman's daughter. The couple married but filed for divorce eighteen months later. A bruising, high-visibility custody battle over Caleigh ensued. According to *New York* magazine, Perelman allegedly told Duff, "I will destroy you—and I will enjoy it." Perelman got Caleigh.

4. Ellen Barkin
Married: 2000–2006   Children: 0   **Settlement: $20 to $60 million**
Actress Barkin met Perelman at the 1999 Oscars. He showered her with fabulous jewels, including a $1.5 million diamond ring just weeks before the divorce. The settlement: Barkin says she got $20 million, plus the baubles that she auctioned off for $20 million. Friends of Perelman say it was closer to $60 million, if you toss in so-called convertible assets—i.e., the jewels and such.

Burkle and Janet were still hammering out the financial terms of the divorce settlement.*

A couple of cases of alleged billionaire peccadilloes came luridly to light in 2006 through a federal suit against private eye Anthony Pellicano, who was accused of illegal wiretapping. (Pellicano, who had just completed a thirty-month jail term for weapons violations, has maintained that he is not guilty of wiretapping and is awaiting trial.) Public documents alleged that Pellicano, a Hollywood detective right out of the movies, was hired to record the private conversations of, among others, two billionaires' wives—Lisa Bonder Kerkorian, third wife of casino king Kirk Kerkorian, and Lisa A. Gores, wife of financier Alec Gores. The tale of Lisa Kerkorian began as a May-December romance. The couple met playing tennis in the mid-1980s, when she was twenty and he was sixty-eight. (Kerkorian is now ninety.) They married in 1998, five months after Lisa gave birth to a daughter, Kira. One month after their wedding the couple divorced, with Kerkorian promising $50,000 a month in child support. So concerned was Kerkorian with maintaining privacy that, according to court papers, he reportedly paid Lisa more than $10 million to help ensure her silence. But Lisa slapped him with a lawsuit two years later, asking for $320,000 a month in child support to cover a long list of necessities: $14,000 a month for parties, $5,900 for eating out, $4,300 for eating in, $436 for taking care of Kira's pets, and $144,000 for travel on private jets, among other things. She later reportedly upped the amount to $1.5 million a month, one of the largest child-support claims ever. During the course of the suit, the Pellicano case revealed, discussions between Lisa and her lawyers were allegedly being intercepted by Pellicano. But in the end the judge in the Kerkorian child-support case was kinder to the mogul than to Lisa: He increased child-support payments by only $316 a month.

The Pellicano investigation also affected the Beverly Hills household of Alec Gores, head of private equity firm Gores Technology Group. Gores, an Israeli immigrant, is now married to third wife Hedi. But back in 2000, while he was married to Lisa, wife number two, Alec allegedly suspected that Lisa

---

*Around the same time, Burkle drew more press attention when he accused a *New York Post* contributor, Jared Paul Stern, of trying to extort $220,000 from him in exchange for keeping false stories about him out of the *Post*'s gossip column. Burkle released six minutes of videotape showing two meetings he had had with Stern, as well as copies of e-mails in which Stern mentions expected payments. Stern, who was immediately fired by the *Post*, claimed that Burkle had set him up and that he had met with the billionaire to discuss a potential investment in his clothing company, Skull & Bones. In early 2007, the federal investigation of Stern was dropped and Stern announced that he would sue Burkle.

was having an affair with his brother Tom, his sometime business competitor and fellow member of the Forbes 400 (2006 net worth: $2 billion), and allegedly hired Pellicano to spy on her, according to the *New York Times*. (A third Gores brother, Sam, is a Hollywood talent agent, married to a former soap-opera star.) Alec admitted to the FBI, according to the *Times*, that he had listened to Pellicano's tapes on several occasions. (Gores was merely a witness in the case, the *Times* reported, and was not charged.) One recording was said to have been an hour-long conversation that took place one evening in early January 2001, just after Lisa and Tom had met at a Beverly Hills hotel. Alec divorced Lisa later that year. His movie-star handsome, forty-something brother Tom, whose Platinum Equity company Web site boasted in early 2007 that he is on "the Forbes World Billionaires and Richest Americans lists, and is noted as one of the youngest individuals added to the roster," is married with three children. (A representative for Tom Gores responded to a request for comment with a blanket denial of the story.)

Battles over the wills and testaments of some Forbes 400 members have also reached epic proportions. Generally—almost stereotypically—they involve a rich and powerful man, a bitter, long-suffering ex-wife, a new love, and a host of neglected and disgruntled offspring. At the core of the battles is the fact that the late billionaire, who may have been meticulous in accumulating his wealth, was less so when it came to bequeathing it, leaving behind an ambiguous will or one signed under uncertain circumstances. But family skirmishes over a will, say estate lawyers, are often the result of animosity that already existed within the family. As one litigator puts it, "What we see a lot of in estate and trust litigation has deep roots."

That was the case with South Florida tycoon Victor Posner, who died in 2002. Posner, a seventh-grade dropout, started out as a Baltimore slumlord and later became a master of hostile takeovers. Some had other names for Posner, such as plunderer and corporate vulture. (*Forbes* magazine once likened him to an arrogant banana republic dictator.) Over three decades, starting in the 1960s, Posner acquired about forty companies, typically installing himself as chairman and awarding himself a huge salary before running the business into the ground. Posner had his share of run-ins with the law. In 1987 he pleaded no contest to tax evasion and fraud; seven years later he was found guilty of concealing a fraudulent scheme to take over electrical and mechanical contracting company Fischbach Corporation. Posner and his son Steven were then barred from running a publicly traded company.

A few years later father and son were slugging it out in the courtroom, feuding over millions of dollars in trust payments that Steven accused his father of withholding. Posner famously settled the dispute in 1995 in his own flamboyant way: He gave his son $11 million in cash and agreed to divvy up the family's assets by tossing a gold-dollar coin in the courtroom, before the judge. Steven won the toss and left the room with some $58 million in real-estate holdings; in return he agreed to forgo future claims to his father's estate.

Posner's death sparked even more controversy, setting off one of the largest will contests in Florida history. Posner was married twice and had two children from each marriage: twins Steven and Gail from the first marriage, and Tracy and Troy from the second. Aside from Posner's tussles with Steven, he had also battled with Gail over her inheritance but had eventually written her into a will he wrote in 1996. But then, shortly before he died at age eighty-three, Posner removed his children and all but one of his grandchildren from that will. Instead, he left nearly all his estate—valued at between $200 million and $1 billion—to former girlfriend Brenda Nestor Castellano, whom he had met in New York in the 1970s when she was a young actress (she played one of Robert Redford's girlfriends in *The Way We Were*). Over the years he had given her executive positions at some of his companies. Castellano, now married and the mother of five children, is chairman of Victor Posner Enterprises, a Miami-based real-estate development firm, and oversees the vestiges of the Posner empire.

Needless to say, being cut out of the will did not sit well with Posner's offspring. Daughter Gail sued Castellano for fraud, claiming she was owed

---

2003

from the pages of *Forbes*

Donald Bren, who made his fortune developing Southern California, has been hauled into court over two illegitimate children; he also has five children from several marriages. (2003 net worth: $4 billion)

David Murdock, of Dole Food and other investments, including real estate, has lined the gardens of his California estate with more than three hundred boulders shipped to the States from Thailand's River Kwai. (2003 net worth: $1.5 billion)

Media baron and septuagenarian **Rupert Murdoch** just had his sixth child, with third wife, Wendi. (2003 net worth: $7.2 billion)

Harold Clark Simmons (investing whiz) may finally have won a long-sought license from Texas to bury nuclear waste in the western part of the state. (2003 net worth: $1.4 billion)

Do you want to marry a billionaire?

Some 46 men and 9 women who appeared on the Forbes 400 list in 2006 are reportedly unmarried. That, of course, doesn't mean that they are looking for a partner; but perhaps some of them are. The individuals below are listed in order of their wealth.

Name	Age	Worth (in millions of dollars)	Status
Men			
Paul Allen *(WA)*	53	16,000	Single
Larry Page *(CA)*	33	14,000	Single
Kirk Kerkorian *(CA)*	89	9,000	3 divorces, 2 children
George Soros *(NY)*	76	8,500	2 divorces, 5 children
Ronald Perelman *(NY)*	63	7,000	4 divorces, 6 children
Michael Bloomberg *(NY)*	64	5,300	1 divorce, 2 children
John Menard Jr. *(WI)*	66	5,200	2 divorces, 6 children
David Geffen *(CA)*	63	4,600	Single
H. Ty Warner *(IL)*	62	4,500	Single
Bradley Hughes *(CA)*	73	4,100	1 divorce, 3 children
George Lucas *(CA)*	62	3,600	1 divorce, 3 children
Bruce Kovner *(NY)*	61	3,000	1 divorce, 3 children
Mitchell Rales *(DC)*	50	2,600	1 divorce, 2 children
Ronald Burkle *(CA)*	53	2,500	1 divorce, 3 children
Steven Rales *(DC)*	55	2,500	1 divorce, 2 children
T. Denny Sanford *(SD)*	70	2,500	2 divorces, 2 children
Mort Zuckerman *(NY)*	69	2,500	1 divorce, 1 child
Glen Taylor *(MN)*	65	2,300	1 divorce, 5 children
Charles Butt *(TX)*	68	2,200	Single
Herbert Allen Jr. *(NY)*	66	2,000	2 divorces, 4 children
Austin Hearst *(NY)*	54	2,000	2 divorces, 3 children
David Hearst Jr. *(CA)*	61	2,000	Single
James Pritzker *(IL)*	55	2,000	1 divorce, 3 children
Tamir Sapir *(NY)*	59	2,000	1 divorce, 4 children
Robert Turner *(FL)*	67	1,900	3 divorces, 5 children
Jon Stryker *(MI)*	48	1,700	Single, 2 children
Neil Bluhm *(IL)*	68	1,600	1 divorce, 3 children
H. Fisk Johnson *(WI)*	48	1,600	1 divorce, 1 child
William Wrigley Jr. *(IL)*	42	1,600	1 divorce, 3 children

Name	Age	Worth (in millions of dollars)	Status
Men *(cont'd.)*			
Marc Rich *(Abroad)*	71	1,500	2 divorces, 2 children
Fayez Sarofim *(TX)*	77	1,500	2 divorces, 5 children
Daniel Ziff *(NY)*	34	1,500	Single
Peter Lewis *(FL)*	72	1,400	1 divorce, 3 children
Gary Michelson *(CA)*	57	1,400	1 divorce
Phillip Ruffin *(KS)*	70	1,400	1 divorce, 3 children
Ollen Smith *(NC)*	79	1,400	1 divorce, 4 children
John Sperling *(AZ)*	85	1,300	2 divorces, 1 child
Leslie Alexander *(TX)*	63	1,200	1 divorce, 1 child
Edmund Ansin *(FL)*	70	1,200	1 divorce, 3 children
Thomas Bailey *(CO)*	69	1,200	1 divorce, 2 children
William Boyd *(NV)*	74	1,200	1 divorce, 3 children
Richard Mellon Scaife *(PA)*	74	1,200	2 divorces, 3 children
James Clark *(FL)*	62	1,100	1 divorce, 2 children
Timothy Headington *(TX)*	56	1,100	Single
Robert Johnson *(DC)*	60	1,000	1 divorce, 2 children
Charles Simonyi *(WA)*	58	1,000	Single
Women			
Alice Walton *(TX)*	57	15,500	2 divorces
Anne Cox Chambers *(GA)*	86	12,600	2 divorces, 3 children
Jacqueline Mars *(NJ)*	67	10,500	2 divorces, 3 children
Mary Dorrance Malone *(PA)*	56	2,200	1 divorce, 2 children
Linda Pritzker *(MT)*	52	2,000	1 divorce, 3 children
Marion Pictet *(Abroad)*	74	1,600	1 divorce, 1 child
Oprah Winfrey *(IL)*	52	1,500	Single
Patricia Stryker *(CO)*	50	1,400	1 divorce, 3 children
Charlotte Weber *(FL)*	63	1,300	1 divorce, 4 children

$100 million. Gail settled out of court in 2002 for an undisclosed sum. But many of the Posner grandchildren fight on. "It was already there," said Castellano in 2003, of all the feuding. "So I just don't pay attention to it anymore."

Similarly, animosity within the families of two other Forbes 400 members—John Seward Johnson, heir to the Johnson & Johnson health-care fortune and oil baron J. Howard Marshall II—sent their widows and children scurrying to the courthouse even before the funerals ended. The lives of both men were a recipe for conflict: huge fortunes, a penchant for womanizing, and late-life marriages to women less than half their age. Johnson was married twice and had six children when, barely one week after he divorced his second wife of thirty years, he married Barbara "Basia" Piasecka, a Polish immigrant who had been his chambermaid. He was seventy-six; she was thirty-four. By the time he died eleven years later, he had cut his children out of the will, leaving a fortune of roughly $500 million to Basia. She received, among other assets, the $30 million, 140-acre mansion in Princeton, New Jersey, that she called Jasna Polana (Polish for Bright Glade) after Leo Tolstoy's country estate; it boasted an air-conditioned kennel and a greenhouse for orchids. A lurid three-year trial ensued as the Johnson children contested the will, claiming that their father was mentally incompetent when he signed it in 1983, a few weeks before his death. (During the course of his marriage to Basia, Johnson drew up or modified twenty-two wills, giving her ever-increasing shares of his estate.)

The reclusive Johnson would have been mortified at the family skeletons that came to light. The children accused their stepmother of bullying and terrorizing their father; one witness testified that he once even saw Basia slapping her elderly husband's face. Basia countered that the children had been an embarrassment to him. Daughter Mary Lea, for example, had at one point accused her second husband of having a homosexual affair and of plotting to murder her. (Mary Lea died in 1990.) And the ex-wife of son J. Seward Johnson Jr., the well-known sculptor, reportedly once shot a private detective hired to record her extramarital affairs. Even more damaging was the later revelation by Mary Lea, then a successful stage and film producer, that Johnson had sexually abused her as a child. The day before the case was slated to go to the jury, the feuding parties reached a settlement. The Johnson children received a total of $42.5 million (in addition to the trusts they already had). Basia took home the prize: more than $300 million, plus Jasna Polana, which she later converted into a tournament-level golf club. Today, nearly seventy years old, Basia resides full-time in Monaco, with an estimated net worth of $2.8 billion.

The saga of Texas oil tycoon J. Howard Marshall II has a more tragic ending. Marshall will be remembered less for his business acumen than for his late-life marriage to troubled former *Playboy* playmate Anna Nicole Smith, whose death in early 2007 sparked a media frenzy. Marshall was born in 1905 near Philadelphia. After graduating from Haverford College and Yale Law

School, he served in a series of influential positions, both at Yale and in Washington, D.C., where he helped develop America's energy policy during World War II. Later he became president of Ashland Oil, held a sizable share of energy firm Koch Industries, and, at age seventy-nine, founded Marshall Petroleum. When Marshall died at age ninety in 1995, he left a fortune valued at more than $500 million—and a nasty trail of events beyond anyone's imagination.

On paper, at least, Marshall's personal life appeared fairly stable. He was married twice, with each marriage lasting about thirty years. He had two sons from his first marriage: James Howard Marshall III and E. Pierce Marshall. But as his second wife, Bettye, started to show signs of Alzheimer's (she died in 1991), Marshall befriended Texas stripper Jewell Dianne "Lady" Walker, forty years his junior. For many years he showered her with gifts—some $6 million in houses, cars, cash, and other luxuries. While undergoing a face-lift, Walker died (also in 1991), and Marshall discovered that she had been cheating on him with several other men. He and son Pierce sued her estate and recovered much of the money.

But Marshall clearly had not learned his lesson. It was in the late 1980s that he first met voluptuous topless dancer Anna Nicole Smith, a former waitress at Jim's Krispy Fried Chicken in Mexia, Texas, and later an actress, model, and *Playboy* centerfold. In 1994, at age eighty-nine and wheelchair-bound, Marshall married Smith, then age twenty-six, at the White Dove Wedding Chapel in Houston. Shortly thereafter, Marshall gave his son Pierce power of attorney over his fortune. "I know people think I married Howard for his money," Smith said soon after their wedding. "But it's not true. I love him." Pierce was one of those who doubted her intentions. Court records show that at one point he stopped Smith's $50,000 monthly allowance, accusing her of defrauding his father. After one year of marriage Marshall died of pneumonia. Marshall's immediate family and pre-Smith friends did not attend the funeral organized by his widow—who, as *People* magazine reported, wore a white dress with a plunging neckline.

Noticeably absent from Marshall's will were older son James Howard Marshall III, who had been alienated from his father, and Anna Nicole Smith, who got nothing beyond the $6 million in gifts that Marshall had given her. Not surprisingly, Smith took Pierce to court to lay claim to Marshall's estate. The suit wrangled its way through Texas and California courts, where it became mired in jurisdictional disputes. At first Smith won a $474 million judgment. But that was later cut to $89 million, and eventually to zero. In

2006, in a much-publicized event, the U.S. Supreme Court agreed to hear the case. It ruled that Smith could revive her pursuit of her late husband's oil fortune—in other words, that she deserved another day in court. But for many reasons, that was not to be. One month after the ruling, at age sixty-seven, her former stepson and longtime opponent E. Pierce Marshall died of a massive infection. And Smith's life took a downward spiral as well, all extensively chronicled in the media. In the fall of 2006, one week after his mother gave birth to a baby girl in a Bahamas hospital, Smith's twenty-year-old son from an early first marriage died of a prescription drug overdose in her hospital room. And in a bizarre twist to the already baroque tale, in February 2007 the thirty-eight-year-old Smith was found dead in a Florida hotel room. The cause of her death, too, was an accidental overdose of prescription medicine.

Meanwhile, even after the death of all the major parties—tycoon J. Howard Marshall II, his son Pierce, and Anna Nicole Smith—the specter of Marshall's money still haunted courtrooms. At the heart of the legal wrangling was the paternity of Smith's then five-month-old daughter, Dannielynn Hope Marshall Stern, who potentially stood to lay claim to Marshall's estate. Possible fathers included Smith's longtime friend and lawyer, Howard K. Stern; her boyfriend of two years, Larry Birkhead; and the eighth husband of actress Zsa Zsa Gabor, Prince Frederic von Anhalt, who claimed a ten-year affair with Smith and a tryst nine months before the baby's birth. By spring 2007 tests showed that photographer Birkhead was Dannielynn's father, but the drama had yet to play itself out. With hundreds of millions at stake, the denouement may well be years away.

So how can the superrich avoid the pitfalls that lead to such nasty family feuds? "One of the great conundrums of the modern world," says management professor Astrachan, "is that people think families should just exist, that one does not need to learn how to manage them and does not have to actively manage them, which often leads to these kinds of fantastic family fights." As wealth creation has taken off in recent years, an entire cottage industry has sprung up to teach the burgeoning ranks of the rich and superrich how to manage their families and fend off family discord. There are more than one hundred programs at universities across the country that study wealthy family businesses, and legions of family, wealth, and values consultants, some independent and many associated with financial services firms. Some view them with skepticism. But many ideas promoted by such consultants seem sensible, especially when it comes to having a succession plan in place that won't be misinterpreted and building safeguards into an estate, such as a clause calling for mediation rather than litigation. The latter strategy, of course, is essential for maintaining at least an appearance of family unity by avoiding high-profile court battles.

Another way to maintain family unity is to defuse family spats before they have a chance to flare up, but that involves lots of family openness. Says therapist Judith Stern Peck, "More and more people realize that they need to do some of this work preemptively." The Ford family, now some ninety members strong, knows that lesson well. The clan rarely talks to the media, except through appointed spokesperson Bill Ford Jr., chairman of Ford Motor Company, and great-grandson of company founder, Henry Ford. But they talk plenty among themselves. Every six months or so the family gathers—in 2006 they met at a Sea Island, Georgia, resort—to catch up on family business. At that particular meeting, Bill Ford (2005 net worth: $1.2 billion) had some bad news to deliver: The company was suspending dividend payments for the final quarter of that year, the first time that Ford Motor Company had done so since 1982. Turning off the dividend stream would hit the family hard, since it controls about 40 percent of the company's voting shares. But the clan pulled together for the greater good. "We can afford to take a hit for a while," one unnamed family member told the *Wall Street Journal.* "The most important thing is the long-term financial health of Ford."

Working It Out

Not all family dynasties fall apart through succession squabbles. While second- and third-generation heirs are notoriously prone to problems in keeping the family business going, some Forbes 400 offspring seem to be managing just fine. Take the Ziffs, for example. In 1994 William Ziff sold his Ziff Communications publishing empire, which included Ziff-Davis Publishing, to buyout firm Forstmann Little & Company for $1.4 billion and retired to Florida.* His sons Dirk, Robert, and Daniel have since nurtured the family fortune via Ziff Brothers Investments, a New York–based hedge fund firm. The result: While in 1994 *Forbes* pegged the brothers' net worth at $500 million apiece, by 2006 they had each tripled that figure.

Another publishing powerhouse, the Newhouses, are keeping their magazines, newspapers, and broadcast and cable TV operations very much in the family. Since the death in 1979 of founder S. I. Newhouse Sr., who was born into poverty on Manhattan's Lower East Side and had bought his first newspaper by the time he was sixteen, the company has been run by his sons Si and Donald, and younger Newhouses are scattered throughout the company. Among them are Si's eldest son, Sam III, and Donald's son Steve. And the family appears destined to run the business for decades to come. As *Forbes* reported in a 1979 article on the family, "They've done their best to see that future ownership won't go outside. Long ago, the principal stockholders—Si, Donald, Ted [brother of S.I. Sr.], Norman [also a brother], and Si's widow Mitzi—signed an agreement requiring that if any of their heirs ever decide to sell, it must be to the others."

New York's Tisch family is also displaying strong survival skills. Brothers James and Andrew Tisch, along with their first cousin Jonathan, are proving to be competent second-generation custodians of the Loews empire.† Since their fathers, Laurence (2003 net worth: $2 billion) and Preston Robert Tisch

---

*Ziff died in 2006.

†Two other of Laurence Tisch's sons, Daniel and Thomas, are not involved in Loews. Likewise, Steven Tisch and Laurie Tisch Sussman, Bob Tisch's other children, do not work at Loews. Steve is a television and movie producer in Hollywood, with credits including *Forrest Gump*, which won the Academy Award for Best Picture in 1994, and more recently *The Pursuit of Happyness*, starring Will Smith. He is also vice chairman and executive vice president of the New York Giants football team, which his father owned. Thomas Tisch, who runs a private investment firm, was elected the twentieth chancellor of Brown University in early 2007.

(2005: $3.9 billion), died in 2003 and 2005, respectively, the trio has surmounted myriad problems within Loews' disparate businesses. Their energy business, for one, took a hit as a result of a drop in oil prices. Their Lorillard Tobacco Company was threatened by smoker lawsuits, while their CNA insurance firm was faced with massive payouts over asbestos claims. Furthermore, their hotel business slumped after the terrorist attacks of September 11, 2001, caused a lull in tourism. Despite the troubles in all four sectors, however, Loews' share price more than tripled from 2003 through 2006, in part as a result of eight stock offerings and a rise in oil prices. As Jim Tisch, who serves as Loews' CEO, said recently, "I learned from the master," referring to his father's investing acumen. But it's too early to say where the empire is headed, just as it's too soon to say when the Tisch troika (all now in their fifties) and their siblings will make an appearance on the Forbes 400 list. As of 2006 Tisch family members on the list were Laurence's widow, Wilma (known as Billie; net worth: $1.9 billion), and Preston's widow, Joan ($3.4 billion).

It's even possible to find amicable divorces among the very rich (although they are rare). When Ted Turner and Jane Fonda's marriage unraveled after ten years, the divorce was private, civilized, and quick. She filed in April 2001; it was finalized one month later. Both had plenty of past experience: Turner had been married twice before, as had Fonda, whose first two husbands were movie director Roger Vadim and Vietnam War activist Tom Hayden. And when land baron Tim Blixseth and second wife, Edra, decided to call it quits in 2007 after twenty-five years of marriage, their parting, too, was notable for its civility. Together the couple had built up assets worth between $1.5 billion and $2 billion, including the Yellowstone Club, a ritzy, members-only resort in Montana. (See Chapter 9, Conspicuous Consumption.) They were famous for hosting lavish parties in "the Party Pad," an auditorium in their Palm Springs–area mansion. But when they realized that their "lives and interests were growing apart," as Edra told the *Wall Street Journal,* they decided on a friendly ending. The pair met in the Beverly Hills Hotel over a bottle of wine, and methodically drew up a list. He got the house in Mexico and his real-estate businesses; she received Porcupine Creek, their 420-acre Palm Springs estate, with its thirty-thousand-square-foot mansion, nineteen-hole golf course, and eight cottages (total estimated value: $200 million). Each got a Rolls-Royce, and they agreed on joint use of their three jets. No judges, no courts, no fodder for late-night show monologues—assuming, that is, neither one has a change of heart.

12

Giving It Away

Ted Turner had an epiphany in the autumn of 1997. Flush with profits from the sale of Turner Broadcasting to media giant Time Warner the year before, business's bad boy decided to show the world a kinder, gentler side: He would give away the largest single sum in philanthropic history.

The gesture made great sense. "Mouth of the South" Turner had put off more than a few tycoons earlier when he complained to the *New York Times* that America's superrich were a stingy lot. They hoarded their stashes, he charged, rather than give away a few million and risk slipping down a rung or two on the Forbes 400 list. He had come down especially hard on billionaire Bill Gates, the richest man in America, and Warren Buffett, the second richest; Buffett had long said he would wait until his death to part with his billions. In contrast, Turner would put his money where his mouth was.

Turner's stage was a Manhattan ballroom, where a black-tie international crowd had gathered for a United Nations association dinner. As Turner prepared to be recognized for his international giving, he leaned over and asked tablemate Vartan Gregorian, president of the Carnegie Corporation of New York and former president of Brown University:

"What is the largest philanthropic gift ever given?"

Gregorian joked that if Turner had to ask, he couldn't afford to match it. Turner whispered that he was about to give $1 billion to benefit the UN. He had discussed it with his wife, Jane Fonda, earlier, Turner said, and she had cried.

"Why?" asked Gregorian, chuckling. "Because you've now impoverished yourself?"

"No," Turner replied. "Because now I am a philanthropist."

Turner gave Gregorian a high five and sauntered to the podium. With his famous gap-toothed grin, reading from notes he had scribbled on the back of an envelope, Turner pledged $100 million a year for ten years to bolster the work of the international organization. As expected, the audience—and the philanthropic world—was floored.

But what a difference a decade makes. Ten years later, Fonda is no longer on his arm; they divorced in 2001. As for the $1 billion pledge, Turner has donated some $600 million, but deep stock losses after the merger of Time Warner and AOL forced him to extend his payout period from ten to fifteen years. Meanwhile, perhaps Turner's prodding was starting to have some effect on Forbes 400 skinflints after all. Gates, for example, gave away some $80 million in 1997, but within two years of Turner's challenge upped donations to $2.8 billion. And by mid-2006 the Bill and Melinda Gates Foundation was a behemoth, with more than $30 billion in assets.

But it was Warren Buffett who, on a rainy Monday morning in Manhattan in June 2006, relegated Turner's beneficence to a philanthropic footnote. At the invitation of Bill and Melinda Gates, more than three hundred international officials, philanthropists (including the dean of donors, David Rockefeller, then ninety years old), scientists, students, journalists, and members of the Buffett and Gates families gathered under the thirty-foot-high, saucer-dome ceiling in the elegant Celeste Bartos Forum of the main New York Public Library building on Fifth Avenue. There the crowd stood witness as legendary investor Buffett signed over nearly 85 percent of his fortune—some $31 billion—to charity. The bulk, about 70 percent of his net worth, would go to the Gates Foundation, at a rate of about $1.6 billion a year;* the rest was earmarked for the individual foundations of Buffett family members.†

What was behind Buffett's change of heart? The simple fact that, while he had no interest in running a philanthropy, his good friend and bridge buddy Bill Gates (who ten days earlier had announced that he would leave daily management of Microsoft in 2008 to devote his time to the Gates Foundation) was the right man for the job. Entrusting his money to Gates, said the plainspoken Buffett, was "a no-brainer." So natural was the transfer, in fact, that it was a nonevent in his mind. The night before the big day, Buffett

---

*The donation took the form of Berkshire Hathaway stock. Buffett stipulated that the Gates Foundation had to disburse its yearly allotment during the year it was received.

†Buffett never intended to give huge sums to his three children, and he remained true to his word. The $1 billion he earmarked for each of them was a gift to their foundations. Still, the Buffett children, now middle-aged, aren't exactly penniless. They inherited $10 million each from their late mother and are likely to receive a more modest amount on their father's death.

How generous are the Forbes 400's top givers?

Here are the estimated lifetime charitable donations and pledges, as of 2006, of the Forbes 400 top givers.

	Estimated lifetime giving (billions)	Net worth ('06, billions)	Source of wealth	Causes supported
Warren Buffett	$40.7	$46.0	Investments	Global health, education
Bill & Melinda Gates	$28.0	$53.0	Microsoft	Global health, education
Gordon & Betty Moore	$7.4	$3.4	Intel	Science, environment
George Soros	$5.9	$8.5	Hedge funds	Open societies, education
Eli & Edythe Broad	$2.1	$5.8	Investments	Arts, biomedical research
Walton family*	$1.8	$82.5	Wal-Mart	Education (K–12)
Alfred Mann	$1.7	$2.2	Biomedical	Biomedical research
Herbert & Marion Sandler	$1.4	$2.2 ('05)	Golden West	Medical research
Ted Turner	$1.3	$1.9	Cable TV	Health, environment
Michael & Susan Dell	$1.2	$15.5	Computers	Children's health, education
Donald Bren	$0.95	$8.5	Real estate	Education, environment
David Rockefeller Sr.	$0.9	$2.6	Oil, banking	Arts, environment
Michael Bloomberg	$0.88	$5.3	Bloomberg LP	Arts, education, health care
Paul Allen	$0.87	$16.0	Microsoft	Science education, research
Bernard Osher	$0.8	$0.9 ('05)	Banking	Arts, education, medicine
Larry Ellison	$0.79	$19.5	Oracle	Health research
John Kluge	$0.75	$9.1	Metromedia	Libraries
George Kaiser	$0.72	$8.5	Oil, gas	Antipoverty
Kirk Kerkorian	$0.7	$9.0	Investments	Humanitarian
Bernard Marcus	$0.65	$1.9	Home Depot	Brain disorders
Irwin & Joan Jacobs	$0.58	$1.7	Qualcomm	Culture
Pierre & Pam Omidyar	$0.58	$7.7	eBay	Microfinance investing
Shelby White**	$0.5	$0.75 ('02)	Investments	Arts, humanities
H. F. & Marguerite Lenfest	$0.47	$0.8 ('04)	Cable	Higher education, arts
Thomas Monaghan	$0.47	$0.45	Domino's	Catholic higher education
Frank Sr. & Jane Batten	$0.4	$1.4	Landmark	Education, child development
Peter Lewis	$0.4	$1.4	Progressive Corp.	Arts, education, social services
David & Cheryl Duffield	$0.33	$1.2	PeopleSoft	Animal welfare
Oprah Winfrey	$0.3	$1.5	Media	Education for women & children
T. Boone Pickens	$0.3	$2.7	Energy	Higher education, athletics
David Geffen	$0.27	$4.6	Media	Higher education, medicine
Frances Comer***	$0.26	$1.0	Lands' End	Environment, scientific research
James Simons	$0.26	$4.0	Hedge funds	Science & math education
Charles & Helen Schwab	$0.23	$4.6	Brokerage	Childhood learning, social issues
George Lucas	$0.21	$3.6	Films	Education, film school
Dan L. Duncan	$0.16	$7.5	Energy	Higher education, health

*includes 7 members   **widow of Leon Levy   ***widow of Gary Comer

Sources: Forbes, BusinessWeek, The Chronicle of Philanthropy

Global Giving, the Gates Way

With more than $30 billion in assets, the Bill and Melinda Gates Foundation towers over the philanthropic world. It is three times the size of the venerable Ford Foundation, ten times the size of the Rockefeller Foundation, and larger than the GDP of many countries. Toss in Warren Buffett's $1.5 billion or so annual pledge, and its grant making is set to double to about $3 billion a year, rendering it even more of a global force. Since 2000, when two smaller Gates trusts merged, it has given away nearly $9 billion. More than $800 million a year goes to global health projects alone, focused mainly on developing new drugs and vaccines for diseases such as AIDS, malaria, and tuberculosis.

Big as it is, Patty Stonesifer, chief of the Gates Foundation and former Microsoft executive, says its aim is not to supplant governments but to form partnerships with them: "Our giving is a drop in the bucket compared to the government's responsibility." That is certainly true: Although the foundation's grants are significant, they are still often smaller than government funding and, indeed, tiny in terms of solving the world's monumental problems.

Meanwhile, it's hard to overstate the foundation's impact. As a lengthy profile of the organization in *The New Yorker* observed, "The research programs of entire countries have been restored, and fields that have languished for years, like tropical medicine, have once again burst to life," thanks largely to the Gates Foundation.

joined his children Howard, Susie, and Peter, two grandchildren, Bill and Melinda Gates, and other family members for dinner at a small Italian restaurant in midtown Manhattan. When asked how he would feel turning over billions the next day, Buffett calmly replied, in the words of the old Paul McCartney tune: "It's just another day."

In the philanthropic universe, however, it was decidedly not just another day. Giving of this magnitude, wrote Peter Singer, bioethics professor at Princeton University, in the *New York Times*, makes it clear that "the first decade of the twenty-first century is a new golden age of philanthropy." Not only was Buffett's bequest the single largest act of charitable giving ever in America, but it was also, as even cynics agree, a rare display of unadulterated generosity. By funneling his riches through the Gates Foundation, Buffett gave up a huge perk of charitable giving—the legacy of his name living on in perpetuity through his own foundation. "He demonstrated an astonishing lack of ego," says Richard Conniff, author of *The Natural History of the Rich*. "That was one of the most flamboyant gestures in the history of wealth on earth."

Private philanthropy, naturally, has long been a hallmark of business titans. Even before the Carnegies and Rockefellers became philanthropic legends, there was George Peabody, considered to be the father of modern philanthropy. Born in 1795 in Danvers, Massachusetts, Peabody was the son of a poor farmer and leather worker. Through hard work and wise investments, Peabody became a hugely successful merchant and international financier. He accumulated some $12 million, or $185 million in today's dollars, before shifting his focus to philanthropy. He gave away more than two-thirds of his fortune, mainly to two causes: to help alleviate the poverty he saw during his travels, and to enrich lives by creating Yale University's Peabody Museum of Natural History, as well as Baltimore's Peabody Institute, America's first academy of music.

During the latter part of the nineteenth century, philanthropy grew along with fortunes. Measured in today's dollars, industrialist Andrew Carnegie gave away $7.2 billion to underwrite libraries and church organs, and to support educational causes. Just as Turner would later do, Carnegie publicly challenged other wealthy industrialists to part with their money; he warned that "he who dies thus rich, dies disgraced." One person Carnegie influenced was Standard Oil titan John D. Rockefeller, who with his eponymous son disbursed a combined $12.6 billion (in today's dollars) largely to the arts and to fight malaria, yellow fever, hookworm, and other diseases. Rockefeller could be ruthless in his business affairs, but he was also an austere Baptist who famously said, "God gave me my money"; and as steward of his riches, he believed he would be held accountable in heaven. Philanthropy also held an earthly reward for Rockefeller: It helped transform his legacy from that of a predatory monopolist to one of the most generous donors of his century.

Over the years, donations among the superrich have crested and fallen with the vagaries of the economy, although the Buffett bonanza of 2006 far surpassed even the combined giving of Peabody, Carnegie, and the two Rockefellers. But the motivations that drove some early philanthropists are no longer valid for many of today's givers, says James Allen Smith, who holds the Waldemar Nielsen chair in philanthropy at Georgetown University. "That language of stewardship is not heard very often today," he says. Heavenly rewards are generally not a big motivator these days, either: As Princeton's Peter Singer points out, Buffett is an agnostic, "not motivated by any belief that it will benefit him in an afterlife."

So what is it that moves today's megawealthy—many of whom have spent their lives amassing their wealth, often in a highly driven way—to give it away? Where are the Forbes 400 putting their money, and why? Are they more or less generous than average Americans? If not, why not? And, more important, is the dollar-to-impact ratio of those donations making a difference in society? Those are the key questions; the answers, as one might imagine, are as complex as the donors themselves.

To begin with, motivations for giving among the Forbes 400 vary widely. "They range from narcissism to altruism to a passionate need from their heart and souls to make a difference," says Joan DiFuria, a principal in the Money, Meaning & Choices Institute, which advises high-net-worth families. Certainly, as French novelist Gustave Flaubert aptly put it, "Every good deed is more than three parts pride." But many philanthropy experts say that desire to improve the lives of the less fortunate is really what drives many to give. "They place their values at the heart of their giving," says Joe Breiteneicher, president of the Philanthropy Initiative, a nonprofit group that advises donors. "And they have a vision of a societal endgame that goes beyond their own accumulation of wealth." There are other motivations for giving as well—generous tax benefits, the goodwill that comes from grand-scale giving, the doors it opens to society's elite, getting one's kids into a big-name college, to name just a few. "Philanthropy is a funny business," says William H. Dietel, who heads the F. B. Heron and Pierson-Lovelace foundations, and who was formerly president of the Rockefeller Brothers Fund (one of several Rockefeller family foundations). "People give for every conceivable reason and get satisfaction from it for a number of reasons, even selfish ones." Or, as Nelson Aldrich, author of *Old Money* and himself a member of the Rockefeller clan, maintains: "They are titanic figures with titanic egos trying to do great, if not impossible, things."

For some Forbes 400 givers, religion does play a significant role. Philanthropic gifts to organizations with a religious affiliation account for roughly 35 percent of charitable gifts in the United States. For example, Robert B. Pamplin Jr., head of an Oregon textile and building materials company and sometime member of the Forbes 400, believes he is an instrument of good. A self-described "businessman, philanthropist, farmer, minister, and author of thirteen books," Pamplin became an ordained minister after surviving a five-year battle with skin cancer. "I believe that God spared me to do good," Pamplin said. "He had a use for me." Pamplin founded Christ Community Church, which provides food for the hungry through organizations in the Portland metro area. In the tradition of church tithing, Pamplin also gives 10 percent of his company's pretax profits each year to nearly two hundred charities.

2004

from the pages of *Forbes*

Charles Ergen, founder of satellite TV company EchoStar, is an avid hiker who recently led twenty interns up 14,433-foot Mount Elbert, Colorado's highest peak. (2004 net worth: $7.3 billion)

Gerald J. Ford, a banker and investor, spends downtime flying his jet from Dallas to Los Angeles to shop for cowboy hats. (2004 net worth: $1.4 billion)

Roger Penske, truck leasing and auto parts maker and founder of Penske Corporation, was a star race-car driver who retired in 1965 at age twenty-eight. (2004 net worth: $1.7 billion)

Michael Ilitch, founder of Little Caesars Pizza, is a former minor-league shortstop. (2003 net worth: $750 million)

For Thomas Monaghan, founder of Domino's pizza, philanthropy seems to be a way to promote his religious convictions. After selling Domino's for $1 billion in 1998, Monaghan announced that he was taking a "millionaire's vow of poverty." He promptly unloaded his antique car collection, stopped flying first class, and pledged to give most of his fortune to Catholic charities and education. An ultraconservative Catholic, Monaghan is bankrolling the construction of a new Catholic university in southwest Florida, flanked by a controversial development (a virtual "Catholic town," his critics charge) of nearly two thousand homes by 2016.

Within the Rockefeller family, the religious pull of patriarch John D. Rockefeller has slackened. The driving factor for many members of the Rockefeller clan today, according to former Rockefeller advisor Dietel, is the euphoria that can come from doing good. "They get a tremendous high out of their philanthropy," he says. Aside from the joy of giving, the younger Rockefellers donate for a number of other reasons, such as family tradition, society's expectations that they should give, and the formal philanthropic training they get, says Georgetown's Smith.

The Rockefellers' sense of responsibility, even if divorced from religious beliefs, is echoed by others of the Forbes 400. When asked what drives him to give generously, John Anderson, owner of Topa Equities Ltd., a huge family holding company, is unabashedly moralistic: "Giving is the right thing to do. You see a need, you help out." Nearly age ninety, Anderson (2006 net worth: $1.9 billion) lives in Los Angeles, not far from the UCLA campus, which he crosses on the five-mile walk he takes several times a week. A barber's son, Anderson grew up poor in a tough Minneapolis neighborhood but ended up at UCLA on an ice-hockey scholarship. In the late 1980s, when the school's chancellor approached him about donating, Anderson says he felt an "obligation" to do so. He promptly gave $15 million to the business school that now bears his name. His reward: "It's amazing how many kids come by and thank me as I walk through campus. It comes back to you in so many ways," he says.

The sense of duty that compels Anderson to share his wealth is typical of many self-made billionaires, who feel a need to repay society for the opportunities that brought them their riches. "This country's been good to me," says Los Angeles· real-estate developer and insurance executive Eli Broad, now in his midseventies and the son of Lithuanian immigrants. "Once you decide your children have more than they'll ever need, and you know that you can't take it with you, of course you want to give back and make a difference." Broad has given back to the tune of $1.8 billion so far, more than 30 percent of his fortune, to causes such as education and medical research.

Sometimes an intensely personal experience or a difficult childhood sets off an interest in giving, as the cases of Oprah Winfrey and financier Theodore Forstmann illustrate. For Oprah (2006 net worth: $1.5 billion), it was a Dickensian family incident that happened when she was twelve years old. Funds were especially tight that year, and her mother informed the family that there would be no Christmas presents. Just as Oprah had resigned herself to the fact, three nuns came to the door bearing a turkey and toys. "I remember feeling that I mattered to these nuns—who I had never met and to this day still do not know their names—and what it meant that they remembered me. I wasn't forgotten." Oprah started her own foundation in 1987 to fund education and empowerment programs for women, children, and families around the world. Ten years later she founded Oprah's Angel Network, now with assets of nearly $30 million, to inspire her fans to follow her philanthropic lead.

A turbulent childhood also explains, at least in part, the giving of Forstmann (2005 net worth: $900 million) to children's causes. "I know what a lonely child feels like," says Forstmann, who had an alcoholic father. "It's a desperate feeling." Forstmann may play hardball buying and selling companies at the negotiating table, but when it comes to philanthropy, he's a modern-day Daddy Warbucks. A lifelong bachelor (though he confessed to a *New York Times* reporter in early 2007 that he had a brief romantic relationship with Princess Diana, and the media once referred to him as a "close friend" of actress Elizabeth Hurley), Forstmann has no children, but he is the guardian of two South African boys, Everest and Siya, whom he is putting through American colleges. Forstmann says he supports "kids all over—one here, one there," including a Bosnian girl ("a great kid, now living in Iowa") who was injured in a mortar attack during the war in her region. "My money saved her life," says Forstmann.

On a broader scale Forstmann teamed up with the late John Walton, heir to the Wal-Mart fortune, to found the Children's Scholarship Fund in 1998, each putting up $50 million. (Walton, who died in 2005 when the small plane he was piloting crashed, wanted Forstmann to give more. As Forstmann says, "You think you're doing okay, until you go up against a Walton.") More than seventy thousand elementary-school children have received vouchers that their families use to help pay tuition at schools of their choice. "What a lousy life it would be if you only thought about yourself and making money," says Forstmann.

A sense of sympathy for the less fortunate can also play a decisive role. "They have so much, can buy everything they want, but at the same time they are bombarded with news about those less well off," says DiFuria of the Money, Meaning & Choices Institute, speaking of the wealthy. And that can lead to feelings of anxiety and guilt: "Some feel only a little, so they don't act on it; some feel so much that it's paralyzing to the extent they want to give all their money away." Philanthropy not only helps assuage those feelings but apparently can also make further personal spending more palatable. A study by researchers at the Yale School of Management and Carnegie Mellon University, for example, found that at all economic levels, donating removes the guilt associated with self-indulgence and helps ease the giver's conscience.

Some, like media magnate Walter Annenberg, onetime owner of *TV Guide* and the *Racing Form* who gave away more than $2 billion during his lifetime and left a foundation with $2.6 billion in assets, advance a more straightforward explanation for their philanthropic generosity. "I certainly feel no guilt," said Annenberg, before he died in 2002 at age ninety-four. "I get great joy out of what I have. And I'm a great believer that you must philanthropically give at least as much as is in keeping with your own good fortune in life."

Another practical reason for donating is the tax breaks that make philanthropy good for the bottom line. "It's only a bit of an exaggeration that

Giving It All Away

A growing group of philanthropists is heeding Andrew Carnegie's call to give it all away before they die. In a 2005 survey of ninety-one people with assets of more than $30 million, 65 percent said they planned to give away most of their personal fortunes during their lifetime, according to Boston College's Center on Wealth and Philanthropy.

Working aggressively toward that goal, for example, is Gordon Moore, who has already given nearly two-thirds of his wealth to conservation and science, leaving Moore and wife, Betty, some $3.4 billion in 2006 to disburse. American Century Investments founder James Stowers Jr. (2001 net worth: $1.6 billion) has handed over more than two-thirds of his fortune to his Stowers Institute for Medical Research in Kansas City. Stowers and his wife, Virginia, both cancer survivors, plan to pump the rest into the institute during their lifetimes. And Herbert and Marion Sandler (2006 net worth: $3.4 billion), cofounders of savings and loan company Golden West, donated $814.7 million in 2006 to a charity whose name they kept secret; that was only part of the total $1.3 billion in stock they gave that year. So far, the Sandlers have disbursed more than half of their net worth to medical research, social reforms, and education. And then there is the example of the $3.8 billion Atlantic Philanthropies, funded by Charles Feeney, former owner of a duty-free shopping empire. A big supporter of higher education, disadvantaged children, human rights, and programs in Ireland, the foundation will give away some $350 million a year until 2016, when it will close its doors. By that time, Feeney will be eighty-five years old. Limiting the life of a foundation gives it "a sense of urgency and impending accountability," says John Healy, former president of the charity.

Among other Forbes 400 members who pledge to die empty-handed: Eli Broad, Alfred Mann, Michael Milken, T. Boone Pickens, Sandy Weill, and South Dakota banking billionaire T. Denny Sanford, who in 2006 gave $400 million to a local hospital system—one of the largest donations ever to a medical institution.

philanthropy is a field held together by a section of the tax code," says Paul Brest, president of the Hewlett Foundation. (The foundation was started by William R. Hewlett, cofounder of Hewlett-Packard and a member of the Forbes 400 until his death in 2001.) Under the tax code, most charitable contributions are tax deductible. So setting up charitable foundations lets donors and trustees support causes and enjoy huge tax breaks as long as the foundation gives away at least 5 percent of its assets each year in grants.

Another reasonable argument for giving is the perceived meaninglessness of simply piling up riches. Princeton's Singer argues that once you amass great wealth, a "diminishing marginal utility" sets in. More money still means more satisfaction, but at a diminishing rate. Indeed, Charles Feeney, founder of the duty-free shops empire, seems to agree. He truly sees little personal utility in his nearly $4 billion fortune. "Money has an attraction for some people," Feeney has said, "but nobody can wear two pairs of shoes at a time." The New Jersey–born businessman, who flies coach class and reportedly wears $5 watches, gave away more than $600 million in twenty years.

Perhaps more surprising than Feeney's largesse was his secretiveness: Even his business partner had no clue of his beneficence. To avoid U.S. tax-disclosure regulations, Feeney had incorporated his foundation in Bermuda; it was only through a lawsuit over a stock sale that his giving became public. (Feeney graced the Forbes 400 list throughout much of the 1990s, even though he had already secretly transferred most of his fortune to his foundations. Forbes dropped him from the list in 1998, after news about his philanthropy came to light.) There's another twist to Feeney's giving, too. He expects his foundation to spend down its assets and close up shop by 2016. (See "Giving It All Away," page 285.)

So where is all the money going? Traditionally, the superrich have channeled their funds into four major areas: education, health, the arts, and the environment.* Of these, not surprisingly, the alma mater gets some of the largest gifts. Data from the *Chronicle of Higher Education*, which tracks individual gifts to colleges above $50 million, shows the extent of largesse showered on America's campuses. Between 1985 and 2006, members of the Forbes 400 have donated or pledged at least $7.5 billion to higher education. Two parallel trends appear from the data: More than $5 billion of that amount was donated *after* 2000, and the size of individual gifts is ballooning. One of the largest on record went to the California Institute of Technology in 2001: $600 million in cash and stock from Intel cofounder Gordon Moore, who has a PhD in chemistry and physics from the school. Moore made the bequest to keep Cal-Tech on the "forefront of research and development."

---

*While there is anecdotal evidence that many wealthy Americans actively support religious organizations and charities, these groups do not seem to be attracting multimillion-dollar gifts.

Another megagift, $400 million, was pledged to Columbia University in spring 2007. Media magnate John W. Kluge, a 1937 grad, promised the funds upon his death, earmarking them for scholarships and other financial aid. MIT received a $350 million gift in 2000. Benefactor Patrick McGovern (2006 net worth: $3 billion), an MIT alum and founder of the International Data Group, gave the funds to create the McGovern Institute for Brain Research. Two other outsize gifts in the past five years: $200 million from entertainment mogul David Geffen in 2002 to the UCLA David Geffen School of Medicine, and $165 million from oil baron T. Boone Pickens to Oklahoma State University in 2005 to support his alma mater's athletics program.

Once considered massive, gifts of $100 million have now become routine, including David Rockefeller's 2005 donation to Rockefeller University, the research institution his grandfather started more than a century ago; two gifts of $100 million each from Sanford Weill and his wife, Joan, to the Weill Medical Center at Cornell University; and Peter B. Lewis's $101 million donation to alma mater Princeton University. The list goes on: Philip Knight, cofounder of Nike, gave alma mater Stanford University $105 million in 2006. West Coast developer John Arrillaga, another Stanford grad, gave the school $100 million the same year. A former basketball star at the school in the late 1950s (he averaged 12.2 points per game), Arrillaga is such a huge supporter of its sports department that he is known as "the patron saint of Stanford athletics."

While donations to one's alma mater can produce concrete results—a new dorm or a business school bearing a donor's name, for example—the billions that members of the Forbes 400s regularly pump into improving the nation's underperforming public schools often seem to evaporate. The effort to improve school systems is, to be sure, worthy, but the results can be a long time in coming, as a string of philanthropists—Walter Annenberg, Bill Gates, Eli Broad, and others—have learned.

One of the first to pour massive sums into solving the seemingly intractable problem of mending broken public schools was Annenberg. His experience has become a philanthropic case study, with lessons to be drawn by donors and recipients alike. Annenberg's big dream was to make secondary education a national priority and really shake America's public schools into action. "To do that I felt I had to drop a bomb," he told Christopher Ogden, author of *Legacy: A Biography of Moses and Walter Annenberg*. The bomb he dropped was a then unimaginable $500 million gift to education, an amount that set a record in 1993 as the largest single philanthropic donation ever. By insisting that private sources match his gift, the "Annenberg Challenge," he raised another $550 million. In total, Annenberg diverted some $1.5 billion to education, including $150 million to the Corporation for Public Broadcasting to create educational television programming. He dispensed study materials to more than forty-seven thousand schools nationwide on subjects from math to poetry, and delivered a digital satellite television channel at no cost to nearly all of the nation's schools and colleges, as well as 60 million homes.

How effective was the massive infusion of funds? The record is mixed. A 2000 report by the Thomas B. Fordham Foundation found that by the late 1990s, the Annenberg Challenge had left only "small footprints" on the vast terrain of public schools it had intended to revitalize. In Philadelphia the gifts were used to start full-day kindergarten, which resulted in better student scores in later years. San Francisco saw similar results, with scores rising at eleven out of fourteen schools. But the grants, sprinkled across nearly twenty cities, were too diffuse to have a major impact, and institutionalizing the few successes largely eluded the program.

"Obviously there were lessons to be learned," says Eli Broad, another big giver to public schools, who is more narrowly funneling funds toward programs that provide awards, scholarships, and training grants, rather than making broad-based gifts to school systems. "It would have been a lot easier to just write the checks," Broad says. Instead, his foundation takes a top-down approach, providing management programs for "overwhelmed principals and administrators," who, he found, are lacking in such skills. Programs span the country from Los Angeles to Boston.

So far, Broad admits, progress is "uneven." But he prefers to focus on the successes. "We've trained more superintendents than any other group in America," says Broad. "We have placed fifty-seven MBAs with experience into large urban schools. We feel good about that." Meanwhile, in New York City, hedge fund manager Bruce Kovner (2006 net worth: $3 billion) is (like Ted Forstmann) deeply involved with education vouchers as well as in creating small, independent charter schools. Kovner sees competition and freedom of choice as a way for children and their families to break out of huge, crime-ridden, dead-end schools. "More than one out of every three hundred people in the United States is in New York City public schools," says Kovner. "And 25 percent are in schools that are failures and destructive. It's one of the great scandals of the city." However noble the sentiments, there's little evidence so far that vouchers have succeeded in greatly ameliorating the myriad problems.

A huge player in the primary and secondary education arena is the Gates Foundation. (World health gets the foundation's largest share of assets—

$6 billion to date.) Gates has spent $1 billion so far in scholarships to high-school graduates and $1.2 billion to improve high schools, largely by creating some fifteen hundred small high schools in forty states and Washington, D.C. The currently popular notion that small schools perform better than large ones has galvanized the foundations of many other Forbes 400 members, including those of Dell's Michael and Susan Dell; Wal-Mart's Walton family; Jerri-Ann and Gary Jacobs (son of Qualcomm founder, Irwin Jacobs); Donald and Doris Fisher, founders of retailer the Gap; and others.

But results of spending to create smaller schools remain mixed. Graduation rates are up somewhat, according to the Gates Foundation, but math scores are "on par with or lagging behind other schools" in their districts, and—just as the Annenberg Challenge found—duplicating successes is a challenge. The Gateses openly discuss their difficulties and setbacks and say they are learning from them. "If you want to equate being naive with being inexperienced," Melinda Gates told *BusinessWeek,* "then we were definitely naive when we first started." She vows to redesign the program and pay closer attention to the curriculum at the schools.

Health research also attracts a high percentage of donations, second only to educational causes. And just as with donations to alma maters, giving is often for very personal reasons. There's nothing like a brush with a frightening illness to open up purse strings and seek treatments, if not solutions and cures. One of the best-known examples is that of former junk-bond king Michael Milken (2006 net worth: $2.1 billion), who discovered that he had prostate cancer in 1993 just after being released from prison. At the time, prostate cancer was a hush-hush disease that received little medical attention and few research dollars. Milken made it his mission to raise its profile and help find a cure.

Using a pseudonym, Milken attended a medical seminar on prostate cancer at Houston's M. D. Anderson Cancer Center. The lectures were not encouraging. From what he knew of the size of his tumor, his life expectancy was very short. After listening to an especially knowledgeable prostate cancer expert from Johns Hopkins, Milken approached the doctor and revealed his identity: "I am Mike Milken," he said. "I want to be cured."

Since its founding in 1993, Milken's Prostate Cancer Foundation (PCF) has raised more than $260 million and provided funding for twelve hundred prostate cancer researchers at one hundred institutions around the world. With his cancer in remission, Milken continues to head the group, focusing on ways to speed up the fight against cancer by streamlining grant making, pumping cash into the research system, and getting private researchers, government agencies, and academics to join forces. One notable result of Milken's giving is his group's annual prostate cancer conference, which is considered an important and much-needed forum for researchers to share data and report progress. And more than eighty Milken-funded human clinical trials have reportedly led to improved prostate cancer treatments. Milken still dabbles in investing, but most of his time is devoted to PCF and his other philanthropies: the Milken Family Foundation and FasterCures.

The list of megamillionaires funding research for cures of ailments and diseases, some of which afflict them or family members, goes on and on: Eli Broad; real-estate tycoon Mort Zuckerman; and California billionaires Ray Dolby (sound pioneer) and William Gross (Pimco investment firm), who are both backing stem-cell research. But are they seeing returns on their investments? Not if they are looking for medical miracles, say philanthropy experts. That's partly due to the time-intensive nature of medical research. Broad, for one, is convinced that the $200 million he has given in the past two years to the Broad Institute at MIT and Harvard is already showering him with rewards. "One week doesn't go by that a scientific journal doesn't write about our research," he says. One such advance came in the fall of 2006: a new kind of genetic "road map" that connects human diseases with potential drugs to treat them. And Mort Zuckerman, who had been a supporter of cancer treatment and research for thirty years, donated $100 million to Memorial Sloan-Kettering Cancer Center in New York after a newly developed procedure cured his daughter of a rare tumor that was pressing on her brain. "It was research that saved her life," he says.

The view from Ronald Lauder's office, high atop Fifth Avenue in the company headquarters of Estée Lauder, is stunning. Not just the sweeping views north over Central Park, but the equally sumptuous vista of art that fills every wall, pedestal, table, and shelf throughout the corridors and conference rooms—with unopened packing crates everywhere attesting to Lauder's insatiable collecting bug. On one wall of the reception area is an exquisite Gerhard Richter painting of a stag. Across from it is a shadowed Anselm Kiefer, the modern German artist and sculptor whose work tries to come to terms with his country's Nazi past. And between the windows is Sledge, a major work by iconic German artist Joseph Beuys, who worked with fur, animal fat, and found objects. "To me, business allows you to do what you really want to do," says Lauder, which in his case includes collecting world-class art in five different

In a Class by Themselves

Why is giving to the arts so popular? One reason is the prestige that comes with supporting museums, as well as the symphony, opera, and ballet (this triumvirate is sometimes called "the SOBs"). Another is the chance that a board position offers to schmooze with people who define high society.

Not all boards are equal, of course. Among the most coveted are New York's Metropolitan Museum of Art and Museum of Modern Art (MoMA), Washington, D.C.'s Kennedy Center, and the Los Angeles County Museum of Art. The price of admission for the New York Metropolitan Opera board is reputedly a commitment to give a minimum of $250,000 a year. The boards of MoMA and the Metropolitan Opera tie—nine each—for the most Forbes 400 members (or their wives).

The king of glitzy boards is financier Stephen Schwarzman (2006 net worth: $3.5 billion), who is chairman of the Kennedy Center, a trustee of New York's Frick Collection, and on the boards of the New York Public Library, the Film Society of New York's Lincoln Center, and the New York City Ballet.

A few superrich board members have both coasts covered, among them Eli Broad (MoMA and the Los Angeles County Museum) and Ronald Burkle (Kennedy Center and the J. Paul Getty Trust). The 400 members, and their spouses, who sit on some of the most sought-after boards include:

Los Angeles
Los Angeles County Museum of Art

Wallis Annenberg: Daughter of deceased media mogul Walter Annenberg, whose foundation has given more than $21 million to LACMA since 1991.

Donald L. Bren: The richest man in Orange County, made his fortune in real estate. Also a big Republican donor and skiing pal of Arnold Schwarzenegger.

Eli Broad: Made his money in real-estate development and investing. Gave $60 million in 2004 to help build a new museum at LACMA that will bear his name.

Robert A. Day: Billionaire money manager chairs the W. M. Keck Foundation; $1 billion endowment funds liberal arts and sciences.

Tom Gores: Israeli immigrant (brother Alec is also a Forbes 400 member). Made his fortune in leveraged buyouts and now heads Platinum Equity, one of the country's largest companies.

Edward P. Roski Jr.: Los Angeles real-estate mogul also gave $23 million to alma mater USC's fine arts school in 2006.

New York City
Metropolitan Opera

Mrs. Walter H. Annenberg: The late media mogul's second wife, Leonore (Lee). Chief of protocol under Ronald Reagan.

Mercedes Bass: Vice chairman; gave the largest unrestricted donation ($25 million) in the Met's history. Wife of oil tycoon Sid Bass.

Gordon P. Getty: Heir to Getty fortune and himself an opera composer; worth $2.3 billion in 2006.

Mrs. Leon Hess: Widow of Leon, who made a $1 billion fortune in oil and helped build the Opera House.

Frederick R. Koch: Son of energy company founder; major art collector who has given pieces to the Carnegie Museum and the Frick, among others.

Bruce Kovner: Huge supporter of NYC's Lincoln Center, including the Met and the Juilliard School of Music.

Mrs. Jeannette Lerman-Neubauer: Husband Joseph, an Israeli immigrant, made his fortune from facilities management company Aramark.

Vivian Milstein: Widow of real-estate investor Seymour Milstein, last on the Forbes 400 list in 1990 with $325 million.

Mrs. William B. Ziff Jr.: Widow of publishing company head, worth $500 million the last time he was on the Forbes 400 in 1994.

Museum of Modern Art

Wallis Annenberg.

Sid R. Bass: Texas oil billionaire; with wife Mercedes sits on Metropolitan Opera board.

Leon Black: Private equity investor and art lover; owns an outstanding collection of impressionist, modern, and old masters, as well as Chinese bronzes.

Michael Bloomberg: Honorary trustee. New York City mayor known to be a big anonymous donor to many causes.

Eli Broad.

Marie-Josée Kravis: Economist wife of multibillionaire Henry Kravis; president of MoMA in 2006.

Ronald S. Lauder: Cosmetics heir. Chairman emeritus—on the board since 1976. Also started the Neue Galerie, dedicated to Austrian art.

David Rockefeller: Honorary chairman. His mother helped found the museum; has given more than $120 million and promised $5 million a year until his death.

Washington, D.C.
Kennedy Center

Stephen Schwarzman: Chairman of the board; donated $10 million in 2004, just after being named chair. Studied at Yale with President George W. Bush.

Nancy G. Kinder: Wife of Richard Kinder, president of Enron Corporation who left the company before the scandal broke (2006 net worth: $2.8 billion).

Stephen A. Wynn: Casino impresario appointed to board by President George W. Bush.

Ronald W. Burkle: Swashbuckling supermarket mogul. Longtime Democratic fundraiser and close pal of Bill Clinton.

fields, from old-master drawings to arms and armor to nineteenth- and twentieth-century paintings and objects.

Lauder, a tall, imposing man in his early sixties who talks a hundred miles a minute and radiates a passion for art, has had a number of careers. "I've always divided my life into chapters, each roughly a decade long," he says. The first was working in Belgium and France for Estée Lauder, the cosmetics company founded by his parents in 1946, and developing the Clinique brand. Next, in the 1980s, came a decade of government service. He served during the first Reagan administration as deputy assistant secretary of defense for Europe and NATO Affairs, and in 1986 was appointed U.S. ambassador to Austria, a posting that led to his increased interest in Jewish survivors in Europe and the eventual founding of fifteen schools in Jewish studies there. His passion also led him to his current business interest, building up media in the region: His Central European Media Enterprises operates thirteen networks in six countries; Apax Partners, a private equity investment group, acquired a 49.7 percent stake in his shares in 2006 for $190 million in cash.

Now, while Lauder continues his business activities at the family-owned firm, he is deeply entrenched in the worlds of collecting and philanthropy. He joined the board of the Museum of Modern Art in 1976 and served as chairman for ten years. But his most lasting philanthropic legacy will undoubtedly be the sumptuous Neue Galerie on Fifth Avenue in New York. Housed in a former Vanderbilt mansion, the gallery is the brainchild of Lauder and the late art dealer Serge Sabarsky, with whom Lauder collaborated for decades. It is devoted to early-twentieth-century German and Austrian art and design, a passion of Lauder's from his early teens and something that previously lacked visibility in the great museum collections of New York. The Neue Galerie's crown jewel is Gustav Klimt's 1904 *Portrait of Adele Bloch-Bauer,* which literally shimmers: The gold background is redolent of Byzantine mosaics. Lauder paid a reported $135 million for it. "This is the great painting of Vienna at the turn of the century," says Lauder. "For our museum, it is our *Mona Lisa.*"

Of all the philanthropic areas, giving to the arts has always attracted major money. "People in the arts have a kind of social power that you can't get unless you're willing to pay," says Rockefeller consigliere Dietel. Adds Nelson Aldrich, "Giving to the arts is the social pinnacle. It's a well-worn path to social success."

Like Ronald Lauder, many donors find their lives transformed once they've been bitten by the collecting bug. Take the case of Norton Simon,

☙

Opera's Tragic Hero

Alberto Vilar had two passions in life: opera and philanthropy. The billionaire was legendary in the late 1990s for his lavish giving to opera houses as far-flung as the Kirov Opera in St. Petersburg, the Royal Opera House in London, and the Metropolitan Opera in New York. He was known to attend fifty operas a year at the Met alone. For many years, the Met's two front-and-center seats, A101 and A102, were reserved for Vilar. His name was etched in brass on the Met's Grand Tier. And a spectacular renovation of a glass atrium in the Royal Opera House was named Vilar Floral Hall in his honor.

The tale of Vilar's life and downfall rivals the drama and intrigue in *The Ring* (Richard Wagner is one of his favorite composers). Now in his mid-sixties, Vilar has described himself as a Cuban exile whose once-affluent family fled the country after the Castro-led revolution. He grew up in Puerto Rico and came to the United States to study, receiving a bachelor's degree in economics from Washington & Jefferson College in Pennsylvania and a master's degree from New York's Iona College. In the late 1970s he and investing partner Gary Tanaka founded Amerindo Investment Advisors, a firm that grew to be a financial giant by investing early in technology and Internet companies like Cisco Systems, Yahoo, and Microsoft. In 2000, Amerindo had nearly $10 billion in assets. The following year, *Forbes* estimated Vilar's net worth at $1 billion.

But Vilar misjudged the depth of the high-tech market crash; as the NASDAQ plunged in 2001, Amerindo began to pay a hefty price. Still, his declining fortunes apparently didn't rein in his urge to give. He pledged to donate more than $100 million that year to the Kennedy Center in Washington, D.C., Columbia University's medical school, NYU, and, of course, opera houses. "Asking Alberto for money was like offering an alcoholic a drink," a friend of Vilar's told *New Yorker* writer James B. Stewart.

Not surprisingly, Vilar was finding it tough to follow through on his pledges. He began to miss payment due dates. For the first time since he had joined the Met's board in 1996, Vilar skipped a meeting in spring 2003. Meanwhile, a meeting in mid-2002 with Lily Cates, a friend and client, would prove the beginning of his undoing. Cates, whose daughter is actress Phoebe Cates (best remembered for her topless poolside scene in *Fast Times at Ridgemont High*), was a wealthy woman. Her second husband, entrepreneur and horse breeder Marshall Naify (whose fortune Forbes put at $1.7 billion in 1999), died one year after their marriage, leaving her $10 million. At Vilar's suggestion, Cates gave him $5 million to invest. But two years later Cates had yet to see any return. During that time, Vilar was reportedly funneling hundreds of thousands to various philanthropies, trying to meet his obligations. In 2005, as he stepped off a plane at Newark Liberty Airport, Vilar was arrested for allegedly defrauding investors. Unable to raise $10 million in cash for bail, he spent nearly one month in prison. Two years later, Vilar remained under house arrest in his Manhattan apartment, awaiting a trial.

The opera world, meanwhile, quickly set out to eradicate Vilar's name from their halls. The Royal Opera House reverted to calling its atrium simply Floral Hall but retained Vilar's name on the Donor and Benefactors Board, in deference to the 4.4 million pounds (about $8 million) he had already donated. The Met was less deferential: Despite the $12 million or so it had actually received from Vilar, it removed his name from the Grand Tier, dropped him as a managing director, and gave away his reserved seats.

Suspicions about Vilar's real background, meanwhile, had been swirling for years. He called himself a lifelong bachelor, but it turned out that he had been married twice—the second time for ten years. He referred to himself as "a shy, shy, shy boy with girls," yet he was often seen in the company of high-powered women, including soprano Renée Fleming. As for his Cuban exile story, it may have been just that. A suspicious former fiancée, a Harvard musicologist, revealed that she had looked at his passport and that his name was not Alberto, but just plain Albert—and that he was born not in Cuba, but in East Orange, New Jersey. "My whole feeling is that this man was insecure," Stewart quotes a source close to the opera world as saying. "He needed the adulation."

Vilar still ranks as one of the Met's top three donors. Should his fortunes reverse once again, however, the opera house will lose out, he has said: "The Met is not going to get my money, but it will not kill my love of music."

founder of Hunt Foods and one of the Forbes 400 until his death in 1993. Simon didn't start collecting art until he was forty-seven, but it wasn't long before he had seven Cézannes in his bedroom alone. Simon's voracious appetite turned into an obsession as he built up one of the finest art collections around, with twelve thousand works ranging from old masters and impressionist paintings to ancient Asian sculpture. "Art," said Simon, "is my religion." His massive collection is now housed in the Norton Simon Museum in Pasadena, California.

Art had a similar effect on Eli Broad, now one of the world's leading art collectors. "You become addicted to art, and you can't live without it," he says. Broad wasn't always an art enthusiast. His urge to collect originated with his wife, Edythe, who often entertained herself by shopping for art pieces when her husband traveled for business. "I'd come back and see something else she bought," he says. "I became curious and became a student of art." That's about the time "the acquisition budget increased," as his wife likes to point out. One salutary effect of collecting, says Broad, is that art expands one's worldview: "It makes you a better citizen, rather than just being a business person dealing with bankers and lawyers all day."

The Broad Art Foundation, started in 1984, has amassed a collection of 750 pieces by more than one hundred international contemporary artists. It serves as a sort of lending library for more than four hundred museums and galleries worldwide. Broad's personal collection, meanwhile, focuses on pop and postwar masterpieces by such artists as Andy Warhol, Jasper Johns, and Roy Lichtenstein. Eventually, Broad will donate the entire collection: "We'll give it all away. We don't want it to go into storage and not be seen by the public." Part of it will be housed in a seventy-thousand-square-foot museum now under construction.

But the quintessential patron of the arts remains nonagenarian David Rockefeller. Rockefeller inherited close ties to New York's Museum of Modern Art from his mother, Abby Aldrich Rockefeller, who helped found the museum in 1929. Rockefeller has supported the museum with donations of more than $120 million over his lifetime and has promised to give more. That doesn't include donating more than twenty works of art by Cézanne, Picasso, Matisse, and others to the museum. His strategy toward giving to the arts, as to other causes, is to pick good people with smart ideas and get out of their way, says Dietel. Rockefeller's explanation for his hands-off policy: "I felt they know most what are the most urgent needs, and there was no need for me to specify a particular place to put it." Meanwhile, his private fifteen-thousand-piece art collection is housed in residences on Manhattan's East Side, the family estate at Pocantico Hills in Westchester County, New York, and a third home on Mount Desert Island in Maine.

Along with arts patronage, a tradition that dates back to ancient times but has flourished since the Middle Ages, preservation of the environment is another favorite blue-blood cause. Environmental giving, says Nelson Aldrich, is "a traditional hand-me-down charity," passed on from generation to generation. It goes back to Teddy Roosevelt, who launched the conservation movement and helped created the national parks system, and John D. Rockefeller, who scooped up eleven thousand pristine acres in Maine for what became Acadia National Park, as well as thirty-five thousand stunning acres for a national park in the Grand Tetons. Old-money philanthropists such as the late Laurance and Winthrop Rockefeller, J.D.'s grandsons and David's brothers, also saw themselves as catalysts for conserving the environment; accordingly, they gave generously. Laurance bought and then deeded two-thirds of St. John, in the U.S. Virgin Islands, plus five thousand offshore acres, to the federal government in the 1950s. The pristine marine areas and unspoiled forests are now national parkland.

But environmental giving is not limited to old money. Although stock losses have put a damper on his entire philanthropic portfolio, Ted Turner's heart has always been in the environment: "When I was a kid, I read a lot of books about animals in Africa, about butterflies, birds, whales, plants, flowers, trees, everything," Turner says. "The natural world fascinated me." In the 1990s he wrote an ecological version of the Ten Commandments. Number one: "I love and respect planet Earth and all living things thereon, especially my fellow species, mankind." Other promises: To have no more than two children (although Turner has five), to use "as little nonrenewable resources as possible," and "as little toxic chemicals, pesticides and other poisons as possible."

Through the Turner Foundation and personally, he has donated more than $1 billion to environmental causes. He started the foundation in 1990 (all five Turner children are directors) to support eco-friendly groups, such as ones that run hands-on ecology programs for kids, or teach seniors and non-English speakers about ways to prevent ecological damage. Turner is also almost single-handedly out to preserve natural, open spaces. He is said to be the nation's largest landowner. "I don't want all the land. I just want the ranch next door," he once said. Joke or not, when you sum up his holdings in eleven states, including Montana, New Mexico, and South Dakota, his domain covers nearly 2 million acres.

His effort to bring back bison in the West worked so well that it resulted in an excess of bison meat (more than 10 percent of the herd of bison in America roams on his land). Turner saw a way to parlay the thriving population into a business venture: Ted's Montana Grill, now a chain of more than forty-five eco-friendly eateries in eighteen states. Another Forbes 400 conservationist, John Malone (the billionaire chairman of Liberty Media) has bought some six hundred thousand acres in Colorado, Wyoming, New Mexico, and

Maine in an effort to save it from "developers who are eating up land like mad in this country." One of Malone's more recent purchases is fifty-four thousand acres of forest near the western Maine–Québec border, where he paid above-market rates to keep land from going to liquidation harvesters who sell off the timber. "I just love land, and I love open spaces," says Malone. "I'm kind of an Irish farmer at heart."

And then there are the save-the-earth visionaries. Lands' End founder Gary Comer, a world-class sailor who had a lifelong fascination with the Arctic, set out several years ago on a campaign against global warming. While crossing the Northwest Passage in 2001, Comer and his crew encountered a lower percentage of sea ice than they expected, completing the trip in his 150-foot yacht, *Turmoil*, in just nineteen days. Arctic explorer Roald Amundsen, by comparison, took three years in the first decade of the twentieth century to make the crossing over the top of North America. Still others who attempted the trip in the mid-1800s never returned. "We were able to do it, and so many people had failed," he told *Science* magazine. "Something happened." Comer decided global warming was the culprit.

Two other events motivated Comer to move quickly toward funding climate research. First, his sale of the Lands' End catalog business to Sears netted him about $1 billion. Second, a diagnosis of prostate cancer in December 2001 lent greater urgency to his decision.* Comer consulted a Nobel-laureate geochemist and other prominent scientists, and with their help devised a simple, no-strings-attached method of underwriting smart research, cutting red tape to a minimum, and keeping a close tab on results. All told, Comer gave more than $30 million to conduct research on global warming.

Some results are coming in. Comer-funded researchers at the University of California–Irvine reported in 2006 that levels of the greenhouse gas methane in the atmosphere can indeed be controlled and decreased by tightening emissions from things like coal mining and leaking oil and gas lines. Their seven-year study, based on measuring sea-level air in locations from Alaska to New Zealand, proves that society can do something to slow global warming. Comer's funds are also helping to underwrite wind-powered machines that suck carbon dioxide from the air. The gas, which also contributes to the greenhouse warming effect, would then be safely stored underground. As Comer once said, "Who needs to go to the moon? Take care of Earth."

*Comer died of cancer in 2006, at age seventy-eight.

Not Your Typical Charitable Donation

While such popular causes as alma maters, museums, and symphonies attract big bucks, it's a lot tougher for "unusual, possibly harebrained ideas" to get support, as Intel cofounder and hugely generous philanthropist Gordon Moore has noted. Among the quirky or off-the-beaten-track giving by some Forbes 400 members:

Paul Allen: Microsoft cofounder Allen (2006 net worth: $16 billion) donated $100 million to establish the Allen Institute for Brain Science in Seattle. Since 2002 eighty researchers at the institute have been mapping the brain of a mouse. Four years and $41 million later, they had created a digital atlas of a mouse brain that showed 20,000 genes and contained 85 million photos and 250,000 slides. The purpose: to help researchers better understand how the human brain works.

Philip Anschutz: Founder of telecommunications company Qwest, Anschutz (2006 net worth: $7.8 billion) has spent some $23 million to promote "positive values" through two foundations: Random Acts of Kindness Foundation and the Foundation for a Better Life. Among the organizations' projects is a nationwide billboard campaign that features individuals performing a good deed and encourages viewers to PASS IT ON.

Bill Gates: In a little-publicized donation, the Gates Foundation put up $10 million to buy high-tech greenhouses built by Jewish settlers in Gaza and transfer them to the Palestinians just before Israel evacuated the area in early 2006. Two other Forbes 400 members, publisher Mort Zuckerman (2006 net worth: $2.5 billion) and real-estate investor Leonard Stern ($3.7 billion), also lent some support. The hyperefficient greenhouses accounted for more than $100 million a year in high-quality, insect-free vegetables to Europe and supplied Israel with 75 percent of its produce. But the investment had a poor return: Some of the greenhouses were stripped and looted by Palestinian gunmen and even by the security officers hired to protect them.

Gordon and Betty Moore: Ocean research is high on the Moores' giving agenda. One ten-year, $145 million project studies the role of microorganisms in the ocean. The Moores are sticklers for measurable results. Researchers will keep close track of the number of new organisms identified, and their discoveries will be cited in scientific journals.

The couple is also a major supporter of Conservation International, a group that seeks to preserve the earth's "hot spots." These areas make up only 1.4 percent of land surface but contain some 60 percent of terrestrial plant and animal species.

Gordon Moore, Paul Allen, William Hewlett, David Packard: Congress ridiculed NASA's controversial Search for Extraterrestrial Intelligence program and cut its funding in the mid-1990s. At that point, SETI managers ran to the Forbes 400 list to find potential funders. Moore, Allen, Hewlett, and Packard were among those willing to fund the search for alien life within our galaxy. They put up a cumulative $20 million to extend the program, but the search is proving painstakingly slow.

Steven Spielberg: Filmmaker Spielberg donated $70 million, partly profits from his 1993 Oscar-winning movie, *Schindler's List* (the true story of Oskar Schindler, who saved more than one thousand Jews from concentration camps during the Holocaust), to fund his Righteous Persons Foundation (RPF), which supports Jewish life and tolerance issues. Spielberg also gave many millions more to help preserve oral testimonies of Holocaust survivors and witnesses.

Jon Stryker: Billionaire grandson of Homer Stryker, an orthopedic surgeon who invented the mobile hospital bed, gave nearly $4 million to help rescue some three hundred chimpanzees that had lived for years in small cages at a research lab in New Mexico. The funds helped build and operate a chimp sanctuary in Florida and transport the animals in an air-conditioned trailer outfitted with a window seat for each chimp.

Ted Waitt: Founder of Gateway, Waitt gave about $1 million toward a National Geographic Society project devoted to one of the Bible's most despised characters: Judas. The project included a translation of the ancient Gospel of Judas, which states that Judas was not a traitor but Jesus' closest friend.

Just how much of their fortunes America's richest (or donors in general) give is hard to pin down for many reasons. Publicly available data is seldom comprehensive, and some gifts are anonymous. Another factor is that donations are often made in the form of stock, so bequest values rise and fall with the market, making precise comparisons nearly impossible. But a onetime

IRS calculation in 2000 of the income, assets, and donations of America's four hundred richest individuals sheds some light on the question. (Because the IRS always keeps names secret, it's not known whether the IRS 400 were the same as the Forbes 400.) Aggregate assets came to $273 billion; actual donations by the group amounted to $10 billion. The NewTithing Group, a research and educational resource on philanthropy, studied the data and found the IRS 400 were responsible for 7 percent of all individual donations. The superrich appear even less generous if you look at tax filers with assets of $125 million or more (6,126 of them in 2003). Donations as a percentage of their assets came to 1.4 percent. By comparison, those with assets of a lowly $145,000 were the largest givers, donating 1.5 percent, according to NewTithing.

Forbes 400 member Ted Forstmann, for one, believes that many of his counterparts lack generosity. "I don't think they give enough money, or enough anything," he says. Indeed, a glance at the chart of top givers on page 278 shows that even among the most generous of the Forbes 400, there is often a huge chasm between the sums donors give and their net worth. Some, including Gordon Moore and Thomas Monaghan, are giving at percentages that surpass even such supergivers as Buffett, Soros, and Turner; although others, including Paul Allen, Larry Ellison, and the Walton family have given away 5 percent or less of their wealth. (Keep in mind that Allen, Ellison, and the Waltons are still gifting sums worth nearly $1 billion each.) But what about the remaining scores of members of the Forbes 400 over the years? Why do they seem to be giving so little?

For some, not giving is based on philosophical, political, and sometimes very personal reasons. Some want to avoid the limelight and the constant

2005

from the pages of *Forbes*

Ronald Burkle, California supermarket magnate, ferries former president Bill Clinton around on his private jet, which Clinton has dubbed "Ron Air." (2005 net worth: $2.3 billion)

Harvey Chaplin, whose family fortune comes from wine and liquor, stuffs his office with Charlie Chaplin memorabilia— even though the legendary comedian is no relation. (2005 family net worth: $1.2 billion)

Timber baron **Timothy Blixseth** writes songs for his own record label, which is distributed by Warner Bros. (2005 net worth: $1 billion)

James E. Cayne, head of Bear Stearns investment house, was originally hired in part because of his card skills and is a ten-time national bridge champion. (2005 net worth: $900 million) solicitations it brings. You won't find Viacom chairman Sumner M. Redstone (2006 net worth: $7.5 billion) on lists of top philanthropists, for example. According to his spokespeople, that's not because he is miserly; he simply prefers to give privately, and donates generously to battling AIDS and cancer as well as to programs researching burn therapies. Forbes 400 member Eli Broad, for one, has his doubts about huge anonymous bequests: "I'm not aware of any large gifts that are anonymous," he says. The data seems to bear out Broad's suspicion: A survey by Indiana University's Center on Philanthropy found that only about 1 percent of gifts of $1 million or more were anonymous. Meanwhile, Redstone may be changing his views. In spring 2007, he announced that he was giving $105 million to three nonprofit health-care organizations to advance cancer care and burn recovery.

Others believe that philanthropy is only a temporary Band-Aid on deep social ills. The late H. L. Hunt, founder of the Hunt oil fortune and father of fourteen (most of whom have graced the Forbes 400 list over the years), was vocal about his aversion to charity. For one thing, Hunt was a notorious tightwad who once said he was "more interested in the acquisition of wealth than its disbursement." Second, Hunt equated receiving charity to being on the public dole; both, in his mind, stripped recipients of the drive to succeed.

More recently, critics of traditional giving have turned to new ways of donating. South Dakota multibillionaire T. Denny Sanford made the largest gift ever to a hospital system—$400 million in 2007—but not before he was guaranteed that his money would create a world-class medical center for pediatrics as renowned as the Mayo Clinic is for geriatrics. "It's the entrepreneurial Sanford coming out in me," he says. "Just to write a big check without a specific mission or project in mind—I have no interest in that." T. Boone Pickens put a novel twist on his gifts of $50 million each to two University of Texas medical institutions in 2007. He stipulated that each gift had to grow to $500 million within twenty-five years. If the medical centers did not meet the goal, they would be obliged to hand over any amount more than $50 million to Pickens's alma mater, Oklahoma State. More philanthropists, such as Bruce Kovner, are increasingly hands-on givers. Besides his involvement with New York City schools, Kovner is also deeply involved with the renovation of Lincoln Center, where he is vice chair, and its celebrated Juilliard School, where he is chairman. "Music is a passion for me," says Kovner, who each day plays one of two Steinway B pianos in his Fifth Avenue mansion. "But I don't believe in vanity giving. I've convinced myself we are building the preeminent performing arts and learning institution in the world."

One watchdog concept taking hold is *venture philanthropy*, in which hard-nosed business practices are used to bring more accountability to the some-times vague disbursements. A leading practitioner is David Duffield, founder of software company PeopleSoft. Animal lovers Duffield and his wife, Cheryl, created the $300 million Maddie's Fund after their miniature schnauzer, Maddie, died in 1997. (The couple now has nine children—six of them adopted—six grandchildren, three dogs, and a parrot.) The sole focus of the foundation is to create a "no-kill" zone by ensuring that homes are found for all dogs and cats housed in shelters. Toward that goal, the Duffields keep a close eye on their grantees.

Maddie's Fund president, Rich Avanzino, says grantees must report to the foundation monthly and show how well they are meeting mutually agreed-upon goals, such as how many pets have been placed. Grant renewals are based on their performance. Groups are also monitored for their ability to cooperate in a field not known for civility among competing groups. "They cannot bash or trash each other in the media," says Avanzino. He believes the fund will achieve its goal within ten years. Now flush with profits from the $11 billion sale of PeopleSoft to Oracle's Larry Ellison, the Duffields are pre-pared to give up to $1 billion to make that happen.

Pierre Omidyar, founder of eBay, and his wife, Pam, are also at the fore-front of creative philanthropy, applying lessons learned from the Internet marketplace to giving. "When you create wealth in a short time, you think about philanthropy as you think about a business," Omidyar told *Forbes.* At the height of the dot-com frenzy in the late 1990s, the Omidyars (2006 net worth: $7.7 billion) traded in life in high-charged Silicon Valley for the anonymity of Paris, where they pondered the heavy burden of their wealth. Neither felt comfortable with their new riches and vowed to give it all away.

The couple now lives in a low-key suburb of Las Vegas, where they devote their time to running the Omidyar Network, a sort of hybrid philanthropy they started in 2004. The operation is part foundation and part venture-capital fund that invests in for-profit companies. Each arm has assets of $200 million, and all potential recipients must meet tough mission criteria. Most important, "They must have some shared interest, some sense of own-ership," says Omidyar spokesperson Daniela Reif, "some 'skin in the game,' as Pierre calls it."

Omidyar is especially enamored of so-called microfinancing, giving small loans to poor people with a business plan—no matter how modest—to help them become self-supporting. The approach, pioneered three decades ago by Bangladeshi economist and Nobel Prize winner Muhammad Yunus, is now one of the hottest notions in American philanthropy. Omidyar's successes include a Latin American mother who opened a produce stand with a $68 loan and made enough to send her children to school. Microlending has even influenced Omidyar's more traditional giving. For example, when he and his wife endowed $100 million in 2005 to their alma mater, Tufts University, they stipulated that the school use the money not for campus improvements or a new research center, but to set up a microfinance investment fund.

At the same time, a small number of 400 donors are beginning to find organizations that have been largely ignored. Some, particularly those promoting social and economic causes, are moving up the agenda. Among the recent examples: Peter Lewis gave $8 million to the American Civil Liberties Union (ACLU) in 2003; Herbert and Marion Sandler gave $15 million, and a five-year matching grant, to Human Rights Watch in 2004; and Jon Stryker, heir to a medical-supply fortune, donated $1 million to the National Gay and Lesbian Task Force in Washington, D.C., in 2006. (Stryker also funds a Save the Chimps organization; see "Not Your Typical Charitable Donation," page 300.) Still, the truly big contributions—the $100 million range bequests—are missing, with the exception of hedge fund billionaire George Soros's contributions to his Open Society Institute.

In the end, though, what really matters is not so much the size of the gifts but their impact on society. The question then becomes: Are the billions that the Forbes 400 have given over the past twenty-five years making a difference? The answer appears to be yes—although a qualified yes. The problem, says philanthropy scholar James Allen Smith of Georgetown, arises when people expect philanthropy to solve problems quickly and permanently. "Sometimes people set the bar for judging philanthropy too high," he says, when success in solving intractable problems is often better measured in baby steps. Take the Measles Initiative, for example, a partnership among Turner's UN Foundation, the American Red Cross, and several international bodies. The groups have worked since 2001 and spent more than $144 million, yet have not eradicated the disease. But they have vaccinated more than 200 million children in more than forty African countries, cutting measles cases and deaths by 60 percent.

Far better, says Smith, is to take a long historical view of giving. "Philanthropy in America has often risen to the occasion," he says. "It has had a huge impact in transforming the intellectual capital that we employ to confront a succession of problems over the last one hundred years." Perhaps the greatest example of all is how philanthropy has transformed higher education in the United States "from sectarian liberal arts colleges of no particular distinction into the greatest university system in the world." At a time of dwindling budgets—and reputations—of the great universities abroad, that is indeed no small achievement.

13

Power and Politics

W hen George Soros was a young boy in Nazi-occupied Hungary, he was given a mission by the Jewish Council, a community organization set up by the Germans for the identification and registration of Jews. His task was to go through Budapest serving deportation papers on Jewish lawyers. When Tivadar, George's father, found out about the job, he forbade the boy to return to work. Years later, Soros could trace the roots of his dislike of philanthropic organizations, particularly Jewish ones, to that formative experience. Yet Soros was destined to become one of the most influential philanthropists the world has ever seen, altering the social and political fabric of thousands of lives from South Africa to the Soviet Union.

Many members of the Forbes 400 have their own foundation or charitable organization. But some of the superrich go a step further: They are sometimes overcome by a zeal to influence the social and political fabric of society. And they do so by channeling their money and their considerable energies and talents through the corridors of power—though, it must be noted, with decidedly mixed results.

For some, to be sure, politics is simply a way of developing advantageous business conditions. In a 1998 essay entitled "Robber Barons," J. Bradford DeLong, a professor of economics at the University of California–Berkeley, writes that during the second half of the nineteenth century the most successful entrepreneurs were either "well-connected enough to fend off political attempts to curb their wealth (or well-connected enough to make political favors the foundation of their wealth)." These days, of course, there are hordes of lobbyists and lawyers swarming Washington, D.C., and state capitals, trying to influence legislation and public opinion, and lobbying is an accepted and generally above-the-board part of the game. And while the Forbes 400, to be sure, aggressively push their business interests, their public activities also spring from a sense of duty as well as a variety of other motivations. With billions of dollars at his fingertips and, more often than not, a highly successful business career behind him, who would not want to influence the events of the day? And no one has tried more aggressively, persistently, and on as broad a canvas as Soros, a perennial Forbes 400 member.

Soros was born into a well-to-do, nonpracticing Jewish family in Budapest, Hungary. The surname Soros was an invention of his father's. A devotee of the international language Esperanto, Tivadar Soros apparently liked the word because it was a palindrome. In order to survive the German occupation, the Soros family lived separately under false identities. When the war ended and the Communists took over Hungary, young George fled to London alone. There, at age seventeen, he entered the London School of Economics, where he discovered the Austrian philosopher Karl Popper. Popper's ideology of an "open society" would guide Soros for the rest of his life.

The very name of Soros's philanthropic arm, the Open Society Fund (now the Open Society Institute), is taken from a book written by Popper in 1945, *The Open Society and Its Enemies.* According to Popper, Communism and Nazism had one trait in common—a belief that they possessed the ultimate truth and that in order to impose that truth, they had to resort to oppression. Popper contrasted this with an "open society" in which a plurality of views and interests constantly collided and were safeguarded by freedom of speech. For the young man who had fled Nazism and Communism, Popper's thoughts were an inspiration. In his biography *Soros: The Life and Times of a Messianic Billionaire,* Michael Kaufman says that during his mainly miserable university days in London, Soros would take "refuge in what he has termed 'messianic' fantasies, he read about [the famous economist John Maynard] Keynes and dreamed of leading a similar life of meaningful impact."

By age fifty, Soros, founder of the hugely successful Quantum Fund, was one of the leading money managers in the world. Yet according to Jane Mayer, writing in *The New Yorker,* Soros felt that his life lacked meaning. He found that meaning in the Open Society Fund, which he established in 1979 and which has since given away more than $4.5 billion. The first program was providing scholarships to black students at the University of Cape Town in South Africa. Since then Soros has spent billions of dollars trying to nudge nations, particularly those under totalitarian control, toward a more democratic and open society.

When the Berlin Wall fell in 1989, Soros saw it as an opportunity for the

West to rescue the East. At a conference in the former East German city of Potsdam, Soros says he was literally laughed at when he suggested launching an aid program for the former Soviet Union similar to the post–World War II Marshall Plan. So he took it upon himself to act alone. He put the day-to-day running of his huge hedge fund in the hands of his longtime deputy, Stanley Druckenmiller. And he set about helping the emerging democratic movement in Eastern Europe. Among his many philanthropic quests were two $25 million loans to the newly formed Republic of Macedonia and financial support for reform in Ukraine.

But by far the biggest beneficiary of Soros's largesse was Russia. During the 1990s Soros reportedly spent $1 billion there. Aryeh Neier, who has been president of the Open Society Institute since 1993, says the figure is an exaggeration. But Soros undoubtedly spent hundreds of millions of dollars. He paid $100 million alone to link Russia's provincial universities to the Internet. Another $100 million was spent on grants for Russian scientists, many of whom had been involved in weapons programs. "It probably prevented a lot of the Russian scientists from leaving science or leaving the country," Neier says. "And it probably prevented them from selling their services to the highest bidder in different parts of the world."

In the 1990s Soros's gaze turned toward America. During the 1994 congressional election the Republicans retook the House of Representatives for the first time in forty years, and Speaker Newt Gingrich famously brandished a copy of his *Contract with America,* whose conservative ideas included curtailing government powers and cutting welfare programs. (Many of the proposals made in the *Contract* originated in the Heritage Foundation— a conservative think tank established by Forbes 400 member Joseph Coors, of the Coors brewing family, and financed by banking heir Richard Mellon Scaife, who is discussed later in this chapter.)

Neier says that what particularly offended Soros was the way in which he saw professions such as law and medicine, which Soros believed should be about more than just money, being dominated by free-market ideology. So he poured money into social causes: immigrants' rights, criminal justice, and education. He also donated more than $1 million toward successful ballot proposals in Arizona and California to legalize the medicinal use of marijuana (insurance tycoon and Forbes 400 member Peter Lewis donated $800,000), and he continued questioning the excesses of capitalism and individualism: Of the approximately $400 million that the Open Society Institute now spends annually, about one-fifth is allocated to U.S. causes.

The seismic shift in U.S. foreign and domestic policy that followed the terrorist attacks of September 11 had a profound effect on Soros. A natural supporter of the Democratic Party (in 1996 he gave $100,000 to the Democratic National Committee), Soros opposed the invasion of Iraq. As the Bush administration's War on Terror rhetoric reverberated around the world, Soros saw a new enemy of the open society. He said the statements of Attorney General John Ashcroft "reminded me of Germany under the Nazis. It was the kind of talk that Goebbels used to line the Germans up. I remember; I was thirteen or fourteen. It was the same kind of propaganda about how 'We are endangered' and 'We have to be united.' "

Soros perceived in the Bush administration a threat so great that he turned against some of the ideals he had espoused throughout the previous decade. During those years he had spent about $18 million supporting various campaign finance reform groups, which were pushing for the abolition of *soft money*, the extremely large donations individuals could give to national political parties on top of the limited donations they could give to candidates.* During the 2002 election, for example, the Democrats received over $9 million from media mogul Haim Saban and almost $7 million from movie producer Steven Bing, both members of the Forbes 400.

In 2002, however, soft money was outlawed under new legislation known as the McCain-Feingold Bill. "It was a huge step in the right direction," says Forbes 400 member Jerome Kohlberg, who launched a lengthy campaign to clean up the campaign finance laws in the mid-1990s, rallying many businessmen to the cause. "I don't think you are ever going to keep the money out of politics, but we came close." Soros should have been happy, too. But two years later he was among a small group of billionaires who met to discuss how they could help defeat President Bush in the upcoming election. Blocked from funding the Democratic Party by McCain-Feingold, the group turned to 527 committees. These groups, named after the section of tax code that allowed for their creation, were authorized to raise unlimited sums of money as long as they were not affiliated with a particular party or candidate. According to the Center for Responsive Politics, Soros donated about $7.5 million to America Coming Together, the largest single 527 group that fought the Republicans in the 2004 election, as well as $2.5 million to MoveOn.org and $12 million to the Joint Victory Campaign 2004, a group comprised of America Coming Together and another anti-Bush group, the Media Fund.

---

*Before 2002, individuals were limited to a $1,000 donation per candidate. Since then, the limit has increased to $2,300.

Soros was hardly alone in his highly visible crusade to unseat President Bush. During the 2004 election members of the Forbes 400 weighed in heavily on both sides. Soros was the largest single donor to pro-Democrat groups—a total of $23.5 million. But he was closely followed by Peter Lewis ($23 million), real-estate heir and movie producer Steven Bing ($14 million), and banking tycoons Herb and Marion Sandler ($13 million). On the other side of the aisle, pro-Republican donors included real-estate tycoon Alexander Spanos ($5 million), oil and investment billionaire T. Boone Pickens ($4.1 million), and media tycoon A. Jerrold Perenchio ($4 million). President Bush felt so threatened by the combined 527 clout of the Left that he lodged a complaint with the Federal Election Commission in March 2004, accusing his rival John Kerry's campaign of coordinating political attacks with the 527 groups. Of course, the Bush campaign benefited from the activities of 527 groups as well. The much-publicized Swift Boat Veterans for Truth criticized Democratic candidate John Kerry's military record and was supported by major donors to the Republican Party.

Politics has always been an expensive business. So it should come as no surprise that the wealthiest people in America are involved in all aspects of political life, from funding think tanks to making major contributions to 527 groups to actually running for office themselves. Notes Celia Wexler, advocacy vice president of Common Cause (a group that describes itself as a "nonpartisan nonprofit advocacy organization"), these high-flying donors aren't in it just to buy power and influence; they're also thinking about their legacy. Although successful entrepreneurs may feel they have contributed to mankind with their products and services—and the capital they generate—they have an urge to make an even larger contribution, observes Wexler. "At some fundamental level," she says, "they want to change the world."

But as the historic record shows, the most obvious way of influencing the world—running for office oneself—has not been successful for most members of the Forbes 400 and their heirs. Few have made it into power, and even fewer have been a success in office. "Statistically, people who spend a great deal of money trying to get elected—don't," says Wexler. During the 2002 midterm elections, for example, the ten biggest-spending, self-financed candidates were all defeated. Indeed, being wealthy may be a detriment to getting elected. GOP consultant John Grotta commented in 1998 that the most successful presidential challengers are not the wealthiest candidates but the ones who can raise the most small contributions—one hundred to two hundred dollars—from a wide swath of the electorate.

The biggest political prize for any tycoon, the presidency, has proved the most elusive. Nelson Rockefeller, governor of the state of New York from 1959 to 1973, launched three failed presidential campaigns in 1960, 1964, and 1968; in the end, he made do with a short-lived stint as vice president in 1974, which ended when President Ford dropped him from the Republican ticket two years later.* Ross Perot ran unsuccessfully for the presidency in 1992 and 1996. Even Donald Trump considered putting his name forward for the Reform Party ticket in the 2000 election.

The presidential race has proved very costly for the families of the Forbes 400. According to David Rockefeller's *Memoirs,* the expense of the gubernatorial and presidential campaigns was "almost ruinous" for his brother Nelson, who financed them with money from his trust fund, as well as modest support from relatives. Rockefeller says that in 1967 Nelson was so strapped for cash that he "demanded" David buy his share in their Brazilian ranch for $2 million to fund his next presidential campaign. David Koch of Koch Industries is estimated to have spent $1.6 million as the vice presidential candidate on the Libertarian ticket in the 1980 presidential campaign. And in 1992 Ross Perot spent an estimated $63 million on his failed presidential bid. He spent less during his subsequent race in 1996, but only because he qualified for fed-

2006

from the pages of *Forbes*

Richard Egan, who made his fortune in data storage and is a former ambassador to Ireland, is fighting an IRS claim that he used a sham shelter to save $62 million in 2001 taxes; he paid in full and now is suing for a refund. (2006 net worth: $1.3 billion)

Major philanthropist **Gordon Moore,** of Intel, has a pygmy owl named after him. (2006 net worth: $3.4 billion)

Kenny Troutt, of Excel Communications, attends a weekly Bible-study session. (2006 net worth: $1.2 billion)

Robert Rich Jr. of Rich Products food company, had a tough taskmaster for a father. Robert Sr., founder of the company, routinely woke his two sons at 5 a.m. and made them do push-ups until their arms burned. (2006 net worth: $1.5 billion)

---

*Rockefeller was never on the Forbes list. He died in 1979, three years before the first 400 list was published. In 1982 fourteen Rockefellers were on the list, including two of Nelson's four brothers.

eral funding, which provided almost all of the $30 million spent on that campaign.*

While the presidency has eluded members of the Forbes 400, millions more have been spent on campaigns, often unsuccessful, for the governor's mansion or the legislature. Here the Rockefellers, at least, have had extraordinary success. John D. Rockefeller's grandson Winthrop Rockefeller was governor of Arkansas from 1967 to 1971. And Winthrop's son, Winthrop Paul Rockefeller, was lieutenant governor of Arkansas from 1996 until his death in 2006. Meanwhile, John D. Rockefeller's great-grandson John D. Rockefeller IV, known as Jay Rockefeller, was governor of West Virginia from 1977 to 1985 and has been a senator from the state ever since.

Another success story is that of Jon Huntsman Jr., son of chemicals tycoon Jon Huntsman, who is at the beginning of his political career. At age forty-four he was elected the Republican governor of Utah in 2004. Huntsman is typical of another kind of Forbes 400 family—those who have had plenty of experience within presidential administrations. Huntsman Jr., a Mormon, learned Mandarin after spending two years as a missionary in Taiwan. While working for his father in the family business, Huntsman Chemical, he also served under presidents Reagan, both Bushes, and Clinton, mainly in the field of international politics. He has spent a good part of his career zigzagging between the public and private sectors and traveling around the world. It was only when his daughter complained during his last job as a U.S. trade ambassador that he was away too much that he considered running for political office in his home state.†

But most campaigns waged by Forbes 400 members or their heirs end in failure. Bill Simon, son of Forbes 400 member William E. Simon, spent $19 million on his failed 2002 bid for the governorship of California. Dick DeVos (son of Amway founder Richard DeVos Sr.) contributed almost $35 million to his $42 million failed Republican campaign for the governorship of Michigan in 2006. And payroll-processing tycoon Thomas Golisano

*Steve Forbes, current publisher of *Forbes* and son of Malcolm, who appeared on the list from 1982 to 1987, campaigned for the Republican nomination in 1996 and 2000.

†Another famous political clan bankrolled by the family fortune is the Kennedys. John, of course, made it to the presidency after being a Massachusetts congressman for six years and a senator for eight. His brother, Robert, served as attorney general and then ran successfully for the Senate from New York before he was assassinated in 1968, while running for the presidency. Edward (Teddy), the youngest brother, now age seventy-five, has been a senator from Massachusetts since 1962. All were aided by the family fortune accumulated by their father, Joseph. But no Kennedy has made it onto the Forbes 400 list.

spent a record $74 million on a failed bid as an Independence Party candidate for New York governor in 2002. Then there's conservative Peter Coors, who spent $1 million on his 2004 Republican bid for a Colorado Senate seat; and Michael Huffington, who spent a then-record $27 million on a failed California Senate campaign in 1994. (Huffington had earlier won election to the House of Representatives in 1993, in a hard-fought campaign that cost him a little over $5 million.)

Huffington, whose father landed the family among the Forbes 400 with a combined net worth of $387 million in 1995 thanks to his energy company Huffco, says he does not perceive his losing 1994 California Senate campaign as a failure. He started out thirty-five points behind the Democratic incumbent Dianne Feinstein, in a state that—because of its size, population, and the cost of advertising in four major media markets (Los Angeles, San Diego, San Francisco, and Sacramento)—is one of the most difficult and expensive to contest. "If I wanted to buy myself a Senate seat, I would have moved to New Hampshire or Rhode Island," Huffington says. As with billionaire presidential candidates who seem to face impossible odds, Huffington says he believed he could win. "Some people run just to get the message out, but I think most of us have to think we can win or we wouldn't do it," Huffington says. "I come from a family where we didn't think about what we can't do. I thought I could win, or I wouldn't have run."

Since losing the Senate race Huffington has not run again for public office. Now he concentrates on influencing policy by other means. He helped on successful campaigns to implement Proposition 184, a California "three strikes" law, and Proposition 10, which raised taxes on cigarettes to pay for childhood health care and education. "I did more good with Proposition 10 and Proposition 184 than I could have done as a congressman or a senator," Huffington says.

Huffington's marriage to noted author and media commentator Arianna Huffington broke up very publicly in 1997, and the following year he announced that he was bisexual, prompting yet another media flurry. Since then he has become more involved with the gay, lesbian, and bisexual section of the Republican Party, supporting the rights of gays to serve in the military and contributing about $250,000 to the Log Cabin Republicans' campaign against George W. Bush's constitutional amendment banning gay marriage. In 2006 Huffington became a director of It's My Party Too, a fiscally conservative but socially liberal Republican political action committee.

One of the problems with Forbes 400 members seeking political office is that it's difficult for corporate commanders in chief to function in the give-and-take of the public sector. CEOs who are used to controlling the world around them can find it difficult to adapt to that loss of control when they step into public life. As NYU economics professor George Smith puts it: "I think entrepreneurs are control freaks generally, and I think people who enter politics have to be collegial."

It was precisely his desire for control and his executive take-charge nature that led the mayor of New York, Michael Bloomberg, to politics in the first place—but not to collegial politics. In the late 1990s, while heading up his hugely successful Bloomberg media and financial services company, Bloomberg published an autobiography, *Bloomberg by Bloomberg.* "And in it I wrote that I'd be a good executive, but not a good legislator," he says. "A good president, governor, or mayor, but not a good congressman or city councilman. Because I want to do things—and do it myself. I'm not a spectator. And some guy a year later picked up on it and wrote, 'He thinks that he'd be a good mayor.' And people started joking about it and talking about it. And then I started thinking about it. Because how do you leave a company after twenty years without indicating to people that you don't have confidence in the future? The perfect answer is to go and try something different. Besides, I wanted to go and do the things that everyone said that you couldn't do. Bring down crime, improve the schools, create a strong economy. If you want to wave a red flag in front of me, tell me something is impossible. Those are the challenges that I like."

Bloomberg's is a classic story of coming from behind—except that he had a huge private war chest to finance his campaign. A liberal Democrat who registered as a Republican to avoid a crowded Democratic primary field, Bloomberg was trailing well behind the Democratic front-runner Mark Green in the spring preceding the 2001 New York mayoral election. In a city where Democratic voters outnumber Republicans five to one, Democratic strategists were confident the city would reject a Republican businessman as mayor. Douglas Muzzio, a professor at Baruch College and political analyst for WABC-TV, told *New York Newsday* in June 2001, as Bloomberg trailed Green by thirty-eight points, that with crime down and the economy not doing too badly, Bloomberg had little to offer. "Who needs a man on horseback to save us?" Muzzio quipped.

The terrorist attacks of September 11, just two months before the election, changed everything. The city plunged into turmoil, especially in downtown Manhattan, an area that Bloomberg knew well from his days at

Salomon Brothers on Wall Street. Bloomberg's campaign team argued that a leading businessman was just the person to lift the city out of the possible recession ahead. By October Bloomberg had cut Green's lead to twenty-two points, and his campaign strategist, Bill Cunningham, was telling the *New York Daily News,* "The world changed for us all on September 11. . . . Now the central question that Mike is talking about is: Who is best equipped to rebuild New York?" Bloomberg was also helped by his seemingly endless supply of money. He spent $72 million on that first election campaign, outspending his opponent by five to one. Trailing by twelve points with two weeks to go, Bloomberg squeaked in by a margin of 40,000 votes out of 1.3 million.

Bloomberg started by shaking up the way city government worked. His first step was to copy the informality of his own company. No one at city hall, not even the mayor, has a private office. Instead, everyone sits in cubicles in a former nineteenth-century hearing room, with Bloomberg's cubicle in the middle of a long row and no bigger than the rest. He conducts interviews at one of three conference tables at one end of the vast, high-ceilinged space. Most mayors are beholden to supporters, but Bloomberg was free to choose whomever he wanted as top lieutenants. For Bloomberg, that is a key virtue of a self-financed campaign: "Nobody gives big dollars unless they expect to get something back," he says, calling it the "Where's mine?" syndrome. "It's true that it has been easier for me *not* to staff my administration with people who got their jobs because of their party affiliation, their campaign contributions, their ethnicity, gender, or orientation. The one thing that's clear is that you need the best people you can name, no matter what." Writing in the *New York Times,* Jonathan Mahler described Bloomberg's choice of senior staff members as "unusual" not only for its lack of patronage but because Bloomberg "has given his deputies an unusual amount of power, particularly compared with [former mayor Rudolph] Giuliani, a notorious micromanager."

When Bloomberg took office in January 2002, the city was running a $5 billion deficit that soon soared as high as $6.5 billion. He set about solving the deficit with a series of hard-nosed measures that won the billionaire mayor few friends. He borrowed $2.5 billion, cut spending by $3 billion, and raised taxes—including a 20 percent hike in property tax. In those first years of his mayoralty, Bloomberg scored the lowest approval ratings of any New York mayor: 24 percent in a *New York Times* mayoral poll at his nadir. A 2004 Quinnipiac University poll found that three times as many New

Yorkers thought their mayor "cold" and "businesslike" (66 percent) than those who found him "warm" and "friendly" (20 percent). He has taken his philosophy of efficiency to great and unpopular lengths, even closing firehouses in the face of public outcry. Police Commissioner Ray Kelly, who has served the NYPD for over thirty years (his first stint as commissioner was between 1992 and 1994, and then from 2002 to the present), told *The New Yorker,* "The Mayor focuses on efficiency, getting the most out of your resources. . . . It's more like a business than any administration I have ever worked for."

And yet in 2005 the mayor who squeaked to victory in 2001 won by a landslide—a 19 percent margin. He spent $85 million on the campaign, more than the first time around, but arguably he would have won easily without it, as during the intervening years his approval ratings soared. Although little had been achieved at Ground Zero by the end of 2006, the city was booming, with a $3.7 billion surplus; crime was down 20 percent; and the mayor's controversial smoking ban had proved a success. (Bloomberg's own $125 million foundation, which he may head up after leaving city hall, funded as its first project a worldwide campaign against smoking. "Nothing will save more lives," claims the mayor.) Nowadays, Bloomberg is considered one of the city's most popular mayors, surpassing even Rudy Guiliani in recent polls. "When the poll numbers are up, they're flattering," says Bloomberg. "When they're down, they're challenging. I've experienced both, and I try to do my job the same way: do the right thing and hold myself accountable for the results."

Aside from Bloomberg and the few other successes in electoral politics, Forbes 400 members seeking power and influence have arguably achieved better results financing foundations and think tanks. Among them is banking heir Richard Mellon Scaife. Born in Pittsburgh in 1932, Scaife is the son of Sarah Mellon, whose uncle, famed banker Andrew Mellon, funded some of America's greatest oil and steel firms at the beginning of the twentieth century. Scaife is one of the leading conservative philanthropists of his generation, generally credited with funding the ideological ascendancy of American conservatism that reached its apex in 1980, when Ronald Reagan was elected president. Three decades earlier, liberal-leaning organizations including labor unions and civil rights groups were setting the terms of policy debates in Washington and around the country. But Scaife, along with other big donors such as Joseph Coors and Charles and David Koch, helped fund

The World's Richest People

Americans have dominated another Forbes list—the World's Richest People—since it first appeared twenty years ago. But other nationalities are catching up fast. While the 2007 list includes 415 American billionaires, 44 more than the year before, their number as a percentage of the list fell by about 3 percent, to 44 percent. That's because the Forbes list grew by 153 names in 2007. The latest list includes billionaires from fifty-three nations. The twenty richest people in the world, worth a total $537 billion, were divided among eleven countries.

Barring royals and dictators (*Forbes* excludes those who make their money directly from the state), Bill Gates has been the world's richest man for the past thirteen years.* It's conceivable, however, that he might lose that title before long. In 2007 *Forbes* estimated that Mexican industrialist Carlos Slim Helú's fortune had increased by about $20 billion in the past year, ranking him third in the world with $49 billion, just behind Gates and Warren Buffet ($56 billion and $52 billion, respectively). Slim made his fortune in banking, construction, mining, auto parts, real estate, insurance, and a seven-year monopoly over the Mexican telecom market during the 1990s. His fortune ballooned in 2007, thanks to soaring Mexican telecom stocks.

Slim is followed on the 2007 list by IKEA founder and legendary penny-pinching Swede Ingvar Kamprad ($33 billion), who is renowned for flying economy and eating in cheap restaurants. Other Europeans among the top ten include seventh-ranked Frenchman Bernard Arnault, with a $26 billion fortune founded on Louis Vuitton and other luxury goods, and eighth-placed Spaniard Amancio Ortega, with a $24 billion fortune from his Zara clothing stores.

America is not the only country whose share of the world's wealth has shrunk. Other industrial nations, including Germany and Japan, have seen their influence wane over the past twenty years. In 2007 India overtook Japan as the Asian nation with the most billionaires. (India had thirty-six billionaires in 2007, compared to Japan's twenty-four billionaires.) The leading Indian billionaire is steel tycoon Lakshmi Mittal, fifth on the 2007 list with a $32 billion fortune. Meanwhile, Japanese real-estate mogul Yoshiaki Tsutsumi, the world's richest man in 1987 with a $20 billion fortune, slipped off the list as the value of his land holdings waned.

*Yoshiaki Tsutsumi was the richest man in the world before Gates. *Forbes* estimated his fortune at $8.5 billion in 1994.

Even countries such as China and Russia are part of the billionaire establishment nowadays. In 1997 mainland China saw its first billionaire, Larry Yung, emerge with a $1.3 billion fortune founded on his conglomerate CITIC Pacific. That same year Russian oligarchs, including Mikhail Khodorkovsky and Boris Berezovsky, burst onto the scene with fortunes built on previously state-owned industries such as Aeroflot and oil giants Sibneft and Yukos. Today Russia has fifty-three billionaires, just two fewer than Germany; but the combined wealth of Russia's billionaires, $282 billion, exceeds that of Germany's $245 billion.

And what of the newcomers? In 2007 Kazakhstan had five billionaires worth a total $13.1 billion from mining, finance, and banking, while Romania, Serbia, and Cyprus made their first appearance on the list. But let's not forget one thing. In 2007 the combined net worth of the world's billionaires was $3.5 trillion. Of that figure, almost 40 percent—a total of $1.36 trillion—belonged to citizens of the United States.

the growth of conservative institutions that fueled the victory of Reaganomics in the 1980s and the triumph of the Gingrich revolution in 1994. Indeed, after being elected Speaker of the House in 1995, Gingrich paid tribute to Scaife, saying he was among those who "really created modern conservatism." David Brock, a former conservative journalist-turned-whistleblower and agent provocateur who published a 2002 book entitled *Blinded by the Right: The Conscience of an Ex-Conservative*, called Scaife "the Daddy Warbucks of the radical Right."

Scaife is not exactly a textbook conservative. He has supported abortion rights, donating substantial sums to Planned Parenthood, and opposed such free-trade agreements as the North American Free Trade Association (Nafta). But when it comes to supporting the overall Republican Party, Scaife has been unwavering. During the 1960s he backed conservative front-runners Barry Goldwater and Richard Nixon. In 1970 he pledged $100,000 to the Republican congressional campaigns; in 1972 he donated $1 million to the Nixon-Agnew presidential campaign. He then went on to fund many of the most influential conservative foundations of the 1970s, including the Heritage Foundation, established by Joseph Coors in 1973 with $250,000, and libertarian think tank the Cato Institute, established with the help of the Koch brothers in 1977 with a $500,000 gift. Through the 1980s, these foundations and institutes provided the intellectual firepower, and occasionally the man-power, that fueled Ronald Reagan's presidency.

When Bill Clinton was elected president in 1992, Scaife became one of his most powerful opponents. He poured over $1.6 million into an investigation by the *American Spectator* magazine, known as the Arkansas Project, which dredged through Clinton's past in search of evidence of marital infidelity, financial irregularities, and even allegations of a possible murder following the suicide of White House lawyer Vincent Foster in 1993. The relentless attacks on the Clintons prompted then First Lady Hillary Rodham Clinton to complain of a "vast right-wing conspiracy."

Allied with Scaife in funding right-leaning think tanks, and arguably most in line ideologically with the Bush White House, is Bruce Kovner, the hedge fund king and New York philanthropist. Kovner had a youthful fling with lib-eralism: "I remember as a fifteen-year-old sneaking into the Democratic Convention of 1960," says Kovner. "As a young person I was very committed on the Left." But after studying as an undergraduate at Harvard with Henry Kissinger and influential conservative political scientist Edward Banfield, Kovner's political views changed. These days he functions as the chairman of the neoconservative American Enterprise Institute, noted not only for its strong ties to the Bush administration but for its backing of free competition in the marketplace and a strong national defense. Kovner has been called "the right-wing George Soros"—a label he vigorously denies. "My own views are not diametrically opposed to Soros's," says Kovner, "but they are grounded in a different set of priorities. I am skeptical of complex government programs and believe in relying on economic incentives and market forces whenever possible."

More recently Kovner has joined Scaife and other Forbes 400 members who buy newspapers and media in order to influence public opinion. Kovner is a backer of the conservative *New York Sun*, which was founded in 2002, and which includes conservative commentary and a staunchly pro-Israel editorial policy along with its first-rate arts coverage. For his part, Scaife has owned the *Pittsburgh Tribune-Review* since 1969, and he has not been afraid to wield it as a weapon. He has used the newspaper to attack adversaries like former Senate Republican leader Hugh Scott, who he thought was too moderate. Scaife says his influence on the editorial page of the *Pittsburgh Tribune-Review* varies, but "I have such a good editorial page editor that very rarely do I even have to make suggestions to him."

Using the power of the press to spread a political message is, of course, hardly new for the very rich, whatever their political views. One extreme example is Henry Ford. Ford owned the Michigan weekly the *Dearborn Independent*, which during the 1920s spread his anti-Semitic views through a series of almost one hundred articles entitled "The International Jew: The World's Problem." The *Dearborn Independent* even republished as fact the fabricated and virulently anti-Semitic *The Protocols of the Learned Elders of Zion*. And in the 1950s H. L. Hunt spread his anti-Communist message through a radio and television show, *Facts Forum*, which was carried on 360 radio stations and 22 television channels.

More moderate members of the Forbes 400 have found the media, especially newspapers, to be an excellent pulpit from which to preach their political views, whether liberal or conservative. The Sulzberger family, which controls the *New York Times*, and the Graham family, controlling owners of the *Washington Post*, have used the editorial pages of both newspapers to shape the liberal left agenda for decades. Meanwhile, Mort Zuckerman, a newspaper junkie and wannabe journalist while growing up, bought the *Daily News* in New York in 1993 and revels in the power of its editorial page. "*The Daily News* endorsed [former mayor Rudolph] Giuliani, and he won by about one percent of the vote, and the paper's endorsement carried more than that one percent," says Zuckerman. "And the paper endorsed Bloomberg for mayor, and he will say that he wouldn't have been successful without that endorsement. For that contribution to the city of New York alone, I'm thrilled with my involvement."

And then there is the famously—and flamboyantly—outspoken Ted Turner, who has chosen to leverage his position as CNN founder to tell the world exactly what he thinks about almost every subject. Asked in September 2005 about the brutality meted out to the people of North Korea, Turner told CNN's *The Situation Room:* "I saw a lot of people over there. They were thin and they were riding bicycles, instead of driving in cars, but . . . I didn't see any brutality." Turner first turned to politically motivated philanthropy in the mid-1980s. But he also began speaking out on U.S. defense spending (too high) and U.S. environmental spending (too low). His television channels have carried powerful messages, airing a proabortion documentary, an antinuclear drama, and an environmentalist children's cartoon series. Although his twenty-four-hour news channel, CNN, which launched in 1980, largely remained one step removed from the influence of its outspoken boss, it has not been without controversy. Dubbed by some of its most vehement critics on the right the "Communist News Network," CNN famously broadcast a controversial and inaccurate 1998 report, "Valley of Death," that accused the U.S. military of using Sarin nerve gas on defectors in Laos during the Vietnam War. Turner apologized to a California audience of television critics who lambasted the report: "I couldn't hurt any more if I was bleeding." *Time* magazine (whose parent company had not yet acquired CNN) noted in a 1990 profile that "in an industry in which executives are careful to keep political views to themselves (except perhaps for flag waving during Bicentennial celebrations), Turner is that rare bird: a TV chieftain with an outspoken conscience."*

If Ted Turner has sought to influence the world through his public statements and philanthropic activities, Rupert Murdoch has taken a more overtly political route. In the United Kingdom, where he controls many of the country's most powerful newspapers, a front-page article in the Murdoch-owned *Sun* ran on the day of the 1992 general election, warning that if Labour won, the last person out of the country should "please turn out the lights." Some political commentators regard the article as the final nail in the coffin of the Labour Party that year. Several years later, HarperCollins, the book publishing company owned by News Corporation, dropped a book that was likely to be critical of the Chinese government, just as Murdoch was negotiating a satellite-TV deal with the Chinese. In the United States Murdoch has arguably had even more impact. When he launched twenty-four-hour Fox News in the 1990s, Murdoch provided a conservative slant that was missing from American TV. Explaining his rationale in February 1996, Murdoch told the National Press Club in Washington, D.C., that although 40 percent of Americans described themselves as "conservative," only 5 percent of journalists did the same. Fox provided an alternative. Although Murdoch's news outlets display a general right-of-center bias, they have been known on occasion to support left-of-center parties, such as Tony Blair's New Labour. More recently, Rupert Murdoch has taken to wooing presidential candidate Senator Hillary Rodham Clinton.

Funding think tanks, using media outlets to promote one's agenda, running for office: All three are highly visible ways of wielding power and influence. But the power of corporate lobbying and behind-the-scenes spending are, of

---

*Time's parent company, Time Warner, merged with CNN's parent company, Turner Broadcasting System, in 1996.

course, important as well in burnishing images and exercising clout. Political contributions, for example, can be as much a form of insurance as a form of investment, with many members of the Forbes 400 hedging their—and their companies'—bets and supporting both major political parties. Seagram's billionaire Edgar Bronfman Sr. has contributed over the years to both Republicans and Democrats. Investors Carl Lindner and Ronald Perelman have raised money for both parties, too. "The way they justify the expenditure is because it is cost-effective," Common Cause's Wexler says. "And it's cost-effective because they get the right public policy outcome. These are people who don't spend money frivolously. I think it's fair to say that year on year, you do see connections between giving and public policy outcomes."

The case of Microsoft and Bill Gates is interesting. For a long time, Wexler says, Microsoft shunned the political arena. In a September 2000 report, *The Microsoft Playbook,* Common Cause found that during the 1993–94 election cycle, Microsoft and its executives contributed a measly $43,000 to national parties and federal candidates, and had just one lobbyist in Washington. But after the company was sued by the Department of Justice in 1997 for anticompetitive practices, the software giant couldn't donate fast enough. Between the end of 1997 and 2000 Microsoft spent $16 million, including more than $10 million lobbying in Washington and a total of $2.6 million in soft-money contributions to both parties. In the first eighteen months of the 2000 election cycle, Common Cause calculated that Microsoft was the fifth-largest soft-money contributor. Common Cause president Scott Harshbarger was quoted as saying in the report, "Microsoft seems to have taken a page from the [tobacco firm] Philip Morris's playbook, combining large political contributions with strategic giving to the favorite charities of lawmakers, substantial support to think tanks that agree with them, ad campaigns, and other efforts to stir up grassroots support. What is extraordinary, besides the breadth and speed of the Microsoft conversion from Washington outsider to consummate insider, is how blatantly and shamelessly and without any sense of irony Microsoft made the transition."

In the past Microsoft had favored one party over the other. In the early to mid-1990s it gave more to the Democrats, and in 1997 and 1998 it gave more to Republicans. But the report found that by the end of the decade Microsoft had "hedged its bets" and begun giving almost equally to both parties. It also gave considerable support to the leadership political action committees (PACs) of influential congressmen from both parties and to PACs of influential congressional committee members. In 1995 Microsoft spent $12,000 in PAC contributions to members of the House Committee on Commerce. In 1999 and 2000 it gave seven times as much: $84,000. Between 1999 and 2000, Microsoft and the Gates Foundation also donated a further $10 million to charities and organizations that were favorites of certain members of Congress.

Wal-Mart and the Walton family have also found that ignoring political giving can lead to problems on Capitol Hill. During the 1998 election cycle the company made only $140,000 in political contributions and had no representatives in Washington, D.C. *Roll Call,* a weekly Washington publication covering Capitol Hill, quoted a senior House GOP source saying that the bottom line "is they don't give money, they don't have Washington representation—so nobody here cares about them." By 2002 Wal-Mart had increased its contributions to federal candidates to a total $1 million, with 85 percent of its funds going to Republicans. Despite these cautionary tales, many corporate giants remain outside the campaign finance world. During the 2000 presidential election many of America's largest companies sat on the sidelines and never made any corporate contributions. Those companies included IBM and Dell. But if a government agency were to turn on them in the way it did Microsoft in the mid-1990s, how long would it be before they, too, took a more active interest in politics?

Hand in hand with political contributions, of course, can go political favors, and while some may be symbolic or purely social, they're not without a certain cachet. During Bill Clinton's presidency, for example, there was intense interest in wealthy supporters who were invited to spend the night in the Lincoln Bedroom. In 1996 the White House released a list of 938 guests who stayed over during President Clinton's first term. The release divided them into groups such as "friends" or "public officials and dignitaries." And many of them were members of the Forbes 400. Among the Clintons' Arkansan friends, whom they had known prior to their White House days, were Wal-Mart heirs Alice, Christy, Helen, and John Walton; among their "longtime friends" were real-estate mogul Eli Broad and Hollywood agent Lew Wasserman; among "friends and supporters since 1992" were investors Ronald Burkle, Carl Lindner, and Dirk Ziff; and among their "arts and letters" guests were music mogul David Geffen, director Steven Spielberg, and cable-television billionaire Ted Turner.

And as many members of the Forbes 400 also realize, further fundraising beyond their own individual donations often reaps rewards as well. Mortgage-firm billionaire Roland Arnall, founder of Ameriquest, and his

The Ultimate B and B

In Lincoln's day, the room on the second floor of the White House now known as the Lincoln Bedroom was actually Lincoln's office and cabinet room. If he ever slept there, it was probably on the sofa. Now the slightly cramped room, recently redecorated by First Lady Laura Bush and stuffed with rococo revival furniture, is arguably the most expensive bed-and-breakfast in the world—an overnight reward for key donors to the Republican and Democratic parties.

Along with stars such as Barbra Streisand, many members of the Forbes 400 have been overnight guests. They include Wal-Mart's Walton family; Steven Spielberg; grocery store magnate and FOB (Friend of Bill) Ronald Burkle; real-estate tycoon Lewis Rudin (now deceased); and LBO whiz Peter May. Although the room can hardly be described as palatial, it does have a number of impressive features. Visitors can, for instance, mull over Lincoln's handwritten copy of the Gettysburg Address before flopping onto the eight-foot-by-six-foot rosewood bed that Mary Todd Lincoln bought in 1861. The room has a few modern conveniences, too, like a giant plasma screen TV.

After Clinton presidency guest David Geffen complained about the former president and his wife to *New York Times* columnist Maureen Dowd at the beginning of 2007, the writer asked Geffen if he regretted the fact that he may have blown his chances of being invited back to the famous guest room. "No," Dowd claims he replied, with a "puckish" smile: " 'It's not as nice as my bedroom.' "

wife, Dawn, contributed about $1 million each to Republican and Democrat election campaigns between 2000 and 2004. But according to the *Washington Post*, they have raised an additional $12 million for President Bush since 2002, with Mrs. Arnall contributing a further $5 million to a pro-Bush 527 group, Progress for America Voter Fund, in 2003. Arnall is now ambassador to the Netherlands.

Indeed, as is commonly suspected but rarely acknowledged publicly, a plum ambassadorial post is often a gratifying reward for political donations. According to a confidential memo listing the eighty-one people who raised over $53,000 during the Clinton-Gore 1996 campaign, one-quarter became ambassadors or "received some other choice offer from the Clinton administration." Examine the Forbes 400 list and you can find the names of many ambassadors: cosmetics heir Ronald Lauder (ambassador to Austria during George H. W. Bush's administration), publishing tycoon Walter Annenberg (ambassador to the United Kingdom during the Reagan administration), technology tycoon Richard Egan (ambassador to Ireland during George W. Bush's first term), and real-estate tycoon George Argyros (ambassador to Spain during George W. Bush's first term). David Rockefeller, during his tenure as head of the Chase Bank, functioned as a sort of ambassador at large for foreign policy, crisscrossing the world on diplomatic missions, including meetings with Fidel Castro and Mikhail Gorbachev. His involvement in foreign policy dates back to the late 1940s, when he joined the Council on Foreign Relations (a body that had been partly funded by his father). "Part of the reward if you are loyal, helpful, bright, and capable is a good position overseas," says Michael Huffington, whose father was ambassador to Austria during the first Bush administration.

But in the end, how successful have all the millions and machinations been? No matter how much money members of the Forbes 400 pour into the political machine, it still pales in comparison to the total raised and spent. George Soros was the largest individual donor of the 2004 election, but his $23.5 million in contributions seems tiny next to the amounts the two parties spent: a total of $4.2 billion. And Soros's man, Democrat John Kerry, did not even win.

In fact, while the sums of money that Soros and Perot, Bloomberg and Scaife, and other Forbes 400 members have poured into political quests may seem enormous to outsiders, to the donors they represent only a fraction of their wealth. The $72 million price tag of Michael Bloomberg's first mayoral campaign came to less than 2 percent of his net worth in 2001. Indeed, Bloomberg risked far more than his wealth when he ran for mayor: He risked his reputation. "Once you're in, it's harder to get out," says Bloomberg. "There's the embarrassment; you can't quit."

Before Perot ran for president he was one of the country's most successful, albeit quirky, entrepreneurs. Two presidential races later, he was something of a figure of fun—an eccentric with big ideas and a never-ending supply of aphorisms. He was a winner in business but a loser in the public popularity contest. Likewise, for a short period, Huffington was a businessman-turned-politician before becoming widely regarded as an heir who blew a fortune running for office. With his first mayoral run, Bloomberg came awfully close to suffering a similar fate. But if fortune is fickle, so is public opinion. In two terms he has gone from obscure businessman to wildly popular statesman, even having to deflect speculation about a possible presidential bid. And although Bloomberg has devoted the last six years to his mayoral duties, for which he is officially paid $1 a year, his net worth during his time in office, according to *Forbes,* has increased to $5.5 billion, or even more if other estimates are to be believed—up from $4 billion when he first became mayor. What billionaire could ask for more?

AFTERWORD

Money and Happiness

F inally, the age-old question that fascinates people about big, big money: Does it make millionaires and billionaires happy—or at least happier? Do Forbes 400 members think that fortune has literally smiled upon them?

In his recent book *Stumbling on Happiness,* Daniel Gilbert, a professor of psychology at Harvard University, observes that "economists and psychologists have spent decades studying the relation between wealth and happiness, and they have generally concluded that wealth increases human happiness when it lifts people out of abject poverty and into the middle class but that it does little to increase happiness thereafter. Americans who earn $50,000 per year are much happier than those who earn $10,000 per year, but Americans who earn $5 million per year are not much happier than those who earn $100,000 per year." Once you've bought your way beyond hunger, sickness, fear, and fatigue, writes Gilbert, "the rest of your money is an increasingly useless pile of paper."

No doubt he's right, but he may also underestimate the joy that this piling up can bring to certain people who delight in the swelling abstraction of their fortunes. As Cary Reich wrote in *Financier,* his biography of investment banker André Meyer, another prominent banker marveled at Meyer's "almost erotic attachment to money. Just to have it, to feel it, to be in possession of it gave him an enormous kick. Money was the symbol of success, and it was the symbol that attracted him, and not the practical use of it."

Predictably, when asked for their thoughts about money and happiness, Forbes 400 respondents did not agree among themselves, although overall (and perhaps not surprisingly) they endorsed a link between the two. Below is a sampling of their responses, along with a few bon mots about money and happiness from, among others, B. C. Forbes, the founder of *Forbes,* who in 1918 compiled a list of the thirty richest Americans of that time.

> The money or place or fame which our endeavors may bring when crowned with so-called success will not yield all the joy we anticipated. Such things may charm, may tickle our vanity, may effervesce a hectic sort of happiness for a while. But consciousness of the worthwhileness of the achievement itself can alone produce in us a state of happiness. Riches are mental, not material.
>
> —B. C. Forbes (reprinted in *Forbes,* Forbes 400 issue, Oct. 1, 1984)

> It's almost obvious to say that I wouldn't be very happy if I didn't have my health. But it's much better to be healthy, knowledgeable and, yes, wealthy too.
>
> —Charles Simonyi (Microsoft; Forbes 400 member for eight years)

> While it will seem like a cliché, I've come to the absolute conclusion that the only measure of success is an individual's satisfaction with his own character. I'm not so naive as to think that money doesn't help, but I know more people who have substantial wealth who are unhappy than I do who are happy.
>
> —Robert F. X. Sillerman (CKX, media/entertainment; Forbes 400 member for one year)

> Money may not bring happiness, but it brings such a good imitation that it is often hard to tell from the real thing.
>
> —William Feather (publisher, author)

> A happy person with money is probably happier, and an unhappy person with money is never happy. Money is not going to fix it. At least that's what my mother used to tell me—and it's true.
>
> —T. Boone Pickens (BP Capital, oil/gas; Forbes 400 member for three years)

Would I be just as happy today with no money? Absolutely. But I have to be very frank. Once you've had it, it's good to look back and know you don't have to make it again. Had I been a guy working in a lumber mill in Roseburg, Oregon, I might have been like my father [a minister whose family was on welfare], looking across the fence and seeing what I might have done and could have done.

—Tim Blixseth (timber, real estate; Forbes 400
member for two years)

My life is a fairy tale, except it's real.

—Alfred Mann (inventor, entrepreneur;
Forbes 400 member for eight years)

Money may not make you happy, but it makes life more convenient. And it puts us in the position to help poor people.

—J. B. Hunt (trucking, transportation;
Forbes 400 member for seven years)

Money does not bring happiness. It brings complexity.

—Kavitark Ram Shriram (Google; Forbes 400
member for two years)

But there was the spending of money and there is no doubt about it, there is no pleasure like it, the sudden splendid spending of money and we spent it.

—Gertrude Stein

All the studies suggest that riches bring happiness, but only for a moment. I read one study that found that the only surefire thing that leads to happiness, except maybe doing something for other people, was to dance.

—Nelson Aldrich Jr. (author, *Old Money: The Mythology
of Wealth in America*)

Right after my company got successful, as a young man I met some of the wealthiest people in the world and found that they were such unhappy, lonely people. Howard Hughes, for example, was a recluse when he was helping with the work we did on the POWs. But he would never ever surface. I learned that money and happiness are unrelated.

—Ross Perot (computer service, real estate; Forbes 400
member for twenty-five years)

I measure my success by how often I'm smiling. If I wake up smiling and looking forward to the day, then I'm successful. That's how I felt when I was dirt-poor and with five roommates and how I feel today. Money can't make you happy, but it sure can make your life a lot easier. If you were happy without money, it's easy to be ecstatic with it!

—Mark Cuban (Broadcast.com; Forbes 400
member for eight years)

We never cared about money. Far more important than being rich is family and friends and cleaning up the environment. My wife and I each have a Prius.

—David Gold (founder, 99 Cents Only stores;
Forbes 400 member for two years)

I believe that wealthy people who lack real happiness sometimes fall back on a poor substitute—ostentation.

—Wilbur Ross Jr. (leveraged buyouts; Forbes 400
member for three years)

I'm opposed to millionaires, but it would be dangerous to offer me the position.

—Mark Twain

Appendix: The Forbes 400, 1982–2006

Listed below, in alphabetical order, are the 1,302 individuals who have appeared on the Forbes 400 list from 1982 through 2006.

	YEARS ON LIST	YEAR OF HIGHEST NET WORTH	PEAK NET WORTH (in millions of dollars)
Abele, John E.	13	2004	4,500
Abercrombie, Josephine E.	1	1982	100
Abraham, S. Daniel	10	2006	1,900
Abramson, Leonard	12	1999	875
Ackerman, Peter	4	1995	350
Adams, Kenneth Stanley, Jr.	4	1985	160
Adams, Richard L.	4	1999	1,400
Adderley, Terence E.	1	1998	570
Adelson, Sheldon	12	2006	20,500
Albertson, Joseph Albert	11	1992	930
Albertson, Kathryn	4	1996	1,200
Alessandrini, Walter	1	2000	770
Alexander, Leslie	1	2006	1,200
Alexander, Norman E.	7	1991	455
Alkek, Albert B.	5	1982	350
Allbritton, Joe Lewis	12	1989	600
Allen, Charles, Jr.	12	1991	430
Allen, Herbert, Sr.	15	1996	800
Allen, Herbert Anthony, Jr.	25	2006	2,000
Allen, Paul Gardner	20	1999	40,000
Allison, Fred M., Jr.	1	1982	100
Anderson, John Edward	20	2006	1,900
Anderson, Robert Orville	6	1982	500
Andreas, Dwayne O.	4	1991	335
Annenberg, Leonore	4	2006	2,000
Annenberg, Walter Hubert	21	1998	4,200
Anschutz, Philip Frederick	25	2000	18,000
Anselmo, Mary & family	10	2000	1,100
Ansin, Edmund Newton	16	2006	1,200
Anthony, Barbara Cox	25	2006	12,600
Appleton, Arthur Ivar	1	1984	200
Argyros, George Leon	11	2006	1,600
Arison, Micky	12	2005	5,800
Arison, Ted	12	1993	3,650
Arnall, Roland	3	2006	3,000

	YEARS ON LIST	YEAR OF HIGHEST NET WORTH	PEAK NET WORTH (in millions of dollars)
Arnold, Issac, Jr.	1	1982	500
Arnow, Robert H.	2	1985	150
Arrillaga, John	19	2000	1,500
Ashton, Alan C.	6	1992	840
Autry, Orvon Gene	10	1994	340
Avery, Alice O'Neill	11	1986	375
Bacon, Louis Moore	3	2006	1,000
Bailey, Thomas	7	2006	1,200
Bainum, Stewart, Jr.	1	1997	880
Bainum, Stewart, Sr.	6	1996	610
Baker, Jay	2	2002	680
Bakke, Dennis	3	2000	2,000
Ballmer, Steven Anthony	17	1999	23,000
Bancroft, Bettina	2	1984	150
Bancroft, Christopher	3	1987	225
Bancroft, Hugh, III	3	1987	225
Barrack, Thomas J.	1	2006	1,000
Bartmann, Kathryn A.	2	1998	700
Bartmann, William R.	2	1998	700
Bass, Anne Hendricks	6	1998	560
Bass, Edward Perry	24	2006	2,500
Bass, Lee Marshall	24	2000	4,700
Bass, Perry Richardson	16	2000	1,500
Bass, Robert Muse	24	2006	5,500
Bass, Sid Richardson	25	2000	4,300
Bastian, Bruce W.	5	1992	840
Batten, Frank	25	1999	2,100
Batten, Frank, Jr.	1	1999	1,100
Bauer, Charles T.	1	2001	800
Beal, Carlton	5	1982	400
Bechtel, Riley P.	14	2001	3,500
Bechtel, Stephen Davison, Jr.	25	2001	3,500
Bechtel, Stephen Davison, Sr.	7	1983	800
Beckerman, David A.	1	1993	420
Behring, Kenneth Eugene	9	1998	495
Belfer, Arthur Bejer	10	1984	550
Benenson, Charles B.	5	1986	200
Bennett, William Gordon	16	2001	675
Benson, Craig Robert	9	2000	920
Berg, Carl Edwin	9	2000	1,500
Berkley, William Robert	5	1989	440
Bernhard, Arnold	6	1984	400
Berrie, Russell	3	1987	420
Berry, Jack Monteith, Sr.	11	1990	400
Berry, John William, Sr.	15	1997	750

	YEARS ON LIST	YEAR OF HIGHEST NET WORTH	PEAK NET WORTH (in millions of dollars)
Bettingen, Burton Green	5	1986	235
Bezos, Jeffrey P.	9	1999	7,800
Biggs, Electra Waggoner	1	1982	150
Bing, Stephen L.	1	2004	750
Binger, Virginia McKnight	18	2002	770
Birck, Michael	5	1999	2,700
Bisciotti, Stephen J.	5	2006	1,100
Black, Leon	1	2006	2,000
Blank, Arthur	15	2000	1,800
Blaustein, Morton K.	9	1990	700
Blavatnik, Leonard	3	2006	7,000
Blech, David	1	1992	295
Blixseth, Timothy	2	2006	1,200
Bloch, Henry W.	2	1994	375
Block, Paul, Jr.	3	1984	150
Block, William, Sr.	5	1993	300
Bloomberg, Michael Rubens	15	2006	5,300
Bluhm, Neil Gary	14	2006	1,600
Boesky, Ivan Frederick	5	1986	200
Booth, Franklin Otis, Jr.	9	2006	1,900
Borg, Malcolm Austin	11	1989	450
Bose, Amar G.	12	2006	1,500
Boudjakdji, Millicent Hearst	15	2002	900
Bowes, William	5	2005	900
Boyd, William Samuel	4	2005	1,400
Boyle, Timothy	3	2004	860
Braddock, Richard S.	1	1999	1,200
Brandes, Charles H.	2	2006	2,000
Bredin, Octavia Mary du Pont	14	1997	500
Breed, Allen Kent	1	1994	485
Bren, Donald Leroy	25	2006	8,500
Brennan, Bernard F.	6	1995	450
Bright, Harvey Roberts (Bum)	5	1987	600
Brin, Sergey	3	2006	14,100
Briscoe, Dolph, Jr.	4	1985	200
Broad, Eli	18	2004	6,000
Bronfman, Edgar Miles, Sr.	24	2001	6,800
Brown, George R.	1	1982	100
Brown, Harold	5	1990	500
Brown, Jack Eugene	14	1982	550
Brown, John W.	6	2005	1,100
Brown, William Lee Lyons, Jr.	1	1982	125
Buck, Peter	3	2006	1,500
Bucksbaum, Matthew & family	2	2006	3,000
Buffett, Susan	13	2003	2,600

	YEARS ON LIST	YEAR OF HIGHEST NET WORTH	PEAK NET WORTH (in millions of dollars)
Buffett, Warren Edward	25	2006	46,000
Bullitt, Dorothy Stimson	3	1986	300
Burkle, Ronald	9	2006	2,500
Burrell, Gary L.	3	2006	1,500
Busch, August Anheuser, Jr.	7	1987	1,300
Butler, Sarah Turner	11	1999	850
Butt, Charles Clarence & family	19	2003	2,300
Buttner, Jean Bernhard	1	1988	350
Cafaro, William Michael & family	9	1997	800
Calamos, John P.	3	2005	2,100
Cantor, Bernard Gerald	3	1993	300
Carell, Monroe J.	3	1998	900
Cargill, James R.	24	2005	1,800
Cargill, Margaret	24	2005	1,800
Carlson, Curtis Leroy	17	1998	1,700
Carpenter, Ben H.	3	1985	250
Carpenter, Robert Ruliph, Jr.	7	1982	333
Carpenter, William Kemble	5	1982	333
Carr, Oliver Taylor, Jr.	2	1988	240
Carsey, Marcy	3	2003	600
Caruth, William Walter, Jr.	8	1987	600
Carver, Lucille	7	1992	525
Casden, Alan I.	4	2006	1,500
Case, Steve	6	2000	1,500
Cathy, S. Truett	2	2006	1,200
Catsimatidis, John Andreas	2	1993	375
Cayne, James	2	2006	1,100
Chace, Malcolm G.	8	2002	1,000
Chambers, Anne Cox	25	2006	12,600
Chambers, John	1	2000	1,000
Chambers, Raymond George	1	1986	185
Chan, Ronnie	3	1995	860
Chandler, Harrison Gray	2	1984	150
Chang, JoMei	1	2000	825
Chaplin, Harvey & family	2	2005	1,200
Chase, David Theodore	6	1991	355
Checchi, Alfred A.	3	1997	600
Chen, Pehong	1	2000	1,700
Chernick, Aubrey	5	1999	700
Chowdry, Michael	3	2000	920
Clapp, Norton	5	1988	465
Clark, Alfred James	4	1990	450
Clark, Emory T.	1	1983	220
Clark, James H.	10	1999	1,800
Clark, Richard Wagstaff	1	1986	180

	YEARS ON LIST	YEAR OF HIGHEST NET WORTH	PEAK NET WORTH (in millions of dollars)
Clayton, James Lee	9	2001	680
Cockrell, Ernest H.	1	1982	130
Cohen, Arthur G.	2	1989	350
Cohen, Edward Baron	3	1985	165
Cohen, Sherman	3	1985	165
Cohen, Steven A.	4	2006	3,000
Cohn, Seymour	13	1989	450
Colket, Tristram C.	9	1998	725
Collier, Miles Carnes	7	1987	500
Comer, Gary Campbell	17	1999	1,100
Congel, Robert J.	7	2003	700
Connell, Grover	23	2005	900
Connell, William	3	1997	650
Connelly, John E.	1	1993	370
Connor, William E., II	7	2006	1,200
Conover, Catherine Mellon	11	1993	300
Cook, Jane Bancroft	15	1987	900
Cook, Scott D.	9	2006	1,300
Cook, William Alfred	19	2006	3,200
Cooke, Jack Kent	15	1989	1,250
Cooke, Phoebe Hearst	24	2006	2,000
Copeland, Gerret van Sweringen	1	1985	150
Copeland, Lammot du Pont, Jr.	1	1985	150
Copeland, Lammot du Pont, Sr.	1	1982	400
Copeland, Pamela Cunningham	1	1985	150
Copley, David C.	2	2005	1,200
Copley, Helen Kinney	22	2003	960
Corn, Elizabeth Turner	11	1999	850
Corrigan, Leo F., Jr.	2	1983	150
Cosby, William Henry, Jr.	3	1994	325
Cotsen, Lloyd Edward	3	1989	345
Coulter, Joseph R.	4	1992	495
Coulter, Wallace Henry	9	1991	800
Cox, Edwin Lochridge, Sr.	8	1982	450
Cox, John Lee	8	1991	500
Cox, William Coburn, Jr.	8	1987	450
Crain, Gertrude Ramsay	6	1989	330
Crocker, Ruth Chandler	1	1982	100
Crow, Fred Trammell	8	1988	775
Crown, Henry	4	1985	550
Crown, Lester & family	25	2006	4,100
Cuban, Mark	8	2006	2,300
Cullen, Roy H.	1	1982	500
Culverhouse, Hugh Franklin	8	1989	365
Cumming, Ian M.	1	1995	345

	YEARS ON LIST	YEAR OF HIGHEST NET WORTH	PEAK NET WORTH (in millions of dollars)
Cummings, Nathan	3	1984	160
Currier, Andrea B.	3	1993	300
Currier, Lavinia M.	5	1993	300
Currier, Michael S.	5	1993	300
Dabah, Morris	1	1991	420
Dai, Weili	1	2006	1,000
Dalitz, Morris Barney	1	1982	110
Daniels, Bill	5	1999	1,100
Danner, Raymond L.	3	1988	310
Darden, Constance Simons Du Pont	15	1997	500
Darrin, David M.	1	1982	100
Dart, William A.	7	1996	700
Davenport, Elizabeth Lupton	15	2001	750
Davidowitz, Joseph Morton	5	1988	275
Davidson, Janice G.	1	1996	475
Davidson, Robert M.	1	1996	475
Davidson, William Morse	24	2006	4,000
Davis, Artemus Darius	2	1993	300
Davis, Barbara & family	1	2005	4,000
Davis, James Elsworth	5	1992	540
Davis, Jim & family	2	2006	2,000
Davis, Kenneth William, Jr.	3	1984	250
Davis, Leonard	3	1985	230
Davis, Marvin Harold	23	2004	5,800
Davis, Shelby Cullom	8	1993	800
Davis, T. Cullen	3	1984	250
Davis, William Selden	3	1984	150
Day, Robert Addison	9	2006	1,300
Day, Willametta Keck	3	1983	168
Dayton, Alida Rockefeller	5	1985	200
De Menil, Dominique	5	1986	200
Deak, Nicholas Louis	2	1984	400
DeBartolo, Edward John, Jr.	12	2006	1,500
DeBartolo, Edward John, Sr.	11	1991	1,400
Dedman, Nancy & family	2	2003	870
Dedman, Robert H.	7	1999	1,200
Dedman, Robert Henry, Sr.	10	1992	800
Dehaan, Christel	4	2001	770
DeLeon, J. Russell	2	2006	1,800
Dell, Michael	15	1999	20,000
DeLuca, Fred	3	2006	1,500
Dempsey, John Cornelius	5	1986	300
Desantis, Robert J.	1	2000	1,000
Deshpande, Gururaj E.	1	2000	7,600
DeVos, Richard Marvin	22	1994	4,500

	YEARS ON LIST	YEAR OF HIGHEST NET WORTH	PEAK NET WORTH (in millions of dollars)
Diller, Barry	10	2003	1,600
Dillon, Clarence Douglas	5	1986	180
Dinner, Richard	2	1985	150
Disney, Lilian Bounds	1	1990	315
Disney, Roy Edward	25	2006	1,200
Dittmer, Thomas Henry	3	1987	400
Dixon, Fitz Eugene, Jr.	15	1988	450
Dixon, Harold R.	1	2000	875
Dixon, Suzanne Searle	8	1983	310
Doerr, L. John	6	2006	1,000
Dolan, Charles Francis	20	1999	3,200
Dolby, Ray Milton	2	2006	1,700
Donaldson, Evelyn du Pont	2	1986	200
Dorrance, Bennett	18	1998	2,700
Dorrance, John Thompson, II	8	1987	1,300
Dorrance, John Thompson, III	5	1991	1,250
Doubleday, Nelson, Jr.	2	1984	150
Douglas, Jean W.	3	1999	700
Doyle, David M.	1	2000	775
Draper, Irene Carpenter	8	1982	333
Dreiseszun, Sherman W.	6	1989	330
Drexler, Millard S.	2	1999	1,000
Druckenmiller, Stanley	12	2006	2,000
Du Pont, Alexis Felix, Jr.	15	1996	490
Du Pont, Irenee, Jr.	16	1998	525
Du Pont, Edward Bradford	2	1982	200
Du Pont, Evelyn Rebecca	2	1983	125
Du Pont, Helena Allaire Crozer	4	1987	300
Du Pont, Henry Eleuthere Irenee	2	1986	200
Du Pont, Joan Wheeler	1	1985	150
Du Pont, John Eleuthere	4	1986	200
Du Pont, Marion	1	1982	300
Du Pont, Pierre Samuel, III	6	1982	300
Du Pont, William, III	2	1983	125
Du Pont, Willis Harrington & family	13	1995	350
Dubinsky, Donna L.	1	2000	730
Duchossois, Richard Louis	5	1989	360
Duemling, Louisa Copeland	1	1985	150
Duffield, David A.	12	2001	1,900
Duke, Doris	12	1987	875
Duke, Jennifer Johnson	3	1997	700
Duncan, Dan L.	3	2006	7,500
Durst, David M.	10	1988	350
Durst, Royal H.	10	1988	350
Durst, Seymour B.	10	1988	350

	YEARS ON LIST	YEAR OF HIGHEST NET WORTH	PEAK NET WORTH (in millions of dollars)
Durwood, Stanley Hugh	1	1985	165
Dyson, Charles Henry & family	13	1988	600
Earhart, Anne Catherine Getty	16	2004	775
Ebbers, Bernard J.	3	1999	1,400
Ebrahimi, Farhad Fred	4	1996	425
Edson, John Orin	20	2006	1,100
Egan, Michael S.	1	1997	540
Egan, Richard J.	13	2000	2,600
Eisner, Michael D.	11	2000	800
Ellis, Alpheus Lee	13	1994	525
Ellison, Lawrence Joseph	20	2000	58,000
Emmerson, Archie Aldis (Red)	10	2006	1,600
Engelhard, Jane B.	15	1996	430
Engelstad, Ralph L.	3	1996	425
Englander, Israel	1	2006	1,200
Ergen, Charles	10	2000	11,000
Eulich, John F.	1	1986	200
Evans, James Emmett & family	11	1990	400
Evans, Thomas Mellon	11	1989	345
Ewing, Marc	1	1999	670
Farb, Harold	3	1982	200
Farish, William Stamps, III	3	1984	150
Farley, William Francis	2	1985	250
Farmer, Richard T.	16	2001	1,800
Fasken, David	1	1982	170
Faulkner, Mary Belin Du Pont	5	1982	300
Feeney, Charles F.	9	1990	1,900
Feinberg, Peter	1	1982	100
Feld, Kenneth	11	2001	780
Ferry, Sandra Rockefeller	5	1985	200
Fetzer, John Earl	3	1984	175
Fickling, William Arthur, Jr.	7	1989	355
Field, Frederick Woodruff	23	2003	1,200
Field, Marshall V.	11	1990	540
Filo, David	9	2000	6,500
Fireman, Paul B.	16	2006	1,000
Fisher, Donald George	19	1999	4,100
Fisher, Doris F.	15	1999	4,100
Fisher, John J.	10	1999	2,200
Fisher, Kenneth L.	2	2006	1,300
Fisher, Lawrence	15	1996	500
Fisher, Max Martin	23	1999	975
Fisher, Robert J.	10	1999	2,100
Fisher, William F.	9	2005	1,400
Fisher, Zachary	15	1996	500

	YEARS ON LIST	YEAR OF HIGHEST NET WORTH	PEAK NET WORTH (in millions of dollars)
Flatley, Thomas John	15	2006	1,300
Fleischer, Ernest Melvin	1	1987	320
Flinn, Lawrence, Jr.	8	1999	2,000
Flint, Lucile Evelina Du Pont	13	1995	480
Flowers, J. Christopher	2	2006	1,200
Forbes, Malcolm Stevenson	6	1987	1
Ford, Gerald J.	6	2006	1,600
Ford, Henry, II	4	1986	250
Ford, Josephine Clay	16	1999	800
Ford, Kenneth William	4	1982	500
Ford, William Clay	24	1999	1,400
Forman, Michael Robert	5	1989	450
Forstmann, Theodore	7	1999	925
Foss, Donald	1	1996	550
France, James C.	8	2005	1,600
France, William C.	8	2005	1,600
Franchetti, Anne	5	1990	425
Frank, Sidney	2	2005	1,800
Frankino, Samuel Joseph	3	1987	350
Frazier, Owsley Brown	1	1982	93
Freeman, Houghton	1	1993	580
Freeman, Mansfield	5	1991	425
Fribourg, Michel & family	17	1997	2,400
Frick, Helen Clay	3	1984	150
Friedkin, Thomas H.	4	2006	1,200
Friedland, Robert M.	3	2005	1,100
Friedman, Phyllis Koshland	1	1996	490
Frist, Thomas F., Jr.	15	2006	1,800
Fritz, Lynn C.	1	1995	450
Frontiere, Georgia Rosenbloom	1	1982	300
Frost, Phillip	12	2006	1,400
Fuld, Richard S., Jr.	1	2006	1,000
Fung, Victor	6	2006	1,600
Fuqua, John Brooks	4	1992	275
Furst, Austin Owen, Jr.	2	1987	230
Gabelli, Mario	1	2005	1,000
Gage, Barbara Carlson	8	2006	2,000
Galbreath, Daniel Mauck	8	1988	500
Galbreath, John Wilmer	4	1986	200
Galesi, Francesco	8	1990	435
Gallo, Ernest	25	2006	1,300
Gallo, Julio	11	1987	425
Galvin, Robert William	24	1999	2,000
Galan, Victor J.	1	2004	800
Garofalo, Stephen A.	2	2000	3,200

	YEARS ON LIST	YEAR OF HIGHEST NET WORTH	PEAK NET WORTH (in millions of dollars)
Gary, Samuel	1	1982	125
Gates, Charles Cassius, Jr.	23	2004	1,300
Gates, William Henry, III	21	1999	85,000
Gaylord, Edward Lewis	21	2002	1,800
Geballe, Frances K.	6	1996	1,200
Geffen, David	19	2006	4,600
George, Mary Hulman	2	1998	500
Gerry, Alan	14	2000	2,600
Gerstner, Louis, Jr.	4	1999	640
Getty, Caroline Marie	16	2004	775
Getty, Eugene Paul (J. Paul), Jr.	8	1994	530
Getty, Gordon Peter	25	1984	4,100
Getty, J. Paul, Jr.	3	1997	1,000
Getty, Tara Gabriel Galaxy Gramaphone	1	1994	355
Giannulli, Mossimo	1	1996	490
Gilbert, Daniel	2	2006	1,100
Gill, Timothy	4	1996	425
Gilmore, James Stanley, Jr.	3	1985	160
Glaser, Robert D.	2	2000	2,400
Glazer, Guilford	19	2005	900
Glazer, Malcolm	7	2006	2,000
Goergen, Robert B.	2	1997	600
Goizueta, Roberto Crispulo	6	1997	1,300
Gold, David	2	2003	860
Goldman, Alfred Dreyfus	4	1989	400
Goldman, Lillian	4	1989	400
Goldman, Monte Henry	3	1986	200
Goldman, Rhoda Haas & family	5	1992	475
Goldman, Richard N.	6	2001	1,500
Goldman, Sol	6	1987	1,100
Goldman, Sylvan Nathan	2	1983	200
Goldsbury, Christopher	12	2006	1,400
Golisano, Blase Thomas	10	2000	2,000
Gonda, Leslie L.	14	2000	1,800
Gonda, Louis L.	14	2001	2,000
Goodan, Alice May Chandler	1	1983	125
Goodman, Murray Henry	1	1988	230
Goodnight, James	11	2000	8,000
Goodson, Mark Les	7	1992	450
Gordy, Berry	1	1986	180
Gores, Alec	5	2003	1,600
Gores, Tom T.	6	2006	2,000
Gosman, Abraham D.	1	1996	480
Gottesman, David	3	2006	2,500
Gottwald, Bruce Cobb	7	1997	510

	YEARS ON LIST	YEAR OF HIGHEST NET WORTH	PEAK NET WORTH (in millions of dollars)
Gottwald, Floyd Dewey, Jr.	7	1997	560
Gould, Kingdon, Jr.	2	1990	300
Graham, Donald E.	2	1989	390
Graham, Katharine	9	1987	875
Graham, William A.	1	1982	100
Grainger, David William	6	1994	340
Grant, Charles B.	1	1982	200
Green, David	4	2005	2,000
Green, Dorothy (Dolly)	7	1988	240
Green, Holcombe T., Jr.	1	1998	640
Green, Joshua, III	6	1998	760
Green, Pincus	22	2006	1,200
Greenberg, Jerry A.	1	2000	1,400
Greenberg, Maurice Raymond	23	2000	4,400
Greenewalt, Margaretta Lammot	8	1990	350
Gregory, John M.	1	2001	810
Griffin, Ben Hill, Jr.	8	1989	390
Griffin, Ken	4	2006	1,700
Griffin, Mervyn Edward	4	1989	300
Gross, William H.	3	2006	1,200
Groves, Franklin Nelson	3	1985	160
Gruss, Joseph S.	4	1990	500
Guccione, Robert Charles Joseph Edward	12	1987	350
Guirlinger, Austin Edward	1	1988	325
Haas, Evelyn Danzig	4	1996	1,100
Haas, Fritz Otto	7	1993	550
Haas, John Charles	14	1999	1,300
Haas, Josephine B. & family	9	1996	1,200
Haas, Peter E., Jr. & family	9	1996	1,200
Haas, Peter E., Sr. & family	10	1996	3,100
Haas, Robert D. & family	9	1996	1,100
Haas, Walter A., Jr. & family	4	1994	490
Haft, Herbert Herman	1	1987	225
Haft, Robert Michael	1	1987	225
Hahn, Ernest Walter	5	1986	300
Hall, Donald Joyce	25	2003	1,900
Hall, Evelyn Annenberg	3	1986	200
Hall, Joyce Clyde	1	1982	200
Hamilton, Dorrance (Dodo) Hill	25	1998	2,000
Hammer, Armand	5	1984	200
Hammons, John Quentin	7	1990	340
Hamon, Jake Louis, Jr.	3	1982	250
Hanson, John Kendrick	2	1983	207
Harbert, John Murdoc, III	12	2006	1,500
Harbert, Marguerite	10	1999	1,600

	YEARS ON LIST	YEAR OF HIGHEST NET WORTH	PEAK NET WORTH (in millions of dollars)
Harbert, Raymond	1	1995	600
Hardesty, Floyd Roger	5	1998	500
Hardie, Mary Jane Hoiles	9	1995	400
Hardy, Joseph Alexander	4	1989	370
Harriman, William Averell	3	1984	150
Harris, Ann Clark Rockefeller	1	1982	100
Hascoe, Norman & family	12	2004	800
Haupt, Enid Annenberg	3	1986	200
Hawkins, Jeffrey C.	1	2000	1,300
Haworth, Richard	6	2001	725
Hayne, Richard A.	1	2005	1,500
Hazen, Lita Annenberg	3	1986	200
Headington, Timothy	1	2006	1,100
Hearst, Austin	14	2006	2,000
Hearst, David Whitmire, Jr.	22	2006	2,000
Hearst, George Randolph, Jr.	24	2006	2,000
Hearst, Hope Chandler	2	1987	500
Hearst, Randolph Apperson	19	2000	1,800
Hearst, William Randolph, Jr.	11	1989	876
Hearst, William Randolph, III	14	2006	2,100
Hefner, Robert A., III	1	1982	150
Heinz, Henry John, II	4	1984	440
Heinz, Henry John, III	6	1990	500
Heinz, Teresa F.	11	1996	800
Heisley, Michael E., Sr.	4	2006	1,000
Helmsley, Harry Brakmann	15	1996	1,700
Helmsley, Leona	10	2006	2,500
Hemmeter, Christopher Bagwell	1	1988	225
Hendricks, Kenneth	3	2006	2,600
Hendrix, Helen Hunt	4	1986	200
Hendrix, John	1	1982	150
Herb, Marvin J.	16	2006	1,100
Herma, John	3	2002	850
Hess, Leon	18	1999	1,020
Hewlett, William Redington	19	2000	9,000
Heyman, Samuel J.	7	1992	1,100
Hicks, Thomas O.	6	2001	760
Hilbert, Stephen C.	1	1998	445
Hildebrand, Jeffrey	1	2006	1,000
Hill, Margaret Hunt	14	1985	1,400
Hillman, Henry Lea	25	1991	3,300
Hillman, Howard Butcher	5	1990	620
Hillman, Tatnall Lea	5	1990	620
Hilton, William Barron	13	1989	1,250
Hines, Gerald Douglas	6	1985	300

	YEARS ON LIST	YEAR OF HIGHEST NET WORTH	PEAK NET WORTH (in millions of dollars)
Hobby, Oveta Culp	13	1987	800
Hoiles, Harry Howard	10	1996	400
Holden, Ronald	2	1997	560
Holding, Robert Earl	13	2006	4,200
Hollingsworth, John D.	8	1990	760
Holst Ross, Courtney	2	2000	800
Honickman, Harold	9	2003	850
Hooker, Jeanette Annenberg	3	1986	200
Hope, Leslie Townes (Bob)	2	1982	280
Horton, Donald R.	1	2005	1,400
Horvitz, Harold R.	1	1988	260
Horvitz, Leonard C.	1	1988	260
Horvitz, William D.	1	1988	260
Hostetter, Amos Barr, Jr.	21	1999	4,000
Houghton, Amory, Jr.	1	1991	420
Howard, Robert Staples	13	1989	600
Hsieh, Ming	1	2005	1,600
Hubbard, Stanley E.	22	1996	1,800
Huber, David R.	1	2000	8,200
Hudson, Harris Whitfield	1	1997	475
Hudson, Mary	1	1982	100
Huffington, Roy Michael	11	1989	410
Hughes, Bradley Wayne	11	2006	4,100
Huizenga, H. Wayne	16	2006	2,100
Hulman, Mary Fendrich	2	1986	180
Hunt, Caroline Rose [was Schoellkopf]	17	1985	1,300
Hunt, Haroldson L. (Hassie), III	2	1982	600
Hunt, Helen	1	1982	200
Hunt, Johnnie Bryan	7	1993	415
Hunt, Lamar	5	1982	1,000
Hunt, Nelson Bunker	5	1984	1,400
Hunt, Ray Lee	25	2006	3,500
Hunt, Ruth June	5	1986	200
Hunt, Ruth Ray	5	1986	200
Hunt, Swanee	5	1986	200
Hunt, William Herbert	5	1984	1,000
Huntsman, Jon M.	18	2000	4,100
Hwang, Kyupin Philip	2	1983	575
Hyde, Joseph Reeves, III	5	1996	480
Icahn, Carl Celian	20	2006	9,700
Ilitch, Michael	11	2006	1,500
Imperatore, Arthur Edward	1	1988	230
Ingersoll, Ralph McAllister, II	1	1989	345
Ingram, Erskine Bronson	5	1994	1,300
Ingram, Martha & family	12	1998	4,700

	YEARS ON LIST	YEAR OF HIGHEST NET WORTH	PEAK NET WORTH (in millions of dollars)
Jackson, Jess Stonestreet	7	2006	2,200
Jacobs, David H.	2	1988	300
Jacobs, Irwin Lawrence	3	1987	250
Jacobs, Irwin Mark	8	2006	1,700
Jacobs, Jeremy Maurice	14	2006	1,000
Jacobs, Richard E. J.	8	1989	505
Jaeger, James Leroy	1	1985	175
Jaharis, Michael	2	2005	1,500
Jain, Naveen	2	2000	2,200
Jamail, Joseph Dah, Jr.	18	2006	1,400
Jannard, Jim	12	2005	1,500
Jobs, Steven Paul	18	2006	4,900
Johnson, Abigail	12	2006	13,000
Johnson, Barbara Piasecka	21	2006	2,800
Johnson, Belton Kleberg	5	1986	190
Johnson, Bobby Ray	3	2000	2,300
Johnson, Charles B.	15	2006	4,500
Johnson, Edward Crosby, III	22	2006	7,500
Johnson, H. Fisk	3	2006	1,600
Johnson, Imogene Powers	3	2006	1,600
Johnson, James Loring	3	1997	700
Johnson, John Harold	5	1986	185
Johnson, John Seward	1	1982	170
Johnson, Robert L.	4	2003	1,300
Johnson, Rupert, Jr.	15	2006	3,700
Johnson, S. Curtis	3	2006	1,600
Johnson, Samuel Curtis	22	2003	7,400
Johnson-Leipold, Helen	3	2006	1,600
Johnson-Marquart, Winnie	3	2006	1,600
Johnston, Summerfield K., Jr.	4	1997	960
Jones, Arthur	1	1983	125
Jones, Jerral Wayne	12	2006	1,300
Jones, Margaret E.	3	1996	770
Jones, Paul Tudor, II	4	2006	2,500
Jordan, Thomas	2	1983	125
Joseph, George	10	2005	1,200
Kadisha, Neil	1	2001	690
Kaiser, George B.	15	2006	8,500
Kalikow, Harold	1	1982	100
Kalikow, Peter Stephen	9	1989	570
Kalmanovitz, Lydia	2	1988	280
Kalmanovitz, Paul	4	1986	250
Kamins, Philip Evan	4	1996	490
Kao, Min H.	4	2006	2,200
Karmanos, Peter, Jr.	2	1999	690

	YEARS ON LIST	YEAR OF HIGHEST NET WORTH	PEAK NET WORTH (in millions of dollars)
Karp, Stephen R.	1	2006	1,000
Kaskel, Howard	9	1989	560
Katzenberg, Jeffrey	7	2001	820
Kauffman, Ewing Marion	10	1989	1,300
Kauffman, Muriel Irene	1	1993	500
Kavadas, Kathryn Bancroft	3	1987	225
Keck, Howard Brighton	14	1995	400
Keck, William Myron, II	9	1991	290
Keinath, Pauline MacMillan & family	19	2006	1,600
Kelley, Brad M.	2	2006	1,500
Kellogg, Peter R.	8	2006	2,500
Kellogg, William S.	9	2002	1,400
Kelly, William Russell	13	1989	550
Kerkorian, Kirk	25	2005	10,000
Khosla, Vinod	5	2001	1,000
Kieckhefer, Robert Hazelwood	3	1984	150
Kim, James	7	2000	2,700
Kim, Jeong H.	1	1998	560
Kimmel, Sidney	12	2001	1,000
Kinder, Richard D.	6	2006	2,800
Klink, Bettina	1	1987	225
Kluge, John Werner	25	2000	13,000
Knapp, Cleon T. (Bud)	1	1989	300
Knight, James Landon	8	1986	385
Knight, Philip Hampson	25	2006	7,900
Koch, Charles de Ganahl	25	2006	12,000
Koch, David Hamilton	25	2006	12,000
Koch, Frederick Robinson	20	2003	650
Koch, William Ingraham	22	2006	1,300
Kogod, Arlene Smith	1	1988	290
Kohlberg, Jerome Spiegel, Jr.	21	2006	1,200
Kohler, Herbert & family	7	2006	4,500
Kohler, Ruth	1	2000	750
Koll, Donald Michael	1	1987	300
Koogle, Timothy	1	2000	1,100
Kordestani, Omid	1	2006	1,900
Korein, Sarah	1	1982	100
Koshland, Daniel E., Jr.	5	1996	795
Kovner, Bruce	15	2006	3,000
Kozmetsky, George	4	1988	240
Krach, Keith J.	2	2000	3,000
Kraft, Robert	2	2006	1,300
Krasny, Michael	10	2006	1,600
Kravis, Henry R.	21	2006	2,600
Krehbiel, Frederick A.	8	2000	1,100

	YEARS ON LIST	YEAR OF HIGHEST NET WORTH	PEAK NET WORTH (in millions of dollars)
Krehbiel, John Hammond, Jr.	12	2000	1,600
Krehbiel, John Hammond, Sr. & family	9	1993	515
Kriens, Scott	2	2000	2,800
Kroc, Joan Beverly	20	1999	3,200
Kroc, Raymond A.	2	1983	450
Kroenke, Ann Walton	12	2001	3,200
Kroenke, E. Stanley	8	2006	2,100
Krohn, Tracy W.	2	2006	1,400
Lampert, Edward S.	5	2006	3,800
Landegger, Carl Clement	7	1989	450
Landegger, George Francis	7	1989	450
Lane, Raymond J.	1	2000	850
Langone, Kenneth G.	8	2001	1,300
Lansky, Meyer	1	1982	100
Lauder, Estée	14	1995	1,000
Lauder, Joseph	1	1982	125
Lauder, Leonard Alan	25	1999	4,100
Lauder, Ronald Steven	25	1999	4,000
Lauren, Ralph	21	2006	3,900
Laurie, Nancy Walton	12	2003	2,900
Lawrence, M. Larry	10	1989	500
Lear, Norman Milton	2	1986	225
Lebensfeld, Harry	5	1993	350
LeBow, Bennett Stephen	2	1988	330
Lee, David L.	1	1999	675
Lee, Thomas H.	14	2006	1,400
LeFrak, Samuel Jayson	21	2001	2,800
Leininger, James Richard	1	1992	285
Lenfest, Harold Fitzgerald	9	1999	2,300
Lennon, Fred A.	8	1997	1,000
Leonsis, Theodore	1	1999	675
Leprino, James	2	2006	1,500
Lerner, Alfred	14	2001	4,900
Lerner, Nancy Beck	4	2006	1,500
Lerner, Norma	4	2006	1,500
Lerner, Randolph D.	7	2003	1,900
Lerner, Theodore N.	1	2006	1,500
Lesher, Dean Stanley	3	1991	360
Levine, Leon	10	2003	1,200
Levine, Stuart Robert	13	1996	830
Levine, William S.	6	2000	1,400
Levinson, Frank	2	2000	2,000
Levitt, William Jaird	1	1982	100
Levy, Leon	9	2002	750
Lewis, Peter Benjamin	13	2005	1,900

	YEARS ON LIST	YEAR OF HIGHEST NET WORTH	PEAK NET WORTH (in millions of dollars)
Lewis, Reginald F.	2	1992	400
Liemandt, Joseph A.	5	2000	1,500
Lindemann, George L.	18	2006	1,500
Lindner, Carl Henry, Jr. & family	24	2006	2,300
Little, John	2	2000	1,900
Littlefield, Edmund Wattis	12	2000	2,300
Litwin, Leonard	16	2006	1,000
Loeb, John Langeloth	3	1983	175
Lopker, Pamela M.	1	1996	425
Louis, John Jeffry, Jr.	13	1994	900
Lovelace, Jonathan, Jr. & family	1	2006	1,100
Lucas, George	12	2006	3,600
Ludwig, Daniel Keith	10	1983	2,000
Lund, Sharon Disney	2	1992	320
Lunger, Mary Jane du Pont	5	1990	260
Lupton, John Thomas	23	2004	800
Lurie, Robert Alfred	12	1990	500
Lurie, Robert Harris	4	1989	425
Lusk, John David	1	1987	225
Lyon, Frank, Jr.	7	1999	700
Lyon, William	5	1991	350
MacElree, Jane Cox	9	1987	450
MacMillan, Cargill, Jr.	19	2006	1,600
MacMillan, John Hugh, III	21	2006	1,600
MacMillan, W. Duncan	21	2006	1,600
MacMillan, Whitney	19	2006	1,600
Magerko, Maggie Hardy	9	2006	2,000
Magness, Bob John	16	2000	2,300
Magness, Gary	8	2000	2,300
Malkin, Judd David	7	1990	775
Malone, John C.	14	1999	3,400
Malone, Mary Alice Dorrance	18	1998	3,000
Mandel, Jack N.	12	1996	600
Mandel, Joseph C.	12	1996	615
Mandel, Morton Leon	11	1996	630
Mandelbaum, David	1	2005	900
Manges, Clinton	1	1984	325
Mann, Alfred	8	2006	2,200
Manning, John P.	1	2006	1,100
Manoogian, Alex	4	1988	260
Manoogian, Richard Alexander	19	2005	1,000
Mansueto, Joseph D.	2	2006	1,200
Marcus, Bernard	15	2000	3,200
Marino, Roger M.	1	2000	1,200
Marion, Anne Windfohr	20	2006	1,300

	YEARS ON LIST	YEAR OF HIGHEST NET WORTH	PEAK NET WORTH (in millions of dollars)
Maritz, Paul A.	1	1999	650
Maritz, William Edward & family	4	1990	500
Markkula, Armas Clifford, Jr.	9	1991	675
Marks, Nancy Smith Lurie	5	1996	520
Marriott, Alice Sheets	4	1989	466
Marriott, John Willard, Jr.	17	2006	1,700
Marriott, John Willard, Sr.	2	1983	373
Marriott, Richard Edwin	17	2006	1,800
Mars, Forrest Edward, Jr.	23	2006	10,500
Mars, Forrest Edward, Sr.	17	1998	4,000
Mars, Jacqueline [was Vogel]	21	2006	10,500
Mars, John Franklyn	23	2006	10,500
Marshall, Barbara Hall	19	2003	960
Marshall, E. Pierce	11	2005	1,700
Marshall, James Howard, II	6	1990	725
Marshall, James Howard, III	1	1995	375
Marshall, Margaret Cullen	1	1982	500
Marsico, Thomas	5	2004	825
Marx, Leonard Maximilian	8	1988	330
Mashouf, Manny & family	1	2006	1,500
Massey, Jack C.	2	1984	150
Mathile, Clayton Lee	16	2006	2,000
Maughan, Rex	3	2002	600
May, Cordelia Scaife	23	2004	825
May, Irene Sophie Du Pont	15	1997	500
May, Peter	3	1992	300
Mays, L. Lowry	10	2000	2,300
McCaw, Bruce R.	18	1999	2,400
McCaw, Craig O.	21	2000	7,700
McCaw, John Elroy, Jr.	18	1999	2,200
McCaw, Keith W.	15	1999	2,400
McCaw, Wendy	3	2000	2,000
McClendon, Aubrey K.	1	2006	1,600
McCombs, Billy Joe (Red)	11	1999	2,100
McCormack, Mark	7	2002	1,000
McCulloch, A. Donald, Jr.	2	1990	470
McEvoy, Nan Tucker	7	2003	640
McGlothlin, James & family	7	1991	515
McGovern, Patrick Joseph	25	2006	3,000
McGuire, William W.	1	2006	1,200
McKelvey, Andrew	4	2000	2,100
McLane, Robert Drayton, Jr.	15	2004	1,300
McLean, Malcolm Purcell	4	1984	475
McLendon, Gordon Barton	4	1985	200
Mcleod, Clark	1	2000	1,000

	YEARS ON LIST	YEAR OF HIGHEST NET WORTH	PEAK NET WORTH (in millions of dollars)
McMahon, Vincent K.	3	2000	1,100
McNair, Robert C.	11	2006	1,500
McNealy, Scott G.	3	2000	3,500
McNeil, Henry Stack	1	1982	168
McVaney, C. Edward	5	1998	1,500
Mecom, John W., Jr.	1	1982	150
Meijer, Frederik G. H.	1	1988	350
Mellon, Paul	17	1998	1,400
Mellon, Richard Prosser	7	1993	300
Mellon, Seward Prosser	7	1993	300
Mellon, Timothy	11	1993	300
Menard, John R., Jr.	13	2006	5,200
Mendik, Bernard H.	7	1989	370
Merage, David	1	2002	550
Merage, Paul	1	2002	550
Meredith, Thomas J.	1	2000	750
Meyer, August Christopher	9	1989	400
Meyerhoff, Joseph	1	1982	100
Michelson, Gary Karlin	2	2006	1,400
Milbury, Cassandra Mellon	7	1993	300
Milken, Lowell Jay	10	2004	800
Milken, Michael Robert	21	2006	2,100
Millard, William H.	4	1984	600
Miller, Diane Disney	1	1990	315
Miller, Sydell	8	1999	1,700
Milliken, Gerrish Hill	12	1989	900
Milliken, Minot King	9	1990	810
Milliken, Roger	23	1989	1,400
Mills, Alice Francis du Pont	16	1998	540
Milstein, Monroe Gary & family	6	1997	530
Milstein, Paul	10	2006	3,500
Milstein, Seymour	9	1989	420
Miner, Robert N.	2	1994	685
Mitchell, George Phydias	23	2006	2,500
Monaghan, Thomas Stephen	16	1999	950
Moncrief, William Alvin, Jr.	14	2006	1,000
Moncrief, William Alvin, Sr.	4	1985	200
Moody, Robert Lee	8	1989	590
Moore, Gordon Earle	24	2000	26,000
Moore, J. Stuart	1	2000	1,400
Moore, Jerry J.	8	1990	650
Moores, John Jay	7	2004	750
Moran, James Martin	18	2006	2,400
Morean, William	8	2000	2,600
Moreno, Arturo	8	2000	1,400

	YEARS ON LIST	YEAR OF HIGHEST NET WORTH	PEAK NET WORTH (in millions of dollars)
Morgan, Frank Sherman	6	1989	330
Morgan, Mary Clark Rockefeller	3	1984	150
Morgridge, John P.	11	2000	5,600
Morris, William Charles	2	2001	600
Morris, William Shivers, III	7	1990	380
Mosbacher, Robert Adam	3	1982	200
Mugar, David Graves	4	1990	300
Munger, Charles	14	2006	1,600
Murchison, Clint W., Jr.	3	1983	350
Murdoch, Keith Rupert	22	2000	11,000
Murdock, David Howard	25	2006	4,200
Murphy, Charles Haywood, Jr. & family	5	1993	550
Murphy, Wendell H.	2	1997	1,000
Muss, Stephen	5	1986	200
Myhvold, Nathan	1	1999	650
Naify, Marshall	11	1999	1,700
Naify, Robert Allen	19	1999	2,500
Nash, Jack	7	2004	750
Nathanson, Marc B.	1	2004	800
Nelson, Marilyn Carlson	8	2006	2,000
Neubauer, Joseph	2	2003	675
Neukom, William	1	1999	625
Newhouse, Donald Edward	25	2003	7,700
Newhouse, Samuel Irving, Jr.	25	2003	7,700
Nicholas, Henry T.	9	2000	10,000
Nicholas, Peter M.	13	2004	3,800
Nichols, Miller	5	1987	325
Nielsen, Arthur Charles, Jr.	6	1987	315
Nielson, Glenn E.	1	1983	125
Noorda, Raymond J.	6	1999	1,100
Noyce, Robert N.	1	1983	155
Oates, Marvin (Buzz) L.	4	2005	900
Oelschlager, James	1	2001	600
Oki, Scott	1	1999	750
Olde, Ernest J.	4	1997	760
Olenicoff, Igor	1	2006	1,600
Olnick, Robert	3	1985	225
Olsen, Kenneth Harry	7	1987	490
Omidyar, Pierre M.	8	2004	10,400
O'Neill, Abby M. Rockefeller	2	1985	425
O'Neill, Abby Mitton	3	1984	300
O'Neill, Laura Simpson	2	1983	150
O'Neill, Richard Jerome	11	1986	375
Ono, Yoko	3	1984	150
Opperman, Dwight D.	12	2006	1,000

	YEARS ON LIST	YEAR OF HIGHEST NET WORTH	PEAK NET WORTH (in millions of dollars)
Oros, David S.	1	2000	1,100
Osher, Bernard A.	4	2004	960
Ottaway, James Haller, Sr.	1	1987	255
Packard, David	14	1995	3,700
Page, Larry E.	3	2006	14,000
Palevsky, Max	6	1988	240
Paley, William S.	9	1989	530
Pamplin, Robert Boisseau, Jr.	7	1994	700
Pamplin, Robert Boisseau, Sr.	5	1993	350
Pan, Jing Jong	1	2000	1,900
Pan, Theresa	1	2000	1,800
Parasol, Ruth	2	2006	1,800
Park, Raymond P.	4	1997	1,000
Park, Roy Hampton	12	1989	600
Parker, Jack	11	1990	350
Parrish, Jesse J., Jr.	1	1982	110
Pasculano, Lynne	7	2005	950
Pasquerilla, Frank James	2	1989	350
Paulson, Allen Eugene	8	1983	500
Paulucci, Luigino Francesco	9	1988	550
Paxson, Lowell W.	2	1987	385
Payson, Charles Shipman	3	1984	150
Pearson, Edith Du Pont & family	13	1995	350
Peery, Richard Taylor	19	2000	1,500
Peltz, Nelson	18	2006	1,300
Pennington, Claude Bernard	13	1985	600
Pennington, Irene Wells	2	1998	600
Pennington, William Norman	14	1998	520
Penske, Roger	4	2006	2,200
Perdue, Franklin Parsons	11	1997	825
Perelman, Ronald Owen	20	2006	7,000
Perenchio, Andrew Jerrold	22	2000	3,100
Perez, Jorge M.	2	2006	1,800
Perot, Henry Ross	25	2006	4,300
Perry, Claire Eugenia Getty	16	2004	775
Petersen, Robert Einar	21	1999	725
Petrie, Milton Jack	12	1987	1,300
Phipps, Howard, Jr.	8	1996	430
Pickens, T. Boone, Jr.	3	2006	2,700
Pictet, Marion MacMillan	21	2006	1,600
Pilaro, Anthony Martin	3	1990	390
Pittman, Robert	1	1999	725
Pogue, Alfred Mack	3	1988	350
Pohlad, Carl Ray	23	2005	2,800
Pontikes, Kenneth Nicholas	3	1987	295

	YEARS ON LIST	YEAR OF HIGHEST NET WORTH	PEAK NET WORTH (in millions of dollars)
Pope, Generoso Paul, Jr.	4	1985	150
Porter, Barry	1	1999	625
Posner, Victor & family	7	1995	460
Price, David G.	2	1997	570
Price, Michael F.	11	2006	1,400
Price, Sol	4	1991	335
Primm, Gary Ernest	1	1994	340
Pritt, Frank	2	1996	500
Pritzker, Abram Nicholas	4	1985	500
Pritzker, Anthony	3	2006	2,000
Pritzker, Daniel	3	2006	2,000
Pritzker, James	3	2006	2,000
Pritzker, Jay Arthur	17	1997	6,000
Pritzker, Jay Robert (J. B.)	3	2006	2,000
Pritzker, Jean (Gigi)	3	2006	2,000
Pritzker, John A.	3	2006	2,000
Pritzker, Karen	3	2006	2,000
Pritzker, Linda	3	2006	2,000
Pritzker, Nicholas J., II	3	2006	1,600
Pritzker, Penny	3	2006	2,100
Pritzker, Robert Alan	22	2003	7,600
Pritzker, Thomas J.	8	2003	7,600
Pulliam, Eugene Smith	3	1987	650
Pulte, William J.	5	2005	1,800
Quadracci, Harry V.	7	2001	780
Rady, Ernest S.	3	2006	2,200
Rahr, Stewart	2	2006	1,500
Raikes, Jeffrey S.	1	1999	650
Rains, Liliore Green	5	1986	235
Rainwater, Richard Edward	20	2006	2,500
Rales, Mitchell	12	2006	2,600
Rales, Steven	12	2006	2,500
Rangos, John G., Sr.	3	1991	545
Redstone, Sumner Murray	23	2000	14,000
Reed, William Garrard, Sr.	2	1983	300
Rees-Jones, Trevor	1	2006	1,500
Reid, Elizabeth Ann	19	2003	960
Reinhart, Dewayne B.	6	1995	550
Rennert, Ira L.	2	2006	1,000
Resenberg, Henry A., Jr.	1	1982	133
Resnick, Burton Paul	6	1989	400
Resnick, Jack	1	1982	100
Reyes, Gregory	1	2000	1,000
Reynolds, Donald Worthington	11	1989	1,100
Rhoads, D. Dean	2	1991	300

	YEARS ON LIST	YEAR OF HIGHEST NET WORTH	PEAK NET WORTH (in millions of dollars)
Rich, Marc	25	2006	1,500
Rich, Robert E., Jr.	1	2006	1,500
Rich, Robert Edward, Sr.	23	2005	2,500
Richards, Roy	1	1982	100
Ricketts, J. Joe	8	2005	2,500
Riggio, Leonard	2	1999	800
Riklis, Meshulam	5	1990	620
Rinker, Marshall Edison (Doc), Sr.	11	1987	400
Rizzuto, Leandro P.	4	2005	925
Roberts, Ann Clark Rockefeller	2	1984	150
Roberts, Brian L.	5	2001	1,000
Roberts, George R.	21	2006	2,600
Roberts, Ralph J.	4	1998	680
Robertson, Julian H., Jr.	10	1999	1,700
Robertson, Michael L.	1	1999	1,000
Robertson, Wilhelmina Cullen	1	1982	500
Robins, E. Claiborne	3	1983	235
Robinson, Jesse Mack	18	2005	1,000
Rock, Arthur J.	11	2000	2,000
Rockefeller, David, Sr.	25	2006	2,600
Rockefeller, Hope Aldrich	5	1985	200
Rockefeller, John Davison, IV	5	1985	200
Rockefeller, Laurance Spelman	22	2003	1,500
Rockefeller, Rodman Clark	3	1984	150
Rockefeller, Steven Clark	3	1984	150
Rockefeller, Winthrop Paul	24	2005	1,200
Rogers, Richard Raymond	2	1983	252
Rollins, Orville Wayne	10	1991	930
Root, Chapman Shaw	8	1989	290
Rosenberg, Henry A., Jr.	3	1984	250
Rosenberg, Ruth Blaustein	10	1990	350
Roski, Edward, Jr.	8	2006	1,800
Ross, Stephen M.	1	2006	2,500
Ross, Wilbur L., Jr.	3	2006	1,200
Ross, Wilhelmina du Pont	3	1985	150
Roth, Steven	2	2006	1,400
Rowland, Pleasant	1	1998	700
Rowling, Reese McIntosh & family	6	1996	1,100
Rowling, Robert	10	2006	5,200
Rudin, Jack	10	1990	750
Rudin, Lewis	10	1990	750
Ruffin, Philip	8	2006	1,400
Rust, Eleanor Francis Du Pont	11	1992	430
Ryan, Patrick George	19	1998	1,300
Saban, Haim	6	2006	2,800

	YEARS ON LIST	YEAR OF HIGHEST NET WORTH	PEAK NET WORTH (in millions of dollars)
Sackler, Arthur Mitchell	2	1986	190
Sakioka, Katsumasa (Roy) & family	5	1995	350
Sall, John	11	2000	3,900
Sammons, Charles A.	1	1988	1,300
Samueli, Henry	9	2000	10,000
Sandler, Herbert M.	3	2005	1,100
Sandler, Marion O.	3	2005	1,000
Sanford, T. Denny	1	2006	2,500
Sant, Roger W.	4	2000	2,200
Saperstein, David I.	1	2002	575
Sapir, Tamir	1	2006	2,000
Sarofim, Fayez Shalaby	20	2000	2,000
Saul, Bernard Francis, II	14	2006	1,800
Saylor, Michael	2	2000	1,200
Scaife, Richard Mellon	25	2006	1,200
Scharbauer, Clarence, Jr.	13	1991	450
Schmidt, Eric	3	2006	5,200
Schneider, Donald J.	13	2006	1,300
Schuler, Barry	1	1999	750
Schuler, James K.	1	1993	345
Schultz, Howard S.	1	2006	1,100
Schulze, Richard M.	9	2005	3,700
Schwab, Charles R.	14	2000	10,000
Schwab, Leslie B.	2	1998	510
Schwan, Marvin Maynard	4	1992	1,000
Schwartz, Ted	2	1996	1,100
Schwarzman, Stephen A.	3	2006	3,500
Scifres, Donald R.	1	2000	1,300
Scott, Walter, Jr.	11	1999	3,800
Scripps, Edward Wyllis	5	1993	1,600
Scurlock, Eddy Clark	1	1983	125
Searle, Daniel Crow	8	1983	310
Searle, William Louis	8	1983	310
Sedwick, Jud	1	1990	315
Selig, Martin	1	1988	230
Shakarian, David B.	3	1983	530
Sharp, Bayard	5	1994	325
Sharp, Hugh Rodney, Jr.	4	1985	225
Sharp, Hugh Rodney, III	5	1998	540
Sharp, Peter Jay	10	1991	330
Shaw, David E.	1	2006	1,000
Sheehan, Jean Ellen du Pont	4	1986	200
Shelton, Robert	3	1984	150
Shirley, Jon	5	1999	1,200
Shoen, E. Leonard & family	3	1986	300

	YEARS ON LIST	YEAR OF HIGHEST NET WORTH	PEAK NET WORTH (in millions of dollars)
Shorenstein, Walter Herbert	24	2005	900
Shriram, Kavitark Ram	2	2006	1,500
Shvidler, Evgeny (Eugene) Markovich	3	2006	2,200
Sidamon-Eristoff, Anne Phipps	7	1996	430
Sidhu, Sanjiv	5	2000	9,800
Siebel, Thomas M.	8	2000	6,400
Siegel, Herbert	7	2006	1,300
Sillerman, Robert F. X.	1	2005	975
Silliman, Mariana Du Pont	11	1992	430
Silverman, Henry	4	1999	650
Silverstein, Larry Abraham	7	1989	420
Simmons, Harold Clark	24	2006	4,100
Simmons, Richard Paul	5	1997	530
Simon, Esther Annenberg	3	1986	200
Simon, Herbert	8	2006	1,200
Simon, Melvin	23	2006	2,600
Simon, Norton Winfred	8	1989	750
Simon, William Edward	6	1987	400
Simons, James H.	3	2006	4,000
Simonyi, Charles	8	1999	1,500
Simplot, John Richard	24	2000	4,700
Simpson, Abby Rockefeller	4	1985	200
Sindhu, Pradeep	1	2000	2,500
Singh, Rajendra	3	2000	1,400
Singleton, Henry Earl	17	1997	1,000
Skaggs, Leonard Samuel, Jr.	14	1996	950
Skeen, Dale M.	1	2000	1,000
Slavik, James D. & family	1	1991	350
Smart, Richard Palmer Kaleioku	7	1990	325
Smith, Athalie Joan Irvine	7	1995	360
Smith, Charles E.	1	1988	290
Smith, Daniel E.	1	2000	7,000
Smith, Delford Michael	1	1991	500
Smith, Frederick Wallace	19	2006	2,200
Smith, Kelvin	1	1982	100
Smith, Margaret Lewis Du Pont	2	1982	200
Smith, Marian Uldine Day	3	1987	300
Smith, Mark C.	1	2003	610
Smith, Ollen Bruton	12	2005	1,500
Smith, Rankin McEachern, Sr.	1	1982	100
Smith, Richard Alan	17	1993	955
Smith, Robert H.	1	1988	290
Smith, Vincent C.	2	2000	2,000
Smith, Vivian Leatherberry	7	1988	400
Snyder, Richard Wesley	3	1987	350

	YEARS ON LIST	YEAR OF HIGHEST NET WORTH	PEAK NET WORTH (in millions of dollars)
Sobrato, John Albert	9	2006	2,400
Solheim, Karsten	4	1993	500
Solomon, Russell	6	1994	400
Solow, Sheldon Henry	22	2006	1,700
Sommer, Viola	9	1997	560
Soon-Shiong, Patrick	4	2006	3,400
Sorenson, James LeVoy	24	2006	4,300
Soros, George	21	2006	8,500
Spangler, Clemmie Dixon & family	17	2006	2,500
Spanos, Alexander Gus	22	2006	1,100
Speer, Roy Merrill	10	2000	1,100
Spelling, Aaron	7	1989	345
Sperling, John	6	2005	1,900
Sperling, Peter	6	2004	1,700
Spiegel, Abraham	1	1987	300
Spielberg, Steven Allen	14	2006	2,900
Stahl, Stanley Irving	9	1989	430
Stanley, John R.	4	1994	700
Stanton, John W.	2	2000	1,100
Stark, Ray	3	1984	175
Stein, Doris Jones	2	1982	150
Stein, Jay	2	1993	365
Steinberg, Saul Philip & family	13	1987	660
Steinhardt, Michael	1	1993	300
Stempel, Ernest E.	16	2000	2,100
Stephens, Jackson Thomas	22	2000	1,600
Stephens, Wilton Robert	9	1987	500
Stern, Leonard Norman	25	2006	3,700
Stewart, Martha	3	2000	1,000
Stowers, James Evans, Jr.	9	2000	1,600
Strawbridge, George	13	1998	920
Strong, Richard S.	6	2001	850
Stryker, Jon L.	6	2005	2,000
Stryker, Patricia A. Short	6	2005	1,700
Stryker, Ronda E.	6	2005	2,200
Stuart, Dwight Lyman	5	1984	350
Stuart, Elbridge Hadley, Jr.	5	1983	265
Sturm, Donald L.	4	1999	3,000
Subotnick, Stuart	6	2000	840
Sulzberger, Arthur Ochs	3	1987	440
Sulzberger, Iphigene Ochs	3	1987	440
Sun, David,	4	1996	900
Sutardja, Sehat	1	2006	1,000
Sutton, Robert B.	1	1982	150
Swig, Melvyn	2	1985	150

	YEARS ON LIST	YEAR OF HIGHEST NET WORTH	PEAK NET WORTH (in millions of dollars)
Swig, Richard	2	1985	150
Sykes, John H.	1	1996	520
Syms, Sy	4	1987	240
Tandon, Sirjang Lal	1	1983	150
Taper, Sydney Mark	13	1994	350
Tate, Jack P.	1	1995	475
Tauber, Laszlo Nandor	10	1990	525
Taubman, A. Alfred	24	1989	2,150
Taylor, Glen	10	2006	2,300
Taylor, Jack Crawford	17	2006	13,900
Taylor, Patrick F.	2	2004	1,200
Taylor, Phyllis Miller	2	2006	1,600
Teel, Joyce Raley	13	2006	1,100
Tepper, David	2	2006	1,500
Terra, Daniel James	10	1995	790
Thalheimer, Louis	7	1990	350
Tharaldson, Gary	2	1998	520
Thompson, B. Ray	1	1984	160
Thorn, Laura Simpson	2	1985	200
Thorne, Oakleigh Blakeman	21	2004	800
Thouron, Esther Driver Du Pont	2	1982	300
Tisch, Joan H.	1	2006	3,400
Tisch, Laurence Alan	22	1997	2,400
Tisch, Preston Robert	24	2005	3,900
Tisch, Wilma Stein	3	2006	1,900
Tow, Leonard	3	2001	1,400
Tramiel, Jack	3	1987	375
Trefler, Alan N.	1	1997	650
Troutt, Kenny	11	2001	1,400
Trump, Donald John	19	2006	2,900
Trump, Fred Charles	3	1984	200
Tu, John	4	1996	900
Tuchman, Kenneth	3	2000	1,200
Turner, Robert Edward (Ted)	25	2000	9,100
Turner, Tom E.	2	1983	150
Turner, William Butler	11	1999	850
Tyson, Barbara	9	1995	785
Tyson, Donald John	18	1997	1,200
Tyson, Randal William	1	1986	275
Udvar-Hazy, Steven F.	14	2006	3,100
Ueltschi, Albert Lee	23	2006	1,600
Van Andel, Jay	20	1994	4,500
Van Beuren, Hope Hill	25	1998	1,700
Van Kampen, Robert Donald	2	1989	290
Vesco, Robert Lee	3	1984	150

	YEARS ON LIST	YEAR OF HIGHEST NET WORTH	PEAK NET WORTH (in millions of dollars)
Vilar, Alberto	4	2001	1,000
Vinciarelli, Patrizio	4	2000	800
Viterbi, Andrew	1	2001	640
Vollum, Howard	4	1983	250
von Bechtolsheim, Andreas	1	2004	1,000
Von Platen, Ruth Chandler	4	1987	300
Vose, Charles Alden, Jr.	3	1984	150
Vose, Charles Alden, Sr.	3	1984	150
Wadhwani, Romesh T.	1	2000	1,300
Wagner, Cyri, Jr.	14	1982	550
Wagner, Todd	8	2006	1,400
Waitt, Norman W.	11	2000	2,200
Waitt, Theodore W.	13	2000	8,400
Walker, Jay S.	2	1999	4,100
Wallace, Lila Acheson	2	1983	250
Walls, Carmage	1	1982	100
Walsh, F. Howard	1	1982	200
Walton, Alice L.	18	2003	20,500
Walton, Christy	2	2005	15,700
Walton, Helen	15	2003	20,500
Walton, James Lawrence	9	1992	1,250
Walton, Jim C.	18	2003	20,500
Walton, John T.	16	2003	20,500
Walton, S. Robson	18	2003	20,500
Walton, Sam Moore	10	1987	8,500
Wang, An	7	1983	1,600
Wang, Charles B.	7	1999	1,600
Wang, Lorraine C.	1	1982	120
Ward, Louis Larrick	12	1988	650
Ward, Tom L.	1	2006	1,600
Warner, H. Ty	8	2003	6,000
Wartels, Nat	1	1982	100
Washington, Dennis	18	2006	2,800
Wasserman, Lewis Robert	16	1998	500
Watkins, Edward G.	5	2005	950
Weaver, J. Wayne	1	1993	385
Weber, Charlotte Colket	22	1998	1,600
Wege, Peter M.	1	1998	590
Weiler, Alan	2	1985	150
Weiler, Jack D.	2	1985	150
Weill, Sanford	10	2000	1,800
Weinberg, Harry	9	1990	950
Weinberg, John Livingston	1	1987	225
Weis, Robert Freeman	15	1987	510
Weis, Sigfried	13	1987	620

	YEARS ON LIST	YEAR OF HIGHEST NET WORTH	PEAK NET WORTH (in millions of dollars)
Welch, John F. (Jack)	1	2001	680
Wendt, Richard C.	4	2000	750
Werner, Tom	3	2003	600
West, Alfred P.	5	2006	1,200
West, Gary L.	1	2006	1,100
West, Mary E.	1	2006	1,100
Wetherell, David S.	2	1999	1,900
Wexner, Bella	8	1991	490
Wexner, Leslie Herbert	25	2006	3,100
Wharton, Albert Buckman, III	1	1982	150
White, Dean	11	2006	1,400
Whitehead, Edwin Carl (Jack)	3	1982	200
Whitman, Margaret	8	2004	1,600
Whitney, Betsey Cushing Roosevelt	16	1991	775
Whittier, Leland K.	1	1982	100
Whittier, N. Paul	1	1982	100
Wien, Lawrence Arthur	6	1988	350
Williams, Arthur L., Jr.	10	2000	1,800
Williams, Clayton Wheat, Jr.	3	1983	200
Williams, Max	1	1985	175
Wilson, Gary	3	1997	515
Winfrey, Oprah	12	2006	1,500
Winnick, Gary	5	2000	3,200
Wirtz, Arthur M.	1	1982	300
Wiskemann, Elizabeth S.	3	2005	1,400
Wister, Diana Strawbridge Norris	12	1998	900
Wold, Elaine Johnson	2	1997	560
Woodner, Ian	3	1989	345
Woodruff, Robert Winship	3	1984	250
Woodward, Helen Whittier	1	1982	100
Wrigley, William	12	1998	2,700
Wrigley, William, Jr.	8	2004	4,000
Wyly, Samuel	7	2006	1,100
Wynn, Stephen A.	5	2006	2,600
Yang, Jerry	9	2000	6,400
York, Marie Denise DeBartolo	3	1998	820
Young, Robert F.	1	1999	670
Yuen, Henry C.	3	2000	1,900
Zachry, Henry Bartell, Jr.	2	2003	1,100
Zarrow, Henry	1	1982	100
Zell, Samuel	21	2006	4,500
Ziff, Daniel Morton	13	2006	1,500
Ziff, Dirk Edward	13	2006	1,500
Ziff, Robert David	13	2006	1,500
Ziff, William Bernard, Jr.	12	1993	1,500

	YEARS ON LIST	YEAR OF HIGHEST NET WORTH	PEAK NET WORTH (in millions of dollars)
Zilkha, Ezra Khedouri	3	1985	150
Zilkha, Selim	1	2001	700
Zimmerman, William	3	1983	220
Zucker, Jerry	2	2006	1,100
Zuckerman, Mortimer Benjamin	18	2006	2,500
Zwan, Bryan J.	1	2001	600
Zweben, Monte	1	2000	1,400

Notes

Introduction

3   His favorite form of transportation: Forbes's antics were regularly chronicled not only in his own magazine but in the wider press. See Chapter 9, Conspicuous Consumption.

4   The gross domestic product (GDP) in the United States: St. Louis Federal Reserve Bank, Series: GOPC1, Real Gross Domestic Product.

4   In 1982 only thirteen billionaires: Forbes data.

4   More generally, in 2005 the wealthiest 1 percent: David Cay Johnston, "Income Gap Is Widening, Data Shows," *New York Times*, Mar. 29, 2007.

4   In 1982 twenty-four Du Pont heirs: See chart "Tough Times for 'Old Money' " on p. 231. Information on the Du Ponts and other famous fortunes comes from data compiled from *Forbes* magazine back issues and files. Many statistics included in this book have been compiled for the first time.

4   What does it say: Forbes data, which tracks the share of national wealth controlled by the Forbes 400 over the course of the list.

6   In the first Forbes 400: Forbes data. See chart "Where the 400 Make Their Money," p. 112.

6   With the emergence of new technology-based: See chart "New York's Down, California's Up," p. 135.

6   Only 13 working women: See chart "Where Are the Women?," p. 7.

8   The average net worth in 2006: See chart "The Value of a College Degree," p. 31.

10   The biggest paychecks went: Compared to the hedge fund kings, even rich Wall Street bankers feel poor. See Chapter 8, Beyond Wall Street.

10   Seventeen of the eighty-three financiers: See "The Really Big Money Men (and One Woman)," p. 181, which lists Forbes 400 members who have accrued their wealth over the course of the list from leveraged buyouts, hedge funds, mutual funds, or venture capital.

10   In 2006 the highest-paid founder: *Institutional Investor*'s *Alpha* magazine, May 2007, www.institutionalinvestor.com.

10   His fortune now equals: See chart "Counting Bill Gates's Billions: It Takes a Continent," p. 11.

10   In 1982 Bob Hope was a member: See chart "Old Media vs. New Media," p. 163.

12   "Time and again he's confounded skeptics": [Unsigned,] "Murdoch Does It—Again," *Forbes*, Oct. 9, 2006.

12   Over its twenty-five years, at least 175 "blue-collar billionaires": Forbes data. See Chapter 5, Blue-collar Billionaires.

13   Microsoft didn't become Microsoft: In fact, Microsoft has made a practice of crushing the competition, thereby earning the enmity of many in Silicon Valley. See Chapter 4, Winning Is Everything, and Chapter 6, West Coast Money.

13   "My experience is that the rich": Paul Johnson, "When Are You Seriously Rich?" *Forbes*, Forbes 400 issue 2004.

13   "What I do is work": Kenneth W. Ford, quoted in *Woodsman,* special edition, www
.rfpco.com/pdfs_wood.pdf.

14   Twelve families who possess "old money": See Chapter 10, Heirs, and also "Tough Times
for 'Old Money' " chart, p. 231.

14   Among the 400 founders: Forbes data; see "25 Years: The Founders' Club," p. 71.

14   In 1982 there were 75 women: Forbes data. One of the most fascinating and underre-
ported aspects of the Forbes 400 is the small—and dwindling—number of women on
the list. See "Where Are the Women?" chart, p. 7.

14   In 1982, 212 members: Forbes data; see "Inherited Wealth vs. Self-Made Wealth" chart,
p. 65.

15   The American heiress who marries: Perhaps the most famous examples of the species
can be found in the novels of Henry James and Edith Wharton.

15   For Protestants such as John D. Rockefeller: David Rockefeller Sr. provides fascinating
insights into the Calvinism of his grandfather in his *Memoirs* (New York: Random
House, 2003). See Chapter 12, Giving It Away.

15   Divorces, second wives: Causes of dissension among the very rich are discussed in Chapter 11, Family Feuds.

15   The very public battles: See Chapter 11, Family Feuds.

15   The Rockefellers have proven particularly adept: The Rockefeller trusts are discussed in
Chapter 10, Heirs.

16   Few have put on: For more details on Ira Rennert's villa-by-the-sea, see Chapter 9, Conspicuous Consumption.

16   American research universities: For a discussion of giving to higher education, see
Chapter 12, Giving It Away, and specifically philanthropy scholar James Allen Smith of
Georgetown University, pp. 280–81.

16   As for the influence that money can buy: See Chapter 13, Power and Politics.

16   George Soros, through his Open Society Institute: See the lengthy discussion of Soros in
Chapter 13, Power and Politics.

17   By this standard: See "All-Time Richest Americans" chart, p. 17.

18   "The traditional mantra about inequality": Dinesh D'Souza, "The Moral Limits of
Wealth," *Forbes,* Oct. 9, 2000.

18   The Vanderbilts alone: Details of the Vanderbilts' sumptuous lives come primarily from
Arthur T. Vanderbilt II, *Fortune's Children: The Fall of the House of Vanderbilt* (New York:
William Morrow, 1989).

18   "I remember an old gentleman": Louis Auchincloss, "Ah, What Would Veblen Say?"
Forbes, Forbes 400 issue, Oct. 1, 1984.

18   In 1991 Kevin Phillips: Kevin Phillips, "The Pendulum Swings Back," *Forbes,* Forbes 400
issue, Oct. 21, 1991.

19   Andrew Carnegie said 120 years ago: Johnson, "When Are You Seriously Rich?"

1. Education, Intelligence, Drive

Sources interviewed for this chapter: Raphael Amit, professor, the Wharton School, University of Pennsylvania; Timothy Blixseth (Forbes 400); Michael Bloomberg (Forbes 400); Red
Emmerson (Forbes 400); K. Anders Ericsson, professor of psychology, Florida State University; Alexander Horniman, professor, Darden School of Business, University of Virginia; J. B.
Hunt (Forbes 400); Anthony Mayo, director, Leadership Initiative, Harvard Business School;
Charles Simonyi (Forbes 400); Robert J. Sternberg, professor of psychology and dean of
the School of Arts and Sciences, Tufts University. Unless otherwise noted, quotations in the

text from the above sources come from interviews conducted by the editors and writers of the book.

24 "My success just proves": Bill Gates, quoted in *Forbes,* Forbes 400 issue, Oct. 17, 1994.

24 "I was wired at birth": Warren Buffett, quoted in Geoffrey Colvin, "What It Takes to Be Great," *Fortune,* Oct. 30, 2006.

24 It seems hard to argue: Daniel Seligman, "Want to Get Rich? Don't Get Born in Afghanistan," *Forbes,* Oct. 13, 1997.

25 "The road to success": Daniel Goleman, "Can You Raise Your Social IQ?" *Parade,* Sept. 3, 2006.

25 "CEOs are hired": Daniel Goleman, *Emotional Intelligence: Why It Can Matter More Than IQ* (New York: Bantam Books, 2005), p. xv.

27 "I'll make money": William M. Adler, "Born an Adult," *L.A. Business,* May 1988.

27 "very high rating": Rhonda L. Rundle, "Dole Food Owner Pours His Fortune into Health Ventures," *Wall Street Journal,* July 28, 2006.

27 "They excited my mind incredibly": David Murdock, quoted in John Heins, "I Just Make Ideas Happen," *Forbes,* Oct. 26, 1987; Michael Leahy, "Our Most Elusive Multimillionaire," *Los Angeles,* Oct. 1981.

27 "Dave was a bulldog": Quoted in John Quirt, "The Man Who Collects Companies," *Fortune,* Mar. 25, 1979.

27 "It was very important to him": Leahy, "Our Most Elusive Multimillionaire."

28 "I had all my eggs in one basket": David Murdock, quoted in Heins, "I Just Make Ideas Happen."

28 Boyish and casual: Eugenia Levenson, "Privacy Does Have a Price," *Fortune,* June 26, 2006.

31 "I was willing to try solutions": Fred DeLuca, quoted in Tom Nawrocki, "The Billionaire Bootstrapper," *FastCompany,* July 26, 2006.

32 By the end of the first semester: Claire Poole, "The Kid Who Turned Computers into Commodities," *Forbes,* Forbes 400 issue, Oct. 21, 1991.

32 Harvard Business School's Anthony Mayo and Nitin Nohria: Mayo and Nohria's study forms the basis of their book *In Their Time: The Greatest Business Leaders of the Twentieth Century* (Boston: Harvard Business School Press, 2005).

33 "Intelligence and drive": Eric Schmidt, quoted in Dinesh D'Souza, *The Virtue of Prosperity: Finding Values in an Age of Techno-Affluence* (New York: Touchstone/Simon & Schuster, 2000), p. 87.

33 "Paul saw that the technology": Bill Gates, quoted in "Dropping Out of Harvard Pays Off for a Computer Whiz Kid," *People,* Dec. 26, 1983/Jan. 2, 1984.

34 "I was amazed": Patrick McGovern, quoted in Alan R. Earls, "IDG Chairman Patrick McGovern: Content for Readers Is Top Priority," American Society of Business Publication Editors Web site: www.asbpe.org.

38 "That meant I built the first 25 Suns": Scott McNealy, quoted in "Fun Days at the Sun Frat House," *Fortune,* May 23, 1988.

38 "At least I graduated": Scott McNealy, quoted in "Microsoft Makes Peace with Sun, Its Loudest Critic," Reuters News Service, Apr. 2, 2004.

38 "Colleges like Harvard": Eric Schmidt, quoted in D'Souza, *The Virtue of Prosperity,* p. 87.

39 A 2005 study: Violina P. Rindova, Ian O. Williamson, and Antoaneta P. Petkova, "Being Good or Being Known," *Academy of Management Journal* 48, no. 3 (Dec. 2005/Jan. 2006).

39 "The school's prominence provides legitimacy": Violina P. Rindova, quoted in Abby Ellin, "Was Earning That Harvard MBA Worth It?" *New York Times,* June 11, 2006.

42 Famed filmmaker Steven Spielberg: Greg Easterbrook, "Who Needs Harvard," *The Atlantic Monthly*, Oct. 2004.

42 "Buy straw hats in winter": Charles Brandes, *Value Investing Today*, 2nd ed. (New York: McGraw-Hill, 1997), p. 19.

42 As for the MBAs so popular: MBA data comes from U.S. Department of Education statistics, as cited in "Gauging the Worth of a Harvard MBA," *New York Times*, June 11, 2006.

42 When *Forbes* once asked: All of the quotations about MBAs come from interviews with Forbes 400 members on Forbes.com.

45 "Certainly people who get rich": Stephen Goldbart, quoted in Josh Hyatt, "What It Takes to Be Rich," *Money*, Aug. 22, 2006.

45 "What I do is work": Kenneth Ford, quoted in *Woodsman*, special edition, www.rfpco .com/pdfs/Ford_wood.pdf.

45 "I don't think I've ever 'worked' ": John Werner Kluge, quoted in Vicki Contavespi, "Tips from Winners in the Game of Wealth," *Forbes*, Oct. 22, 1990.

2. Risk

Sources interviewed for this chapter: Sheldon Adelson (Forbes 400); Mark Buchman (banker for, among others, Jon Huntsman); Richard Conniff, author, *The Natural History of the Rich: A Field Guide* (2002); Red Emmerson (Forbes 400); Jon Huntsman (Forbes 400); Andrew Keyt, executive director, Chicago Family Business Center, Loyola University; T. Boone Pickens (Forbes 400); George Smith, Stern School of Business, New York University; Donald Trump (Forbes 400), interview conducted by e-mail; Jerry White, Caruth Institute of Entrepreneurship, Cox School of Business, Southern Methodist University. Unless otherwise noted, quotations in the text from the above sources come from interviews conducted by the editors and writers of the book.

46 Hedge fund honcho Steve Cohen: Ianthe Jeanne Dugan and Anita Raghavan, "Private Money: The New Financial Order," *Wall Street Journal*, Sept. 16, 2006.

46 Media magnate John Kluge: Vicki Contavespi, "Tips from Winners in the Game of Wealth," *Forbes*, Oct. 22, 1990.

46 "I'd just won a hand": Henry Kravis, quoted in Colin Leinster, "Greed Really Turns Me Off," *Fortune*, Jan. 2, 1989.

46 And odd couple Bill Gates and Warren Buffett: Daniel Roth, "The $91 Billion Conversation," *Fortune*, Oct. 31, 2005.

46 And billionaire industrialist Dennis Washington: Contavespi, "Tips from Winners in the Game of Wealth."

46 Shipping magnate Daniel Ludwig: "Daniel Ludwig, Billionaire Businessman Dies at 95," obituary, *New York Times*, Aug. 29, 1992.

46 Donald Trump borrowed: Mark Singer, "Trump Solo," *The New Yorker*, May 19, 1997.

47 And oilman and corporate raider T. Boone Pickens: Joseph Nocera, "Return of the Raider," *Fortune*, May 27, 2002.

47 Among the men: Christopher Palmeri and Marla Matzer, "The Plaza Hotel, That's Not My Style," *Forbes*, Feb. 26, 1996.

47 "I figured my worst risk": Richard L. Stern, "Denny's Always the Low-Cost Producer," *Forbes*, May 15, 1989.

50 Hunt stayed afloat: Harry Hurt, *Texas Rich* (New York: W. W. Norton, 1982), pp. 41–43.

50 The well was situated: Ibid., p. 91.

50 "a man of contradictions": Ibid., p. 118.

50 Another time he came: Ibid., p. 167.

51   "the most remarkable billionaire": Larry King, quoted in the foreword to Jon Hunts-
      man, *Winners Never Cheat* (Upper Saddle River, N.J.: Wharton School Publishing,
      2005), p. xxi.

51   By his late thirties: This and all information on the Shell deal in subsequent paragraphs
      is taken from Phyllis Berman and Dolores Lataniotis, "This Guy Is Going to Lose Every-
      thing," *Forbes*, Nov. 27, 1989.

53   But while many a business: Nina Andrews, "Hunts' Assets Will Pay Creditors, Court
      Rules," *New York Times*, Dec. 17, 1989.

53   By 1986, when he filed for personal bankruptcy: Lisa M. Keefe, "Texas Broke," *Forbes*,
      Oct. 26, 1987.

53   The founder of the Dallas Cowboys: Peter H. Frank, "C. W. Murchison Jr. Dies in Texas
      at 63," *New York Times*, Apr. 1, 1987.

53   William Gordon Bennett filed for personal bankruptcy: Ed Koch and Judy Odierna,
      "Gaming Pioneer Bennett Dies," *Las Vegas Sun*, Dec. 23, 2002.

53   His personal bankruptcy case in 2001: Dan Lynch, "Divorce Not Legal, So $66 Million Is
      Due; Bankruptcy," *Daily Business Review* [Palm Beach, Fla.], Mar. 16, 2005.

54   Emmerson built timber company Sierra Pacific: Jim Carlton, "Forest Fire," *Wall Street
      Journal*, May 27, 2004.

54   He rode out two recessions: Information about Emmerson comes primarily from a per-
      sonal interview, plus Carleen Hawn, "What the Spotted Owl Did for Red Emmerson,"
      Forbes, Oct. 13, 1997.

55   "Entrepreneurs have a fundamental need": Jerry White, "Striking It Rich," *Time*, Feb. 15,
      1982.

55   Such a belief in oneself: Suzanne Oliver, "Al Lerner's Got an Affinity," *Forbes*, Forbes 400
      issue, Oct. 14, 1996. Most of the information on Lerner in the subsequent section comes
      from this article.

56   Between 2004 and 2006, Adelson's wealth: Forbes.com.

56   Adelson, the son of a Boston taxi driver: Matthew Miller, "The Gambler," *Forbes*, Mar. 28,
      2005. Most of the material on Adelson in the subsequent section comes from this article.

58   Adelson was first through the gates: Peter Sanders and Bruce Stanley, "Rolling the Dice,"
      Wall Street Journal, Sept. 7, 2006.

58   The Sands Macau raked in $400 million: Ibid.

58   Meanwhile, in Macau: Forbes.com.

58   Though Adelson will own: Miller, "The Gambler."

59   Wynn is credited with leading: Much of the information here comes from Tyler
      Maroney, "Steve Wynn's Growing Pains," *Fortune*, Nov. 22, 1999. See also Matthew
      Miller, "Courtesy Callers," *Forbes*, Oct. 9, 2006.

59   Kerkorian ran a small air-charter service: Most of the information here comes from
      Matthew Miller, "Cash Kings," *Forbes*, Oct. 9, 2006; David Welch, "Kerkorian's Retreat
      Another Good Sign for Wagoner," *BusinessWeek* online, Dec. 4, 2006; Monica Langley,
      "Exit Ramp," *Wall Street Journal*, Dec. 2, 2006; Ralph King Jr., "Kerkorian in the Emerald
      City," *Forbes*, Nov. 26, 1990.

60   Trump began building: Alan Farnham, *Forbes Great Success Stories: Twelve Tales of Vic-
      tory Wrested from Defeat* (New York: John Wiley & Sons, 2000), p. 130.

60   In hindsight, being outbid: Richard L. Stern and John Connelly, "How Merv Griffin Got
      Taken to the Cleaners," *Forbes*, June 11, 1990.

60   Trump, who had retained: Farnham, *Forbes Success Stories*, p. 135.

61   "excessively friendly bankers": Singer, "Trump Solo."

61   In his 1997 book: Donald J. Trump with Kate Bohner, *Trump: The Art of the Comeback*
      (New York: Random House, 1997), introduction.

61   The resulting company: Stephane Fitch, "The Real Apprentices," *Forbes*, Oct. 16, 2006. Also Stephane Fitch, "What Is Trump Worth?" Forbes.com, Sept. 21, 2006.

61   "I took a big risk": E-mail interview with Donald Trump. *The Apprentice* dominated ratings during its first three seasons (2004 and early 2005), then trailed off.

61   "Pressure can bring out the best": E-mail interview with Donald Trump.

62   Born in 1897: "Daniel Ludwig, Billionaire Businessman Dies at 95," obituary, *New York Times*, Aug. 29, 1992. Much of the material in the subsequent section comes from this obituary.

62   When Ludwig ran into difficulties: Warren Hoge, "Ludwig May Cut Brazil Project," *New York Times*, Oct. 16, 1980.

62   As if the Amazon weren't trouble: Larry Rohter, "Delusions of Economic Grandeur Deep in Brazil's Interior," *New York Times*, Nov. 9, 1999.

63   It often cost: Nocera, "Return of the Raider." Subsequent material in this section is also taken from this article.

64   "During 2001/2002": Riva D. Atlas, "Even the Smartest Money Can Slip Up," *New York Times*, Dec. 30, 2001.

65   "In effect, money center banks": Farnham, *Forbes Great Success Stories*, p. 39.

66   Hundreds of millions of dollars: Singer, "Trump Solo."

66   "I've never borrowed": Timothy L. O'Brien, "Fortune's Fools," *New York Times*, Sept. 17, 2006.

3. Luck—and Timing

Sources interviewed for this chapter: Sheldon Adelson (Forbes 400); Mark Cuban (Forbes 400); Daniel Gilbert (Forbes 400); J. B. Hunt (Forbes 400); Christopher Jencks, professor of social policy, Harvard University; Ross Perot (Forbes 400); Mort Zuckerman (Forbes 400). Unless otherwise noted, quotations in the text from the above sources come from interviews conducted by the editors and writers of the book.

68   By the time of his death: "Johnnie B. Hunt, 79, Trucking Company Owner, Is Dead," obituary, *New York Times*, Dec. 8, 2006.

68   Hunt was born in 1927: Claire Poole, "Once You're Hungry, You're Different," *Forbes*, Oct. 19, 1992.

68   There was no CB or radio: J. B. Hunt interview and Poole, "Once You're Hungry, You're Different." Much of the subsequent information about Hunt comes from these two sources.

72   Media tycoon John Kluge: Vicki Contavespi, "Tips from Winners in the Game of Wealth," *Forbes*, Oct. 22, 1990.

72   "neither family background": Christopher Jencks, *Inequality: A Reassessment of the Effect of Family and Schooling in America* (New York: Harper & Row, 1972), pp. 226–28.

72   The "luck" that Jencks cited: Daniel Seligman, "Luck and Careers," *Fortune*, Nov. 16, 1981.

72   "Given the choice": Harry Hurt III, *Texas Rich* (New York: W. W. Norton, 1982), p. 373.

72   "The way the ball bounces": Mark M. Colodny, "Ross Perot on His Good Luck," *Fortune*, June 3, 1991.

75   "skilled at creating and noticing": Richard Wiseman, "The Luck Factor," *Skeptical Inquirer*, May/June 2003.

77   "Unlucky people miss chance opportunities": Ibid.

77   He plunged into debt: Jaclyn Fierman, "Great Fortunes Lost," *Fortune*, July 18, 1988.

77   But that was due: Ken Auletta, "Rising Son," *The New Yorker*, June 6, 1994; Connie

Bruck, "Bronfman's Big Deals," *The New Yorker*, May 11, 1998; and Edward Klein, "Edgar Bets the House," *Vanity Fair*, July 1995.

78 "I suppose you can": Colin Leinster, "The Second Son Is Heir at Seagrams," *Fortune*, Mar. 17, 1986.

78 Although there was little doubt: Klein, "Edgar Bets the House."

78 "I think the Bronfman kid": Michael Oneal, Ronald Grover, and William C. Symonds, "The Mogul: Just How Risky Is Edgar Bronfman's Gamble," *BusinessWeek*, Apr. 24, 1995.

78 "The taking of Edgar": Bruck, "Bronfman's Big Deals."

79 "Of course he is going to make mistakes": Ibid.

79 One year later: Jeff Leeds, "Wipe Egg Off Face. Try Again. Voila," *New York Times*, Apr. 17, 2004.

79 In March 2002 Vivendi Universal: Leslie Kaufman and John Schwartz, "New Divide: Those Who Sold and Everyone Else," *New York Times*, July 14, 2002.

80 Not that the belt tightening stopped: [Unsigned,] "Maestro Bronfman Keeps Tuned to Mission," *Financial Times*, June 16, 2004.

80 In October 2004: John Carreyrou, "Fortou's Coups at Vivendi Turn Some Investors' Heads," *Wall Street Journal*, Oct. 25, 2004.

82 "I hedged 100 percent": Kaufman and Schwartz, "New Divide."

82 "I'm the stupidest person": Patricia Sellers, "Ted Turner Is a Worried Man," *Fortune*, May 26, 2003.

82 He has launched three companies: Fred Moody, "A Billionaire at Play," *Wall Street Journal*, Oct. 22, 1999.

83 In 1995, the same year: Adam Lashinsky, Oliver Ryan, and Patricia Neering, "Remembering Netscape," *Fortune*, July 25, 2005.

83 It was sold in 1987: Fleming Meeks, "Would You Believe It?" *Forbes*, Mar. 1, 1993.

84 But as cellular grew: Ellie Winninghoff, "Craig McCaw's Bold Gamble on 'Pop' Finance," *Corporate Finance*, Feb. 1990.

84 It was the largest cellular operator: Ibid.

84 So in 1989: O. Casey Corr, "Going Public," *Seattle Times*, Apr. 7, 1993.

84 "In the future": Fleming Meeks, "Winning Is Only the First Step," *Forbes*, Dec. 25, 1989.

84 "Craig is an amazing person": Andrew Kupfer and Erin M. Davies, "Craig McCaw's Cosmic Ambition," *Fortune*, May 27, 1996.

85 "You arrive at moments": Ibid.

85 Internet loans billionaire Daniel Gilbert: Monte Burke, "Net Game," *Forbes*, Oct. 10, 2005.

86 Sure enough, in 2002: Ibid.

86 Even Intuit's Bennett said: Ibid.

4. Winning Is Everything

Sources interviewed for this chapter: Dr. Paul Babiak, industrial psychologist and coauthor, with Dr. Robert Hare, of *Snakes in Suits* (2006); Ron Chernow, author, *Titan: The Life of John D. Rockefeller, Sr.* (1998); Jim Clark (Forbes 400); Richard Conniff, author, *The Natural History of the Rich* (2002); Edward Jay Epstein, author, *Dossier: The Secret Life of Armand Hammer* (1996); Charles Geisst, professor of finance, Manhattan College, New York; Bruce Kovner (Forbes 400); Dr. Michael Maccoby, psychoanalyst and author, *The Productive Narcissist: The Promise and Perils of Visionary Leadership* (2003); David A. Skeel Jr., professor of corporate law, University of Pennsylvania, and author, *Icarus in the Boardroom* (2005); Matthew Symonds, writer, *The Economist*, and author, *Softwar: An Intimate Portrait of Larry Ellison and Oracle*

(2004). Unless otherwise noted, quotations in the text from the above sources come from interviews conducted by the editors and writers of the book.

87   Like Rockefeller, fellow industrial giant Andrew Carnegie: David Nasaw, *Andrew Carnegie* (New York: Penguin, 2006), pp. x, 346.

89   He paid his hourly employees: Sam Walton with John Huey, *Sam Walton: Made in America* (New York: Bantam, 1993). Walton wrote in his autobiography, "In the beginning, I was so chintzy I didn't pay my employees very well. We really didn't do much for the clerks except pay them an hourly wage, and I guess that wage was as little as we could get by with at the time" (p. 127).

89   And he sued: Bob Ortega, *In Sam We Trust: The Untold Story of Sam Walton and Wal-Mart, the World's Most Powerful Retailer* (New York: Times Business, 1999), p. 86.

89   According to Bob Ortega: Ibid., pp. 105, 107.

89   Although Walton was unusual among retailers: Ibid., pp. 90, 92, 210.

89   In 2006 fines of at least $78 million: Steven Greenhouse, "Wal-Mart Told to Pay $78 Million," *New York Times,* Oct. 14, 2006.

89   A policy of wage caps: Paul Krugman, "The War Against Wages," *New York Times,* op-ed, Oct. 6, 2006. Also see Paul Krugman, "Wal-Mart's Excuse," *New York Times,* op-ed, Dec. 12, 2006.

89   In addition, the company faces: Steven Greenhouse, "Court Approves Class Action Suit Against Wal-Mart," *New York Times,* Feb. 7, 2007.

89   Even now it offers: Michael Barbaro and Robert Pear, "Wal-Mart and Union Unite, at Least on Health Policy," *New York Times,* Feb. 7, 2007.

89   And, according to the *New York Times:* Michael Barbaro, "Bare-Knuckle Enforcement of Wal-Mart's Rules," *New York Times,* Mar. 29, 2007.

90   "Only the little people": At Leona Helmsley's tax evasion trial, Helmsley's housekeeper attributed this quote to her employer. Linda Greenhouse, "High Court Rejects Leona Helmsley's Appeal in Tax Fraud Case," *New York Times,* Feb. 25, 1992. The remark was originally quoted in the *New York Times* on July 12, 1989.

90   "It is a sort of disease": Lee Penn, "The United Religions Initiative," *New Oxford Review,* Dec. 1998.

90   "For some reason": Stanley Bing, *Throwing the Elephant* (New York: Harper Business, 2002), p. 55.

90   "I felt I had": As quoted by Tina Brown, "The Dish on Liz Smith," Salon.com, Feb. 6, 2003.

90   "Jeffrey [Katzenberg] was my retriever": Stewart, *Disney War,* p. 72.

90   "All I want in life": Devon Leonard and Peter Elkin, " 'All I Want in Life Is an Unfair Advantage,' " *Fortune,* Aug. 8, 2005.

91   "The Nike product has become": John H. Cushman Jr., "Nikes Pledges to End Child Labor and Apply U.S. Rules Abroad," *New York Times,* May 13, 1998. For a critical history of Nike's overseas labor practices and boycotts, see www.newacademy.ac.uk/ publications/keypublications/documents/nikereport

91   "It's not sufficient": Karen Southwick, *Everyone Else Must Fail: The Unvarnished Truth About Oracle and Larry Ellison* (New York: Crown Business, 2003), p. 1.

91   These aggressive tactics: Ibid., pp. 3, 76, 86–89, 96, 112.

92   "Ellison, ahead of nearly everyone else": Ibid., p. 2.

93   Once they had defeated such 1980s competitors: Ibid., p. 267.

93   "They basically said": John Heileman, "The Whole Truth and Nothing But the Truth," *Wired,* Nov. 2000.

93   "The only thing J. D. Rockefeller did": Ibid.

94   "My job": Ibid.

95 Reflecting upon Murdoch's battles: Jon Heilemann, "The Power Grid: Rupert, White Knight," *New York,* May 14, 2007.

95 Jack Welch was similarly tough-minded: Anthony Bianco, "Jack Welch: The Fall of an Icon," *BusinessWeek* online, Sept. 23, 2002.

96 Had the insurance unit been adequately reserved: Jonathan R. Laing, "You Don't Know Jack," *Barrons,* Dec. 28, 2005.

96 Friedland was chairman and CEO: E-mail from Ivanhoe Mines spokesman Bob Williamson, Apr. 13, 2007.

97 The EPA and the state of Colorado: Richard Read, "Mining's Bad Boy Sees Lucrative Haven in Mongolia," *Star-Ledger* [Newark, N.J.], Nov. 6, 2005.

97 U.S. officials now admit: Patrick Barta, "Mongolia Is Roiled by Miner's Huge Plans," *Wall Street Journal,* Jan. 4, 2007. The U.S. government paid Friedland $1.25 million as reimbursement for his legal fees, according to an e-mail from Ivanhoe Mines spokesman Bob Williamson.

97 An attorney for Friedland: Barta, "Mongolia Is Roiled."

97 When one of his traders: *Wall Street Journal,* Nov. 6, 2001, from a review of *No Bull: My Life In and Out of Markets,* by Michael Steinhardt, online at Amazon.com.

97 Steinhardt traces part of this monstrousness: Robert Lenzer, "Michael Steinhardt's Voyage Around His Father," *Forbes,* Nov. 8, 2001.

97 With its buoyant calypso tunes: James B. Stewart, *Disney War* (New York: Simon & Schuster, 2005), p. 104.

98 Boosted by more runaway hits: Ibid., p. 124.

98 Katzenberg then asked Eisner: Ibid., pp. 235–37.

98 After the trial: Ibid., pp. 235, 238.

98 "live in the grip of a vision": Michael Meyer, *The Alexander Complex: The Dreams That Drive Great Businessmen* (New York: New York Times Books, 1989), quoted in Peter Finch, "What Do Empire Builders Really Want?" *BusinessWeek,* Sept. 4, 1989.

98 Meyer refers to Apple founder: Ibid.

98 "People think I'm an asshole": David A. Kaplan, *The Silicon Boys and Their Valley of Dreams* (New York: William Morrow, 1999), p. 104. Kaplan attributes the story about Jobs allegedly cheating Wozniak to Nolan Bushnell, founder of Atari, a video games company.

99 When the famed Jari Project: Gwen Kinkead, "Trouble in D. K. Ludwig's Jungle," *Fortune,* Apr. 20, 1981.

99 "All I want in life": Devon Leonard and Peter Elkin, "Inside Hank Greenberg's Big Fall," *Fortune,* Aug. 8, 2005.

99 "Why do I have to die?": Sally Bedell Smith, *In All His Glory: The Life and Times of William S. Paley and the Birth of Modern Broadcasting* (New York: Random House, 1990), p. 606.

99 Rupert Murdoch, for example: Julia Angwin, "News Corp. Provides Murdoch a $50,000-a-Month Residence," *Wall Street Journal,* Sept. 8, 2006.

100 Because of a brief meeting: Edward Jay Epstein, *Dossier: The Secret History of Armand Hammer* (New York: Random House, 1996), pp. 61, 62, 65, 67–68.

101 Drawing in the 1990s: Ibid., pp. 113–45.

101 One of his mistresses: Ibid., p. 20.

101 Though the FBI and the State Department: Ibid., pp. 5–23.

101 Measures to accomplish this: Jeff Stein, "The Greatest Vendetta on Earth," *Salon,* Aug. 30, 2001, tells how freelance journalist Janice Pottker was harassed after her 1990 article in a Washington, D.C., business magazine exposed secrets about the secretive Feld family, especially about its patriarch, Irvin Feld.

101 By pleading guilty: Ibid., pp. 339–43.

103   "The rules are": J. Winokur, *The Rich Are Different* (New York: Pantheon, 1996), p. 28.

104   With his sharp business skills: obituary, *New York Times,* Jan. 16, 1983.

104   WorldCom collapsed: ABC Online, July 14, 2005, www.abc.net.au/news/newsitems/200507/s1413797.htm.

5. Blue-collar Billionaires

Sources interviewed for this chapter: John E. Anderson, Topa Equities; Diane Byrne, editor, *Power & Motoryacht;* S. Truett Cathy (Forbes 400); Chuck Collins, cofounder, Responsible Wealth, and coauthor, with Bill Gates Sr., *Wealth and Our Commonwealth: Why America Should Tax Accumulated Fortunes* (2004); David Gold (Forbes 400); Alexander Horniman, professor of business administration and organizational behavior, Darden School of Business, University of Virginia; Wayne Huizenga (Forbes 400); S. M. Miller, professor emeritus of sociology, Boston University. Unless otherwise noted, quotations in the text from the above sources come from interviews conducted by the editors and writers of the book.

109   But few could have measured up: Interview with Diane Byrne, editor, *Power & Motoryacht.*

109   "piercing, right to the soul": Gail DeGeorge, *The Making of a Blockbuster: How Wayne Huizenga Built a Sports and Entertainment Empire from Trash, Grit, and Videotape* (New York: John Wiley & Sons, 1996), p. 201.

109   Huizenga, with an estimated net worth: *CIA Factbook,* www.cia.gov.

109   As winner of the 2005 World Entrepreneur Award: Interview with Hilary Mariassy, Ernst & Young, LLP.

110   Think of Forbes 400 members: www.ey.com.

110   Huizenga's grandfather: DeGeorge, *The Making of a Blockbuster,* p. 26.

110   And James Leprino: leprinofoods.com.

111   A self-described "old potato farmer": Lawrence Zuckerman, "The Potato Tycoon Who Is the Force Behind Micron," *New York Times,* Feb. 8, 1996.

111   "Nobody ever put a penny": "A Portrait: J. R. Simplot," Idaho Public Television interview, www.idahotv.org/productions/idahoportrait/about/simplot.html.

111   "Work honestly and build": Scott Carrier, "J. R. Simplot," *Esquire,* Feb. 2001.

113   As head of the company: DeGeorge, *The Making of a Blockbuster,* p. 23.

113   But Huizenga always insisted: Ibid., p. 35.

115   In any case: Ibid., p. 3.

115   During the following years: Ibid., p. 68.

115   "I certainly liked the Blockbuster business": Ibid., p. 23.

115   By the time Huizenga sold it: "Wayne Huizenga Named 2004 National Ernst & Young Entrepreneur of the Year," Ernst & Young press release, Nov. 20, 2004.

115   He turned his energy: Will Flower, vice president of communications, Republic Services.

115   In 1998 he named the scattered car franchises: autonation.com.

115   One key investor: Ida Picker, "Wayne Huizenga, Conglomerateur," *Institutional Investor,* Apr. 1997.

115   "the excitement of making the deal": DeGeorge, *The Making of a Blockbuster,* p. 311.

116   By 2006 Gold had built: www.99only.com.

116   The huge twenty-two-thousand-square-foot stores: Erica Sagon, "Dollar-Store Chains Plan Expansion in the Valley," *The Arizona Republic,* May 2, 2006.

117   Knickknacks and useless trinkets: Brendan Coffey, "Every Penny Counts," *Forbes,* Sept. 30, 2002.

118   The company operates: www.city-data.com/city/Commerce-California.html.

118   "If we operated": Nancy D. Holt, "Workspaces," *Wall Street Journal,* Oct. 15, 2003.

118 It often features: [Unsigned,] "99 Cents Only Stores Will Be Celebrating the Grand Opening," *BusinessWeek*, July 18, 2006.

118 Manoogian struck gold: Masco history, www.masco.com.

118 Then, in an about-face: Masco annual report, www.masco.com.

118 Billionaire Manoogian collects: Scott DeCarlo, "The Best and Worst Bosses," *Forbes*, May 8, 2006.

118 He devotes a good chunk: Forbes.com.

119 He came up with the odd company name: Richard Read, "Jeld-Wen Keeps Plants Humming in the U.S. and Abroad," *The Oregonian*, June 12, 2005.

119 "Dick can walk the main street": Elisa Williams, "Work Speaks for Itself," *Forbes*, Oct. 9, 2000.

119 "one of the most remarkable success stories": Jimmy Carter, endorsement for *Eat Mor Chikin*, by S. Truett Cathy (Decatur, Ga.: Looking Glass Books, 2002), back cover.

120 More than 70 Forbes 400 members: Information in the "Feeding Frenzies" box comes from Forbes.com. Additional sources are noted below.

120 Ernest Gallo, Julio Gallo: Gallo.com; Martin Weil, "Ernest Gallo, 97; Influential Cofounder of Winery," obituary, *Washington Post*, Mar. 7, 2007.

120 Wendell H. Murphy: Tatiana Serafin, "High on the Hog," *Forbes*, May 8, 2006; Daniel Roth, "The Ray Kroc of Pigsties," *Forbes*, Oct. 13, 1997.

120 Luigino "Jeno" Paulucci: Trang Ho, "Entrepreneur Jeno F. Paulucci," *Investor's Business Daily*, Nov. 27, 2006.

120 Frank Perdue: familybusinessmagazine.com.

120 Robert Rich Sr., Robert Rich Jr.: familybusinessmagazine.com.

121 Donald J. Tyson: www.familybusinessmagazine.com/top150.html.

121 William Wrigley, William Wrigley Jr.: Ibid.

121 "no clearer case study": Cathy, *Eat Mor Chikin*, p. vi.

121 His father, an insurance salesman: Ibid., pp. 18–21.

121 The next day she fried it: Ibid., p. 15.

122 "to recognize and seize opportunities": Warren G. Bennis and Robert J. Thomas, *Geeks & Geezers: How Era, Values and Defining Moments Shape Leaders* (Boston: Harvard Business Press, 2002), p. 92.

122 Yet that year Michael Ilitch: Mark Tatge with Miriam Gottfried, "The Forbes 400 Encore," *Forbes*, Oct. 9, 2006.

122 Their success with pizza: Bennis and Thomas, *Geeks & Geezers*, p. 17.

122 "That destroyed my dreams": Michael Ilitch interview on Fox Sports Network, www.littlecaesars.com, Sept. 22, 2006.

122 While he rolled the dough: Ibid.

123 "My idol was Ray Kroc": Ibid.

123 His "Pizza, pizza" campaign: Michael Oneal, "Pizza Pizza and Tigers, Too," *BusinessWeek*, Sept. 14, 1992.

123 By 2006 Little Caesars: Tatge and Gottfried, "The Forbes 400 Encore."

123 The following year he traded: Forbes.com.

123 None other than his old competitor: Oneal, "Pizza Pizza and Tigers, Too."

123 Successful entrepreneurs, he says: Josh Hyatt, "What It Takes to Be Rich," *Money*, Aug. 22, 2006.

124 "If you're going to build": DeGeorge, *The Making of a Blockbuster*, p. 77.

124 The story goes: Eric Schlosser, *Fast Food Nation* (New York: Harper Perennial, 2005), p. 33.

124 a photo taken by German photographer: Brendan Coffey, "Every Penny Counts," Museum of Modern Art public relations office.

124 Penske's $16 billion enterprise: Forbes.com.

124   "The real success is in the details": Dave Caldwell, "No Shortcuts for Penske: Fastidious Means Fast," *New York Times*, May 28, 2006.

124   "We are never smarter": Jonathan Guthrie, "Lessons from Wayne's World," *Financial Times*, June 8, 2006.

125   Witness the case of H. Ty Warner: "The Forbes 400," *Forbes*, Oct. 11, 1999.

125   At the height of the Beanie Baby craze: Ibid.

125   He bought prime real estate: James M. Pethokoukis, "Money & Business: Ty Warner," *U.S. News & World Report*, Feb. 16, 2004.

126   At the time, supermarket pet food: Erin Davies, "Selling Sex and Cat Food," *Fortune*, June 9, 1997.

126   On weekends he took the samples: Sam Hill and Glenn Rifkin, "Customers Tuning Out? Try an Alternative Approach," *Wall Street Journal*, Dec. 28, 1998.

126   Mathile sold the closely held company: Forbes.com.

126   "We're hoping another Iams": Stephanie Irwin, "Billionaire's Wisdom: Dayton Needs to Find the Next Wright Brothers," *Dayton Daily News*, Aug. 15, 2005.

126   But after selling a used car: Jim Moran, *Jim Moran: The Courtesy Man* (Chicago: Bonus Books, 1996), pp. 2–18.

127   Junk Man: Forbes.com and public.storage.com.

127   Dolls with a Difference: Lisa Bannon, "Hi, Barbie! I'm Samantha; Can I Boost Your Sales?" *Wall Street Journal*, June 16, 1998; Forbes.com.

127   A Ping That Went Ka-ching: Forbes.com; pinggolf.com.

128   A Better Parking Lot: Daniel Roth, "Career Opportunity: Long Hours, Good Pay," *Forbes*, May 19, 1997; Matt Krantz, "Leaders and Success: Central Parking's Monroe Carell," *Investor's Business Daily*, July 24, 1998.

128   Not Just Hot Air: Forbes.com; Jeffrey A. Trachtenberg, "Make My Day," *Forbes*, July 29, 1985; Janet Novack, "Doing Good—in Prison," *Forbes*, Oct. 9, 2006.

128   "I had a television set": Jim Moran, quoted in Graham Button, "Jim Moran, Master Salesman," *Forbes*, Oct. 28, 1989.

129   He signed off with hand kisses: "The American Bazaar," *Time*, Mar. 24, 1961.

129   Moran's business was riding high: www.jimmoranfoundation.org/history02.asp.

129   As Moran recounted: Moran, *Jim Moran: The Courtesy Man*, p. 136.

129   That same year he pleaded guilty: Button, "Jim Moran, Master Salesman."

129   Daughter Pat is on the board: company press release.

129   "If I hadn't been lucky enough": Moran, *Jim Moran: The Courtesy Man*, p. 155.

130   NBC and McMahon lost: Forbes.com.

130   WWE recovered, though: Joe Flint, "The Advertising Report: Luring New Wrestling Viewers and Getting Back in the Ring," *Wall Street Journal*, Mar. 30, 2005.

130   One wide-open field: B. J. Pine II and James Gilmore, *The Experience Economy: Work Is Theater and Every Business a Stage* (Boston: Harvard Business School Press, 1999).

6. West Coast Money

Sources interviewed for this chapter: David Duffield (Forbes 400); Ken Fisher (Forbes 400); David A. Kaplan, author, *The Silicon Boys and Their Valley of Dreams* (1999); Charles Schwab (Forbes 400); John Sobrato (Forbes 400); Matthew Symonds, author, *Softwar: An Intimate Portrait of Larry Ellison and Oracle* (2004). Unless otherwise noted, quotations in the text from the above sources come from interviews conducted by the editors and writers of the book.

131   Who could have known: The description of Gates and Ballmer's meeting with IBM comes from Paul Carroll, *Big Blues: The Unmasking of IBM* (New York: Crown, 1993), p. 33.

131 Apple Computer, a three-year-old start-up: Jay Cocks, "The Updated Book of Jobs: A Testament of Prophecy, True Belief, Go-getting, and Megabucks," *Time*, Jan. 23, 1983.

131 An impatient IBM: Bill Gates, *The Road Ahead* (New York: Viking Penguin, 1995), pp. 47–48.

132 Gates and his friend Paul Allen: Ibid., p. 17.

132 Gates arrived with Ballmer: Carroll, *Big Blues*, p. 33.

132 When Gates and Ballmer finally showed up: Ibid.

132 Gates looked young for his age: John Seabrook, "Email from Bill," *The New Yorker*, Jan. 10, 1994. See also Carroll, *Big Blues*.

132 IBM, which had been founded: Gates, *The Road Ahead*, p. 47.

132 It was hierarchical: Carroll, *Big Blues*, pp. 3, 6, 7.

132 "IBM wanted to bring": Gates, *The Road Ahead*, p. 47.

134 "One of the most important lessons": Ibid.

134 Gates insisted on a license arrangement: David A. Kaplan, *The Silicon Boys and Their Valley of Dreams* (New York: William Morrow, 1999), pp. 115–16.

134 Gates bought the rights: Ibid., p. 113.

134 Twenty-seven years after: Saul Hansell, "A $500 milestone for Google Believers," *New York Times*, Nov. 22, 2006.

136 In 1999, when David Kaplan: Kaplan, *The Silicon Boys*, pp. 17, 13.

136 One of the youngest people: Ibid., p. 99.

136 In 1998 Google's founders: John Battelle, *The Search: How Google and Its Rivals Rewrote the Rules of Business and Transformed Our Culture* (New York: Portfolio, 2005), p. 86.

137 One class exercise: Kaplan, *The Silicon Boys*, p. 5.

138 "Even back in the late seventies": Charles Simonyi, quoted ibid., p. 259.

138 The Valley's relatively contained geography: AnnaLee Saxenian, *Regional Advantage: Culture and Competition in Silicon Valley and Route 128* (Cambridge, Mass.: Harvard University Press, 1994), p. 29.

138 "From the outset": Ibid. Much of the information on the history of Silicon Valley comes from Saxenian's book.

140 They had become friends: Kaplan, *The Silicon Boys*, p. 34.

140 Later he encouraged the duo: Saxenian, *Regional Advantage*, p. 20.

140 Hewlett and Packard are the iconic models: The information on Hewlett and Packard's early days in Silicon Valley comes mainly from John Markoff, "William Hewlett Dies at 87: A Pioneer of Silicon Valley," obituary, *New York Times*, Jan. 13, 2001.

141 In a 1983 *Esquire* article: Tom Wolfe, "The Tinkerings of Robert Noyce: How the Sun Rose on the Silicon Valley," *Esquire*, Dec. 1983.

141 At Fairchild, Noyce designed: Kaplan, *The Silicon Boys*, p. 56.

141 It was at Intel in late 1971: "How the West Kicked Butt," *Forbes*, Aug. 25, 1997.

142 But like Hewlett-Packard: Richard S. Tedlow, *Andy Grove: The Life and Times of an American* (New York: Penguin, 2006), p. 124.

142 He arranged funding: Saxenian, *Regional Advantage*, p. 26.

144 He realized that large numbers: John Kador, *Charles Schwab: How One Company Beat Wall Street and Reinvented the Brokerage Industry* (Hoboken, N.J.: John Wiley & Sons, 2002), pp. 17, 42.

145 "I could never have done it": Most of the information on Charles Schwab comes from the interview with him.

146 "A lot of it is focus": The information on John Sobrato comes from the interview with him.

146 Before he started Apple Computer: Cocks, "The Updated Book of Jobs."

146 "Why did you send me this renegade": Kaplan, *The Silicon Boys*, p. 97.

146 Markkula, who had recently retired: Ibid.

146   In 1966, after dropping out: Matthew Symonds, *Softwar: An Intimate Portrait of Larry Ellison and Oracle* (New York: Simon & Schuster, 2004), p. 57.

147   "He had to be rich": Ibid., p. 130.

147   Ellison and his partners: Ibid., p. 61.

147   And as Oracle grew: Alan Farnham, *Forbes Great Success Stories: Twelve Tales of Victory Wrested from Defeat* (New York: John Wiley & Sons, 2000), pp. 57–58.

147   "Too many companies here": Thomas Siebel, quoted in Symonds, *Softwar,* p. 215.

148   "PeopleSoft prided itself": The information on David Duffield comes primarily from the interview with him.

148   Only half of the top forty: AnnaLee Saxenian, *The New Argonauts: Regional Advantage in a Global Economy* (Cambridge, Mass.: Harvard University Press, 2006), p. 34.

149   Soon Silicon Graphics was earning billions: Michael Lewis, *The New New Thing: A Silicon Valley Story* (New York: Penguin, 2001), p. 47.

149   Clark also foresaw: Ibid., p. 50.

149   "Bill Gates sent a memo": Ibid., p. 70.

150   "The speed with which Clark": Ibid., p. 75.

150   When the bubble burst: Ken Kurson, "Don't Worry Be Happy: Yacht Designers Say They've Got a Depression-Proof Business. Could That Be True?" *Forbes,* Oct. 9, 2000.

151   Their software calibrated that ranking: Battelle, *The Search,* p. 75.

152   At one point, their student search-engine project: Ibid., p. 78.

152   One of them, Vinod Khosla: Ibid., p. 83.

152   In 1998, however, they got $100,000: Ibid., p. 85.

153   "It wasn't clear": Sergey Brin, quoted in Jeffery Toobin, "Google's Moonshot," *The New Yorker,* Feb. 5, 2007.

154   After all, Google's market value: Hansell, "A 500 Milestone for Google Believers."

155   Companies there account for one-third: Saxenian, *The New Argonauts,* p. 30.

155   "Google is doing more damage": Gary Rivlin, "Relax Bill Gates; It's Google's Turn as the Villain," *New York Times,* Aug. 24, 2005.

7. Entertainment and Media

Sources interviewed for this chapter: Ken Auletta, media critic, *The New Yorker,* and author; Michael Bloomberg, mayor, New York City (Forbes 400); George Cooke, entertainment lawyer, Manatt, Phelps & Phillips, LLP; Edward J. Epstein, author, *The Big Picture: The New Logic of Money and Power in Hollywood* (2005); Janet Healy, former Walt Disney Company studio executive and producer, *Shark Tale;* Stanley S. Hubbard, chairman of Hubbard Broadcasting Corporation (Forbes 400); John Malone, chairman of Liberty Media Corporation (Forbes 400); Tom Pollock, ex-chairman of MCA/Universal Pictures and co-owner of Montecito Pictures; Roy C. Smith, professor of entrepreneurship and finance, New York University; Jonathan Taplin, adjunct professor, Annenberg School for Communication, University of Southern California; David Waterman, professor of telecommunications, Indiana University, and author, *Hollywood's Road to Riches* (2005).

156   The audience was standing: Dennis McDougal, *The Last Mogul: Lew Wasserman, MCA, and the Hidden History of Hollywood* (New York: Crown, 1998), p. 427.

157   Edgar Bronfman Jr.: In 2003 *New York* magazine called Bronfman "possibly the stupidest person in the media business." Bronfman family biographer Nicholas Faith dubbed Edgar Jr. "the Clown Prince" (www.iht.com/articles/2006/06/23/arts/idbriefs24a.php). *BusinessWeek* named Bronfman one of the worst managers in 2002. And Connie Bruck, in *When Hollywood Had a King: The Reign of Lew Wasserman, Who Leveraged Talent into*

Power and Influence (New York: Random House, 2003), wrote, "Perhaps Bronfman's worst sin in the eyes of Hollywood was that he had been taken in a deal [selling USA cable networks to Barry Diller for too low a price].... And it was not the first time Bronfman had been bested since he took over MCA.... Hollywood denizens chortled at Edgar Jr.'s combination of arrogance and pratfalls" (pp. 454–56).

158 He'd helped build MCA: Bruck, *When Hollywood Had a King*, pp. 15–83. Music Corporation's founder, Jules Stein, started off booking bands into nightclubs in Chicago. The clubs were controlled by Chicago's Mob. Stein paid off and was "sometimes partners" with the Mob as he expanded into booking dance bands, orchestras, floor shows, even liquor for new nightclubs around the country. When MCA came to Hollywood in the 1930s, the Mob had already infiltrated the studios and was entwined with Hollywood society, according to Bruck (pp. 55–64).

158 "I run all the studios": Wendy Smith, review of *The Last Mogul*, Amazon.com.

158 Once he had a ton of snow: Caroline Sutton and Collin Willis, "Inside the World of Mr. Hollywood . . . and the House That Tack Built!" *Sunday Mirror*, June 20, 1996.

158 Among other things, he visited: Bruck, *When Hollywood Had a King*, p. 408.

158 Journalist Edward Jay Epstein: Edward Jay Epstein, *The Big Picture: The New Logic of Money and Power in Hollywood* (New York: Random House, 2005), p. 125. A single episode of *ER*, for example, could fetch $300,000.

159 As part owner of the show: Richard Zoglin, "He Has a Hot TV Series, a New Book and a Booming Comedy Empire," *Time*, Sept. 28, 1987.

159 Although he had flunked out: Robert Sam Anson, "David Geffen Talks a Little," *Esquire*, Nov. 1982.

159 "I felt sure": Playboy interview with David Geffen, *Playboy*, Sept. 1994, p. 57.

159 He quickly sold Asylum: John Seabrooke, "The Many Lives of David Geffen," *The New Yorker*, Feb. 23, 1998.

160 Geffen, said Sandy Gallin: Lisa Gubernick and Peter Newcomb, "The Richest Man in Hollywood," *Forbes*, Dec. 24, 1990.

160 Profits largely settled in Geffen's pocket: Ibid.

160 He cashed out his MCA stock: *Forbes*, Oct. 9, 2006.

160 By 2006 that nest egg: Patricia Sellers, "The Best Investor of His Generation," *Fortune*, Feb. 8, 2006.

160 The three each invested $33 million: Andrew E. Serwer, "Analyzing the Dream," *Fortune*, Apr. 17, 1995, p. 71.

161 Geffen netted at least $300 million: Geraldine Fabrikant and Sharon Waxman, "A Mogul Ponders Becoming a Publisher, But Others Have the Same Idea," *New York Times*, Nov. 9, 2006.

161 Besides, Geffen, Paul Allen, and Katzenberg: Gary Gentile, "DreamWorks Animation Pays CEO Katzenberg $1 in 2006," Associated Press, Mar. 30, 2007.

161 In 2006 he announced: Merissa Marr, "Geffen's Goodbye," *Wall Street Journal*, Dec. 8, 2006.

161 "He is bored": Fabrikant and Waxman, "A Mogul Ponders."

162 Unlike the old Hollywood movie moguls: John Motavalli, *Bamboozled at the Revolution: How Big Media Lost Billions in the Battle for the Internet* (New York: Viking, 2002). Motavalli cites a 1998 interview with Bob Pittman of AOL Time Warner in which Pittman explained the "phenomenal success of cable in this way: 'The three networks looked at the cable business and chose not to start a cable network because they didn't want to ding their earnings to build a new business. They said, "If it ever gets big, then we'll come in." But by the time they got in, Ted Turner had news, ESPN had sports, MTV had music, Nickelodeon had kids and there was no opportunity' " (p. 15).

162   It was a wild bet: Robert Goldberg with Gerald Jay Goldberg, *Citizen Turner: The Wild Rise of an American Tycoon* (New York: Harcourt Brace, 1995), notes that Ted Turner was worth $100 million when he launched CNN (p. 225). On putting all that at risk, see Ted Turner, "My Beef with Media," *Washington Monthly*, July/Aug. 2004, where Turner writes: "I risked my personal wealth to start CNN." He also says, "Our losses were so high that our loans were called in. I refinanced . . . and stayed just a step ahead of the bankers" (p. 3).

162   He denounced CBS's programming: Goldberg, *Citizen Turner*, p. 266.

162   Though Turner failed: Museum of Broadcast Communications, museum.tv/archives/ctv/P/htm/P/paleywillia-htm.

162   Captain Outrageous, as Turner was sometimes known: pbs.org/wgbh/theymadeamerica/whomade/turnerhi.htm.

163   Philip Anschutz: Glenn Bunting, "Denver Billionaire's Invisible Hand Shapes L.A.," *Los Angeles Times*, July 23, 2006.

163   Michael Eisner: James B. Stewart, *Disney War* (New York: Simon & Schuster, 2005).

163   David Geffen: Lisa Gubernick and Peter Newcomb, "The Richest Man in Hollywood," *BusinessWeek*, Dec. 24, 1990.

163   William Paley: Christopher Buckley, "Success Was Not Enough," *New York Times*, Nov. 4, 1990.

163   Jerry Perenchio: Meg James, "Univision Deal Wins Approval Narrowly," *Los Angeles Times*, Sept. 28, 2006.

163   Sumner Redstone: Bryan Burrough, "Sleeping with the Fishes," *Vanity Fair*, Dec. 2006, p. 246.

163   Haim Saban: Stewart, *Disney War*, pp. 364–76.

163   Aaron Spelling: obituary at cbsnews.com/stories/2006/06/24/ap/entertainment/main D8IEBVGG0.shtml.

163   Martha Stewart: Amazon.com.

163   Lew Wasserman: Bruck, *When Hollywood Had a King*, p. 408.

163   Oprah Winfrey: "Star-Studded Opening for Oprah's School," Associated Press, Jan. 3, 2007.

164   Mark Cuban: For hiring of Dan Rather, see Howard Kurtz, "Rather to Host 'Fearless' Show on HDNet," *Washington Post*, July 10, 2006.

164   Barry Diller: Fabrikant, "Diller, a Late Entry."

164   Charles Dolan: *Forbes*, Oct. 9, 2006.

164   John Malone: Johnnie L. Roberts, "The King of HDTV," *Newsweek*, Jan. 22, 2007.

164   Craig McCaw: Stephanie Mehta, "A New Wireless Winner," *Fortune*, Aug. 6, 2006.

164   Rupert Murdoch: Jon Fine, "Rupert Speaks His Mind," *BusinessWeek* online, Feb. 8, 2007.

164   Larry Page: For company mission, see google.com.

164   Turner's good friend: Ken Auletta, "John Malone: Flying Solo," *The New Yorker*, Feb. 7, 1994, pp. 58–59. Malone is quoted as saying, "I play hardball. But I'm very direct. And I win frequently." Also see Daniel Pearl and Laura Landro, "Uneasy Union: Turner's Frustration Raises Odds of a Split with Cable Partners," *Wall Street Journal*, Apr. 12, 1992.

165   Johnson subsequently fell off: Lea Goldman, *Forbes* coeditor of World's Richest People list, in an online chat, Mar. 3, 2004, at forbes.com/lists/2004/03/03/0303chat_transcript.html.

166   DirecTV plans to launch: Johnnie L. Roberts, "The King of HDTV," *Newsweek*, Jan. 22, 2007, pp. 44–45.

167   Both have recently divorced: Bryan Burrough, "Sleeping with the Fishes," *Vanity Fair*, Dec. 2006, pp. 251, 260, for Redstone's blind date, marriage in April 2003, and plans for succession.

167   "I am Viacom": Thomas S. Mulligan, Charles Duhigg, and Claudia Eller, "Last of the Titans," *Los Angeles Times*, Sept. 18, 2006.

167   In 1990, however, News Corporation owed: Epstein, *The Big Picture*, p. 64.

168   Murdoch's News Corporation: Owen Gibson, "Internet Means End for Media Barons, Says Murdoch," *The Guardian*, Mar. 14, 2006, reports Murdoch's declaration of "a second age of discovery" created by the Internet. Murdoch also said he'd underestimated the power of the Web—"a creative, destructive technology" still "in its infancy yet breaking and remaking everything in its path."

168   "humiliating": Sumner Redstone on *The Charlie Rose Show*, Oct. 4, 2006.

168   "To find something comparable": Spencer Reiss, "His Space," *Wired*, July 2006.

168   His goal, Murdoch says now: Peter Kafka, "Blue Sky," *Forbes*, Feb. 12, 2007.

169   He realized from his exposure: Roy C. Smith, *The Wealth Creators* (New York: St. Martin's Press, 2001), pp. 38–42.

169   Not coincidentally, the company: Carol J. Loomis, "Bloomberg's Money Machine," *Fortune*, Apr. 5, 2007.

170   Murdoch hired Diller to create: Ken Auletta, "Barry Diller's Search for the Future," *The New Yorker*, Feb. 22, 1993. Auletta reports that Diller told Murdoch he wanted "to be a principal, not just a well-paid employee"; Murdoch said no, "there's only one principal," and Diller quit (p. 49).

170   He made another fortune: Bruck, *When Hollywood Had a King*, says that when Diller sold the USA network to Vivendi, he would "essentially get $11.7 billion of value in return for assets . . . bought for $4.1 billion" (p. 454).

170   He also paid himself handsomely: Geraldine Fabrikant, "Diller, a Late Entry, Takes the Prize for Highest Paid," *New York Times*, Oct. 26, 2006. Diller's earnings were $295 million in 2005. Adding in stock options from IAC/Interactive and Expedia gave him even more: $469.7 million.

171   As film historian David Thomson points out: David Thomson, *The Whole Equation: A History of Hollywood* (New York: Knopf, 2004), p. 342.

171   "I've earned enough": Lesley Stahl, *60 Minutes* interview with George Lucas, CBS-TV, Mar. 13, 2005, www.cbsnews.com/stories/2005/03/10/60minutes/main679325.shtml.

172   It's estimated that: Ronald Grover, "Steven Spielberg: The Storyteller, How Hollywood's Most Successful Director Sustains His Creative Empire," *BusinessWeek*, July 13, 1998. The table "Anatomy of a Spielberg Hit" lays out how the director walked away with $294 million of the $951 million his dino thriller earned from ticket sales, merchandising, video sales, and fees from TV/cable. This excludes foreign film sales and sales to airlines, military bases, and other outlets.

173   How ironic, given that: www.answers.com/topic/oprah-winfrey and Oprah's spokesperson. Winfrey was told she needed plastic surgery while she was an anchorwoman in Baltimore; she refused.

173   Her salary as Chicago's most popular TV talk host: Information in this paragraph and the following two paragraphs comes from Robert La Franco, "Piranha Is Good," *Forbes*, Oct. 16, 1995.

174   In 2005 alone, she gave nearly $52 million: Mmoma Ejiofor, "Generous Celebs," *Forbes*, May 5, 2006.

174   "If I lost control of the business": Patrica Sellers, "The Business of Being Oprah," *Fortune*, Apr. 1, 2002.

8. Beyond Wall Street

Sources interviewed for this chapter: Leon Black (Forbes 400); John C. Coffee, professor of law, Columbia University Law School; Steven Drobny, author, *Inside the House of Money* (2006), and cofounder and partner of Drobny Global Advisors, an international macro research firm; Ted Forstmann (Forbes 400); Charles Geisst, professor of finance, School of Business, Manhattan College, New York, and author, *Wall Street: A History* (1997); Vinod Khosla (Forbes 400); Jerome Kohlberg (Forbes 400); Bruce Kovner (Forbes 400); Dick Kramlich, cofounder and general partner of New Enterprise Associates, Menlo Park, Calif., and former chairman and president of the National Venture Capital Association; Steven Pearlstein, business columnist, *Washington Post;* Michael Peltz, executive editor, *Institutional Investor* and *Alpha;* Julian Robertson (Forbes 400); Arthur Rock (Forbes 400); David Skeel, professor of corporate law, University of Pennsylvania Law School, and author, *Icarus in the Boardroom* (2005); Roy Smith, professor of entrepreneurship and finance, New York University, and author, *The Wealth Creators* (2001); Charles Taylor, National Venture Capital Association; David B. Williams, managing partner, Williams Trading LLC, Stamford, Conn. Also brief overview, Stephen Schwarzman (Forbes 400). One Wall Street banker with thirty years of experience on the Street wished to remain anonymous. No negative material was used from this source. Unless otherwise noted, quotations in the text from the above sources come from interviews conducted by the editors and writers of the book.

176 Allowed in once a year: Ianthe Jeanne Dugan and Anita Raghavan, "The Atlas of New Money," *Wall Street Journal,* Dec. 16, 2006.

176 The new crowd: Nina Munk, "Greenwich's Outrageous Fortunes," *Vanity Fair,* July 2006; also Dugan and Raghavan, "The Atlas of New Money."

176 According to *Alpha* magazine: Information on the salaries of Simons and the other hedge fund managers is from Stephen Taub, "The Top 25 Moneymakers: The New Tycoons," *Alpha,* Apr. 20, 2007, alphamagazine.com.

177 Hedge funds now control: financialpolicy.org/fpfspb30.htm. According to financial policy.org, 18 to 22 percent of the trading volume on the New York Stock Exchange and 30 to 35 percent on the London Stock Exchange is by hedge funds. Seventy-five percent of actively traded convertible bonds are held by hedge funds. Hedge funds account for 45 percent of trading volume in emerging market bonds, 47 percent in distressed debt, and 25 percent in high-yield bonds. Plus, they account for over half the trading volume in credit derivatives—an exploding market, thanks to their involvement.

177 In early 2007, for example: Jenny Anderson, "SEC Is Looking at Stock Trading," *New York Times,* Feb. 6, 2007.

177 "Only the final conflagration": Edmund C. Stedman, ed., *New York Stock Exchange* (1905; reprint, New York: Greenwich Press, 1969), p. 100.

177 You can still make a princely fortune: Jenny Anderson, "Record Profits Elicit Big Bonuses on Wall Street," *New York Times,* Jan. 12, 2006.

179 Kohlberg Kravis Roberts & Company: Sarah Bartlett, *The Money Machine: How KKR Manufactured Profits and Power* (New York: Warner Books, 1991). The material on the history of KKR comes primarily from Bartlett, *The Money Machine;* Bryan Burrough and John Helyar, *Barbarians at the Gate: The Fall of RJR Nabisco* (New York: Harper & Row, 1990); and interview with Jerome Kohlberg.

180 "They went out to the state pension funds": Interview with anonymous Wall Street banker, Nov. 2006.

180 Rather than 8 percent from blue-chip stocks: Bartlett, *The Money Machine,* p. 128.

180 By 1983 KKR claimed: Burrough and Helyar, *Barbarians at the Gate,* p. 140.

180 Soon their fees grew: Interview with Kohlberg.

180 They took Gibson private: Burrough and Helyar, *Barbarians at the Gate,* p. 140.

180 Peter G. Peterson: Andy Serwer, "Wall Street's Hottest Hand: Blackstone CEO Has Built a Powerhouse Unlike Any Other," *Fortune,* June 9, 2003.

182 "In the eighties": Interview with anonymous Wall Street banker, Nov. 2006.

183 It was a "casino society": Burrough and Helyar, *Barbarians at the Gate*, p. 515. Most of the information on the LBO frenzy comes from this source.

183 Another new wrinkle: Scott Paltrow, "Junk Bonds Are Now Out and Ted Forstmann Is In," *Los Angeles Times*, Aug. 26, 1990.

183 He based his conclusion: [Unsigned,] "Going After the Crooks," *Time* cover story, Dec. 1, 1986. Also James B. Stewart, *Den of Thieves* (New York: Simon & Schuster, 1990), p. 53.

183 At first Milken underwrote: Stewart, *Den of Thieves*, p. 54. Information about Victor Posner is from ibid., pp. 112–20, which details his predatory financial ploys and his taste for teenage girls.

184 Then, in 1984, Milken began using: Burrough and Helyar, *Barbarians at the Gate*, p. 141.

184 Black famously conceived: Jerry Useem, "20 That Made History," *Fortune*, June 27, 2005, as well as interview with Black.

184 Carl Icahn, for example: Information about Marshall Field's comes from Charles Geisst, *Wall Street: A History* (New York: Oxford University Press, 1997), p. 339; information about Carl Icahn and Texaco is from Roy C. Smith, *The Wealth Creators: The Rise of Today's Rich and Super-Rich* (New York: St. Martin's Press, 2001), p. 107.

184 Not all of his deals: Geisst, *Wall Street*, p. 340. By 2006, Icahn's fortune had ballooned to $9.7 billion.

184 Then he earned $30 million: famoustexans.com entry on Boone Pickens.

185 As Milken once bragged: Stewart, *Den of Thieves*, picture caption opposite p. 240.

185 Kohlberg excoriated: Bartlett, *The Money Machine*, p. 214. Kohlberg stayed a limited partner and sued Henry Kravis and George Roberts for withholding his share of profits. The suit was settled for an undisclosed sum.

185 Undeterred, Kravis and Roberts: Stewart, *Den of Thieves*, p. 469.

185 Drexel Burnham Lambert: Ibid., p. 470.

185 It was a surreal juncture: Ibid., pp. 509–10.

186 Carl Icahn laughed loudest: Smith, *The Wealth Creators*, p. 108. Also see transcripts .cnn.com/TRANSCRIPTS/0008/18/mlld.00.html.

186 Milken pleaded guilty: Stewart, *Den of Thieves*, pp. 511, 536, 519, 506–7.

186 By then, some major LBOs: Burrough and Helvar, *Barbarians at the Gate*, p. 513; Stewart, *Den of Thieves*, pp. 503–4. For West Point–Pepperell, see www.answers.com/topic/west-point-pepperell-inc.

186 But millions of small investors: Stewart, *Den of Thieves*, p. 500.

187 Modest and arrogant at once, Buffett: Information about Berkshire Hathaway's revenues is drawn from the 2006 Fortune 500; www.money.cnn.com/magazines/fortune/fortune500/snapshots/194.html.

187 "If I wanted to": Vanessa Grigoriades, "Billionaires Are Free," *New York*, Nov. 6, 2006.

187 He invested most of that float: Smith, *The Wealth Creators*, pp. 140–58.

188 He added many more companies: Executive Jet data comes from Anthony Bianco, "The Warren Buffett You Don't Know," *BusinessWeek*, July 5, 1999, cover story.

188 Its book value has grown: This figure is Warren Buffett's, from his 2005 annual chairman's report to shareholders, at berkshirehathaway.com/letters/2005ltr.pdf. That report mentions a $49 billion float in 2005. For information on Berkshire Hathaway subsidiaries, see quote.morningstar.com/Quote/Quote.aspx?ticker=BRK.B.

188 Not that Buffett doesn't have: Information on Buffett's several scares in investing comes from Dan Seligman, "Want to Get Rich?" *Forbes*, Oct. 13, 1997. Additional information about General Re fallout appeared in Marcy Gordon, "Fraud Charges for Three Former

General Re Executives, One From AIG," Associated Press, Feb. 2, 2006, and "AIG Delays Report on Accounting Troubles," Associated Press, Mar. 30, 2005.

188   his license plate: Catherine Rentz Pernot, "Warren Buffett's Billion Dollar Secrets," *Missourian,* Mar. 5, 2006.

188   He has beaten the S&P index: 2005 Chairman's Report, Berkshire Hathaway.

188   "There is class war all right": Ben Stein, "In Class Warfare, Guess Which Class Is Winning," *New York Times,* Nov. 26, 2006.

189   Some in the financial world: Geisst, *Wall Street,* p. 358.

189   Number 153 on the Forbes 400 list: The Milken Institute, www.mikemilken.com.

189   However, by the nature of the business: Interview with Arthur Rock; Charles Taylor, vice president of research, National Venture Capital Association. Statistics on NVCA Web site show that only 14 percent of companies VCs seed have the happy outcome of going public; a third are acquired; the rest fail.

190   Since 1986 the average return: "Venture Capital Performance, Q3 '06," under heading "Industry Stats and News" on the the National Venture Capital Association Web site. A chart in that report by Thomson Financial/National Venture Capital Association shows how investors fared over the last twenty years in venture capital and LBOs. VC returned 16.50 percent; LBOs, 13.20 percent. Private equity, which includes LBOs, has returned 14 percent to investors since 1986. All beat the S&P 500 over the last twenty years. It returned 9.7 percent to investors; the NASDAQ, 11.4 percent.

190   The early venture capitalists: Information on Doriot comes from Steven P. Galante, "An Overview of the Venture Capital Industry and Emerging Trends," www.vcinstitute .org/materials/galante.html.

190   But the term *VC* didn't exist: Rock is credited with coining the term *venture capital* in 1965. See www.siliconiran.com.

190   Rock, now an octogenerian: Information on Rock comes primarily from the interview with him.

190   In 2001 his Intel stake: Forbes 400 list, *Forbes,* Oct. 8, 2001.

190   A shy and intimidatingly quiet man: Michael Moritz, "Arthur Rock: The Best Long-Ball Hitter Around," *Time,* Aug. 25, 2006.

191   KPCB was a founding investor: Its $8 million investment in Amazon.com was worth $60 million by the time of the company's initial public offering in 1997. Laura Rich, "How John Doerr, the Old Prospector, Finally Struck Google," *New York Times,* May 3, 2004.

191   KPCB's original $12.5 million investment: Forbes 400 list, *Forbes,* Oct. 9, 2006.

191   Today Doerr has raised funds: Clive Thompson, "New York's Very Weird Five-Year Forecast," *New York,* Nov. 13, 2006.

191   "Green tech," he believes: Terence Chea, "Doerr Firm Invests in 'Green Technology,' " Associated Press, Apr. 10, 2006.

191   "Energy is subject to the same sort": Laura Locke, "The Green-Tech Venture Capitalist," *Time,* Oct. 23, 2006.

192   In 2006 VCs poured $727 million: Matt Richtel, "Tech Barons Take on New Project: Energy Policy," *New York Times,* Jan. 29, 2007.

192   For his investment efforts: www.legalaffairs.org/issues/November-December-2005feature_ skeel_novdec05.msp.

192   Between 1962 and 1966 he outperformed the top: "Brief History of Hedge Funds," www .capmgt.com/brief_history.html.

193   In 1969, at age thirty-nine: Connie Bruck, "The World According to Soros," *The New Yorker,* Jan. 23, 1995. Much of the information on Soros comes from this article. Also Gary Weiss and Gail E. Schares, "The Man Who Moves Markets," *BusinessWeek* cover story, Aug. 23, 1993.

193 Charges of insider trading: *International Herald Tribune*, www.iht.com/articles/2006/12/13/bloomberg/bxsoros.php.

193 But it also earned: Smith, *The Wealth Creators*, pp. 173–76.

193 He sometimes couldn't walk: Jane Meyer, "The Money Man," *The New Yorker*, Oct. 18, 2004.

193 In another gamble: Joshua Cooper Ramo, "The Price of Failure," *Time*, Sept. 7, 1998.

193 In 1977 he signed: Lyle Crowley, "George Soros," *New York Times Magazine*, Apr. 3, 1994.

194 "I don't play the game": Soros, quoted in Steven Drobny, *Inside the House of Money: Top Hedge Fund Traders on Profiting in a Global Market* (Hoboken, N.J.: John Wiley & Sons, 2006), p. 2.

194 Closing his Quantum Fund: Ibid., p. 30.

194 He kept buying: Drobny, *Inside the House of Money*, pp. 257–58, recollected by former Tiger Management trader Dwight Anderson.

195 "Are we right about this situation?": Robertson, quoted ibid., p. 248.

195 "He had a high tolerance": Interview with former Tiger Management trader who requested anonymity.

195 "Some investors probably got": Interview with Julian Robertson. Robertson says he is still liquidating Tiger's investments, which have been under contract until now, including a railroad in Brazil.

195 These days most of the largest hedge funds: *Absolute Return*'s annual ranking of the largest hedge funds, Mar. 5, 2007.

196 If only you had invested: Forbes 400 lists in 2006, 2005, 2002, and 1999; [Unsigned,] "The Berkshire Bunch," *Forbes*, Oct. 12, 1998; and 2005 Chairman's Report for reference to Munger and Buffett tap dancing to work every day.

197 The rise in the value of AutoNation: Patricia Sellers, "Eddie Lampert Is . . . the Best Investor of His Generation," *Fortune*, Feb. 8, 2006.

197 "For Lampert, investing is": Michael Peltz, e-mail exchange with author, Feb. 2007.

197 "Eddie Lampert has not turned around": Steven Pearlstein, "Pearlstein Live," call-in discussion on Oct. 19, 2005, www.washingtonpost.com/wp-dyn/content/discussion/2005/10/18/DI2005101800731.html?nav=rss_business.

198 "Thrashing through a lot of trades": Interview with anonymous financial advisor.

199 He denies the charges: "Lampf, Lipkid, Prupis & Petigrow Announces $4 Billion Class-Action Lawsuit by Biovail Shareholders Filed Against SEC Capital, Steven A. Cohen, Gradient Analytics, Banc of America Securities and B of A Analyst David Maris," *Businesswire*, Mar. 24, 2006.

199 It has an outdoor ice-skating rink: Susan Pulliam, "Private Money: The New Financial Order—the Hedge Fund King Is Getting Nervous," *Wall Street Journal*, Sept. 16, 2006.

200 Private equity firms can afford: www.breakingviews.com; "Private Equity's Buying Spree May Clog Up the Exit Doors Later," *Wall Street Journal Europe*, Jan. 5–7, 2007.

200 The 1980s are no longer the golden age: Jason Singer and Henny Sender, "Growing Funds Fuel Buyout Boom," *Wall Street Journal*, Oct. 26, 2006.

201 "Any fool can buy a company": Henny Sender, "Inside the Minds of Kravis, Roberts," *Wall Street Journal*, Feb. 27, 2007.

9. Conspicuous Consumption

Sources interviewed or corresponded with for this chapter: Nelson Aldrich Jr., author, *Old Money: The Mythology of Wealth in America* (1988); Mark Cuban (Forbes 400); Daniel Gilbert (Forbes 400); Steve Greenberg, Allen & Company; Dr. Lee Hausner, of the family-wealth consulting firm IFF Advisors; Tobias Meyer, worldwide head of contemporary sales, Sotheby's; Todd Millay, executive director of Wharton Global Family Alliance; Farhad Vladi, of Vladi Private Islands. Unless otherwise noted, quotations in the text from the above sources come from interviews conducted by the editors and writers of the book.

205 The average cost of a home in the Hamptons: Kathleen M. Howley, "Hamptons Real Estate Sales Slow as Rising Rates Sideline Buyers," Bloomberg.com, Aug. 4, 2006.

205 In 2005 pharmaceuticals tycoon: Forbes.com.

205 But nothing prepared: Nina Munk, "Greenwich's Outrageous Fortunes," *Vanity Fair,* July 2006.

205 Rennert made his fortune: Ibid. Much of the information on how Rennert made his fortune comes from Munk's article.

206 The centerpiece of the five-building compound: Miriam Hill, "Wealth Makes Waves at N.Y. Beach Resort," *Philadelphia Inquirer,* July 19, 2004.

206 The estate is supplied with energy: Munk, "Greenwich's Outrageous Fortunes."

206 The estate is valued at $185 million: Mary Williams Walsh, "Pension Battle May Entangle Mogul's Home," *New York Times,* Feb. 3, 2006.

206 In 1998 Rennert tried: Munk, "Greenwich's Outrageous Fortunes."

206 Neighbors have called the house "arrogant": Julia C. Mead, "At Home in Versailles on the Atlantic," *New York Times,* July 4, 2004.

206 The writer Kurt Vonnegut: Ibid. Vonnegut stayed put. He died on April 11, 2007.

209 "To gain and to hold the esteem": Thorstein Veblen, quoted in James W. Michaels, "The Mass-Market Rich," *Forbes,* Oct. 9, 2000.

209 In Veblen's day: See Arthur T. Vanderbilt II, *Fortune's Children: The Fall of the House of Vanderbilt* (New York: William Morrow, 1989), for more details on the period.

210 In 2007 timber baron Tim Blixseth: Forbes.com.

210 Media mogul John Kluge: Information on the mansions in this section comes mostly from Forbes.com.

210 On the West Coast: Patricia Leigh Brown, "Techno-Dwellings for the Cyber-Egos of the Mega-Rich," *New York Times,* Aug. 4, 1996.

210 Multimillion-dollar homes: "Real Estate of Bay Area Billionaires," http://blog.360 .yahoo.com/blog-2Ojrgz8zaa.tuoHABvthpbldl6KImA--?cq=1&p=158.

210 Few areas of America: Munk, "Greenwich's Outrageous Fortunes."

211 For a few heady months in 2000: [Unsigned,] "Gates Loses Title as World's Richest Man," news.com, Apr. 2000.

211 In 2007 the online real-estate Web site Zillow.com: Jeffrey M. O'Brien, "What's Your House Really Worth?" *Fortune,* Feb. 19, 2007.

212 The building is about as ecologically friendly: See www.usnews.com/usnews/tech/ billgate/gates.htm; virtual tour of Bill Gates's house taken from *The Road Ahead* CD-ROM viewable at video.google.com/videoplay?docid=8431004719814226551&hl= en. Also see "Mr. Gates and Mr. Allen Build Their Dream Houses," *Forbes,* Oct. 19, 1992.

213 The estate even has: Matthew Symonds, "Absolutely Excessive!" *Vanity Fair,* Oct. 1, 2005.

213 "I'm worried, Larry": Carrie Kirby, "Inside Look at a Billionaire's Budget," *San Francisco Chronicle,* Jan. 31, 2006.

213 The following year Ellison purchased: www.powerandmotoryacht.com/megayachts/ 2006%2Damerica%2Dlargest%2Dyachts.

213 *Vanity Fair* described the interior: Symonds, "Absolutely Excessive!"

213 Allen's boat is noted: Kiri Blakeley, "Bigger Than Yours: Billionaire Yachts," Forbes.com slideshow.

213 And Ellison's conspicuous spending: Adam Cohen, "Peeping Larry," *Time,* July 10, 2000.

213 In recent years he has bought swaths: Symonds, "Absolutely Excessive!"

213 As for women: Ibid.

213 During the 1980s, Trump bought: Robert Frank, "Rich vs. Richer: Old Money Isn't Having a Ball in Palm Beach," *Wall Street Journal,* May 20, 2005.

213 He also bought *Nabila:* Kevin Wheatley, "How to Spend It," *Financial Times,* Aug. 8, 1992.

213 Oprah Winfrey is another big buyer: Bob Goldsborough, "Oprah's Empire: Talk-Show Queen Adds to Her Chicago Real-estate Holdings," *Chicago Tribune,* Dec. 11, 2006.

214 For a few brief seasons: George Vecsey, "Sports of the Times: Will Donald Now Become a Big Wheel?" *New York Times,* Dec. 7, 1988.

214 And in 2004, as an investment: Forbes homes slideshow, www.forbes.com/2006/07/24/cx_sc_0724homeslide_top_3.html?partner=yahoouk%0A%0A.

214 "Through it all": Stephane Fitch, "The Real Apprentices," *Forbes,* Oct. 9, 2006.

214 In New York alone: Information on Trump's various real-estate holdings comes from Stephane Fitch, "What Is Trump Worth?," Forbes.com, Sept. 21, 2006.

214 A 2000 Gallup poll: Theodore Spencer, "What Does Trump Really Want?" *Fortune,* Apr. 3, 2000.

215 In the late nineteenth century: Vanderbilt, *Fortune's Children,* p. 110.

215 When Saul Steinberg's twenty-five-year-old daughter: Leslie Eaton, "Selling the Farm, Park Avenue Style; For a Pair of Socialites, It's Out with the Ormolu," *New York Times,* May 27, 2000.

215 Wedding guests such as Norman Mailer and Barbara Walters: Leslie Eaton, "The Steinbergs' Fixer-Upper," *New York Observer,* Apr. 1, 2002. Also Judith H. Dobrzynski, "Books: Lifestyles of the Rich and Shameless," *BusinessWeek,* Nov. 13, 1989.

215 The following year: Joseph N. DiStefano, "Life Is Grand," *Philadelphia Inquirer,* Dec. 16, 2001.

215 Malcolm Forbes understood the appeal: Alan Riding, "Tangier Journal: As in Old Days, the Jet Set Comes in for a Landing," *New York Times,* Aug. 21, 1989.

215 The almost $2.5 million tab: Michael Mewshaw, "Echoes of Sin City," *New York Times,* Oct. 18, 1998.

215 More recently, financier Stephen Schwarzman spent: Page Six, "No Room for Henry at Bash," *New York Post,* Feb. 15, 2007.

215 Her most famous party: Vanderbilt, *Fortune's Children,* p. 121.

216 The two left the table: Michael Gross, *740 Park* (New York: Random House, 2005), p. 497.

216 The 1990s ushered in: James Reginato and Joseph Steuer, "Gilty Pleasures: At Home with Mercedes and Sid," *Dallas Morning News,* Oct. 4, 1992.

217 New York socialite Nan Kempner: Bob Colacello, "Nan in Full," *Vanity Fair,* Apr. 1, 2005.

217 Therefore, the future wife: Julie Connelly, "The CEO's Second Wife," *Fortune,* Aug. 28, 1989.

217 Georgette Mosbacher told *Texas Monthly* magazine: Ibid.

217 As if to drive home: Page Six, "$3 Million Party."

217 If the Forbes 400 had an address: Gross, *740 Park.* Most of the information about 740 Park comes from Gross's book.

218 "meant he was going up in life": Laura Steinberg, quoted in Johanna Berkman, "The Fall of the House of Steinberg," *New York,* June 19, 2000.

218 "A co-op at 740 Park": Gross, *740 Park,* p. 510.

218 Displays of wealth: Paul Fussell, *Notes on Class: A Guide Through the American Status System* (New York: Touchstone/Simon & Schuster, 1992), p. 30.

218 According to the American novelist Alison Lurie: Lurie, quoted ibid., p. 112.

219 Lauren started his multibillion-dollar empire: Cathy Horyn, "Chasing the Threads in

the Life of Ralph Lauren," *New York Times*, Jan. 12, 2003; and Phyllis Berman, "The Wall Street Fashion Game," *Forbes*, Mar. 4, 2002.

219 Costing $500,000: Vanderbilt, *Fortune's Children*, p. 25.

220 The Top Ten U.S.-Owned Yachts: *Power & Motoryacht* list of America's 100 Largest Yachts, 2006.

221 But by 2005 there were 6,000: J. Bonasia, "Oracle's Ellison Edges Microsoft's Allen in Battle of the Really, Really Big Boats," *Investor's Business Daily*, Mar. 17, 2005.

221 Paul Allen, for one, owns: Diane M. Byrne, "America's Largest 100 Yachts, 2006," powerandmotoryacht.com; Diane M. Byrne, "The World's Largest 100 Yachts, 2004," powerandmotoryacht.com.

221 Taking sailing to the next level: Vanderbilt, *Fortune's Children*, pp. 280, 411.

221 Nowadays billionaires are prepared: Erika Brown and Daniel Fisher, "The Thriller B's: Billionaires by the Boatload Maneuver for the America's Cup," *Forbes*, Sept. 30, 2002.

221 Ellison spent $194 million: Kirby, "Inside Look at Billionaire's Budget."

221 Ted Turner was the first: William C. Symonds, "Captain Comeback—Ted Turner Is Back from the Brink and Thinking Big Again," *BusinessWeek*, July 17, 1989.

221 But with the help: Bryan Burrough, "Wild Bill Koch's Grand Designs," *Vanity Fair*, June 1994.

222 Texas billionaire Bunker Hunt: Most of the information about Bunker and Lamar Hunt's sports activities comes from Harry Hurt III, *Texas Rich* (New York: W. W. Norton, 1982).

222 "All through our school years": Ibid., p. 329.

222 As Warren Buffett wrote: Janet Whitman, "Open Buffett," *New York Post*, Mar. 2, 2007.

222 And at a match between soccer teams: Glenn F. Bunting, "A Denver Billionaire's Invisible Hand," *Los Angeles Times*, July 23, 2006.

223 That cost him $500,000: John Dorschner, "For NBA Owners, a Contrast in Style," *Miami Herald*, June 11, 2006.

223 As head of Kroenke Sports Enterprises: Jack Bell, "Thinking Globally, Rapids and Arsenal See Win-Win Deal," *New York Times*, Feb. 14, 2007.

223 Carnival Cruise Line heir Arison: Dorschner, "For NBA Owners."

223 In 2004 Arison hired: Chris Broussard, "O'Neal Trade Shifts Balance of Power," *New York Times*, July 15, 2004.

223 He bought the Tigers franchise: Forbes.com.

224 Glazer borrowed almost all: Ibid.

224 The Microsoft billionaire bought: Kurt Badenhausen, "How Not to Run a Sports Franchise," *Forbes*, July 3, 2006.

225 It is said that hedge fund head Steve Cohen: Munk, "Greenwich's Outrageous Fortunes."

226 A study by NYU's Jianping Mei and Michael Moses: [Unsigned,] *The Economist*, Jan. 13, 2007.

228 When the apparent double standard: David D'Arcy, *The Art Newspaper*, 2002, republished at www.forbes.com/collecting/2002/07/03/0703/hot.html.

228 "Nobody lucky enough": [Unsigned,] "Perot Miffed with Listing Among Rich," *Kilgore [Texas] News Herald*, Aug. 29, 1982.

228 Warren Buffett, the nation's second-richest man: Forbes.com.

228 Likewise, the recluse Richard Wendt: Elisa Williams, "Work Speaks for Itself," *Forbes*, Oct. 9, 2000.

228 Wynn, who suffers from a rare disease: Nick Poumgarten, "The $40-million Elbow," *The New Yorker*, Oct. 23, 2006.

229 In the late 1990s: Michaels, "The Mass-Market Rich."

229 "Theirs is not old wealth": Dinesh D'Souza, "A Century of Wealth: The Billionaire Next Door," *Forbes*, Oct. 11, 1999.

229 "Earlier this century": David Brooks, *Bobos in Paradise: The New Upper Class and How They Got There* (New York: Simon & Schuster, 2001), p. 47.

10. Heirs

Sources interviewed for this chapter: Nelson W. Aldrich Jr., author, *Old Money: The Mythology of Wealth in America* (1988); Natalie A. Black; Peter Buffett; Susie Buffett; Sara Hamilton of Family Office Exchange; Dr. Lee Hausner, of the family-wealth consulting firm IFF Advisors; Andrew Keyt, executive director of the Chicago Family Business Center at Loyola University; Herbert V. Kohler Jr. (Forbes 400); Todd Millay, executive director of Wharton Global Family Alliance; Ross Perot (Forbes 400); Ross Perot Jr.; Ivanka Trump; Rod Wood, Wilmington Trust. Unless otherwise noted, quotations in the text from the above sources come from interviews conducted by the editors and writers of the book.

230 Huntington Hartford II lost it all: Michael Lewis, "From Riches to Rags," *New York Times,* Feb. 3, 1991.

230 When *Forbes* tracked Hartford down: Lisa Gubernick, "That's My Excuse, Anyway," *Forbes,* Oct. 28, 1985.

230 Seven years later: [Unsigned,] "A. & P. Heir in Bankruptcy," *New York Times,* Mar. 25, 1992.

230 He was groomed for society: Lewis, "From Riches to Rags."

230 "I was in my 20s": Gubernick, "That's My Excuse, Anyway."

230 Hartford's daughter Juliet: *Born Rich,* a 2003 documentary directed by Jamie Johnson, shoutfactory.com.

230 But a succession of bad luck: Lewis, "From Riches to Rags."

232 His philanthropic ventures: Gubernick, "That's My Excuse, Anyway."

232 "The older I get": Nelson W. Aldrich Jr., *Old Money: The Mythology of Wealth in America* (New York: Allworth Press, 1996), p. 129.

232 "To the self who inherits it": Ibid., p. 126.

233 To locate the only inheritor: [Unsigned,] "The Texaco Bankruptcy—Family Feud," *Wall Street Journal,* Apr. 14, 1987.

234 A century before Warren Buffett: Landon Thomas Jr., "A Gift Between Friends," *New York Times,* June 27, 2006.

234 "The parent who leaves his son": James K. Glassman, "A Century of Wealth: Inheritance and Sloth," *Forbes,* Oct. 11, 1999.

234 "From our earliest days": David Rockefeller Sr., quoted in William Davis, *The Rich: A Study of the Species* (London: Sidgwick & Jackson, 1983), p. 15.

235 Warren Buffett has devoted his life: Information in this box comes from annual Forbes 400 lists.

235 In David Rockefeller Sr.'s *Memoirs:* David Rockefeller, *Memoirs* (New York: Random House, 2003), p. 33.

235 Likewise, legendary Texas oilman: Harry Hurt III, *Texas Rich* (New York: W. W. Norton, 1982), p. 107.

235 "Give them enough": Carol Loomis, "Warren Buffett Gives It Away," *Fortune,* July 10, 2006.

236 Although Ivanka went to Choate Rosemary Hall: Chris Weinkopf, "John Kerry's America: Pride, Privilege, and Presumption," *American Enterprise,* Oct. 1, 2004.

236 He amassed a fortune: Tracie Rochon, "Fred C. Trump, Postwar Master Builder of Housing for Middle Class, Dies at 93," obituary, *New York Times,* June 26, 1999.

236 According to *Forbes,* Donald: Alan Farnham, *Forbes Great Success Stories: Twelve Tales of Victory Wrested from Defeat* (New York: John Wiley & Sons, 2000), p. 139.

238   Nicky has her own clothing label: [Unsigned,] "Nicky Hilton Sued for Breach of Contract over 'Nicky O's Chicago' Hotel Project," Associated Press, Feb. 13, 2007.

238   Meanwhile, Paris remains: Julee Greenberg, "Paris Hilton Builds on Risqué Lifestyle," *Women's Wear Daily,* Jan. 5, 2007.

239   Her father told the *New York Times:* Erika Kinetz, "Candy-Colored Dreams," *New York Times,* Jan. 1, 2006.

239   "They work well together": Stephane Fitch, "The Real Apprentices," *Forbes,* Oct. 16, 2006.

240   In turn, Abby Rockefeller's daughter: [Unsigned,] "Philanthropy for the 21st Century," *New York Times,* Nov. 5, 1989.

241   Commodore Vanderbilt's son Corneel: Arthur T. Vanderbilt II, *Fortune's Children* (New York: HarperCollins, 2001), p. 20.

241   During the 1980s: Information on the legal battles and the 1994 reversal of the 1985 ruling that declared Lewis Du Pont Smith mentally incompetent to handle his own affairs can be found in Maureen Orth, "Blueblood War," *Vanity Fair,* Apr. 1993; also Joe McDermott, "DuPont Heir Wants Ridge Ousted," *Allentown* [Pa.] *Morning Call,* July 18, 1996.

243   Perot Jr.'s choice of a career: Allen R. Myerson, "Ross Perot Jr., the Builder, His Stamp on Dallas," *New York Times,* July 11, 1999.

243   It is now home: Penny Cockerell, "Dreams on Steroids," *The Oklahoman,* July 25, 2006.

244   The company continued its weak performance: Kirk Shinkle, "Perot Systems Corp., Plano, Texas; Tech Services Provider Puts on a Brave Face," *Investor's Business Daily,* Dec. 9, 2004.

244   Perot Jr. has also come in for some criticism: Myerson, "Ross Perot Jr., the Builder."

245   Unlike Huntington Hartford: Christopher Winans, "Bookshelf: A Moneyed Life Full of Failure," *Wall Street Journal,* Jan. 2, 1991.

245   The company, which like all chemical companies: Alan Friedman, "Shaken to the Core: DuPont, America's Biggest Chemicals Group, Is in the Process of a Radical Restructuring," *Financial Times,* Aug. 18, 1992.

245   About one-third of the workforce: Robert Lenzner and Carrie Shook, "There Will Always Be a DuPont," *Forbes,* Oct. 13, 1997.

247   But before the wreckers moved in: Rockefeller, *Memoirs,* pp. 188–89.

248   "The Grantor is more concerned": Rockefeller, quoted in Carol Loomis, "The Rockefellers: End of a Dynasty?" *Fortune,* Aug. 4, 1986.

248   Even the original 1932 trusts: Loomis, "The Rockefellers: End of a Dynasty?"

248   By the 1970s and 1980s: Ibid.

248   "Our debates and disagreements": Rockefeller, *Memoirs,* p. 336.

248   Herbert V. Kohler Jr. faced a similar problem: Richard A. Melcher, "Can Kohler Keep It All in the Family?" *BusinessWeek,* May 4, 1998.

248   When he assumed control: Gary Samuels, "Generational Investor," *Forbes,* Oct. 16, 1995.

249   He announced a one-for-twenty reverse stock split: Ibid.

249   A concerted effort by opponents: Carl Hulse, "Battle on Estate Tax," *New York Times,* June 14, 2002.

250   A century ago: Information on family trusts comes mainly from interviews with Sara Hamilton of Family Office Exchange and Todd Millay, executive director of Wharton Global Family Alliance.

11. Family Feuds

Sources interviewed for this chapter: Joseph Astrachan, professor of family business, Kennesaw State University; Joan DiFuria, codirector, Money, Meaning & Choices Institute; Stephen

Goldbart, codirector, Money, Meaning & Choices Institute; Judith Stern Peck, director of the Money, Values and Family Life Project, Ackerman Institute for the Family; James Tisch, president and CEO, Loews Corp.; Thayer Cheatham Willis, author, *Navigating the Dark Side of Wealth: A Life Guide for Inheritors* (2003); William D. Zabel, founding partner, Schulte Roth & Zabel, LLP. Unless otherwise noted, quotations in the text from the above sources come from interviews conducted by the editors and writers of the book.

253   "perhaps the nastiest family feud": Brian O'Reilly and Patty De Llosa, "The Curse on the Koch Brothers," *Fortune,* Feb. 17, 1997.

253   Over the decades: Bryan Burrough, "Wild Bill Koch's Grand Designs," *Vanity Fair,* June 1994.

253   "I know he feels we had bad relations": Ibid.

253   During his youth he often fought: Ibid.

253   His disappointed father had disinherited him: Leslie Wayne, "Brothers at Odds," *New York Times,* Dec. 7, 1986.

253   When his father died: O'Reilly and De Llosa, "The Curse on the Koch Brothers."

253   By the late 1970s: Leslie Wayne, "Pulling the Wraps off Koch Industries," *New York Times,* Nov. 20, 1994.

254   To this day Charles is proud: Michael Arndt, "Koch: Very Private, and a Lot Bigger," *BusinessWeek,* Nov. 16, 2005.

254   "Here I am, one of the wealthiest men": Wayne, "Brothers at Odds."

254   The younger Marshall complied: Ibid.

255   "It was an emotionally wrenching time": Ibid.

255   A temporary truce was signed: Arndt, "Koch: Very Private, and a Lot Bigger."

255   But hostilities flared again: Wayne, "Brothers at Odds."

255   "They wanted a lot of cash": Ibid.

255   The intrafamily Koch battles: Wayne, "Pulling the Wraps off Koch Industries."

255   Kicked out of Koch Industries: O'Reilly and De Llosa, "The Curse on the Koch Brothers."

255   "When people are spreading things about you": Burrough, "Wild Bill Koch's Grand Designs."

255   He hired Marc Nezer: Ibid.

255   The legal wrangling: Arndt, "Koch: Very Private and a Lot Bigger."

255   Under the nation's whistle-blower laws: [Unsigned,] "Near Misses," *Forbes,* Oct. 9, 2000.

256   They issued a joint statement: Associated Press, "Judge Clears Koch Brothers' Settlement Pact," *Wall Street Journal,* May 29, 2001.

256   Meanwhile, Koch Industries: Arndt, "Koch: Very Private and a Lot Bigger."

256   According to the U.S. Small Business Administration (SBA): "Succession Planning: Passing on the Mantle," Success Series, U.S. Small Business Administration, www.sba .gov/gopher/Business-Development.

257   In the first of many Getty lawsuits: Michael Klepper and Robert Gunther, *The Wealthy 100* (Secaucus, N.J.: Carol Publishing Group, 1996), p. 232.

257   An uncaring and cold husband: Ibid., p. 234.

257   In 1959, at the age of sixty-six: Kevin Sessums, "The Getty's Painful Legacy," *Vanity Fair,* Mar. 1992.

257   The principal financial problem: [Unsigned,] "The Texaco Bankruptcy," *Wall Street Journal,* Apr. 14, 1987.

257   For those who worked at the firm: Sessums, "The Getty's Painful Legacy."

258   But at the same time he punished: "The Texaco Bankruptcy."

258   Ronald failed in the family business: Horacio Silva, "Family Ties," *New York Times,* Sept. 23, 2001. See also Philip Coggan, "Books, Misfortunes of the Getty Dynasty,"

Financial Times, Oct. 28, 1995, and Carol Loomis, "The War Between the Gettys," *Fortune,* Jan. 21, 1985.

258   Jean Paul Jr. dropped out: Coggan, "Books, Misfortunes of the Getty Dynasty."

258   Routinely humiliated: "The Texaco Bankruptcy."

258   As with Timmy: Klepper and Gunther, *The Wealthy 100.*

258   Three years later J. Paul died: Peter Kafka, "A Century of Wealth, Decades of Dough," *Forbes,* Oct. 11, 1999.

258   When, during the early 1980s: "The Texaco Bankruptcy."

258   The legal battles raged: Ibid.

259   Eventually, Gordon laid the feud to rest: Silva, "Family Ties."

259   That was the case: Stephane Fitch, "Pritzker vs. Pritzker," *Forbes,* Nov. 24, 2003.

259   And A.N.'s sons Jay and Robert: Ford S. Worthy, "The Pritzkers: Unveiling a Private Family," *Fortune,* Apr. 23, 1988.

259   By the end of the 1990s: Jodi Wilgoren and Geraldine Fabrikant, "Knives Drawn for a $15 Billion Family Pie," *New York Times,* Dec. 11, 2002.

260   "If we are going to have a problem": Worthy, "The Pritzkers."

260   But the challenge: Mark Maremont, "How a Little Princess Won Back Her Inheritance," *SunHerald* [Gulfport, Miss.], Jan. 9, 2006.

260   In protest she adopted the stage name: Joseph Weber, "The House of Pritzker," *BusinessWeek,* Mar. 17, 2003.

260   All of the adult cousins: Wilgoren and Fabrikant, "Knives Drawn for a $15 Billion Family Pie."

260   "I expect our modus operandi": Susan Chandler and Kathy Bergen, "Inside the Pritzker Family Feud," *Chicago Tribune,* June 12, 2005.

260   Within months of Jay's death: Wilgoren and Fabrikant, "Knives Drawn for a $15 Billion Family Pie."

261   But at age eighteen: Jeremy Grant, "Youngest Cousin Puts Spotlight on the Pritzkers," *Financial Times,* Dec. 12, 2002.

261   Liesel claimed that the family: Wilgoren and Fabrikant, "Knives Drawn for a $15 Billion Family Pie."

261   When the family finally settled: Mark Maremont, "Pritzkers Settle Family Lawsuit," *Wall Street Journal,* Jan. 7, 2005.

261   "It's classic fourth-generation stuff": Grant, "Youngest Cousin Puts Spotlight on the Pritzkers."

261   According to a 2005 study: Jay Zagorsky, "Marriage and Divorce's Impact on Wealth," Center for Human Resource Research, Ohio State University, *Journal of Sociology* 41, no. 4 (2005).

263   As the story goes: David A. Kaplan, *The Silicon Boys and Their Valley of Dreams* (New York: William Morrow, 1999), p. 143.

263   Barkin got a reported $20 million: Ruth La Ferla, "Ellen Unloads," *New York Times,* Sept. 21, 2006.

263   "As exquisite as the collection is": Sally Singer, "Siren Song," *Vogue,* Aug. 1, 2006.

263   A former grocery store bag boy: John M. Broder and Patrick Healty, "How a Billionaire Friend of Bill Helps Him Do Good, and Well," *New York Times,* Apr. 23, 2006.

263   Among the items found: Associated Press, "LA Billionaire's Wife: Burkle Spied," May 20, 2006.

264   Some 120 members of the 2006 Forbes 400 list: See "Do You Want to Marry a Billionaire," p. 268.

264   Real-estate heiress Golding: Details on Perelman's multiple marriages come from Geoffrey Gray, "Ronald Perelman vs. Ellen Barkin: Scenes from a Broken Marriage," *New York,* Mar. 27, 2006. Also see Forbes.com.

265 A couple of cases of alleged billionaire peccadilloes: Indictment filed against Anthony Pellicano in the Central District of California (CR No. 05-1046 (C) RMT), Feb. 2005.

265 One month after their wedding: Alex Kuczynski, "Can a Kid Squeeze by on $320,000 a Month?" *New York Times,* Jan. 20, 2002.

265 So concerned was Kerkorian: Jean O. Pasco, "Lawsuit Spotlight Not Part of Bren Plan," *Los Angeles Times,* May 18, 2003.

265 But Lisa slapped him with a lawsuit: Kuczynski, "Can a Kid Squeeze by on $320,000 a Month?"

265 She later reportedly upped: Pasco, "Lawsuit Spotlight Not Part of Bren Plan."

265 During the course of the suit: Indictment filed against Anthony Pellicano.

265 But in the end: Pasco, "Lawsuit Spotlight Not Part of Bren Plan."

265 Gores, an Israeli immigrant: Forbes.com.

265 But back in 2000: David M. Halbfinger and Allison Hope Weiner, "Dispute over Evidence in Pellicano Wiretap Case," *New York Times,* June 13, 2006.

265 Around the same time: John Sullivan, Associated Press, "Manhattan Writer Sues Billionaire and Newspaper," *New York Times,* Mar. 23, 2007.

266 A third Gores brother, Sam: Roger Friedman, "Clinton, Madonna, Pellicano, Kabbalah: Africa Connection," FOXNews.com, Oct. 18, 2006.

266 Alec admitted to the FBI: Halbfinger and Weiner, "Dispute over Evidence in Pellicano Wiretap Case."

266 His movie-star handsome, forty-something brother: "About Platinum: Executive Profiles: Tom Gores," www.platinumequity.com.

266 "What we see a lot of": Rebecca Riddick, "Money, Death and Discord," *Daily Business Review,* Oct. 6, 2006.

266 *Forbes* magazine once likened him: Allan Sloan and Harold Seneker, "How Posner Profited Even Though His Companies Didn't," *Forbes,* Apr. 8, 1985.

266 Over three decades: Kenneth N. Gilpin, "Victor Posner, 83, Master of Hostile Takeover," obituary, *New York Times,* Feb. 13, 2002.

267 Steven won the toss: Nathan Vardi, "All in the Family," *Forbes,* Aug. 11, 2003.

267 Instead, he left nearly all his estate: Darcie Lunsford, "Posner Successor Builds Her Future," *South Florida Business Journal,* Sept. 12, 2003.

269 "It was already there": Ibid.

270 Johnson was married twice: Kristin McMurran, "The Band-Aid Heir Left All He Owned to His Widow," *People,* May 26, 1986.

270 She received, among other assets: Richard Lacayo, "Life-Styles of the Rich and Famous," *Time,* Mar. 24, 1986.

270 During the course of his marriage: McMurran, "The Band-Aid Heir Left All He Owned to His Widow."

270 The children accused their stepmother: Ibid.

270 Daughter Mary Lea, for example: Barbara Goldsmith, "Dark Inheritance: Part One," *Vanity Fair,* Oct. 1986.

270 Basia took home the prize: Frank J. Prial, "A Celebration at the Johnson Estate," *New York Times,* June 5, 1986.

270 Today, nearly seventy years old: Forbes.com.

271 Later he became president of Ashland Oil: Daniel Golden, "College Finally Got Alumnus to Pledge," *Wall Street Journal,* July 24, 2003.

271 For many years he showered her: Anne Maier and Laurel Brubaker Calkins, "Anna Nicole Smith Buries Husband," *People,* Aug. 21, 1995.

271 In 1994, at age eighty-nine: Ibid.

271 "I know people think": Ibid.

271 Marshall's immediate family and pre-Smith friends: Ibid.

271   Noticeably absent from Marshall's will: [Unsigned,] "Celebrity Lawsuits: Show Me the Money," *The Economist,* May 6, 2006.

272   It ruled that Smith could revive: Kaja Whitehouse, "Departing Shot: How to Disinherit Neatly," *Wall Street Journal,* May 6, 2006.

272   One month after the ruling: [Unsigned,] "E. Pierce Marshall, Tycoon's Son," obituary, *Washington Post,* June 28, 2006.

272   And Smith's life took a downward spiral: Jessica Robinson, "Smith's Son Died During Hospital Visit," Associated Press, Sept. 11, 2006.

272   And in a bizarre twist: David Montgomery, "Anna Nicole Smith's Death Ruled Accidental Overdose," *Washington Post,* Mar. 27, 2007.

272   Possible fathers included: Amy Argetsinger and Roxanne Roberts, "Who's Your Daddy?" *Washington Post,* Feb. 18, 2007.

272   As wealth creation has taken off: Rachel Emma Silverman, "Making Peace over Money," *Wall Street Journal,* Oct. 21, 2006.

273   Every six months or so: Gina Chon and Rachel Emma Silverman, "Ford Family's Cash Faucet Goes Dry," *Wall Street Journal,* Sept. 16, 2006.

273   The company was suspending dividend payments: Jeffrey McCracken, Stephen Power, and Joseph B. White, "Sharp Skid: Ford and Chrysler Show Dark Outlook for U.S. Car Makers," *Wall Street Journal,* Sept. 16, 2006.

273   "We can afford to take a hit": Chon and Silverman, "Ford Family's Cash Faucet Goes Dry."

274   In 1994 William Ziff sold: Matthew Miller, "Cash Kings," *Forbes,* Oct. 9, 2006.

274   Since the death in 1979: Information on the Newhouses comes from Jefferson Crosby, "Newhouse, After Newhouse," *Forbes,* Oct. 29, 1979; David Henry, "Tax Collector's Vengeance," *Forbes,* Mar. 5, 1984; and Forbes.com.

274   Brothers James and Andrew Tisch: Robert Lenzer, "High on Loews," *Forbes,* Feb. 26, 2007.

275   She filed in April 2001: James Barron with Adam Nagourney, "Boldface Names," *New York Times,* May 23, 2001.

275   They were famous for hosting lavish parties: Robert Frank, "The Wealth Report: A Billionaire's Divorce—and Not a Lawyer in Sight," *Wall Street Journal,* Jan. 21, 2007.

12. Giving It Away

Sources interviewed for this chapter: Nelson W. Aldrich Jr., author, *Old Money: The Mythology of Wealth in America* (1988); John E. Anderson (Forbes 400); Rich Avanzino, president, Maddie's Fund; Joe Breiteneicher, president, The Philanthropy Initiative; Eli Broad (Forbes 400); Peter Buffett; Kathy Bushkin, chief operating officer, United Nations Foundation; Richard Conniff, author, *The Natural History of the Rich: A Field Guide* (2003); William Dietel, president, F. B. Heron and Pierson/Lovelace Foundation; Joan DiFuria, codirector, Money, Meaning & Choices Institute; Pablo Eisenberg, senior fellow, Public Policy Institute, Georgetown University; Theodore Forstmann (Forbes 400); Stephen Goldbart, codirector, Money, Meaning & Choices Institute; Vartan Gregorian, president, Carnegie Corporation of New York; John Healy, former president, Atlantic Philanthropies; Bruce Kovner (Forbes 400); Ronald Lauder (Forbes 400); John Malone (Forbes 400); Ryan Nguyen, research manager, NewTithing Group; Stacy Palmer, editor, *The Chronicle of Philanthropy;* Daniela Reif, communications specialist, Omidyar Network; Peter Singer, professor of bioethics, Princeton University; James Allen Smith, professor of philanthropy, Georgetown University; Tim Stone, president, NewTithing Group; Jean Strouse, biographer and director of the Dorothy and Lewis B. Cullman Center for Scholars and Writers, New York Public Library; Mortimer B. Zuckerman (Forbes 400). Unless otherwise noted, quotations in the text from the above sources come from interviews conducted by the editors and writers of the book.

276   "Mouth of the South" Turner: Maureen Dowd, "Ted's Excellent Idea," *New York Times,* Aug. 22, 1996.

277   Gates, for example, gave away: www.gatesfoundation.org.

277   Entrusting his money to Gates: Warren Buffett on *The Charlie Rose Show,* June 26, 2006.

279   "Our giving is a drop in the bucket": Patty Stonsifer, interviewed on *The Diane Rehm Show,* NPR, Jan. 30, 2007.

279   "The research programs of entire countries": Michael Specter, "What Money Can Buy," *The New Yorker,* Oct. 24, 2005.

279   Giving of this magnitude: Peter Singer, "On Giving," *New York Times,* Dec. 17, 2006.

280   Even before the Carnegies: Franklin Parker, *George Peabody: A Biography* (Nashville: Vanderbilt University Press, 1995).

280   He gave away more than two-thirds: Christina Wise, "He's the Financier Who Fathered Philanthropy," *Investor's Business Daily,* Sept. 22, 2006.

280   One person Carnegie influenced: Carol Loomis, "Warren Buffet Gives It Away," *Fortune,* July 10, 2006.

281   As Princeton's Peter Singer points out: Peter Singer, "Happiness, Money, and Giving It Away," Project Syndicate, July 2006, http://www.project-syndicate.org/commentary/singer13.

282   "I believe that God spared me": John H. Taylor, "Creative Philanthropy," *Forbes,* Oct. 19, 1992.

282   In the tradition of church tithing: www.pamplin.org/philanthropy-content.html.

282   After selling Domino's for $1 billion: Dinesh D'Souza, *The Virtue of Prosperity: Finding Values in an Age of Techno-Affluence* (New York: Free Press, 2000), p. 112.

283   "I remember feeling that I mattered": Michelle Conlin et al., "The Top Givers," *BusinessWeek,* Nov. 29, 2004.

283   "I know what a lonely child feels like": Jan Hoffman, "A Latter-Day Warbucks," *New York Times,* Apr. 27, 1999.

284   A lifelong bachelor: Richard Sandomir, "Sports Business: Star Struck," *New York Times,* Jan. 12, 2007.

284   More than seventy thousand elementary-school children: Children's Scholarship Fund newsletter, vol. II, issue 7, 2005.

284   A study by researchers: Ravi Dhar and Uzma Khan, "Licensing Effect in Consumer Choice," *Journal of Marketing Research* 43 (May 2006).

284   "I get great joy": Craig Horowitz, "The Respectable Mr. Annenberg," *M,* Apr. 1984.

284   "It's only a bit of an exaggeration": hewlittfoundation.org.

285   In a 2005 survey: John Havens, researcher, Boston College Center on Wealth and Philanthropy, interview.

285   Among other Forbes 400 members: Forbes.com.

286   Moore made the bequest: *Chronicle of Higher Education Almanac,* Aug. 25, 2006.

287   Two other outsize gifts: Ibid.

287   West Coast developer John Arrillaga: Ibid.

287   A former basketball star: Erin Strout, "Stanford U. Gets $100 Million Gift," *Chronicle of Higher Education,* May 2006.

287   "To do that I felt": Christopher Ogden, *Legacy: A Biography of Moses and Walter Annenberg* (New York: Little, Brown, 1999), p. 539.

288   He dispensed study materials: Kathleen Hall Jamieson, "Walter H. Annenberg: Biographical Memoirs," *Proceedings of the American Philosophical Society* 48, no. 2 (June 2004).

288 But the grants: Raymond Domanico et al., "Can Philanthropy Fix Our Schools? Appraising Walter Annenberg's $500 Million Gift to Public Education," Thomas B. Fordham Institute, Apr. 1, 2000.

289 But results of spending: gatesfoundation.org.

289 "If you want to equate": Jay Freene and William C. Symonds, "Bill Gates Gets Schooled," *BusinessWeek,* June 26, 2006.

289 "I am Mike Milken": Cora Daniels, "The Man Who Changed Medicine," *Fortune,* Nov. 29, 2004.

290 One such advance: Nicole Davis, "Genetic 'Roadmap' Charts Links Between Drugs and Human Disease," The Broad Institute, Sept. 29, 2006, web.mit.edu/newoffice/2006/drugs.html.

294 "Asking Alberto for money": James B. Stewart, "The Opera Lover," *The New Yorker,* Feb. 13 and Feb. 20, 2006.

295 In 2005, as he stepped off a plane: *U.S. v. Vilar,* Southern District of New York, Apr. 4, 2007.

295 The Royal Opera House reverted: info.royaloperahouse.org/news/index.

295 Despite the $12 million or so: Stewart, "The Opera Lover."

295 He referred to himself: Ibid.

295 "My whole feeling": Quoted ibid.

295 "The Met is not going to get my money": Stewart, "The Opera Lover."

295 "Art," said Simon: Michael Ybarra, "Passion's Fruits," *ARTnews,* Oct. 11, 1998.

296 Broad's personal collection: Broad Art Foundation brochure.

296 That doesn't include donating: Maria Di Mento, "David Rockefeller Pledges $100 Million to Museum of Modern Art," *Chronicle of Philanthropy,* Apr. 28, 2006.

296 "I felt they know most": Ibid.

296 Meanwhile, his private fifteen-thousand-piece art collection: Karen W. Arenson, "Turning 90, a Rockefeller Gives the Presents," *New York Times,* June 9, 2005.

297 "When I was a kid": turnerfoundation.org.

297 Other promises: Irene Lacher, "Ted Turner's 10 Commandments," *Los Angeles Times,* May 4, 1990.

297 He started the foundation: turnerfoundation.org.

297 He is said to be: Forbes.com.

297 "I don't want all the land": Jack Hitt, "One Nation, Under Ted," *Outside,* Dec. 2001.

297 Joke or not: Forbes.com.

297 His effort to bring back bison: Geraldine Fabrikant, "Plunge in Bison and AOL Weighs on Turner Fortune," *New York Times,* Aug. 26, 2002.

297 Turner saw a way to parlay: www.tedsmontanagrill.com.

298 One of Malone's more recent purchases: Phyllis Austin, "John Malone Purchases," *Maine Environmental News,* May 22, 2002.

298 "We were able to do it": Richard A. Kerr, "Gary Comer Profile: An Entrepreneur Does Climate Science," *Science,* Feb. 24, 2006.

298 First, his sale of the Lands' End catalog business: Forbes.com.

298 Comer consulted a Nobel-laureate geochemist: Andrew Revkin, "Paying the Freight and Relishing the Ride," *New York Times,* Nov. 13, 2006.

298 All told, Comer gave: Maria Di Mento and Nicole Lewis, "Record-Breaking Giving," *Chronicle of Philanthropy,* Feb. 22, 2007.

298 Their seven-year study: "Level of Important Greenhouse Gas Has Stopped Growing," University of California–Irvine, press release, Nov. 20, 2006.

298 The gas, which also contributes: Kerr, "Gary Comer Profile."

299 Paul Allen: [Unsigned,] "Microsoft Co-Founder Unveils 'Brain Atlas,' " *Philanthropy Today,* Sept. 27, 2006.

299   Philip Anschutz: Forbes.com.

299   Bill Gates: Nathan Vardi, "Simply Smashing," *Forbes,* Apr. 24, 2006.

299   Gordon and Betty Moore: www.moore.org/marine-micro.aspx; Forbes.com.

300   Gordon Moore, Paul Allen, William Hewlett, David Packard: www.set1.org; Forbes.com; Jule Pitta, "The Forbes 400 and the Little Green Men," *Forbes,* Oct. 17, 1994.

300   Steven Spielberg: Forbes.com; www.righteouspersonsfoundation.com.

300   Jon Stryker: Forbes.com; Arcus Foundation newsletter, Spring 2006; www.arcus foundation.org; www.savethechimps.org.

300   Ted Waitt: Guy Gugliotta and Alan Cooperman, "Newly Translated Gospel Offers More Positive Portrayal of Judas," *Washington Post,* Apr. 7, 2006.

301   The NewTithing Group: "Study 1: The Generosity of Rich and Poor," NewTithing Group, Apr. 2004, www.newtithing.org.

302   According to his spokespeople: Conlin et al., "The Top Givers."

302   "I'm not aware of any large gifts": David Whelan, "Who Gives?" *Forbes Global,* Oct. 11, 2004.

302   A survey by Indiana University's Center on Philanthropy: Frank Greve, "Secret Giving Often a Challenge," *Miami Herald,* Nov. 13, 2005.

302   Second, Hunt equated receiving charity: Harry Hurt III, *Texas Rich* (New York: W. W. Norton, 1982), p. 123.

302   South Dakota multibillionaire T. Denny Sanford: Ben Gose, "Great Plains Generosity," *Chronicle of Philanthropy,* Feb. 5, 2007.

302   T. Boone Pickens put a novel twist: Debra Blum, "Oil Tycoon Gives $100 Million—with Strings Attached," *Chronicle of Philanthropy,* May 17, 2007.

303   The couple now has nine children: Stacy Lacy, "A Fifth Startup?" *BusinessWeek,* Nov. 13, 2006.

303   "When you create wealth in a short time": Quentin Hardy, "The Radical Philanthropist," *Forbes,* May 1, 2000.

303   Neither felt comfortable: Michelle Conlin with Rob Hof, "The eBay Way," *BusinessWeek,* Nov. 29, 2004.

304   For example, when he and his wife: Robert D. Hof, "A Major Push for Microphilanthropy," *BusinessWeek,* Nov. 4, 2005.

304   Among the recent examples: Pablo Eisenberg, "Top Donors Are Doing Too Little to Help the Needy," *Chronicle of Philanthropy,* Feb. 23, 2006.

13. Power and Politics

Sources interviewed for this chapter: Michael Bloomberg, mayor, New York City (Forbes 400); Michael Huffington, former U.S. Congressman from California and son of Forbes 400 member Roy Michael Huffington; Jon Huntsman Jr., governor of Utah and son of Forbes 400 member Jon Huntsman; David Koch (Forbes 400); Bruce Kovner (Forbes 400); Aryeh Neier, president of the Open Society Institute; H. Ross Perot (Forbes 400); Richard Mellon Scaife (Forbes 400); George Smith, professor of economics and international business, Stern School of Business, New York University; Celia Wexler, vice president for advocacy, Common Cause; Mortimer B. Zuckerman (Forbes 400). Unless otherwise noted, quotations in the text from the above sources come from interviews conducted by the editors and writers of the book.

306   When George Soros was a young boy: Michael T. Kaufman, *Soros: The Life and Times of a Messianic Billionaire* (New York: Vintage, 2003), pp. 32, 67.

306   In a 1998 essay: J. Bradford DeLong, "Robber Barons," University of California–Berkeley and National Bureau of Economic Research, Jan. 1, 1998.

307   The surname Soros: Kaufman, *Soros,* p. 24.

307 In order to survive: Ibid., p. 53.

307 Popper's ideology of an "open society": Ibid., pp. 70–73.

307 In his biography *Soros:* Ibid., p. 166.

307 Yet according to Jane Mayer: Jane Mayer, "The Money Man," *The New Yorker,* Oct. 18, 2004.

307 The first program was providing scholarships: Aryeh Neier interview.

307 When the Berlin Wall fell: Kaufman, *Soros,* pp. 228–29.

308 But by far the biggest beneficiary: Mayer, "The Money Man."

308 During the 1994 congressional election: [Unsigned,] "The Charge of the Think-Tanks," *The Economist,* Feb. 15, 2003.

308 He also donated more than $1 million: Judith Miller, "With Big Money and Brash Ideas, a Billionaire Redefines Charity," *New York Times,* Dec. 17, 1996.

309 He said the statements: Mayer, "The Money Man."

309 Soros perceived in the Bush administration: Ibid.

309 During the 2002 election: Statistics from Center for Responsive Politics, "Top Individual Contributors," 2002.

309 But two years later: Mayer, "The Money Man."

310 Soros was the largest single donor: Center for Responsive Politics, "Top Individual Contributors to 527 Committees, 2004 Election Cycle."

310 President Bush felt so threatened: AP Wire Service, "Republicans File Complaint over Kerry, Group Ads," Apr. 1, 2004.

310 Indeed, being wealthy: Jeffrey H. Birnbaum, Eileen P. Gunn, and Michelle McGowan, "The Money Chase," *Fortune,* Sept. 7, 1998.

311 Even Donald Trump considered: Jerry Useem and Theodore Spencer, "What Does Donald Trump Really Want?" *Fortune,* Apr. 3, 2000.

311 Rockefeller says that in 1967: David Rockefeller, *Memoirs* (New York: Random House, 2002), p. 194.

311 And in 1992 Ross Perot spent: Connie Cass, "For His Second Presidential Bid, Ross Perot Has Turned from a Free-Spending Billionaire into Something of a Penny-Pincher," Associated Press, Oct. 22, 1996.

312 Meanwhile, John D. Rockefeller's great-grandson: Jill Andresky, "Dan Quayle, Boy Exception," *Forbes,* Oct. 24, 1988.

312 But most campaigns waged: Figures from National Institute on Money in State Politics.

312 Steve Forbes, current publisher: Geraldine Fabrikant, "A Forbes Family Fund-Raiser," *New York Times,* Aug. 8, 2006.

314 A liberal Democrat who registered: Philip Lentz, "Bloomberg Prepping for City Hall Race," *Crain's New York Business,* Oct. 30, 2000.

314 In a city where Democratic voters: Michael Saul, "Mike Cuts into Dems' Lead," *New York Daily News,* Oct. 6, 2001.

314 "Who needs a man on horseback": Dennis Duggan, "Hard to Get Excited About This Rich Guy," *Newsday,* June 7, 2001.

315 By October Bloomberg had cut: Saul, "Mike Cuts into Dems' Lead."

315 He spent $72 million: Elizabeth Kolbert, "The Un-Communicator," *The New Yorker,* Mar. 1, 2004.

315 Trailing by twelve points: Michael Powell and Thomas B. Edsall, "Bloomberg Wins N.Y. Mayoral Race," *Washington Post,* Nov. 7, 2001.

315 Writing in the *New York Times:* Jonathan Mahler, "The Bloomberg Vista," *New York Times,* Sept. 10, 2006.

315 When Bloomberg took office: Kolbert, "The Un-Communicator."

315 A 2004 Quinnipiac University poll: Mahler, "The Bloomberg Vista."

316   "The Mayor focuses on efficiency": Kolbert, "The Un-Communicator."

316   And yet in 2005: Mahler, "The Bloomberg Vista."

316   Scaife is one of the leading conservative philanthropists: "The Charge of the Think-Tanks."

318   Indeed, after being elected: Phil Kuntz, "Citizen Scaife," *Wall Street Journal,* Oct. 12, 1995.

318   David Brock, a former conservative journalist-turned-whistleblower: David Brock, "How I Almost Brought Down the President," *The Guardian,* Mar. 12, 2002.

318   Scaife is not exactly: Robert G. Kaiser, "The Conservative Godfather," *Austin American-Statesman,* May 9, 1999.

318   In 1970 he pledged $100,000: Kuntz, "Citizen Scaife."

318   in 1972 he donated: John Kay, Richard Lambert, Geoffrey Owen, and Martin Wolf, "Spending Power," *Financial Times,* Nov. 13, 2004.

318   He then went on to fund: Kuntz, "Citizen Scaife."

319   When Bill Clinton was elected president in 1992: Brock, "How I Almost Brought Down the President."

319   The relentless attacks: Kaiser, "The Conservative Godfather."

320   Ford owned the Michigan weekly: Hardy Green, "A Titan of Industry—and a Bigot," *BusinessWeek,* Jan. 21, 2002.

320   And in the 1950s H. L. Hunt: Harry Hurt III, *Texas Rich* (New York: W. W. Norton, 1982), pp. 154–64, 179–80.

320   Asked in September 2005: CNN transcript of *The Situation Room,* aired Sept. 19, 2005; available at edition.cnn.com/TRANSCRIPTS/0509/19/sitroom.01.html.

320   But he also began speaking out: Richard Zoglin, "The Greening of Ted Turner," *Time,* Jan. 22, 1990.

320   Dubbed by some: Maureen Dowd, "CNN: Foxy or Outfoxed?" *New York Times,* Aug. 15, 2001.

321   Turner apologized to a California audience: Peter J. Boyer, "The People's Network," *The New Yorker,* Aug. 3, 1998.

321   *Time* magazine: Glenn Nelson, "The Greening of Ted Turner," *Time,* Jan. 22, 1990.

321   Several years later, HarperCollins: John Gapper, "News Corp. Joins Patten Book Row" *Financial Times,* Feb. 28, 1998.

321   When he launched: Times Wire Services, "Battle of the Cable Stars," *Los Angeles Times,* Nov. 30, 1995.

321   Explaining his rationale: [Unsigned,] "The Gambler's Last Throw," *The Economist,* Mar. 9, 1996.

322   Seagram's billionaire Edgar Bronfman Sr.: Robert Lenzer, "Creative Giving: The Confrontationist," *Forbes,* Nov. 29. 1999.

322   Investors Carl Lindner and Ronald Perelman: Birnbaum, Gunn, and McGowan, "The Money Chase."

322   In a September 2000 report: Common Cause, *The Microsoft Playbook,* 2002.

323   During the 1998 election cycle: [Unsigned,] "Don't Discount Wal-Mart's Influence After Lott's Prodding, Retail Giant Decides to Expand Lobbying Shop," *Roll Call,* Jan. 13, 2000.

323   By 2002 Wal-Mart had increased: Figures from Common Cause.

323   Mortgage-firm billionaire Roland Arnall: Thomas B. Edsall and Jeffrey H. Birnbaum, "Big-Money Contributors Line Up for Inauguration," *Washington Post,* Jan. 13, 2005.

324   According to a confidential memo: Birnbaum, Gunn, and McGowan, "The Money Chase."

324   Examine the Forbes 400 list: Forbes.com.

325   David Rockefeller, during his tenure: Rockefeller, *Memoirs,* p. 194.

325   George Soros was the largest individual donor: [Unsigned,] "Center for Responsive Politics Predicts '06 Election Will Cost $2.6 Billion," Center for Responsive Politics press release, www.opensecrets.org/pressreleases/2006/PreElection.10.25.asp.

Afterword: Money and Happiness

Most of the responses in the Afterword come either from a questionnaire sent to members of the Forbes 400 in March 2007 or from individual interviews conducted with members of the 400, as well as with essayists and analysts of wealth and money. Other sources are cited below.

327   In his recent book *Stumbling on Happiness:* Daniel Gilbert, *Stumbling on Happiness* (New York: Knopf, 2006), pp. 217–18.

327   As Cary Reich wrote: Cary Reich, *Financier: The Biography of André Meyer* (New York: HarperCollins, 1983), quoted in "Other Comments," *Forbes,* Forbes 400 issue, Oct. 1, 1984.

328   "Money may not bring happiness": William Feather, quoted in *Forbes,* Forbes 400 issue, Oct. 1, 1984.

329   "My life is a fairy tale": Alfred Mann, quoted in "Thoughts on the Business of Life," *Forbes,* Forbes 400 issue, Oct. 6, 2003.

329   "But there was the spending of money": Gertrude Stein, quoted in "Thoughts," *Forbes,* Forbes 400 issue, Oct. 1, 1984.

330   "I'm opposed to millionaires": Mark Twain, quoted ibid.

Index